PENGUIN BOOKS

THE PENGUIN ANTHOLOGY OF TWENTIETH-CENTURY AMERICAN POETRY

RITA DOVE was born in Akron, Ohio, in 1952. A 1970 Presidential Scholar, she received her BA summa cum laude from Miami University of Ohio and her MFA from the University of Iowa. She also held a Fulbright Scholarship at the Universität Tübingen in Germany. She has published the poetry collections *The Yellow House on the Corner* (1980), *Museum* (1983), *Thomas and Beulah* (1986), *Grace Notes* (1989), *Selected Poems* (1993), *Mother Love* (1995), *On the Bus with Rosa Parks* (1999), and *American Smooth* (2004); a book of short stories, *Fifth Sunday* (1985); the novel *Through the Ivory Gate* (1992); essays under the title *The Poet's World* (1995); and the play *The Darker Face of the Earth*, which had its world premiere in 1996 at the Oregon Shakespeare Festival and was subsequently produced at the Kennedy Center in Washington, D.C., the Royal National Theatre in London, and other theaters. *Seven for Luck*, a song cycle for soprano and orchestra with music by John Williams, was premiered by the Boston Symphony Orchestra at Tanglewood in 1998. For America's Millennium, the White House's 1999/2000 New Year's celebration, Ms. Dove contributed—in a live reading at the Lincoln Memorial, accompanied by John Williams's music—a poem to Steven Spielberg's documentary *The Unfinished Journey*. She is the editor of *The Best American Poetry 2000*, and from January 2000 to January 2002 she wrote a weekly column, *Poet's Choice*, for the *Washington Post*. Her latest poetry collection, *Sonata Mulattica*, was published by W. W. Norton in the spring of 2009. Dove served as poet laureate of the United States and Consultant in Poetry to the Library of Congress from 1993 to 1995 and as poet laureate of the Commonwealth of Virginia from 2004 to 2006. She has received numerous literary and academic accolades, among them the 1987 Pulitzer Prize in Poetry and the 1996 Heinz Award in the Arts and Humanities. More recently she was honored with the 2006 Common Wealth Award of Distinguished Service, the 2007 Chubb Fellowship at Yale University, the 2008 Library of Virginia's Lifetime Achievement Award, and the 2009 Fulbright Lifetime Achievement Medal. When President Obama presented her with the 2011 National Medal of Arts, she became the only poet who has been decorated with the two highest U.S. government distinctions in the arts and humanities. (In 1996, President Clinton had bestowed upon her the National Humanities Medal.) She is Commonwealth Professor of English at the University of Virginia in Charlottesville, where she lives with her husband, the writer Fred Viebahn.

THE PENGUIN ANTHOLOGY OF TWENTIETH-CENTURY AMERICAN POETRY

EDITED WITH AN INTRODUCTION BY

RITA DOVE

PENGUIN BOOKS

PENGUIN BOOKS
Published by the Penguin Group
Penguin Group (USA), 375 Hudson Street,
New York, New York 10014, USA

USA | Canada | UK | Ireland | Australia | New Zealand | India | South Africa | China
Penguin Books Ltd, Registered Offices: 80 Strand, London WC2R 0RL, England
For more information about the Penguin Group visit penguin.com

First published in the United States of America by Penguin Books,
a member of Penguin Group (USA) Inc., 2011
This paperback edition published in Penguin Books 2013

Introduction and selection copyright © Rita Dove, 2011
THE LIBRARY OF CONGRESS HAS CATALOGED THE HARDCOVER EDITION AS FOLLOWS:
The Penguin anthology of twentieth-century American poetry / edited with an introduction by Rita Dove. ·
p.   cm.
Includes index.
ISBN 978-0-14-310643-2 (hc.)
ISBN 978-0-14-312148-0 (pbk.)
1. American poetry—20th century.   I. Dove, Rita.
PS613.P47 2011
811'.508—dc23   2011036342

Printed in the United States of America
5   7   9   10   8   6   4

Set in Arno Pro
Designed by Sabrina Bowers

Contents

Introduction by Rita Dove   xxix

Edgar Lee Masters   (1868–1950)   1
FROM *Spoon River Anthology:*
    The Hill · 1
    Fiddler Jones · 2
    Petit, the Poet · 3

Edwin Arlington Robinson   (1869–1935)   4
    Miniver Cheevy · 4
    Mr. Flood's Party · 5

James Weldon Johnson   (1871–1938)   7
    The Creation · 7

Paul Laurence Dunbar   (1872–1906)   10
    The Poet · 10
    Life's Tragedy · 10

Robert Frost   (1874–1963)   12
    The Death of the Hired Man · 12
    Mending Wall · 17
    Birches · 18
    Stopping by Woods on a Snowy Evening · 20
    Tree at My Window · 20
    Directive · 21

Amy Lowell (1874–1925)   23
Patterns · 23

Gertrude Stein (1874–1946)   26
Susie Asado · 26
FROM *Tender Buttons:*
  A Box · 26
  A Plate · 27

Alice Moore Dunbar-Nelson (1875–1935)   28
I Sit and Sew · 28

Carl Sandburg (1878–1967)   29
Grass · 29
Cahoots · 29

Wallace Stevens (1879–1955)   31
Peter Quince at the Clavier · 31
Disillusionment of Ten O'Clock · 33
Thirteen Ways of Looking at a Blackbird · 34
Anecdote of the Jar · 36
The Emperor of Ice-Cream · 36
Of Mere Being · 36

Angelina Weld Grimké (1880–1958)   38
Fragment · 38

William Carlos Williams (1883–1963)   39
Tract · 39
Danse Russe · 41
The Red Wheelbarrow · 41
The Yachts · 42
FROM *Asphodel, That Greeny Flower* (Book I, lines 1–92) · 43

Sara Teasdale (1884–1933)   51
Moonlight · 51
There Will Come Soft Rains · 51

Ezra Pound (1885–1972)   53

The Jewel Stairs' Grievance · 53
The River-Merchant's Wife: A Letter · 53
In a Station of the Metro · 54
Hugh Selwyn Mauberley · 54
FROM *Canto LXXXI* (Libretto: "Yet / Ere the season died a-cold") · 62

Hilda Doolittle (H.D.) (1886–1961)   65

Sea Rose · 65
Helen · 65
FROM *The Walls Do Not Fall:*
  1 ("An incident here and there") · 66
FROM *Hermetic Definition:* "Red Rose and a Beggar":
  1 ("Why did you come") · 68
  2 ("Take me anywhere . . .") · 68
  5 ("Venice—Venus?") · 69

Robinson Jeffers (1887–1962)   70

Gale in April · 70
Shine, Perishing Republic · 70
Clouds at Evening · 71
Credo · 71

Marianne Moore (1887–1972)   73

The Fish · 73
Poetry · 74
Poetry · 75

T. S. Eliot (1888–1965)   76

The Love Song of J. Alfred Prufrock · 76
Preludes · 80
The Waste Land · 81

Claude McKay (1889–1948)   93

If We Must Die · 93
The Harlem Dancer · 93

Archibald MacLeish (1892–1982)   95
Ars Poetica · 95

Edna St. Vincent Millay (1892–1950)   97
First Fig · 97
Recuerdo · 97

E. E. Cummings (1894–1962)   98
in Just- · 98
Buffalo Bill 's · 99
the Cambridge ladies who live in furnished souls · 99
next to of course god america i · 99
somewhere i have never travelled,gladly beyond · 100
r-p-o-p-h-e-s-s-a-g-r · 101

Jean Toomer (1894–1967)   102
Reapers · 102
November Cotton Flower · 102
Portrait in Georgia · 102

Louise Bogan (1897–1970)   104
Medusa · 104
New Moon · 104

Melvin B. Tolson (1898–1966)   106
Dark Symphony · 106
FROM *Harlem Gallery*: Psi ("Black Boy, / let me get up from the white man's
Table . . .") · 110

Hart Crane (1899–1932)   120
FROM *The Bridge* [excerpts]:
Proem: To Brooklyn Bridge · 120
FROM *II: Powhatan's Daughter:* The River · 121

Robert Francis (1901–1987)   126
Silent Poem · 126

Langston Hughes (1902–1967) 127

The Negro Speaks of Rivers · 127
I, Too · 127
Dream Boogie · 128
Harlem · 129

Countee Cullen (1903–1946) 130

Incident · 130
To John Keats, Poet, at Spring Time · 130
Yet Do I Marvel · 132
From the Dark Tower · 132

Stanley Kunitz (1905–2006) 133

Father and Son · 133
The Portrait · 134
Touch Me · 134

W. H. Auden (1907–1973) 136

Musée des Beaux Arts · 136
Epitaph on a Tyrant · 137

Theodore Roethke (1908–1963) 138

My Papa's Waltz · 138
The Waking · 138
In a Dark Time · 139

Charles Olson (1910–1970) 141

FROM The Maximus Poems: I, Maximus of Gloucester, to You · 141
The Distances · 145

Elizabeth Bishop (1911–1979) 147

The Fish · 147
Sestina · 149
First Death in Nova Scotia · 150
Visits to St. Elizabeths · 151
One Art · 153

Robert Hayden (1913–1980)   155
Mourning Poem for the Queen of Sunday · 155
Those Winter Sundays · 156
Frederick Douglass · 156
Middle Passage · 157

Muriel Rukeyser (1913–1980)   162
Effort at Speech Between Two People · 162
Then I Saw What the Calling Was · 163
The Poem as Mask · 163

Delmore Schwartz (1913–1966)   165
The Heavy Bear Who Goes with Me · 165

John Berryman (1914–1972)   167
FROM *The Dream Songs:*
    4 ("Filling her compact & delicious body") · 167
    14 ("Life, friends, is boring. We must not say so") · 167
    29 ("There sat down, once") · 168
    149 ("This world is gradually becoming a place") · 168
Henry's Understanding · 169

Randall Jarrell (1914–1965)   170
90 North · 170
The Death of the Ball Turret Gunner · 171
The Woman at the Washington Zoo · 171
Next Day · 172

Weldon Kees (1914–1955)   174
For My Daughter · 174

Dudley Randall (1914–2000)   175
A Different Image · 175

William Stafford (1914–1993)   176
Traveling through the Dark · 176
At the Bomb Testing Site · 177

Ruth Stone (1915–2011)   178
    Scars · 178

Margaret Walker (1915–1998)   179
    For My People · 179

Gwendolyn Brooks (1917–2000)   181
    The Mother · 181
    A Song in the Front Yard · 182
    The Bean Eaters · 182
    The Lovers of the Poor · 183
    We Real Cool · 185
    The Blackstone Rangers · 186

Robert Lowell (1917–1977)   188
    "To Speak of Woe That Is in Marriage" · 188
    Skunk Hour · 188
    For the Union Dead · 190

Robert Duncan (1919–1988)   193
    Often I Am Permitted to Return to a Meadow · 193
    My Mother Would Be a Falconress · 194

Lawrence Ferlinghetti (1919–)   197
    Populist Manifesto · 197

William Meredith (1919–2007)   201
    Parents · 201

Howard Nemerov (1920–1991)   203
    Because You Asked About the Line Between Prose and Poetry · 203

Hayden Carruth (1921–2008)   204
    The Hyacinth Garden in Brooklyn · 204
    August 1945 · 205

Richard Wilbur (1921–)   207
Love Calls Us to the Things of This World · 207
Cottage Street, 1953 · 208
The Writer · 209

James Dickey (1923–1997)   211
The Sheep Child · 211

Alan Dugan (1923–2003)   213
Love Song: I and Thou · 213

Anthony Hecht (1923–2004)   215
"More Light! More Light!" · 215

Richard Hugo (1923–1982)   217
Degrees of Gray in Philipsburg · 217
The Freaks at Spurgin Road Field · 218

Denise Levertov (1923–1997)   219
The Poem Unwritten · 219
Caedmon · 219
Swan in Falling Snow · 220

Louis Simpson (1923–2012)   221
American Poetry · 221

Carolyn Kizer (1925–)   222
A Muse of Water · 222

Kenneth Koch (1925–2002)   225
Fresh Air · 225
Permanently · 231

Maxine Kumin (1925–)   232
  Morning Swim · 232
  How It Is · 233

Gerald Stern (1925–)   234
  Behaving Like a Jew · 234
  The Dancing · 235
  Another Insane Devotion · 235

A. R. Ammons (1926–2001)   237
  The City Limits · 237
  Corsons Inlet · 238

Robert Bly (1926–)   242
  Snowfall in the Afternoon · 242
  Driving to Town Late to Mail a Letter · 243
  Waking from Sleep · 243

Robert Creeley (1926–2005)   244
  The Flower · 244
  I Know a Man · 244
  The Language · 245
  The Rain · 246
  Bresson's Movies · 246

James Merrill (1926–1995)   248
  The Victor Dog · 248

Frank O'Hara (1926–1966)   250
  Steps · 250
  Poem ("Lana Turner has collapsed!") · 251
  The Day Lady Died · 252

John Ashbery (1927–)   253
  Some Trees · 253
  Self-Portrait in a Convex Mirror · 254
  What Is Poetry · 266

Galway Kinnell (1927–)   268

The Bear · 268

After Making Love We Hear Footsteps · 271

Saint Francis and the Sow · 271

W. S. Merwin (1927–)   273

Air · 273

For the Anniversary of My Death · 274

Yesterday · 274

Chord · 275

James Wright (1927–1980)   277

A Blessing · 277

Autumn Begins in Martins Ferry, Ohio · 277

Lying in a Hammock at William Duffy's Farm in Pine Island, Minnesota · 278

In Response to a Rumor That the Oldest Whorehouse in Wheeling, West Virginia,
    Has Been Condemned · 278

Donald Hall (1928–)   280

My Son My Executioner · 280

Digging · 280

Philip Levine (1928–)   282

Animals Are Passing from Our Lives · 282

They Feed They Lion · 283

You Can Have It · 284

The Simple Truth · 285

Anne Sexton (1928–1974)   287

Her Kind · 287

The Abortion · 288

Wanting to Die · 288

In Celebration of My Uterus · 290

Rowing · 291

Adrienne Rich (1929–)   293

Orion · 293

Planetarium · 294

A Valediction Forbidding Mourning · 296

FROM *Twenty-One Love Poems:* XIII ("The rules break like a
thermometer...") · 296

Gregory Corso (1930–2001)   298

Marriage · 298

Gary Snyder (1930–)   302

Hay for the Horses · 302

Riprap · 303

Mid-August at Sourdough Mountain Lookout · 303

Derek Walcott (1930–)   304

A Far Cry from Africa · 304

Sea Grapes · 305

FROM *The Schooner* Flight (part 11, After the Storm: "There's a fresh light that
follows...") · 306

The Light of the World · 307

FROM *Omeros,* Book VII, LXIV, i ("I sang of quiet Achille, Afolabe's
son...") · 310

Miller Williams (1930–)   312

Let Me Tell You · 312

Etheridge Knight (1931–1991)   314

The Idea of Ancestry · 314

Amiri Baraka (LeRoi Jones) (1934–)   316

Preface to a Twenty Volume Suicide Note · 316

An Agony. As Now. · 317

SOS · 318

Black Art · 318

Ted Berrigan (1934–1983)   320

Wrong Train · 320

A Final Sonnet · 320

Audre Lorde (1934–1992)   322
Power · 322

Sonia Sanchez (1934–)   324
poem at thirty · 324

Mark Strand (1934–)   326
The Prediction · 326
The Night, the Porch · 326

Russell Edson (1935–)   328
A Stone Is Nobody's · 328

Mary Oliver (1935–)   329
Singapore · 329
The Summer Day · 330

Charles Wright (1935–)   331
Reunion · 331
Dead Color · 331
California Dreaming · 332

Lucille Clifton (1936–2010)   335
homage to my hips · 335
[at last we killed the roaches] · 335
the death of fred clifton · 336
to my last period · 336

June Jordan (1936–2002)   337
Poem About My Rights · 337

Frederick Seidel (1936–)   340
1968 · 340

C. K. Williams (1936–)   342
From My Window · 342
Blades · 344

Diane Wakoski (1937–)   346
The Mechanic · 346

Michael S. Harper (1938–)   348
Dear John, Dear Coltrane · 348
Last Affair: Bessie's Blues Song · 349
Grandfather · 351
Nightmare Begins Responsibility · 352

Charles Simic (1938–)   353
Stone · 353
Fork · 354
Classic Ballroom Dances · 354

Paula Gunn Allen (1939–2008)   355
Grandmother · 355

Frank Bidart (1939–)   356
Ellen West · 356

Carl Dennis (1939–)   367
Spring Letter · 367
Two or Three Wishes · 368

Stephen Dunn (1939–)   369
Allegory of the Cave · 369
Tucson · 370

Robert Pinsky (1940–)   371
History of My Heart · 371
The Questions · 377
Samurai Song · 379

James Welch (1940–2003) 380

Christmas Comes to Moccasin Flat · 380

Billy Collins (1941–) 381

Introduction to Poetry · 381
The Dead · 382

Toi Derricotte (1941–) 383

Allen Ginsberg · 383
The Weakness · 384

Stephen Dobyns (1941–) 386

How to Like It · 386
Lullaby · 387

Robert Hass (1941–) 390

Song · 390
The Pornographer · 390
The Return of Robinson Jeffers · 391

Lyn Hejinian (1941–) 394

FROM *My Life:* A name trimmed with colored ribbons · 394

B. H. Fairchild (1942–) 396

The Machinist, Teaching His Daughter to Play the Piano · 396

Haki R. Madhubuti (Don L. Lee) (1942–) 398

But He Was Cool or: he even stopped for green lights · 398
A Poem to Complement Other Poems · 399

William Matthews (1942–1997) 402

In Memory of the Utah Stars · 402
The Accompanist · 403

Sharon Olds (1942–)   405
The Language of the Brag · 405
The Lifting · 406

Henry Taylor (1942–)   408
Barbed Wire · 408

Tess Gallagher (1943–)   409
Black Silk · 409
Under Stars · 410

Michael Palmer (1943–)   411
I Do Not · 411

James Tate (1943–)   414
The Lost Pilot · 414

Norman Dubie (1945–)   416
Elizabeth's War with the Christmas Bear · 416
The Funeral · 417

Carol Muske-Dukes (1945–)   419
August, Los Angeles, Lullaby · 419

Kay Ryan (1945–)   421
Turtle · 421
Bestiary · 421

Larry Levis (1946–1996)   423
Childhood Ideogram · 423
Winter Stars · 424

Adrian C. Louis (1946–)   427
Looking for Judas · 427

Thomas Lux (1946–) 428
The People of the Other Village · 428

Marilyn Nelson (1946–) 429
The Ballad of Aunt Geneva · 429
Star-Fix · 430

Ron Silliman (1946–) 433
Albany · 433

Ai (1947–2010) 435
Cuba, 1962 · 435
The Kid · 435
Finished · 436

Yusef Komunyakaa (1947–) 439
Thanks · 439
Tu Do Street · 440
Facing It · 441
Nude Interrogation · 442

Nathaniel Mackey (1947–) 443
Song of the Andoumboulou: 21 · 443

Gregory Orr (1947–) 445
Gathering the Bones Together · 445
Two Lines from the Brothers Grimm · 447
Origin of the Marble Forest · 448

Roberta Hill Whiteman (1947–) 449
Reaching Yellow River · 449

Albert Goldbarth (1948–) 452
Away · 452

Heather McHugh (1948–)   454
   Language Lesson 1976 · 454
   What He Thought · 455

Leslie Marmon Silko (1948–)   457
   In Cold Storm Light · 457

Olga Broumas (1949–)   458
   Calypso · 458

Victor Hernández Cruz (1949–)   459
   Latin & Soul · 459

Jane Miller (1949–)   461
   Miami Heart · 461

David St. John (1949–)   463
   Iris · 463

C. D. Wright (1949–)   465
   Why Ralph Refuses to Dance · 465
   Girl Friend Poem #3 · 466
   Crescent · 466

Carolyn Forché (1950–)   467
   Taking Off My Clothes · 467

Jorie Graham (1950–)   468
   San Sepolcro · 468

Marie Howe (1950–)   470
   What the Living Do · 470

Joy Harjo (1951–)   472
She Had Some Horses · 472
My House is the Red Earth · 474

Garrett Hongo (1951–)   475
The Legend · 475

Andrew Hudgins (1951–)   477
Begotten · 477
We Were Simply Talking · 477

Brigit Pegeen Kelly (1951–)   479
Imagining Their Own Hymns · 479
Song · 480

Paul Muldoon (1951–)   482
Meeting the British · 482
Errata · 483
The Throwback · 484

Judith Ortiz Cofer (1952–)   485
Quinceañera · 485

Rita Dove (1952–)   486
Parsley · 486
Daystar · 488
After Reading Mickey in the Night Kitchen for the Third Time Before Bed · 489
Claudette Colvin Goes to Work · 490

Alice Fulton (1952–)   492
Our Calling · 492

Barbara Hamby (1952–)   494
Thinking of Galileo · 494
Hatred · 495

Mark Jarman (1952–)   497
    Unholy Sonnet 13 · 497

Naomi Shihab Nye (1952–)   498
    The Traveling Onion · 498
    Arabic · 499
    Wedding Cake · 500

Alberto Ríos (1952–)   502
    Nani · 502
    England Finally, Like My Mother Always Said We Would · 503

Laurie Sheck (1952–)   504
    Nocturne: Blue Waves · 504
    The Unfinished · 505

Gary Soto (1952–)   506
    Field Poem · 506
    Oranges · 506
    Black Hair · 508

Susan Stewart (1952–)   509
    Yellow Stars and Ice · 509
    The Forest · 510

Mark Doty (1953–)   512
    Brilliance · 512
    Esta Noche · 514
    Bill's Story · 515

Harryette Mullen (1953–)   518
    Black Nikes · 518

Franz Wright (1953–)   519
    Alcohol · 519

Lorna Dee Cervantes (1954–)   521
To My Brother · 521
"Love of My Flesh, Living Death" · 522

Sandra Cisneros (1954–)   523
My Wicked Wicked Ways · 523
Little Clown, My Heart · 524

Cornelius Eady (1954–)   525
Jack Johnson Does the Eagle Rock · 525
Crows in a Strong Wind · 525
I'm a Fool to Love You · 526

Louise Erdrich (1954–)   528
Indian Boarding School: The Runaways · 528

David Mason (1954–)   529
Spooning · 529

Marilyn Chin (1955–)   534
How I Got That Name · 534
Composed Near the Bay Bridge · 536
The Survivor · 537

Cathy Song (1955–)   538
The Youngest Daughter · 538

Annie Finch (1956–)   540
Another Reluctance · 540
Insect · 540

Li-Young Lee (1957–)   542
The Gift · 542
Eating Together · 543

Carl Phillips (1959–)   544
   Our Lady · 544
   As from a Quiver of Arrows · 545

Nick Flynn (1960–)   547
   Bag of Mice · 547
   Cartoon Physics, part 1 · 547

Elizabeth Alexander (1962–)   549
   The Venus Hottentot · 549
   Affirmative Action Blues (1993) · 552
   Equinox · 554

Reetika Vazirani (1962–2003)   555
   FROM White Elephants:
      A Million Balconies · 555
      Train Windows · 555

Sherman Alexie (1966–)   556
   What the Orphan Inherits · 556
   The Powwow at the End of the World · 557

Natasha Trethewey (1966–)   558
   Hot Combs · 558
   Amateur Fighter · 558
   Flounder · 559

A. E. Stallings (1968–)   561
   The Tantrum · 561

Joanna Klink (1969–)   562
   Spare · 562

Brenda Shaughnessy (1970–)   563
   Postfeminism · 563
   Your One Good Dress · 564

Kevin Young (1970–)   565

Quivira City Limits · 565
Everywhere Is Out of Town · 566
Whatever You Want · 567

Terrance Hayes (1971–)   568

At Pegasus · 568
Lady Sings the Blues · 569

Acknowledgments

Choosing and representing an entire century of American poetry doesn't happen overnight and certainly not single-handedly. I cannot thank my editor at Penguin Classics, Elda Rotor, enough for her fortitude in seeing this project through, and assistant editor Lorie Napolitano for her attention to detail and her diligence.

My immense gratitude goes out to my assistant Anne Gilliam, proofreader and problem solver extraordinaire. Her focused energy pushed me along when I needed it most.

I also thank the University of Virginia for sabbatical leaves which afforded me the necessary time to compile this anthology, and the university library for supplementing my personal book collection through its extensive holdings and easy inter-library loans.

Last but not least: Completing this collection would have been impossible without the help of my husband, Fred Viebahn. His patience during this four-year enterprise was nothing short of heroic, while his willingness to take time out of his own writing regimen in order to act as a sounding board and creative consultant—as well as emergency proofreader and resident drill sergeant whenever deadlines loomed—has most certainly earned him a marble bust in my personal Walhalla.

Introduction

My Twentieth Century of American Poetry

Dear T.,

When you heard that I was editing this anthology, you wrote: "I look forward to your vision of 20th Century American Poetry and I'm so glad for it." To which I inwardly cringed, for your e-mail arrived just as I found myself so deep inside this enterprise as to be hopelessly blinded by the trees in the forest, the forest, the forest.

But your words reminded me why I accepted this Sisyphean task. I said yes because I believed I had a clear vision—so clear, in fact, that in that one nanosecond following the publisher's query, I saw the whole trajectory of the twentieth century and how it played out poetically for America. I thought the foreword would be the easy part . . . and I should have written it right then, before rereading, discovering, misplacing notes; before tracking down copyright dates, crunching numbers—in short, before the politics of selection could interfere with my judgment. And so I have decided to begin this foreword with an open letter to you, who were so hopeful and clear about the necessity for "my vision," as you put it: to reflect with you on the selections made, both of poets and their poems; to bemoan the reprint fees that kept certain works (and, yes, even their authors) from inclusion, shortened some entries, and forced me to face those horrible, necessary questions—the only relevant questions, really, that should guide a compilation of this scope: Is this a voice that will be remembered? Did he or she make an impact that mattered?

And now we find ourselves with a sticky wicket (as the British would say), because so many factors are at work: the influx of creative writing programs, which give young writers a place to exist as they develop; the economic exigencies and human prejudices that kept many of the poor, the nonwhite, the female voices from being heard for much of the century; the advances in science (birth control, for instance) that resulted in increased independence for women and therefore more women publishing; the impact of wars on existential utterances; the cultural renaissances that have shaped and reshaped African-American poetry; technology (again), which has driven the development of presentation tools, from manual typewriters to IBM Selectrics, mimeographs to photocopies, offset printing to digital print-on-demand, computer diskettes to cyber magazines.

If I could, I'd make this introduction a fold-out book. Open to the first page, and up would pop a forest: a triangle of birches labeled Robert Frost, a solitary Great Oak for Wallace Stevens, a patch of quirky sycamores tagged William Carlos Williams, and a Dutch Elm for Hart Crane, with a double lane of poplars for Elizabeth Bishop and a brilliant autumnal maple tree marked Langston Hughes bearing leaves called Harper, Clifton, Soto. Lift up a birch leaf and find Donald Hall; opposing sycamore branches might bear the names Robert Creeley (with a sprouting Kay Ryan) and Robert Hayden (with shoots labeled Alexander, Dunn, Bidart). Turn the page to a jungle: There are Ginsberg's exuberant vines, with orchids populating the densest entanglements; Sharon Olds perched atop the Sexton/O'Hara thicket; Terrance Hayes latched onto the thick coiled tubers of Gwendolyn Brooks and Robert Lowell. On the next page, a cityscape unfolds with two main thoroughfares, Pound Boulevard and Eliot Avenue, running nearly parallel (after merging early on, then veering off again) through neighborhoods clustered around H. D. Arcade, Auden Gardens, Walcott Plaza.

No matter. Here are the poems I see emblazoned on pennants along the road we have just traversed, my selection from the poetry that accompanied America through the last century, interpolated with the times in which they were forged and upon which they exerted their spirit. This is the proper moment to look back—after the first decade of the twenty-first century has given us the illusion of distance, after we have reconciled ourselves to owning this scary new millennium by looking forward before we've begun to forget. The past is never more truly the past than now.

Yours, as ever,

Rita

*   *   *

The king is dead; long live the king.
—ANONYMOUS

The *Anthology of Twentieth-Century American Poetry* sounds so portentous, so absolute—the borders staked out, the sentries armed—that right away a definition of terms is called for. I thought it would be sheer pleasure to be given permission to indulge in my favorite pastime, reading, while feeding my passion, poetry. However: the entire century, the entire United States of America—where does one begin and where end exactly? Hence, on to the terms.

Anthologies are usually arranged chronologically, with the occasional half-hearted attempt to suggest literary movements by sectioning off decades or inserting special clumpings into the chronological mix—Harlem Renaissance,

Black Mountain school, the Beats. It's the proverbial catch-22: Present the poets in sequential order, and each poem touts its wares standing alone, at the expense of knowing the conditions that spawned and nurtured it; one result of this method is that a love poem from 1908 will invariably sound stilted when compared to this month's similarly inclined but less accomplished lyric. On the other hand, any attempt at a delineation of trends and events coincident with a generation of poets inevitably founders, for there are so many exceptions to whatever grid one tries to superimpose on such living, breathing material: Sara Teasdale was ten years younger than Robert Frost but died thirty years before him, so we will never know how she might have evolved as a poet; the flame of Sylvia Plath's thirty-one years casts a curiously static light next to the brilliant arc inscribed by Derek Walcott, whose gifts became manifest around the same time (Plath was two years his junior) but grew to encompass the epic proportions of his masterpiece *Omeros,* published when the poet was sixty.

So it seems we are doomed from the start. I have resigned myself to the conventional chronological sorting in the hopes that this will be seen not as an attempt to corral poets into historical arenas but rather as a nod to the ineluctable influence of the quotidian—the cultural signatures of the century as well as the significance of being an American poet evolving under those signatures. This foreword shall suggest trends—patterns in a tapestry whose many colorful threads exult in running riot. In other words, although for the most part I will be toeing the line along which we move from the past toward the future, be prepared for a few sidesteps, even a leap or two or a quick glimpse back.

Certain margins hold firm, even if at first glance they might seem arbitrary. All poets live(d) or were born in the United States of America, and their poems were written in English. All poems have been published no earlier than 1900 and no later than 2000. Demarcating the starting line proved unproblematic, with only Stephen Crane missing the cut entirely; certain landmark poems, such as "Richard Cory" and Dunbar's "We Wear the Mask," were also ineligible, although their authors were not. Stretching the finish line, however, was a more dubious endeavor, and I ended up having to exclude many poets who have gained reputations in the first decade of the twenty-first century and will most likely figure in anthologies of the new millennium. Likewise, the last entries in this volume represent the earlier work of poets yet to reach their peak. Some have since gone on to win major awards, while new and younger talents have sprung from the loam of creative writing workshops, suddenly and loudly "in."

Slippages like these invite the question, Why draw a line in the sand and say, Here, and no further? Shouldn't anyone who had already begun to publish in the "old" century be represented by their best work, even if it appeared after 2000? Shouldn't established poets be represented by the fullest trajectory of their oeuvre?

I don't mean to be flip, but one has to stop somewhere. And as it happens, the end of the millennium is not merely "as good a place as any"—it's a unique marker.

We humans assign significance to grand finales—to a century or, in this case, also a millennium. We begin to wrap things up long before the end arrives: Nations reflect upon their history and destiny, ordinary citizens grow sentimental and superstitious by turns, artists shake off complacency to tackle the dreaded monster of mortality with an exalted sense of purpose and doom.

Only when the king is dead may the eulogies begin. Only now that we have stepped firmly over the timeline can we begin to focus on what the twentieth century, with its hundred springs and hundred summers and hundred autumns and hundred winters, was all about.

*   *   *

> The United States . . . is she who is the mother of twentieth century civilization. She began to feel herself as it just after the Civil War. And so it is a country the right age to have been born in and the wrong age to live in.
>
> —GERTRUDE STEIN

The beginning of the twentieth century was still partially populated by those who had crawled out of the wreckage of the Civil War thirty-five years earlier—defeated but defiant former Confederates, victorious but insecure Northerners, an involuntary population of freedmen struggling to create an identity for themselves in hostile environments. Waves of immigrants, mostly European, brought their own cultural riches to the mix, but also their social and economic traumata. While the émigré would need time to acquire the language skills necessary to partake in the literary discourse, those who were already publishing at the turn of the century had either witnessed slavery and the battles fought over that disgraceful institution or had seen how the wounds of remembered strife, prejudice, poverty, humiliation, and deadly turmoil were borne forward, still festering, in the tales of their parents and neighbors. Not surprising, then, that as the new century dawned, many citizens who could afford a little wiggle room were motivated to start afresh, do things differently, embrace the new.

Edgar Lee Masters's *Spoon River Anthology* is so familiar a presence in literature textbooks, it's difficult to imagine how startling the testimonials of his townspeople must have sounded to post-Victorian (read post–Civil War) American ears. The volume begins with what seems to be a lament for times past, an elegy for those who could talk

> . . . of the fish-frys of long ago,
> Of the horse-races of long ago at Clary's Grove,
> Of what Abe Lincoln said
> One time at Springfield.

The offhand, rather abrupt ending is anything but casual; what Masters chose to leave ringing in that silence was the ghostly damage from the injuries this young country had inflicted on itself and whose last living witnesses were buried under the poet's allegorical earth. That was the past, he seemed to be saying; but now we have our own songs to sing.

At first the new century's poets committed themselves to bearing witness. Portraits and dramatic monologues abounded—E. A. Robinson's hapless loners, Frost's taciturn farmers, Amy Lowell's grieving widow. Those sidelined from the mainstream's surging currents seized the opportunity to bring attention to their condition and were more often than not either ignored or confined to stereotype, praised for what Paul Laurence Dunbar called a "jingle in a broken tongue." The impulse driving them all, however, stemmed from the same revelation: that every person contains a story that, if told well, would resonate within us no matter how strange or unfamiliar the circumstances, bound as we are by the instincts and yearnings of human existence.

*   *   *

> Emily Dickinson wrote that she was Nobody at approximately the same time Walt Whitman was claiming to be everybody.
> —ALICIA OSTRIKER

Emily Dickinson and Walt Whitman are generally regarded as the double-yolked egg from which hatched a brood of distinctly American prosodies: Whitman would have thrilled to the multitudes thronging Hart Crane's Brooklyn Bridge and stood shoulder to shoulder, howling, with Allen Ginsberg; Dickinson would have hummed along with the "happy genius" of William Carlos Williams's household. But the century was advancing, acquiring its own demons.

Four men emerged as early monoliths: Robert Frost, Wallace Stevens, William Carlos Williams, and Ezra Pound. Born within eleven years of each other, these four—soon joined by T. S. Eliot and E. E. Cummings—would lay the framework for modern poetry that informed most of the poetic trends specific to the United States of America.

Yes, these six poets were all Caucasian males, but so was then, by design, membership in the cultural elite. For the most part, minority expression was obliged to identify itself in relationship to the establishment; female and nonwhite poets had little choice but to emulate or, if temperamentally suited, argue with the rulers of mainstream perception.

*   *   *

> Style is . . . the mind skating circles around itself as it moves forward.
> —ROBERT FROST

One could explain away the phenomenon of Robert Frost with the adage "He who dies with the most toys wins," but that would be unfair and, in fact, epitomize the dismissive attitude characterizing the Frost-bashing of the 1970s and 1980s. Still, Wallace Stevens preceded him to the grave; William Carlos Williams died the same year but was nine years younger and had not been seen by millions on TV at John F. Kennedy's inauguration. In terms of longevity, only Pound could compete, but with a reputation tarnished by his pro-Fascist and anti-American activities during World War II, he spent the last twenty-seven years of his life incarcerated, institutionalized, or in exile.

Too many readers see Frost as a grandfatherly coot dispensing homespun homilies. His knack for bons mots ("Good fences make good neighbors") can be overwhelming, and there's the temptation to gloss over the complex emotional topographies of his best work.

"The Death of the Hired Man" takes the pith and immediacy of Shakespear-ean drama and places it squarely in the poetic arena. Frost asks us to consider this moment with the mind-eye of poetry; at first, the lengthy exchanges of dia-logue sound curiously flattened, with a nineteenth-century lyricism soaring whenever descriptive passages interpose. Gradually our ear adjusts to the subtle patterns of New England dialect; the prosaic business of stagecraft falls away as a magical layering of traditional rhythms with the cadence of human utterance takes hold; and the dialogue sings:

> "Home," he mocked gently.
>   "Yes, what else but home?
>
> It all depends on what you mean by home.
> Of course he's nothing to us, any more
> Than was the hound that came a stranger to us
> Out of the woods, worn out upon the trail."
>
> "Home is the place where, when you have to go there,
> They have to take you in."
>
>   "I should have called it
> Something you somehow haven't to deserve."
>
> ("The Death of the Hired Man," lines 116–125)

In the lyric narrative that became his signature—"Birches," "Stopping by Woods on a Snowy Evening"—Frost's touch is masterfully ambivalent. Years spent wrapped in the mantle of Poetry's statesman (a distinction he avidly pursued and coveted, even when he grew to chafe under its expectations) produced a cadre of pieces geared toward dispensing wisdom; the satisfaction delivered by poems like "Fire and Ice," "Design," and "Acquainted with the Night" is blunt and somewhat smug. The poem "Directive," however, published when he was seventy-three, finds its way back to an elegiac restraint resonant with dramatic undertones and lyric descants—in short, vintage Frost.

*　　*　　*

> The poet is the priest of the invisible.
> —WALLACE STEVENS

To understand the tremendous importance of modernism as a literary movement in America, we must look back to Victorian England. Although American democracy had gone to great lengths (and through a couple of wars) to distance itself from the former colonial rulers, the two countries, linked by a common language, were still quite close culturally. By the end of the nineteenth century, the Victorians' stolid moral and religious institutions had begun to show cracks: The revelations of Darwinism and rapidly accelerating industrialization, soon to be exacerbated by the horrors of World War I and expanding struggles for workers' rights, challenged the old order with its God-given statutes of right and wrong. Sophisticated readers were now less interested in contemplative entertainment than in words that lent meaning to the confusing changes upon them. Modernism rose from the ruins: Nothing is stable, reality is not necessarily synonymous with truth, truth can be imaginary. Although the impressionist painters had already introduced the unsettling notion that we do not see the world directly but rather the light playing off of the world in our imagination, their take offered aesthetic variations of the factual world with just a mild sense of alienation; modernism—at least its most emphatic representatives—did away with certainties altogether.

Into this disquieting age strode Wallace Stevens, a man with a mind of his own: He married against his parents' wishes (and never spoke with his father again), attended Harvard, was admitted to the New York bar—only to turn his back on the intellectual elite to work as an insurance executive for the rest of his life. As a poet he was a late bloomer, publishing his first book at age forty-four. He argued with Robert Frost, fought with Ernest Hemingway (true to form, Hemingway knocked him down), challenged Frost anew. And his poems were unlike anyone else's.

Stevens has been described as a poet of the mind. More precisely, he believed that the mind imposes its interpretation of reality on our consciousness, that there is no objective reality but that which our mind perceives, interprets, and impresses upon our awareness at any given moment. The emperor of ice cream, then, is a fitting monarch for an empire where each moment quickly melts away while the pleasure experienced in that instant lingers, absolute and powerfully real. In "Thirteen Ways of Looking at a Blackbird" (arguably his most popular poem), Stevens turns an apprehended point in time this way and that, light catching in the interstices. To the observer in "Anecdote of the Jar," a glass jar placed in the landscape makes "the slovenly wilderness / Surround that hill"; the jar, having no mind to adjust its reality, takes "dominion everywhere." Stevens was a modernist poet who exhibited none of the anxiety modernism often engendered; rather than fret over the lack of objective reality, Stevens championed "the supreme fiction" of the mind, content to walk to work every day, write his poems, and savor "the music of what happens."

*   *   *

The image is more than an idea. It is a vortex or cluster of fused ideas and is endowed with energy.

—EZRA POUND

Along came Ezra Pound and wooed an entire generation. Who could resist his vitality, his brilliant outrageousness, his infectious visionary zeal? "Make it new!" he exhorted, before hunkering down in Mussolini's Italy. In 1913, he published the English poet F. S. Flint's essay "Imagisme" in the magazine *Poetry*, which Harriet Monroe had founded the previous year in Chicago and for which Pound worked as its foreign editor. Flint set down the tenets of his and Pound's aesthetic: "1. Direct treatment of the 'thing', whether subjective or objective; 2. To use absolutely no word that does not contribute to the presentation; 3. As regarding rhythm: to compose in the sequence of the musical phrase, not in the sequence of a metronome."

This manifesto became the movement's mantra. "A poem should not mean / But be," proclaimed Archibald MacLeish, and William Carlos Williams's red wheelbarrow proved the point. Hilda Doolittle, who had also come to Europe, whittled her signature down to the initials (Pound, her onetime fiancé, dubbed her "H.D., Imagiste") and set to the task of writing her feminine response, soon to be joined by wealthy Bostonite Amy Lowell.

Under the broad umbrella of modernism, Pound next tried to put his personal stamp on his own fringe. He called it vorticism, decreeing that an image is not reproduced as reality but as a construct, charged with visions of history, cultural allusions, the collective unconscious, and inscribed with the existing sociolinguistic palette. Although his friend T. S. Eliot and a few British artists initially subscribed to its vague terms, vorticism failed to take hold.

Pound pressed on. His expatriate status in London, before and during World War I, afforded him a splendid isolation from the immediacy of American trends, yet offered plenty of European influences, leaving his nimble intelligence free to dip and worm into other cultures. This attitude bore certain dangers—the loss of oneself in a single mythology (as happened to H.D., who became enamored with ancient Greece) or, in Pound's case, the immersion in many traditions, concomitant with an abdication of responsibility . . . which perhaps later contributed to his mounting irrationalism, anti-Semitism, and anti-American rants.

A hundred years after, we can see Pound's manifestos as attempts to invest the physical world with cultural palimpsests of influence; his argument, essentially, was that nothing—no thing—is absolute. "Old news," we might say today, bombarded as we are by the multifarious, conflicting verities advanced by our ever-present audiovisual media. We must remember, however, that until the advent of mass communication, news arrived through narrow, relatively privileged channels, and shaking loose fact from fiction—that is, conflicting facts from useful fictions—was a task akin to soothsaying.

*   *   *

> Where else can what we are seeking arise from but speech?
> —WILLIAM CARLOS WILLIAMS

In many ways, William Carlos Williams was a twentieth-century literary Everyman. He had a full-time professional career as a physician with a private practice in his hometown of Rutherford, New Jersey; he also led a full life as a writer, with an oeuvre that included novels, short stories, plays, autobiography, and of course, poetry. He jotted down lines between patient consultations and hospital visits, claiming that medical training had sharpened his observational skills. (Having been raised on the glazed red wheelbarrow, I have to nod in weary acquiescence.)

It hadn't always been that way. His early literary role models, while a student at the University of Pennsylvania, were the Romantic poets, especially Keats. Williams credited his friendship with Ezra Pound during that time for catapulting him out of the nineteenth century and into the twentieth, though he would eventually veer away from the static aesthetics of imagism in search of, as he put it, "ways of managing the language."

The key to creating an authentic American poetry, Williams believed, lay in the speech patterns of ordinary people. Listening to his patients' stories awoke in him a desire to transmit onto the page the unique vitality of the American idiom. He chastised Eliot for looking backward and considered *The Waste Land* a betrayal. A new prosody was needed: a system that would free American poetry from the tyranny of iambic pentameter yet provide a structure flexible enough to incorporate the improvisational cadences of the spoken word.

What he came up with was the variable foot. Based on musical measure, Williams's "foot" corresponded to a "beat," variable because the number of words contained in each foot varied according to the energy of what was being expressed. (An exclamation might warrant many more words per foot than a calm reflection, for instance.) Furthermore, this variable line was broken into three units and arranged in a series of descending triads, each sub-line indented a bit more than the previous, so that the reader would step from one pulsed exhalation to the next, down the page. This prosodic strategy found its apotheosis in Williams's great book-length love poem, *Asphodel, That Greeny Flower.*

Ironically, Williams's faith in America hindered the recognition he so craved from his countrymen. His books met with muted interest; his belated appointment as Consultant in Poetry at the Library of Congress was thwarted by politicians who decried his leftist affiliations. He died in 1963, two months before receiving the Pulitzer Prize for his volume *Pictures from Brueghel,* as well as the Gold Medal for poetry from the National Institute of Arts and Letters.

*   *   *

Don't try to enjoy it, let it try to enjoy you.
—E. E. CUMMINGS

Almost all serious artists were, at least initially, deeply affected by modernism, even if what in youth might have seemed like a revolt would in later life often deteriorate into surrendering to one's own quirks. T. S. Eliot's Prufrock is a modern-day Hamlet beset not by familial treachery but the betrayal of meaning; his mental pacing dictates the poem's rhythm—just as the Age of Uncertainty is rendered in the fragmentation of *The Waste Land,* whose "heap of broken images" presents a vision of a universe lost to itself. In time, however, Eliot's attempts at hiding his squeamishness vis-à-vis the vox populi behind a mask of world-weary condescension led him to repudiate his American roots by concurrently becoming a British subject and embracing Anglicanism, a sourpuss retreating behind the weathered marble of the Church.

Following Pound's and Eliot's example, many poets plunged headlong into the Long Poem—H.D. (*Trilogy*), William Carlos Williams (*Paterson*), Melvin B. Tolson (*Harlem Gallery*). The exception was E. E. Cummings. Into a hothouse of exotic, overcultivated, and cross-fertilized specimens, he let in a blast of outside air. Where others burrowed deeper into *self*-consciousness, Cummings delighted in the mélange of consciousness, the sheer messiness of living in the quotidian. He treated language as a malleable, evolving ectoplasm; if there were no existing words to express the moment, Cummings invented them, then gave us a soundtrack ("far away and wee," "wish by spirit and if by yes") to his observations of everyday American life—from the joy of a child with his balloon to the snobbery of the "unbeautiful" Cambridge ladies with their "comfortable minds." Through his conscious immersion in linguistic sensations, the arrangements of sound in shifting rhetorical landscapes, Cummings coined language that smashed words and sensory impressions together, up against the act of articulation.

That a poet would go eye-to-eye with his medium was not new. What was different in Cummings was the relentlessness of his shorthand, his insistence that readers navigate his terrain on his terms. The poem "r-p-o-p-h-e-s-s-a-g-r" takes the dismantling one crucial step further: Not only does he strip syntax and syllables down to their barely speakable essentialness, but the very words are dismantled. Squinting at the twentieth-century canon through Cummings's corrective lens, it is easy to see the sepia filter later supplied by Langston Hughes and make out the future contours of John Berryman; further along the spectrum lurk the practitioners of L=A=N=G=U=A=G=E poetry.

*   *   *

It is human nature to stand in the middle of a thing.
—MARIANNE MOORE

It's time to take a break here before we march on. Although men dominated the art of poetry (and its business) throughout much of the twentieth century—no wonder, given society's prevalent role assignments before feminism put up a fight—several women breached the ramparts of male power and self-importance early on. The flowering of Amy Lowell, H.D., Gertrude Stein, and Alice Dunbar could be accepted by the male power structure with a lenient smile and attributed to the feminine mystique; nevertheless, it created the fissures that would later, in the century's fourth quarter, crack open wide enough to admit equity in quantity and quality, if not quite yet in positions of power.

Amy Lowell's "Patterns," though somewhat reserved and stiff, is nonetheless remarkable for its scathing condemnation of societal norms: The traditional behavior prescribed for and expected of women is examined and rejected, yet maintained on the surface—a female Richard Cory who decides to keep on living, a dichotomy that presented a volatile package in its time. Both Lowell's whaleboned Madame and Alice Dunbar's despairing seamstress rage inwardly, giving fair warning of explosions to come. And come they will eventually—Sylvia Plath's rage, Anne Sexton's biting sarcasm, Adrienne Rich's break with traditional mythologies, the unabashed sexual ruminations of Sharon Olds. And let's not forget the women who paved the road before them: Marianne Moore, Edna St. Vincent Millay, Louise Bogan, Muriel Rukeyser, Elizabeth Bishop.

H.D. eventually outgrew Pound's label "Imagiste." After early brief lyrics like "Sea Rose," she perfected a three-line stanza whose cadenced phrases hovered as if caught in the spell of an incantation ("thrall" was one of her favorite words); her late work exemplified the tenets of the 1960s movement écriture féminine, which called for the feminine inscription of the body onto the text.

Stately Marianne Moore, whose orderly poems seemed nearly impregnable, was mentor and friend to Elizabeth Bishop, two dozen years her junior, whose own exquisitely crafted "imaginary gardens" contained their share of Moore's "toads"—iron kettles and oarlocks and stuffed loons—yet somehow managed to chisel the universe into pixilated uncertainties. Reticence and flawless craftsmanship became the accepted manner; like the child drawing "another inscrutable house" (Bishop's "Sestina"), female poets in the first half of the century coded their protest. Beneath the genteel shell of Amy Lowell's maven, the static portraits of H.D.'s Helen or Louise Bogan's Medusa, Sara Teasdale's fervent lyrics, Marianne Moore's sardonic intelligence, and Edna St. Vincent Millay's merry peccadilloes, a subversive dissembling throbbed.

It has always fascinated me how men, even those of "good will" and a benevolent nature, can see and rail against those of society's ills that have affected them and yet have a hard time letting go of their male-centered privileges. Poets have been no exception to this paradox. There is no denying that men ruled not only government and industry throughout the twentieth century but held sway over culture as well, including the politics, economics, and trends of poetry. Outside of the privacy of the home, the environment was mostly male; exceptions were permitted only as long as they didn't threaten the status quo. This does not diminish the great contributions the male masters made to the land- and mindscapes of art, and it is moot to ask now what might have been lost in that environment, but it needs to be said as a warning to keep us from repeating the flaws of the past.

For much of the twentieth century—even in the allegedly progressive USA—women were expected to remain a few steps behind their men. They were not the only discriminated group, of course; racial minorities also had to take a backseat on the bus that was in no hurry to leave the good ole times behind.

*　*　*

The American Mind must reckon with a fundamentally changed Negro.

—ALAIN LOCKE, "THE NEW NEGRO"

By 1925, when Alain Locke's essay "The New Negro" appeared in the magazine *Survey Graphic*, the Harlem Renaissance was already well under way. Six years earlier, Claude McKay had sounded an electrifying call to arms with his sonnet "If We Must Die"; Jean Toomer's *Cane*—a collage of prose pieces, poetry, and song—had appeared in 1923. Duke Ellington was playing regular gigs in New York, and a nineteen-year-old Langston Hughes had published "The Negro Speaks of Rivers" before leaving Columbia University in 1922, after his freshman year, citing his run-ins with prejudice.

Just who was this New Negro, and how did he end up in Harlem? The transformation of a Manhattan neighborhood originally built for the white upper-middle class into the nerve center of black art, music, and literature, which lasted as such for more than a decade, was born from the confluence of several social, economic, and political factors. The Great Migration had started around 1910; impoverished black sharecroppers fleeing an unrepentant and unreconstructed South responded to the siren calls of industry and moved into major urban centers of the North. The war effort created even more jobs; meanwhile, a housing glut in New York induced landlords to lower rents in order to attract tenants. Harlem rapidly became an African-American district.

A taste of economic independence, a ready-made community built on shared experiences, songs, and sorrows—the combination was joyous, galvanizing, and irresistible. For the first time in American history, black artists were not working in isolation; buoyed by racial pride, surrounded by those who understood their backstory, they felt empowered to explore all aspects of their humanity, no longer locked into the roles of militant or minstrel. This gave them freedom to experiment, to stretch previous precepts of prosody, to dip into other artistic modes for inspiration and cross-pollination—Langston Hughes's "Dream Boogie," for example, which simulated the syncopated rhythms of a jazz piano, with the speaker's conflicted stance reflected in the stops and reversals of the music. In his article "The Negro Artist and the Racial Mountain" (published in the *Nation* in 1926), Hughes made his case clear: "We younger Negro artists now intend to express our individual dark-skinned selves without fear or shame. If white people are pleased we are glad. If they aren't it doesn't matter. We know we are beautiful. And ugly, too. . . . If colored people are pleased we are glad. If they are not, their displeasure doesn't matter either. We build our temples for tomorrow, as strong as we know how and we stand on the top of the mountain, free within ourselves."

Or, as Duke Ellington would say, "It don't mean a thing if it ain't got that swing."

* * *

Tomorrow's gone—we'll have tonight!
—DOROTHY PARKER

The Roaring Twenties were the party before the knock on the door; they all knew it couldn't last, so they partied harder. There was relief at having survived the Great War, but the horrors still lingered while the industrial revolution got another jump start. This mixture of exuberance and anxiety found expression in the brittle glee of Edna St. Vincent Millay's flaring candle, E. E. Cummings's syntactical break dances, the cacophony of urban life on Hart Crane's bridge.

The Great Depression burst the bubble; the party was over. Many writers found a new connection to community—not to mention a livelihood—working for government job programs, in particular the Federal Writers' Project. Ironically, once the economy began to turn around, social commitment became suspect as the establishment's growing fear of Communism transmogrified into the true ogre: the U.S. Congress's infamous investigative committees in the late forties and early fifties, so utterly un-American in their callous intrusiveness . . . but that's another (sad) story.

*   *   *

I'd sooner, except the penalties, kill a man than a hawk.
—ROBINSON JEFFERS, "HURT HAWKS"

For the most part, the westward expansion of the nineteenth century had left American poetry behind, safely ensconced in the cultural centers of the East. Intrepid American individualism had persisted on its westward vision, a cheerful Grim Reaper mowing down everything in its path on the march to the Pacific. Toward the middle of the twentieth century, especially after World War II, the view shifted: Pound's antiquities had lost their luster, Eliot's England grown stale, the call of Crane's Brooklyn Bridge faded to an echo. West of the Hudson lay a brave new world: the hardscrabble Appalachia of James Wright's southeastern Ohio, Philip Levine's working-class Detroit, Gwendolyn Brooks's impoverished bean eaters in Chicago, the transcendental hermits of Robert Bly's Minnesotan winters. Richard Hugo described the scarred facades of Montana mining towns while over in Oregon, William Stafford's deadpan lines sketched in the implacable face of the northwestern desert. Gary Snyder rambled up and down the West Coast and finally went so far west as to end up Far East, living for years in Japan studying Buddhism before returning to his native California and the "high still air" of the Sierras.

In North Carolina, Charles Olson returned to Black Mountain College. The year was 1951; the school's experimental interdisciplinary curriculum had been attracting innovative artists like Willem de Kooning, John Cage, Merce Cunningham, and Robert Rauschenberg. For the next few years, Olson coached a group of young poets in the principles of composition described in his 1950 essay "Projective Verse," in which he argued that poetic meter should follow the demands of the human breath, proposing an "open form" of "composition by field," with the text conceived as a web of linked perceptions rather than a logic-driven outline. Prominent Black Mountain poets included Robert Creeley, Denise Levertov, and Robert Duncan; the tenets of projectivism (as it was sometimes called) would influence a later movement known as the Language school.

*   *   *

> The scrimmage of appetite everywhere.
> —DELMORE SCHWARTZ

The experience of the Second World War informed, in one way or another and more or less directly, many poets of that generation who had served in the military—Kenneth Koch, Louis Simpson, Richard Hugo, Richard Wilbur, and Anthony Hecht (army); Randall Jarrell, James Dickey, and James Meredith (air force); and Robert Bly and Lawrence Ferlinghetti (navy)—as well as others, like Robert Lowell and William Stafford, who had been conscientious objectors. In the aftermath, the horrors of indiscriminate human slaughter and exposure to the devastating consequences of totalitarian regimes opened the American consciousness to distinctly European concepts like absurdism, nihilism, *tristesse*. If, as Theodor Adorno famously said, to write a poem after Auschwitz was barbaric, new ways of articulating what poetry used to express would have to be found.

The limbo between despair, resignation, and hope caused many American poets to split ranks. The polished wit of James Merrill's formal verse placed him squarely on the side of the poetry establishment, while the elegant poems of the much-laureled Richard Wilbur, reminiscent of Frost's lyric narratives and Stevens's noble imagination, drew criticism from some—including the sharp-tongued Jarrell—for being *too* beautiful (an opinion I do not share).

No longer indebted to the old British school of articulate reasoned oratory and less beholden to social, ethnic, or regional confines, poets were setting fresh examples across movements and cultural lines: Langston Hughes shifted from the decorous pronouncements of his Harlem Renaissance poems ("I too sing America") to the jazz- and bebop-infused rhythms of his 1951 volume, *Montage of a Dream Deferred*; Theodore Roethke coaxed the rigid contours of formal verse into a gnarled lushness reminiscent of the flora in his father's greenhouses, while Randall Jarrell offered a brutal Western take on haiku with "The Death of the Ball Turret Gunner." Margaret Walker's *For My People*, with its loose-limbed lines reminiscent of black sermon, broke through conventional literary norms so powerfully that in 1942 she became the first African-American poet to win the Yale Younger Poets prize. Three years later, with the publication of her first book, *A Street in Bronzeville*, Gwendolyn Brooks confirmed that black women can express themselves in poems as richly innovative as the best male poets of any race; her second book, *Annie Allen*, even snagged the 1950 Pulitzer Prize—the first (and for the next thirty-seven years only) such recognition of a nonwhite poet.

Increasingly, African-American influences were permeating mainstream life and art, even though the phenomenon often remained unacknowledged.

Around the turn of the century, the blues had come up north, met the city, and birthed jazz, which listened to the scat singer and evolved into bebop, blowing apart melody until it became its own rhythm. Musical innovation and improvisation loosened the screws on other traditions as well—and then, in October 1955 at an experimental art gallery in San Francisco, a slight, bespectacled man in his late twenties tilted his head back and howled.

*   *   *

America how can I write a holy litany in your silly mood?
—ALLEN GINSBERG, "AMERICA"

Half a century later, it's hard to imagine what a jolt Ginsberg's *Howl* gave to the self-satisfied fifties, with broadcast series like *Father Knows Best* crooning peace and prosperity while GIs died in Korea and McCarthyism mocked the forefathers' democratic ideals. The new American export, rock 'n' roll, had just begun to rattle the picket fences of middle-class complacency and would eventually shake up mass culture worldwide. Until *Howl*, poets were generally well behaved (if sometimes curmudgeonly or inebriated), and personal declarations were couched in the crafted restraint befitting the gentleman artist. One simply did not shout in public; those who found occasion to raise their voices did so elegantly, in song or praise or faint lament. Now, suddenly, someone was ranting shamelessly.

Howl set off sparks in all directions. Its keenly personal style, its unabashed antiestablishment stance and confessional rawness, stood as an ultimatum to proponents of New Criticism like Allen Tate and Robert Penn Warren, who posited the ideal poem as a self-contained text untethered by authorial intent or historical context. Ginsberg's liberation of the first person "I" opened the floodgates to a host of literary spin-offs, from the Black Mountain and New York schools to their kissing cousins, the Confessional poets.

Every soup gets cold, however, and by the time the Beat poets were losing verbal steam, their take-no-prisoners approach had cleared a trail for the Confessionals, who were dedicated to uncovering a more intimate post-Beat self. When Robert Lowell published *Life Studies* in 1959, he had shed much of his old traditional verse forms, distanced himself from his former New Criticism views, and begun to insist upon telling all, with no consideration for ethical or social decorum. (What use is decorum to a manic-depressive poet who knows that his "mind's not right"?) Anne Sexton wrote in great detail about birth and abortion, celebrating her uterus and pondering suicide; Sylvia Plath painted her father as a Nazi with a "fat black heart," ending her poem "Daddy" with the unforgettable words "Daddy, daddy, you bastard, I'm through."

The cost of such personal exposure was high. Both Sexton and Plath killed themselves. John Berryman sought to harness his own darkness by pouring a cast of characters (featuring Henry and the mysterious Mr. Bones) into eighteen-line verses he called Dream Songs; but in the end he, too, could no longer resist the Grim Reaper he had carried inside for so long: 385 Dream Songs later, Berryman jumped from the Washington Avenue Bridge in Minneapolis—the city where, forty-five years before, his father had also taken his life.

* * *

I don't look on poetry as closed work. I feel they're going on all the time in my head and I occasionally snip off a length.

—JOHN ASHBERY

The melting pot was simmering: With the Beats drumming up followers in California and the Confessionals telling it all in Boston and beyond, another group began to coalesce in New York City. As had been the case with past artistic movements, they were not only poets but painters, dancers, and musicians as well; their shining star was abstract expressionism, whose exponents, many emerging from the terror of war, rejected complacent doctrines such as realistic representation and harmonious composition and instead emphasized surrealism, nihilism, and spontaneous creation—Willem de Kooning's brooding swirls, the action paintings of Jackson Pollock.

Again, artists traded influences across genres. How to translate into words the improvisational styles of jazz virtuosi like Miles Davis and John Coltrane? How to create a line (of language, paint, melody) and then subvert it, deflecting specific meaning in favor of the process itself, so that the act of composition ended not just in a work of art but, as one art critic put it, "an event"? The self-consciousness of creation became the subject of creation; as John Ashbery asked, "Is there anything / To be serious about beyond this otherness / That gets included in the most ordinary / Forms of daily activity"?

The poets of the New York school (Ashbery, Kenneth Koch, and Frank O'Hara, to name a few) used Manhattan as their template—its energy, its penchant for serendipitous encounters. Nothing in life was predictable, they seemed to be saying, not even what you thought you were about to think—so don't take yourself too seriously.

What a contrast to the Confessional poets, with their outpourings of intimate details! Nowhere is this new attitude made more plain than in Koch's deliciously wicked "Fresh Air," which parodies the genteel, overly sensitized poetry of the day, the young poets "trembling in publishing houses and universities." Koch's influence is not to be underestimated: His fantastical, freewheeling cockiness not only gave the literati permission to laugh at themselves, but ushered in farce as a legitimate mode of High Art—an initiative that also encouraged O'Hara, who is generally crowned with the laurel of lightheartedness. (Koch may have seemed to bow to Ovid, but Alexander Pope was his man.) How can we begin to measure the impact made by his children's books, which led generations to the pools of creativity and bid them drink?

*   *   *

> Calling all black people, come in, black people, come on in.
> —AMIRI BARAKA, "SOS"

The concept of the poet as witness ("I have seen") informed the observational stance of the New York school but also served as paradigm for the accusatory, righteous anger of the Black Arts movement, which was possibly the most cohesive among the many cultural upheavals—second-wave feminism, gay awareness, hippies, the student protests—of the sixties, at least in poetry.

Two historic events precipitated a social and interpretive sea change: The first was the civil rights movement, which obtained a public face with Rosa Parks's action of civil disobedience in 1955, steadily gained steam with the Freedom Riders in the early sixties, rose to international prominence with Martin Luther King Jr.'s philosophy of nonviolence and the March on Washington in 1963, before achieving a significant legal victory with the 1964 Civil Rights Act. The second galvanizer was the Vietnam War, which gave rise to the New Left, epitomized by large-scale demonstrations that shook the country to its core, all the way into the seventies.

The transformation of the gifted Beat poet LeRoi Jones into African nationalist firebrand Amiri Baraka in the midsixties signified more than a name change. By 1965, when Malcolm X was assassinated, Baraka was already deeply dissatisfied with the slow progress of the civil rights struggle; his poems thenceforward were defiant, confrontational, and unapologetic. The nascent Black Arts movement entered a new phase; unlike their counterparts of the Harlem Renaissance, African-American poets now were not only describing and reflecting upon the peculiarities of their place at America's table—they were upturning the benches and walking off to eat by themselves. Whether celebrating the strength of black women (Sonia Sanchez), extolling the triple hipness of the new black man (Haki Madhubuti, formerly known as Don L. Lee), or calling for revolt (Baraka), Black Arts movement proponents united in defining their experience and the future on their terms. The old Euro-American literary standards were rejected, and African culture (or rather, an idealized idea of Africa) and its derivatives this side of the Middle Passage became the rallying cry of the New Black Aesthetic. The poetry that emerged was distinctly oral, using the language patterns and vocabulary of the street to arouse feelings of solidarity and pride among African Americans.

Against such clamor and thunder, introspective black poets had little chance to assert themselves and were swept under the steamroller. As the recipient in 1966 of the grand prize for poetry at the First World Festival of Negro Arts in

Dakar, Senegal, Robert Hayden should have been widely praised by his own race; instead he was held suspect for his ties to the white poetry establishment (he had studied under Auden), and it would be nearly a decade before his poems could regain the recognition they deserved. Melvin Tolson's *Harlem Gallery* shared a similar fate: This rollicking, irreverent pastiche of the black cultural elite (which should have been just what the times demanded) appeared in 1965, at the height of civil and racial unrest; unfortunately, the foreword was written by Karl Shapiro, former editor of *Poetry* magazine, whose glib pronouncement that "Tolson writes and thinks in Negro" prompted Sarah Webster Fabio, in a review for *Negro Digest,* to respond: "Melvin Tolson's language is most certainly not 'Negro' to any significant degree. The weight of that vast, bizarre, pseudo-literary diction is to be placed back into the American mainstream where it rightfully and wrongmindedly belongs." Others joined in, deriding Tolson's book as mere high shenanigans, an Uncle Tom's attempt to impress his masters so that they might admit him into the white-dominated literary pantheon.

And yet, regrettable as such postures were, the Black Arts movement was a necessary explosion, commanding attention for a segment of the literary population that, with a few token exceptions, had been largely ignored since the 1920s. Sounding the battle cry "Black is beautiful!" with a breezy disregard for mainstream approval, these buoyantly brash artists found that their public acceptance was spilling beyond their target group, with white students wearing dashikis and crooning to Marvin Gaye. Such success also encouraged other neglected voices to speak up: Feminist poets took heart; Native Americans, Hispanics, gays, and Asian Americans dared to come forward and explore the range of their differences and similarities.

On the other hand, certainly, and sadly, the willful self-segregation of the Black Arts movement contributed to a new entrenchment of a largely whitewashed poetry establishment. The dearth of pigmentation among the faces found on its broadsides and awards committees would have a profound effect for decades to come.

Around the same time, some of the best white male poets sought inspiration—and guidance—in peculiar places. From the Connecticut village of Stonington came the first strange and exhilarating installments of James Merrill's occult adventures; shedding the jeweled carapaces of formalism in favor of the rules of the Ouija board, Merrill's chronicle of conversations with the spirits of W. H. Auden, deceased friends, and a Greek Jew named Ephraim from the first century A.D. marked the beginning of a journey that would culminate in the dazzling 560-page epic *The Changing Light at Sandover.* Others went off in search of themselves, delving into Eastern philosophies, the Jungian collective unconscious, psychoanalytic approaches and interpretations, or the more straightforward symbolism of folktales. In his 1963 essay "A Wrong Turning in American Poetry," Robert Bly took on the century's early grand masters, dismissing Pound's imagism as "Picturism" and pronouncing the concept of objective correlative "astoundingly passionless." Drawing inspiration from the Spanish-language poets Federico García Lorca, César Vallejo, Antonio Machado, and Juan Ramón Jiménez, Bly expanded the idea of "deep image," following the advice of the late-nineteenth–early-twentieth-century German poet Rainer Maria Rilke to "go into yourself" to find images that may not be fully understood by the rational mind—W. S. Merwin's "rain with its bundle of roads," Russell Edson's stone that will not consent to be owned. The poems of Mark Strand and Charles Simic played out their dream logic in a psychic terrain where the method of narration was often the parable: Simic wrapped the nightmarish experience of his Serbian childhood into the iconic tropes of folklore while Strand went deeper, unimagining the self against a landscape as starkly drawn as a Hopper painting.

* * *

show me someone not full of herself
and i'll show you a hungry person

—NIKKI GIOVANNI

The women's movement was growing. Muriel Rukeyser's plea "Speak to me," made in 1935 (in her prescient poem "Effort at Speech Between Two People"), had changed by the sixties to the triumphant shout "No more masks! No more mythologies!" And so the masks—and the gloves—came off. In 1971, the first issue of *Ms.* magazine was published, and Helen Reddy's "I Am Woman" hit the top of the charts; also that year, Adrienne Rich, already renowned as a poet, delivered a paper before the Modern Language Association's Commission on the Status of Women in the Profession. That speech became the landmark essay "When We Dead Awaken: Writing as Re-Vision," in which Rich described the era as a "time of awakening consciousness" for female poets learning to speak "to and of women . . . out of a newly released courage to name, to love each other, to share risk and grief and celebration."

Outward, inward—openness can travel both ways. As feminist writing became more vocal and more politicized, some poets, heeding Rich's counsel that "until we can understand the assumptions in which we are drenched we cannot know ourselves," began to dismantle the myths of the male-centric culture—the "absurdities of the dinner table" (Anne Sexton), the "secret bleeding of a woman" (Diane Wakoski). Challenging the more or less cloaked misogyny of the Black Power movement (where women were being praised for raising young black warriors) were Audre Lorde and June Jordan, whose depictions of life in the crosshairs of gender and racial oppression refused to privilege one identity over the other. "I have been wrong the wrong sex the wrong age / the wrong skin the wrong nose the wrong hair the / wrong need the wrong dream," Jordan wrote in "Poem About My Rights," but concluded: "Wrong is not my name / My name is my own my own my own"!

*   *   *

It is only a matter of time, Indian
you can't sleep with the river forever.
　　　—LESLIE MARMON SILKO, "INDIAN SONG: SURVIVAL"

During the seventies, while America was licking its self-inflicted Vietnam War wounds and most of her citizens were shaking their heads over the Nixon nightmare, more and more of her poets fell under the spell of higher education. Creative writing programs proliferated in colleges and universities, offering technical training and creative confidence to increasing numbers of students. ("You, too, can write like Whitman!") There were rules of prosody to be consumed and regurgitated, free-form writing exercises dished out to encourage sensitivity and spontaneity (even if the end product had to be turned in by semester's end). Most wondrous of all, the fledgling writer's efforts were rewarded with immediate feedback from an accomplished poet-professor as well as a circle of her peers. All this activity transpired in congregations called workshops, where talent was tested and genius honed—though critique could be merciless, and a kind of inspiration-by-committee was often substituted for the genuine, ragged article. Poets were being raised like broods of chicks.

I write this as a graduate and teacher of—and believer in—workshops. I might have been a bit shy but was not faint of heart when, in the midseventies, I attended the Iowa Writers Workshop, that Grand Smithy in the country's heartland where, for well over half a century, writers have been forged and sent out to captivate America from sea to shining sea. What would be the name for a movement that's already institutionalized? There was a chimera known as the Iowa Poem, whose dispassionate diction, spare vocabulary, and unassailable surface concealed a profound fragility; I struggled diligently against its lure and felt a perilous guardedness creeping into my creative marrow. Competition was fierce, at times cutthroat—but did it trample budding talents before they could blossom or merely guarantee the survival of the fittest? Who knows? As the only African American and one of only three minority students in my two years there, I was spared the most bruising battles simply because the other members of the workshop didn't consider us competition; we sat by, an invisible trio, as our white classmates slugged it out in the Iowa sandbox of American poetry.

*   *   *

life is hopelessly frayed,
all loose ends.
　　　—LYN HEJINIAN

Embedded in the zeal of the University of Iowa's flagship creative writing program were the seeds of its own undoing. A new pluralistic energy sprouted as twenty-somethings were taught how to write, how to publish, and were sent forth to teach others, even to found their own writing programs. Despite—or maybe because of—the growing importance of creative writing as a field of study and practice in American colleges and universities, it became harder and harder to identify trends, to differentiate between movements. A narrative poem could assume many guises, from Stephen Dunn's artful anecdotes to Marilyn Chin's sly pronouncements or the smart chat of Barbara Hamby; a poet might choose to tell his story by orbiting a lyrical instance (like the goldfish in Mark Doty's "Brilliance") or by leading us through a shaggy dog tale (David Mason's "Spooning"). Thought could be interrupted (Joanna Klink) or allowed to amass its own wild logic (Harryette Mullen). An insistence on shapeliness—the Celtic "music of what happens" poured into Keats's Grecian Urn—was preserved in Derek Walcott's majestic chronicles, while the formal constructs of Natasha Trethewey's "Flounder" and A. E. Stallings's "The Tantrum" were built to encase a Pandora's box of sorrows. We had Larry Levis's extended meditations on the nature of memory, Lucille Clifton's honey-and-pepper lyrics, Greg Orr's haunting utterances, Frank Bidart's disturbing explorations into human deviation, and Ai's brutalized souls. Jazz, with its delight in improvisation and the "blue note" of irony, continued to inform the work of many (can I get a witness for Michael S. Harper, C. D. Wright, Cornelius Eady, Charles Simic, Brenda Shaughnessy, Yusef Komunyakaa?), while Stephen Dobyns sang a lullaby to the passing century and Michael Palmer, frustrated by mass communication's ability to usurp meaning from language, declared: "I do not know English!"

Enough declaiming—it is time for disclaimers. I assume all responsibility for the selections in this anthology. I have thought long and deeply about the poems included here, and I have agonized over those that did not make it in the end. Although I have tried to be objective, the contents are, of course, a reflection of my sensibilities; I leave it to the reader to detect those subconscious obsessions and quirks as well as the inevitable lacunae resulting from buried antipathies and inadvertent ignorance. In anticipation of the naysayers, all I can say in my defense is: I have tried my best.

The Introduction's Epilogue

Long gone are the times when a poet laureate was paid in royal barrels of sherry; faded to a rosy smudge is the image of the disheveled poet in a garret, starved to sticks yet mustering enough strength to lift a tattered page from the stained coverlet and declaim softly the verse he has just written. Poetry has become a business, albeit a small one; the laws of supply and demand have taken on an urgency similar to the pressures in the wider world of commerce, though in a quirky, somehow Chaplinesque fashion. This is especially true when copyright and permissions fees become part of the equation.

I learned this the hard way. Once I had made my selections for this anthology, I could not simply apply a predetermined blueprint for annual royalty distribution—a kind of equal rights formula where every contributor receives the same per-line or per-page fees based upon a sales percentage. This method is common in some European countries, and similarly equitable calculations are used in the U.S. music industry. Not so in American book publishing. A number of early-twentieth-century poems are now in the public domain and thereby free of copyright restrictions (those whose authors died at least seventy years ago or, in some cases, those that were published in the early decades—it gets complicated). All others, however, are controlled by publishers, agents, or in rare instances the poets themselves, and these fees need to be negotiated case by case, poem by poem.

It doesn't seem right to weigh poems like cabbage or fish, but that is precisely what the final grueling work of an anthologist becomes. And worse: Each poetrymonger applies his own rate, so the crucial question of "Who matters?" is skewed by fees that range from modest to outrageous and don't necessarily correlate to literary significance and artistic influence. With every rights holder applying his or her own more or less arbitrary criteria, the question twists into: Is Poem X worth five times as much as Poem Y? It's a bothersome process at best, a nasty one at worst; the quagmire grew grimmer the deeper I ploughed on, plagued by fears of miscalculation. Therefore, my last disclaimer: Due to budgetary issues, some major poems—and even a few poets—were perforce eliminated. The closer I came to our new millennium, the more unrealistically some permissions fees skyrocketed, and the almighty dollar finally decreed that I whittle down my choices. In a last-minute salvage operation, I appealed directly to many of the poetry merchants; happily, nearly every poet, agent, and publisher contacted responded to my predicament with generosity—except for one, who insisted on unaffordable fees. I could not spend roughly one fourth of the entire budget on a small fraction of the anthology, and I could not betray the trust of those who had granted me affordable fees under the sine qua non that I would not abuse their largesse by shifting the savings to satisfy extreme demands.

And so there are no poems by Allen Ginsberg and Sylvia Plath (and none by Sterling Brown) to be found in these pages, and astute readers might notice bits and pieces of contemporary poetry that also fell victim to their owners' stranglehold. For these involuntary gaps, I ask you to cut me some slack. Fortunately, Ginsberg and Plath are widely available (and even free of charge in your local public library, for instance). Alas, the legacy of the dead can still be enslaved by the living. I wish I could have asked Allen Ginsberg himself, whom I'd met late in his life and come to know as a magnanimous man, what he thought of this; a "New Millennium Howl" might have resulted.

In the end, I believe I have remained true to the quest I embarked on when Elda Rotor, the director of Penguin Classics, wrote me out of the blue to ask if I would consider tackling this colossus; her unwavering confidence in the project kept me going when the din of voices grew loud. Here, then, my panorama of twentieth-century American poetry—viewed not with a scholar's dissecting eye but from the perspective of a contemporary poet who, although not exactly born into her country's mainstream, nevertheless took possession of mainstream society's intellectual shapes and artistic aesthetics to make them her own.

—RITA DOVE

THE
PENGUIN
ANTHOLOGY
OF
TWENTIETH-
CENTURY
AMERICAN
POETRY

Edgar Lee Masters (1868–1950)

Edgar Lee Masters was born in Garnett, Kansas, and grew up in Illinois. He attended Knox College and became a lawyer in Chicago; in 1920 he moved to New York City as a freelance writer. His poetry books include A Book of Verses *(1898),* Songs and Sonnets *(1910),* Songs and Sonnets: Second Series *(1912),* Spoon River Anthology *(1915),* The Great Valley *(1916),* Songs and Satires *(1916),* Toward the Gulf *(1918),* Starved Rock *(1919),* Domesday Book *(1920),* The Open Sea *(1921),* The New Spoon River *(1924),* Selected Poems *(1925),* Lee: A Dramatic Poem *(1925),* Jack Kelso: A Dramatic Poem *(1928),* The Fate of the Jury: An Epilogue to Domesday Book *(1929),* Lichee Nuts *(1930),* Godbey: A Dramatic Poem *(1931),* The Serpent in the Wilderness *(1933),* Richmond: A Dramatic Poem *(1934),* Invisible Landscapes *(1935),* Poems of People *(1936),* The Golden Fleece of California *(1936),* More People *(1939),* Illinois Poems *(1941),* Along the Illinois *(1942),* The Enduring River: Uncollected Spoon River Poems *(1991), and* The Harmony of Deeper Music: Posthumous Poems *(1976). Among his honors were the Mark Twain Medal, the Poetry Society of America Medal, an Academy of American Poets fellowship and the Shelley Memorial Award. Edgar Lee Masters died in a nursing home in Philadelphia.*

From *Spoon River Anthology*

The Hill

Where are Elmer, Herman, Bert, Tom and Charley,
The weak of will, the strong of arm, the clown, the boozer, the fighter?
All, all, are sleeping on the hill.

One passed in a fever,
One was burned in a mine,
One was killed in a brawl,
One died in a jail,
One fell from a bridge toiling for children and wife—
All, all are sleeping, sleeping, sleeping on the hill.

Where are Ella, Kate, Mag, Lizzie and Edith,
The tender heart, the simple soul, the loud, the proud, the happy one?—
All, all, are sleeping on the hill.

One died in shameful child-birth,
One of a thwarted love,
One at the hands of a brute in a brothel,
One of a broken pride, in the search for heart's desire,
One after life in far-away London and Paris
Was brought to her little space by Ella and Kate and Mag—
All, all are sleeping, sleeping on the hill.

Where are Uncle Isaac and Aunt Emily,
And old Towny Kincaid and Sevigne Houghton,
And Major Walker who had talked
With venerable men of the revolution?—
All, all are sleeping on the hill.

They brought them dead sons from the war,
And daughters whom life had crushed,
And their children fatherless, crying—
All, all are sleeping, sleeping, sleeping on the hill.

Where is Old Fiddler Jones
Who played with life all his ninety years,
Braving the sleet with bared breast,
Drinking, rioting, thinking neither of wife nor kin,
Nor gold, nor love, nor heaven?
Lo! he babbles of the fish-frys of long ago,
Of the horse-races of long ago at Clary's Grove,
Of what Abe Lincoln said
One time at Springfield.

Fiddler Jones

The earth keeps some vibration going
There in your heart, and that is you.
And if the people find you can fiddle,
Why, fiddle you must, for all your life.
What do you see, a harvest of clover?
Or a meadow to walk through to the river?
The wind's in the corn; you rub your hands
For beeves hereafter ready for market;
Or else you hear the rustle of skirts
Like the girls when dancing at Little Grove.
To Cooney Potter a pillar of dust
Or whirling leaves meant ruinous drouth;

They looked to me like Red-Head Sammy
Stepping it off, to "Toor-a-Loor."
How could I till my forty acres
Not to speak of getting more,
With a medley of horns, bassoons and piccolos
Stirred in my brain by crows and robins
And the creak of a wind-mill—only these?
And I never started to plow in my life
That some one did not stop in the road
And take me away to a dance or picnic.
I ended up with forty acres;
I ended up with a broken fiddle—
And a broken laugh, and a thousand memories,
And not a single regret.

Petit, the Poet

Seeds in a dry pod, tick, tick, tick,
Tick, tick, tick, like mites in a quarrel—
Faint iambics that the full breeze wakens—
But the pine tree makes a symphony thereof.
Triolets, villanelles, rondels, rondeaus,
Ballades by the score with the same old thought:
The snows and the roses of yesterday are vanished;
And what is love but a rose that fades?
Life all around me here in the village:
Tragedy, comedy, valor and truth,
Courage, constancy, heroism, failure—
All in the loom, and oh what patterns!
Woodlands, meadows, streams and rivers—
Blind to all of it all my life long.
Triolets, villanelles, rondels, rondeaus,
Seeds in a dry pod, tick, tick, tick,
Tick, tick, tick, what little iambics,
While Homer and Whitman roared in the pines?

Edwin Arlington Robinson (1869–1935)

Edwin Arlington Robinson was born in Head Tide, Maine. He attended Harvard and later moved to New York City, where he worked as a clerk until 1910. He led a solitary life, dividing his time between New York and the MacDowell Colony in New Hampshire. Among his poetry books are The Torrent and the Night Before (1896), The Children of the Night (1897), Captain Craig and Other Poems (1902), The Town Down the River (1910), The Man Against the Sky (1916), Merlin (1917), The Three Taverns (1920), Collected Poems (1921, Pulitzer Prize), Avon's Harvest (1921), Roman Bartholomew (1923), The Man Who Died Twice (1924, Pulitzer Prize), Dionysus in Doubt (1925), Tristram (1927, Pulitzer Prize), Fortunatus (1928), Sonnets, 1889–1917 (1928), Cavender's House (1929), Modred (1929), The Glory of the Nightingales (1930), Selected Poems (1931), Matthias at the Door (1931), Talifer (1933), Amaranth (1934), King Jasper (1935), Collected Poems (1937), and Uncollected Poems and Prose (1975). Edwin Arlington Robinson died in New York City.

Miniver Cheevy

Miniver Cheevy, child of scorn,
    Grew lean while he assailed the seasons;
He wept that he was ever born,
    And he had reasons.

Miniver loved the days of old
    When swords were bright and steeds were prancing;
The vision of a warrior bold
    Would set him dancing.

Miniver sighed for what was not,
    And dreamed, and rested from his labors;
He dreamed of Thebes and Camelot,
    And Priam's neighbors.

Miniver mourned the ripe renown
    That made so many a name so fragrant;
He mourned Romance, now on the town,
    And Art, a vagrant.

Miniver loved the Medici,
    Albeit he had never seen one;
He would have sinned incessantly
    Could he have been one.

Miniver cursed the commonplace
    And eyed a khaki suit with loathing;
He missed the mediæval grace
    Of iron clothing.

Miniver scorned the gold he sought,
    But sore annoyed was he without it;
Miniver thought, and thought, and thought,
    And thought about it.

Miniver Cheevy, born too late,
    Scratched his head and kept on thinking;
Miniver coughed, and called it fate,
    And kept on drinking.

Mr. Flood's Party

Old Eben Flood, climbing alone one night
Over the hill between the town below
And the forsaken upland hermitage
That held as much as he should ever know
On earth again of home, paused warily.
The road was his with not a native near;
And Eben, having leisure, said aloud,
For no man else in Tilbury Town to hear:

"Well, Mr. Flood, we have the harvest moon
Again, and we may not have many more;
The bird is on the wing, the poet says,
And you and I have said it here before.
Drink to the bird." He raised up to the light
The jug that he had gone so far to fill,
And answered huskily: "Well, Mr. Flood,
Since you propose it, I believe I will."

Alone, as if enduring to the end
A valiant armor of scarred hopes outworn,
He stood there in the middle of the road
Like Roland's ghost winding a silent horn.
Below him, in the town among the trees,
Where friends of other days had honored him,

A phantom salutation of the dead
Rang thinly till old Eben's eyes were dim.

Then, as a mother lays her sleeping child
Down tenderly, fearing it may awake,
He set the jug down slowly at his feet
With trembling care, knowing that most things break;
And only when assured that on firm earth
It stood, as the uncertain lives of men
Assuredly did not, he paced away,
And with his hand extended paused again:

"Well, Mr. Flood, we have not met like this
In a long time; and many a change has come
To both of us, I fear, since last it was
We had a drop together. Welcome home!"
Convivially returning with himself,
Again he raised the jug up to the light;
And with an acquiescent quaver said:
"Well, Mr. Flood, if you insist, I might.

"Only a very little, Mr. Flood—
For auld lang syne. No more, sir; that will do."
So, for the time, apparently it did,
And Eben evidently thought so too;
For soon amid the silver loneliness
Of night he lifted up his voice and sang,
Secure, with only two moons listening,
Until the whole harmonious landscape rang—

"For auld lang syne." The weary throat gave out,
The last word wavered, and the song was done.
He raised again the jug regretfully
And shook his head, and was again alone.
There was not much that was ahead of him,
And there was nothing in the town below—
Where strangers would have shut the many doors
That many friends had opened long ago.

James Weldon Johnson (1871–1938)

James Weldon Johnson was born in Jacksonville, Florida. After attending Atlanta University, he worked as a schoolteacher, a lawyer, a journalist, a civil rights advocate, and a diplomat (as U.S. consul in Venezuela and Nicaragua). In his later years, he taught at Fisk University. Together with his brother, the composer Rosamond Johnson, he wrote "Lift Every Voice and Sing," which became the Black National Anthem. His poetry books include Fifty Years and Other Poems *(1917),* Saint Peter Relates an Incident *(1934),* Selected Poems *(1936),* The Creation *(1994),* Lift Ev'ry Voice and Sing *(songs, 1995), and* Complete Poems *(2000). Among his honors were the Spingarn Medal and the W.E.B. Du Bois Prize for Negro Literature. James Weldon Johnson died in a car accident while vacationing in Maine.*

The Creation

And God stepped out on space,
And he looked around and said:
I'm lonely—
I'll make me a world.

And far as the eye of God could see
Darkness covered everything,
Blacker than a hundred midnights
Down in a cypress swamp.

Then God smiled,
And the light broke,
And the darkness rolled up on one side,
And the light stood shining on the other,
And God said: That's good!

Then God reached out and took the light in his hands,
And God rolled the light around in his hands
Until he made the sun;
And he set that sun a-blazing in the heavens.
And the light that was left from making the sun
God gathered it up in a shining ball
And flung it against the darkness,
Spangling the night with the moon and stars.
Then down between
The darkness and the light
He hurled the world;
And God said: That's good!

Then God himself stepped down—
And the sun was on his right hand,
And the moon was on his left;
The stars were clustered about his head,
And the earth was under his feet.
And God walked, and where he trod
His footsteps hollowed the valleys out
And bulged the mountains up.

Then he stopped and looked and saw
That the earth was hot and barren.
So God stepped over to the edge of the world
And he spat out the seven seas—
He batted his eyes, and the lightnings flashed—
He clapped his hands, and the thunders rolled—
And the waters above the earth came down,
The cooling waters came down.

Then the green grass sprouted,
And the little red flowers blossomed,
The pine tree pointed his finger to the sky,
And the oak spread out his arms,
The lakes cuddled down in the hollows of the ground,
And the rivers ran down to the sea;
And God smiled again,
And the rainbow appeared,
And curled itself around his shoulder.

Then God raised his arm and he waved his hand
Over the sea and over the land,
And he said: Bring forth! Bring forth!
And quicker than God could drop his hand,
Fishes and fowls
And beasts and birds
Swam the rivers and the seas,
Roamed the forests and the woods,
And split the air with their wings.
And God said: That's good!

Then God walked around,
And God looked around
On all that he had made.
He looked at his sun,
And he looked at his moon,

And he looked at his little stars;
He looked on his world
With all its living things,
And God said: I'm lonely still.

Then God sat down—
On the side of a hill where he could think;
By a deep, wide river he sat down;
With his head in his hands,
God thought and thought,
Till he thought: I'll make me a man!

Up from the bed of the river
God scooped the clay;
And by the bank of the river
He kneeled him down;
And there the great God Almighty
Who lit the sun and fixed it in the sky,
Who flung the stars to the most far corner of the night,
Who rounded the earth in the middle of his hand;
This Great God,
Like a mammy bending over her baby,
Kneeled down in the dust
Toiling over a lump of clay
Till he shaped it in his own image;

Then into it he blew the breath of life,
And man became a living soul.
Amen. Amen.

Paul Laurence Dunbar (1872–1906)

Paul Laurence Dunbar was born in Dayton, Ohio. During high school he edited and published an African-American newspaper, the Dayton Tattler. *Unable to afford college, he worked as an elevator operator, a clerk, and finally as a freelance writer and lecturer, living in Chicago, then Washington, D.C., Harmon, Colorado, and New York City before returning to Dayton. He was married to the poet Alice Moore (Dunbar-Nelson). His poetry books include* Oak and Ivy *(1893),* Majors and Minors *(1896),* Lyrics of Lowly Life *(1896),* Lyrics of the Hearthside *(1899),* Poems of Cabin and Field *(1899),* Candle-lightin' Time *(1901),* Lyrics of Love and Laughter *(1903),* When Malindy Sings *(1903),* Li'l Gal *(1904),* Chris'mus Is a Comin', and Other Poems *(1905),* Howdy, Honey, Howdy *(1905),* Lyrics of Sunshine and Shadow *(1905),* A Plantation Portrait *(1905),* Joggin' Erlong *(1906), and* The Collected Poetry of Paul Laurence Dunbar *(1993). He also wrote the lyrics for the musical* In Dahomey *(New York, 1903). Dunbar died in Dayton, Ohio, from tuberculosis.*

The Poet

He sang of life, serenely sweet,
    With, now and then, a deeper note.
    From some high peak, nigh yet remote,
He voiced the world's absorbing beat.

He sang of love when earth was young,
    And Love, itself, was in his lays,
    But ah, the world, it turned to praise
A jingle in a broken tongue.

Life's Tragedy

It may be misery not to sing at all
    And to go silent through the brimming day.
It may be sorrow never to be loved,
    But deeper griefs than these beset the way.

To have come near to sing the perfect song
    And only by a half-tone lost the key,
There is the potent sorrow, there the grief,
    The pale, sad staring of life's tragedy.

To have just missed the perfect love,
    Not the hot passion of untempered youth,
But that which lays aside its vanity
    And gives thee, for thy trusting worship, truth—

This, this it is to be accursed indeed;
    For if we mortals love, or if we sing,
We count our joys not by the things we have,
    But by what kept us from the perfect thing.

Robert Frost (1874–1963)

Robert Frost was born in San Francisco, California, and moved to Massachusetts in 1885. He attended Dartmouth College and Harvard University, then worked as a teacher, cobbler, and editor before farming in New Hampshire for nine years. From 1912–1915 he lived in Scotland and England; upon his return to the United States, he bought another farm in New Hampshire. He also taught at Amherst College, Middlebury College, and the University of Michigan; as of 1940 he spent his winters in southern Florida. His numerous poetry books include A Boy's Will *(1913),* North of Boston *(1914),* Mountain Interval *(1916),* New Hampshire *(1923, Pulitzer Prize),* West-Running Brook *(1928),* The Lovely Shall Be Choosers *(1929),* Collected Poems *(1930, Pulitzer Prize),* The Lone Striker *(1933),* From Snow to Snow *(1936),* A Further Range *(1936, Pulitzer Prize),* A Witness Tree *(1942, Pulitzer Prize),* Come In, and Other Poems *(1943),* Masque of Reason *(1945),* Steeple Bush *(1947),* Hard Not to be King *(1951)* Aforesaid *(1954),* In the Clearing *(1962),* Longer Poems: The Death of the Hired Man *(1966), and* Complete Poems *(1968). Among his honors were the Congressional Gold Medal and the Bollingen Prize. Robert Frost was President John F. Kennedy's inaugural poet. He died in Boston.*

The Death of the Hired Man

Mary sat musing on the lamp-flame at the table
Waiting for Warren. When she heard his step,
She ran on tip-toe down the darkened passage
To meet him in the doorway with the news
And put him on his guard. "Silas is back."
She pushed him outward with her through the door
And shut it after her. "Be kind," she said.
She took the market things from Warren's arms
And set them on the porch, then drew him down
To sit beside her on the wooden steps.

"When was I ever anything but kind to him?
But I'll not have the fellow back," he said.
"I told him so last haying, didn't I?
'If he left then,' I said, 'that ended it.'
What good is he? Who else will harbour him
At his age for the little he can do?
What help he is there's no depending on.
Off he goes always when I need him most.
'He thinks he ought to earn a little pay,
Enough at least to buy tobacco with,
So he won't have to beg and be beholden.'

'All right,' I say, 'I can't afford to pay
Any fixed wages, though I wish I could.'
'Someone else can.' 'Then someone else will have to.'
I shouldn't mind his bettering himself
If that was what it was. You can be certain,
When he begins like that, there's someone at him
Trying to coax him off with pocket-money,—
In haying time, when any help is scarce.
In winter he comes back to us. I'm done."

"Sh! Not so loud: he'll hear you," Mary said.

"I want him to: he'll have to soon or late."

"He's worn out. He's asleep beside the stove.
When I came up from Rowe's I found him here,
Huddled against the barn-door fast asleep,
A miserable sight, and frightening, too—
You needn't smile—I didn't recognise him—
I wasn't looking for him—and he's changed.
Wait till you see."

                    "Where did you say he'd been?"

"He didn't say. I dragged him to the house,
And gave him tea and tried to make him smoke.
I tried to make him talk about his travels.
Nothing would do: he just kept nodding off."

"What did he say? Did he say anything?"

"But little."

            "Anything? Mary, confess
He said he'd come to ditch the meadow for me."

"Warren!"

            "But did he? I just want to know."

"Of course he did. What would you have him say?
Surely you wouldn't grudge the poor old man
Some humble way to save his self-respect.

He added, if you really care to know,
He meant to clear the upper pasture, too.
That sounds like something you have heard before?
Warren, I wish you could have heard the way
He jumbled everything. I stopped to look
Two or three times—he made me feel so queer—
To see if he was talking in his sleep.
He ran on Harold Wilson—you remember—
The boy you had in haying four years since.
He's finished school, and teaching in his college.
Silas declares you'll have to get him back.
He says they two will make a team for work:
Between them they will lay this farm as smooth!
The way he mixed that in with other things.
He thinks young Wilson a likely lad, though daft
On education—you know how they fought
All through July under the blazing sun,
Silas up on the cart to build the load,
Harold along beside to pitch it on."

"Yes, I took care to keep well out of earshot."

"Well, those days trouble Silas like a dream.
You wouldn't think they would. How some things linger!
Harold's young college boy's assurance piqued him.
After so many years he still keeps finding
Good arguments he sees he might have used.
I sympathise. I know just how it feels
To think of the right thing to say too late.
Harold's associated in his mind with Latin.
He asked me what I thought of Harold's saying
He studied Latin like the violin
Because he liked it—that an argument!
He said he couldn't make the boy believe
He could find water with a hazel prong—
Which showed how much good school had ever done him.
He wanted to go over that. But most of all
He thinks if he could have another chance
To teach him how to build a load of hay—"

"I know, that's Silas' one accomplishment.
He bundles every forkful in its place,
And tags and numbers it for future reference,
So he can find and easily dislodge it

In the unloading. Silas does that well.
He takes it out in bunches like big birds' nests.
You never see him standing on the hay
He's trying to lift, straining to lift himself."

"He thinks if he could teach him that, he'd be
Some good perhaps to someone in the world.
He hates to see a boy the fool of books.
Poor Silas, so concerned for other folk,
And nothing to look backward to with pride,
And nothing to look forward to with hope,
So now and never any different."

Part of a moon was falling down the west,
Dragging the whole sky with it to the hills.
Its light poured softly in her lap. She saw it
And spread her apron to it. She put out her hand
Among the harp-like morning-glory strings,
Taut with the dew from garden bed to eaves,
As if she played unheard some tenderness
That wrought on him beside her in the night.
"Warren," she said, "he has come home to die:
You needn't be afraid he'll leave you this time."

"Home," he mocked gently.

                          "Yes, what else but home?

It all depends on what you mean by home.
Of course he's nothing to us, any more
Than was the hound that came a stranger to us
Out of the woods, worn out upon the trail."

"Home is the place where, when you have to go there,
They have to take you in."

                          "I should have called it
Something you somehow haven't to deserve."

Warren leaned out and took a step or two,
Picked up a little stick, and brought it back
And broke it in his hand and tossed it by.
"Silas has better claim on us you think
Than on his brother? Thirteen little miles

As the road winds would bring him to his door.
Silas has walked that far no doubt to-day.
Why didn't he go there? His brother's rich,
A somebody—director in the bank."

"He never told us that."

            "We know it though."

"I think his brother ought to help, of course.
I'll see to that if there is need. He ought of right
To take him in, and might be willing to—
He may be better than appearances.
But have some pity on Silas. Do you think
If he had any pride in claiming kin
Or anything he looked for from his brother,
He'd keep so still about him all this time?"

"I wonder what's between them."

                     "I can tell you.
Silas is what he is—we wouldn't mind him—
But just the kind that kinsfolk can't abide.
He never did a thing so very bad.
He don't know why he isn't quite as good
As anybody. Worthless though he is,
He won't be made ashamed to please his brother."

"I can't think Si ever hurt anyone."

"No, but he hurt my heart the way he lay
And rolled his old head on that sharp-edged chair-back.
He wouldn't let me put him on the lounge.
You must go in and see what you can do.
I made the bed up for him there to-night.
You'll be surprised at him—how much he's broken.
His working days are done; I'm sure of it."

"I'd not be in a hurry to say that."

"I haven't been. Go, look, see for yourself.
But, Warren, please remember how it is:
He's come to help you ditch the meadow.

He has a plan. You mustn't laugh at him.
He may not speak of it, and then he may.
I'll sit and see if that small sailing cloud
Will hit or miss the moon."

                                It hit the moon.
Then there were three there, making a dim row,
The moon, the little silver cloud, and she.

Warren returned—too soon, it seemed to her,
Slipped to her side, caught up her hand and waited.

"Warren?" she questioned.

                            "Dead," was all he answered.

Mending Wall

Something there is that doesn't love a wall,
That sends the frozen-ground-swell under it,
And spills the upper boulders in the sun;
And makes gaps even two can pass abreast.
The work of hunters is another thing:
I have come after them and made repair
Where they have left not one stone on a stone,
But they would have the rabbit out of hiding,
To please the yelping dogs. The gaps I mean,
No one has seen them made or heard them made,
But at spring mending-time we find them there.
I let my neighbor know beyond the hill;
And on a day we meet to walk the line
And set the wall between us once again.
We keep the wall between us as we go.
To each the boulders that have fallen to each.
And some are loaves and some so nearly balls
We have to use a spell to make them balance:
'Stay where you are until our backs are turned!'
We wear our fingers rough with handling them.
Oh, just another kind of outdoor game,
One on a side. It comes to little more:
There where it is we do not need the wall:
He is all pine and I am apple orchard.

My apple trees will never get across
And eat the cones under his pines, I tell him.
He only says, 'Good fences make good neighbors.'
Spring is the mischief in me, and I wonder
If I could put a notion in his head:
'*Why* do they make good neighbors? Isn't it
Where there are cows? But here there are no cows.
Before I built a wall I'd ask to know
What I was walling in or walling out,
And to whom I was like to give offense.
Something there is that doesn't love a wall,
That wants it down.' I could say 'Elves' to him,
But it's not elves exactly, and I'd rather
He said it for himself. I see him there
Bringing a stone grasped firmly by the top
In each hand, like an old-stone savage armed.
He moves in darkness as it seems to me,
Not of woods only and the shade of trees.
He will not go behind his father's saying,
And he likes having thought of it so well
He says again, 'Good fences make good neighbors.'

Birches

When I see birches bend to left and right
Across the lines of straighter darker trees,
I like to think some boy's been swinging them.
But swinging doesn't bend them down to stay
As ice-storms do. Often you must have seen them
Loaded with ice a sunny winter morning
After a rain. They click upon themselves
As the breeze rises, and turn many-colored
As the stir cracks and crazes their enamel.
Soon the sun's warmth makes them shed crystal shells
Shattering and avalanching on the snow-crust—
Such heaps of broken glass to sweep away
You'd think the inner dome of heaven had fallen.
They are dragged to the withered bracken by the load,
And they seem not to break; though once they are bowed
So low for long, they never right themselves:
You may see their trunks arching in the woods

Years afterwards, trailing their leaves on the ground
Like girls on hands and knees that throw their hair
Before them over their heads to dry in the sun.
But I was going to say when Truth broke in
With all her matter-of-fact about the ice-storm
I should prefer to have some boy bend them
As he went out and in to fetch the cows—
Some boy too far from town to learn baseball,
Whose only play was what he found himself,
Summer or winter, and could play alone.
One by one he subdued his father's trees
By riding them down over and over again
Until he took the stiffness out of them,
And not one but hung limp, not one was left
For him to conquer. He learned all there was
To learn about not launching out too soon
And so not carrying the tree away
Clear to the ground. He always kept his poise
To the top branches, climbing carefully
With the same pains you use to fill a cup
Up to the brim, and even above the brim.
Then he flung outward, feet first, with a swish,
Kicking his way down through the air to the ground.
So was I once myself a swinger of birches.
And so I dream of going back to be.
It's when I'm weary of considerations,
And life is too much like a pathless wood
Where your face burns and tickles with the cobwebs
Broken across it, and one eye is weeping
From a twig's having lashed across it open.
I'd like to get away from earth awhile
And then come back to it and begin over.
May no fate willfully misunderstand me
And half grant what I wish and snatch me away
Not to return. Earth's the right place for love:
I don't know where it's likely to go better.
I'd like to go by climbing a birch tree,
And climb black branches up a snow-white trunk
Toward heaven, till the tree could bear no more,
But dipped its top and set me down again.
That would be good both going and coming back.
One could do worse than be a swinger of birches.

Stopping by Woods on a Snowy Evening

Whose woods these are I think I know.
His house is in the village though;
He will not see me stopping here
To watch his woods fill up with snow.

My little horse must think it queer
To stop without a farmhouse near
Between the woods and frozen lake
The darkest evening of the year.

He gives his harness bells a shake
To ask if there is some mistake.
The only other sound's the sweep
Of easy wind and downy flake.

The woods are lovely, dark and deep,
But I have promises to keep,
And miles to go before I sleep,
And miles to go before I sleep.

Tree at My Window

Tree at my window, window tree,
My sash is lowered when night comes on;
But let there never be curtain drawn
Between you and me.

Vague dream-head lifted out of the ground,
And thing next most diffuse to cloud,
Not all your light tongues talking aloud
Could be profound.

But, tree, I have seen you taken and tossed,
And if you have seen me when I slept,
You have seen me when I was taken and swept
And all but lost.

That day she put our heads together,
Fate had her imagination about her,
Your head so much concerned with outer,
Mine with inner, weather.

Directive

Back out of all this now too much for us,
Back in a time made simple by the loss
Of detail, burned, dissolved, and broken off
Like graveyard marble sculpture in the weather,
There is a house that is no more a house
Upon a farm that is no more a farm
And in a town that is no more a town.
The road there, if you'll let a guide direct you
Who only has at heart your getting lost,
May seem as if it should have been a quarry—
Great monolithic knees the former town
Long since gave up pretense of keeping covered.
And there's a story in a book about it:
Besides the wear of iron wagon wheels
The ledges show lines ruled southeast northwest.
The chisel work of an enormous Glacier
That braced his feet against the Arctic Pole.
You must not mind a certain coolness from him
Still said to haunt this side of Panther Mountain.
Nor need you mind the serial ordeal
Of being watched from forty cellar holes
As if by eye pairs out of forty firkins.
As for the woods' excitement over you
That sends light rustle rushes to their leaves,
Charge that to upstart inexperience.
Where were they all not twenty years ago?
They think too much of having shaded out
A few old pecker-fretted apple trees.
Make yourself up a cheering song of how
Someone's road home from work this once was,
Who may be just ahead of you on foot
Or creaking with a buggy load of grain.
The height of the adventure is the height
Of country where two village cultures faded
Into each other. Both of them are lost.
And if you're lost enough to find yourself
By now, pull in your ladder road behind you
And put a sign up CLOSED to all but me.
Then make yourself at home. The only field
Now left's no bigger than a harness gall.
First there's the children's house of make believe,
Some shattered dishes underneath a pine,

The playthings in the playhouse of the children.
Weep for what little things could make them glad.
Then for the house that is no more a house,
But only a belilaced cellar hole,
Now slowly closing like a dent in dough.
This was no playhouse but a house in earnest.
Your destination and your destiny's
A brook that was the water of the house,
Cold as a spring as yet so near its source,
Too lofty and original to rage.
(We know the valley streams that when aroused
Will leave their tatters hung on barb and thorn.)
I have kept hidden in the instep arch
Of an old cedar at the waterside
A broken drinking goblet like the Grail
Under a spell so the wrong ones can't find it,
So can't get saved, as Saint Mark says they mustn't.
(I stole the goblet from the children's playhouse.)
Here are your waters and your watering place.
Drink and be whole again beyond confusion.

Amy Lowell (1874–1925)

Amy Lowell was born in Brookline, Massachusetts. Independently wealthy, she traveled and lectured widely, promoting poets as well as reviewing their work. Her own poetry books include A Dome of Many-Colored Glass *(1912),* Sword Blades and Poppy Seed *(1914),* Men, Women and Ghosts *(1916),* Can Grande's Castle *(1918),* Pictures of the Floating World *(1919),* Legends *(1921),* What's O'Clock *(1925, Pulitzer Prize),* East Wind *(1926),* Ballads for Sale *(1927), and* The Complete Poetical Works of Amy Lowell *(1955). Amy Lowell died of a cerebral hemorrhage in Brookline, Massachusetts.*

Patterns

I walk down the garden paths,
And all the daffodils
Are blowing, and the bright blue squills.
I walk down the patterned garden paths
In my stiff, brocaded gown.
With my powdered hair and jewelled fan,
I too am a rare
Pattern. As I wander down
The garden paths.

My dress is richly figured,
And the train
Makes a pink and silver stain
On the gravel, and the thrift
Of the borders.
Just a plate of current fashion,
Tripping by in high-heeled, ribboned shoes.
Not a softness anywhere about me,
Only whale bone and brocade.
And I sink on a seat in the shade
Of a lime tree. For my passion
Wars against the stiff brocade.
The daffodils and squills
Flutter in the breeze
As they please.
And I weep;
For the lime-tree is in blossom
And one small flower has dropped upon my bosom.

And the plashing of waterdrops
In the marble fountain
Comes down the garden-paths.
The dripping never stops.
Underneath my stiffened gown
Is the softness of a woman bathing in a marble basin,
A basin in the midst of hedges grown
So thick, she cannot see her lover hiding,
But she guesses he is near,
And the sliding of the water
Seems the stroking of a dear
Hand upon her.
What is Summer in a fine brocaded gown!
I should like to see it lying in a heap upon the ground.
All the pink and silver crumpled up on the ground.

I would be the pink and silver as I ran along the paths,
And he would stumble after,
Bewildered by my laughter.
I should see the sun flashing from his sword-hilt and the buckles on his shoes.
I would choose
To lead him in a maze along the patterned paths,
A bright and laughing maze for my heavy-booted lover,
Till he caught me in the shade,
And the buttons of his waistcoat bruised my body as he clasped me,
Aching, melting, unafraid.
With the shadows of the leaves and the sundrops,
And the plopping of the waterdrops,
All about us in the open afternoon—
I am very like to swoon
With the weight of this brocade,
For the sun sifts through the shade.

Underneath the fallen blossom
In my bosom,
Is a letter I have hid.
It was brought to me this morning by a rider from the Duke.
"Madam, we regret to inform you that Lord Hartwell
Died in action Thursday se'nnight."
As I read it in the white, morning sunlight,
The letters squirmed like snakes.
"Any answer, Madam?" said my footman.
"No," I told him.
"See that the messenger takes some refreshment.

No, no answer."
And I walked into the garden,
Up and down the patterned paths,
In my stiff, correct brocade.
The blue and yellow flowers stood up proudly in the sun,
Each one.
I stood upright too,
Held rigid to the pattern
By the stiffness of my gown.
Up and down I walked,
Up and down.

In a month he would have been my husband.
In a month, here, underneath this lime,
We would have broke the pattern;
He for me, and I for him,
He as Colonel, I as Lady,
On this shady seat.
He had a whim
That sunlight carried blessing
And I answered, "It shall be as you have said."
Now he is dead.

In Summer and in Winter I shall walk
Up and down
The patterned garden-paths
In my stiff, brocaded gown.
The squills and daffodils
Will give place to pillared roses, and to asters, and to snow.
I shall go
Up and down,
In my gown.
Gorgeously arrayed,
Boned and stayed.
And the softness of my body will be guarded from embrace
By each button, hook, and lace.
For the man who should loose me is dead,
Fighting with the Duke in Flanders,
In a pattern called a war.
Christ! What are patterns for?

Gertrude Stein (1874–1946)

Gertrude Stein was born in Allegheny, Pennsylvania, and grew up in Oakland, California, and Baltimore, Maryland. She attended Radcliffe College and Johns Hopkins Medical School before moving to Paris, France, in 1903. Independently well-to-do, she became an art collector and prolific writer. Her poetry has been collected in numerous books, including Tender Buttons *(1914),* Portraits and Prayers *(1934),* Selected Writings *(1946), and* Unpublished Writings, Vol. 6: Stanzas in Meditation *(1956). Gertrude Stein died of stomach cancer in Neuilly-sur-Seine, France.*

Susie Asado

Sweet sweet sweet sweet sweet tea.
    Susie Asado.
Sweet sweet sweet sweet sweet tea.
    Susie Asado.
Susie Asado which is a told tray sure.
A lean on the shoe this means slips slips hers.
When the ancient light grey is clean it is yellow, it is a silver seller.
This is a please this is a please there are the saids to jelly. These are the wets these say the sets to leave a crown to Incy.
Incy is short for incubus.
A pot. A pot is a beginning of a rare bit of trees. Trees tremble, the old vats are in bobbles, bobbles which shade and shove and render clean, render clean must.
    Drink pups.
Drink pups drink pups lease a sash hold, see it shine and a bobolink has pins. It shows a nail.
What is a nail. A nail is unison.
Sweet sweet sweet sweet sweet tea.

From *Tender Buttons*

A BOX.

A large box is handily made of what is necessary to replace any substance. Suppose an example is necessary, the plainer it is made the more reason there is for some outward recognition that there is a result.

A box is made sometimes and them to see to see to it neatly and to have the holes stopped up makes it necessary to use paper.

A custom which is necessary when a box is used and taken is that a large part of the time there are three which have different connections. The one is on the table. The two are on the table. The three are on the table. The one,

one is the same length as is shown by the cover being longer. The other is different there is more cover that shows it. The other is different and that makes the corners have the same shade the eight are in singular arrangement to make four necessary.

Lax, to have corners, to be lighter than some weight, to indicate a wedding journey, to last brown and not curious, to be wealthy, cigarettes are established by length and by doubling.

Left open, to be left pounded, to be left closed, to be circulating in summer and winter, and sick color that is grey that is not dusty and red shows, to be sure cigarettes do measure an empty length sooner than a choice in color.

Winged, to be winged means that white is yellow and pieces pieces that are brown are dust color if dust is washed off, then it is choice that is to say it is fitting cigarettes sooner than paper.

An increase why is an increase idle, why is silver cloister, why is the spark brighter, if it is brighter is there any result, hardly more than ever.

From *Tender Buttons*

A PLATE.

An occasion for a plate, an occasional resource is in buying and how soon does washing enable a selection of the same thing neater. If the party is small a clever song is in order.

Plates and a dinner set of colored china. Pack together a string and enough with it to protect the centre, cause a considerable haste and gather more as it is cooling, collect more trembling and not any even trembling, cause a whole thing to be a church.

A sad size a size that is not sad is blue as every bit of blue is precocious. A kind of green a game in green and nothing flat nothing quite flat and more round, nothing a particular color strangely, nothing breaking the losing of no little piece.

A splendid address a really splendid address is not shown by giving a flower freely, it is not shown by a mark or by wetting.

Cut cut in white, cut in white so lately. Cut more than any other and show it. Show it in the stem and in starting and in evening coming complication.

A lamp is not the only sign of glass. The lamp and the cake are not the only sign of stone. The lamp and the cake and the cover are not the only necessity altogether.

A plan a hearty plan, a compressed disease and no coffee, not even a card or a change to incline each way, a plan that has that excess and that break is the one that shows filling.

Alice Moore Dunbar-Nelson (1875–1935)

Alice Ruth Moore was born in New Orleans, Louisiana. She attended Straight (now Dillard) University and worked as a public school teacher in New Orleans before moving first to New York, then to Washington, D.C., in 1898 to marry poet and publisher Paul Dunbar. She later lived and taught in Wilmington, Delaware, where she remarried twice and worked as a newspaper and magazine editor and a political activist. Her poems appeared in many magazines and anthologies during her lifetime. Alice Moore Dunbar-Nelson died in Philadelphia, Pennsylvania, three years after moving there from Wilmington.

I Sit and Sew

I sit and sew—a useless task it seems,
My hands grown tired, my head weighed down with dreams—
The panoply of war, the martial tred of men,
Grim-faced, stern-eyed, gazing beyond the ken
Of lesser souls, whose eyes have not seen Death,
Nor learned to hold their lives but as a breath—
But—I must sit and sew.

I sit and sew—my heart aches with desire—
That pageant terrible, that fiercely pouring fire
On wasted fields, and writhing grotesque things
Once men. My soul in pity flings
Appealing cries, yearning only to go
There in that holocaust of hell, those fields of woe—
But—I must sit and sew.

The little useless seam, the idle patch;
Why dream I here beneath my homely thatch,
When there they lie in sodden mud and rain,
Pitifully calling me, the quick ones and the slain?
You need me, Christ! It is no roseate dream
That beckons me—this pretty futile seam,
It stifles me—God, must I sit and sew?

Carl Sandburg (1878–1967)

Carl Sandburg was born in Galesburg, Illinois. He left school at thirteen, worked manual jobs and served in the military during the Spanish-American War. He then attended Lombard College before moving first to Milwaukee as a journalist and then to Chicago. His poetry books include In Reckless Ecstasy *(1904),* Chicago Poems *(1916),* Cornhuskers *(1918),* Smoke and Steel *(1920),* Slabs of the Sunburnt West *(1922),* Selected Poems *(1926),* Good Morning, America *(1928),* The People, Yes *(1936),* Complete Poems *(1950, Pulitzer Prize), and* Harvest Poems *(1960). Among his many honors were the 1940 Pulitzer Prize in history for* Abraham Lincoln: The War Years *and a 1959 Grammy Award for best spoken word performance. In 1945 he moved from the Chicago area to Flat Rock, North Carolina, where he died twenty-two years later.*

Grass

Pile the bodies high at Austerlitz and Waterloo.
Shovel them under and let me work—
        I am the grass; I cover all.

And pile them high at Gettysburg
And pile them high at Ypres and Verdun.
Shovel them under and let me work.
Two years, ten years, and passengers ask the conductor:
        What place is this?
        Where are we now?

        I am the grass.
        Let me work.

Cahoots

Play it across the table.
What if we steal this city blind?
If they want any thing let 'em nail it down.

Harness bulls, dicks, front office men,
And the high goats up on the bench,
Ain't they all in cahoots?
Ain't it fifty-fifty all down the line,
Petemen, dips, boosters, stick-ups and guns—
        what's to hinder?

      Go fifty-fifty.
If they nail you call in a mouthpiece.
Fix it, you gazump, you slant-head, fix it.
      Feed 'em. . . .

Nothin' ever sticks to my fingers, nah, nah,
      nothin' like that,
But there ain't no law we got to wear mittens—
      huh—is there?
Mittens, that's a good one—mittens!
There oughta be a law everybody wear mittens.

Wallace Stevens (1879–1955)

Wallace Stevens was born in Reading, Pennsylvania. He attended Harvard University and New York Law School and worked for several New York law firms before becoming an insurance company executive and, as such, moving to Hartford, Connecticut, in 1916. His poetry books include Harmonium *(1923),* Ideas of Order *(1935),* Owl's Clover *(1936),* The Man with the Blue Guitar *(1937),* Parts of a World *(1942),* Notes toward a Supreme Fiction *(1942),* Transport to Summer *(1947),* The Auroras of Autumn *(1950),* Selected Poems *(1952),* The Collected Poems *(1954, Pulitzer Prize, National Book Award),* Poems by Wallace Stevens *(1959),* The Palm at the End of the Mind *(1971), and* The Emperor of Ice-Cream and Other Poems *(2005). Among his honors were the Bollingen Prize and a gold medal from the Poetry Society of America. Wallace Stevens died in Hartford, Connecticut.*

Peter Quince at the Clavier

I

Just as my fingers on these keys
Make music, so the selfsame sounds
On my spirit make a music, too.

Music is feeling, then, not sound;
And thus it is that what I feel,
Here in this room, desiring you,

Thinking of your blue-shadowed silk,
Is music. It is like the strain
Waked in the elders by Susanna.

Of a green evening, clear and warm,
She bathed in her still garden, while
The red-eyed elders watching, felt

The basses of their beings throb
In witching chords, and their thin blood
Pulse pizzicati of Hosanna.

II

In the green water, clear and warm,
Susanna lay.
She searched

The touch of springs,
And found
Concealed imaginings.
She sighed,
For so much melody.

Upon the bank, she stood
In the cool
Of spent emotions.
She felt, among the leaves,
The dew
Of old devotions.

She walked upon the grass,
Still quavering.
The winds were like her maids,
On timid feet,
Fetching her woven scarves,
Yet wavering.

A breath upon her hand
Muted the night.
She turned—
A cymbal crashed,
And roaring horns.

III

Soon, with a noise like tambourines,
Came her attendant Byzantines.

They wondered why Susanna cried
Against the elders by her side;

And as they whispered, the refrain
Was like a willow swept by rain.

Anon, their lamps' uplifted flame
Revealed Susanna and her shame.

And then, the simpering Byzantines
Fled, with a noise like tambourines.

IV

Beauty is momentary in the mind—
The fitful tracing of a portal;
But in the flesh it is immortal.

The body dies; the body's beauty lives.
So evenings die, in their green going,
A wave, interminably flowing.
So gardens die, their meek breath scenting
The cowl of winter, done repenting.
So maidens die, to the auroral
Celebration of a maiden's choral.

Susanna's music touched the bawdy strings
Of those white elders; but, escaping,
Left only Death's ironic scraping.
Now, in its immortality, it plays
On the clear viol of her memory,
And makes a constant sacrament of praise.

Disillusionment of Ten O'Clock

The houses are haunted
By white night-gowns.
None are green,
Or purple with green rings,
Or green with yellow rings,
Or yellow with blue rings.
None of them are strange,
With socks of lace
And beaded ceintures.
People are not going
To dream of baboons and periwinkles.
Only, here and there, an old sailor,
Drunk and asleep in his boots,
Catches tigers
In red weather.

Thirteen Ways of Looking at a Blackbird

I

Among twenty snowy mountains,
The only moving thing
Was the eye of the blackbird.

II

I was of three minds,
Like a tree
In which there are three blackbirds.

III

The blackbird whirled in the autumn winds.
It was a small part of the pantomime.

IV

A man and a woman
Are one.
A man and a woman and a blackbird
Are one.

V

I do not know which to prefer,
The beauty of inflections
Or the beauty of innuendoes,
The blackbird whistling
Or just after.

VI

Icicles filled the long window
With barbaric glass.
The shadow of the blackbird
Crossed it, to and fro.
The mood
Traced in the shadow
An indecipherable cause.

VII

O thin men of Haddam,
Why do you imagine golden birds?

Do you not see how the blackbird
Walks around the feet
Of the women about you?

VIII

I know noble accents
And lucid, inescapable rhythms;
But I know, too,
That the blackbird is involved
In what I know.

IX

When the blackbird flew out of sight,
It marked the edge
Of one of many circles.

X

At the sight of blackbirds
Flying in a green light,
Even the bawds of euphony
Would cry out sharply.

XI

He rode over Connecticut
In a glass coach.
Once, a fear pierced him,
In that he mistook
The shadow of his equipage
For blackbirds.

XII

The river is moving.
The blackbird must be flying.

XIII

It was evening all afternoon.
It was snowing
And it was going to snow.
The blackbird sat
In the cedar-limbs.

Anecdote of the Jar

I placed a jar in Tennessee,
And round it was, upon a hill.
It made the slovenly wilderness
Surround that hill.

The wilderness rose up to it,
And sprawled around, no longer wild.
The jar was round upon the ground
And tall and of a port in air.

It took dominion everywhere.
The jar was gray and bare.
It did not give of bird or bush,
Like nothing else in Tennessee.

The Emperor of Ice-Cream

Call the roller of big cigars,
The muscular one, and bid him whip
In kitchen cups concupiscent curds.
Let the wenches dawdle in such dress
As they are used to wear, and let the boys
Bring flowers in last month's newspapers.
Let be be finale of seem.
The only emperor is the emperor of ice-cream.

Take from the dresser of deal,
Lacking the three glass knobs, that sheet
On which she embroidered fantails once
And spread it so as to cover her face.
If her horny feet protrude, they come
To show how cold she is, and dumb.
Let the lamp affix its beam.
The only emperor is the emperor of ice-cream.

Of Mere Being

The palm at the end of the mind,
Beyond the last thought, rises
In the bronze decor,

A gold-feathered bird
Sings in the palm, without human meaning,
Without human feeling, a foreign song.

You know then that it is not the reason
That makes us happy or unhappy.
The bird sings. Its feathers shine.

The palm stands on the edge of space.
The wind moves slowly in the branches.
The bird's fire-fangled feathers dangle down.

Angelina Weld Grimké (1880–1958)

Angelina Weld Grimké was born in Boston, Massachusetts, the daughter of a prominent African-American father and a white mother. She attended what is now Wellesley College and taught school in Washington, D.C. In 1926 she retired from teaching and moved to New York City. Some of her poems, originally published in African-American magazines and anthologies, were collected posthumously in Selected Works of Angelina Weld Grimké *(1991). During her lifetime she also published her three-act play* Rachel *(1920, first produced in Washington, D.C., 1916, and in New York City, 1917). Much of her writing centered on lesbian love or the horrors of racism. Angelina Weld Grimké died in Brooklyn, New York.*

Fragment

I am the woman with the black black skin
I am the laughing woman with the black black face
I am living in the cellars and in every crowded place
    I am toiling just to eat
    In the cold and in the heat
        And I laugh
I am the laughing woman who's forgotten how to weep
I am the laughing woman who's afraid to go to sleep

William Carlos Williams (1883–1963)

William Carlos Williams was born in Rutherford, New Jersey, studied medicine at the University of Pennsylvania, and opened a practice in his hometown, where he worked as a pediatrician for the rest of his life. His poetry books include The Tempers *(1913);* Kora in Hell *(1920);* Sour Grapes *(1921);* Spring and All *(1923);* Collected Poems, 1921–1931 *(1934);* The Complete Collected Poems 1906–1938 *(1938);* The Broken Span *(1941);* Paterson, Book I *(1946),* Book II *(1948),* Book III *(1949),* Book IV *(1951),* Book V *(1958),* Books I–V *(1963);* Selected Poems *(1949, National Book Award);* The Collected Later Poems *(1950);* Collected Earlier Poems *(1951);* The Desert Music and Other Poems *(1954);* Journey to Love *(1955);* Pictures from Brueghel and Other Poems *(1962, Pulitzer Prize); and* The William Carlos Williams Reader *(1966). Among his honors were the 1926 Dial Award and the 1952 Bollingen Prize. In 1952 he was appointed Consultant in Poetry at the Library of Congress but did not serve due to right-wing pressures. He died in Rutherford, New Jersey.*

Tract

I will teach you my townspeople
how to perform a funeral
for you have it over a troop
of artists—
unless one should scour the world—
you have the ground sense necessary.

See! the hearse leads.
I begin with a design for a hearse.
For Christ's sake not black—
nor white either—and not polished!
Let it be weathered—like a farm wagon—
with gilt wheels (this could be
applied fresh at small expense)
or no wheels at all:
a rough dray to drag over the ground.

Knock the glass out!
My God—glass, my townspeople!
For what purpose? Is it for the dead
to look out or for us to see
how well he is housed or to see
the flowers or the lack of them—
or what?
To keep the rain and snow from him?
He will have a heavier rain soon:

pebbles and dirt and what not.
Let there be no glass—
and no upholstery, phew!
and no little brass rollers
and small easy wheels on the bottom—
my townspeople what are you thinking of?

A rough plain hearse then
with gilt wheels and no top at all.
On this the coffin lies
by its own weight.
                                  No wreaths please—
especially no hot house flowers.
Some common memento is better,
something he prized and is known by:
his old clothes—a few books perhaps—
God knows what! You realize
how we are about these things
my townspeople—
something will be found—anything
even flowers if he had come to that.
So much for the hearse.

For heaven's sake though see to the driver!
Take off the silk hat! In fact
that's no place at all for him—
up there unceremoniously
dragging our friend out to his own dignity!
Bring him down—bring him down!
Low and inconspicuous! I'd not have him ride
on the wagon at all—damn him—
the undertaker's understrapper!
Let him hold the reins
and walk at the side
and inconspicuously too!

Then briefly as to yourselves:
Walk behind—as they do in France,
seventh class, or if you ride
Hell take curtains! Go with some show
of inconvenience; sit openly—
to the weather as to grief.
Or do you think you can shut grief in?
What—from us? We who have perhaps

nothing to lose? Share with us
share with us—it will be money
in your pockets.
                              Go now
I think you are ready.

Danse Russe

If when my wife is sleeping
and the baby and Kathleen
are sleeping
and the sun is a flame-white disc
in silken mists
above shining trees,—
if I in my north room
dance naked, grotesquely
before my mirror
waving my shirt round my head
and singing softly to myself:
"I am lonely, lonely.
I was born to be lonely,
I am best so!"
If I admire my arms, my face,
my shoulders, flanks, buttocks
against the yellow drawn shades,—

Who shall say I am not
the happy genius of my household?

The Red Wheelbarrow

so much depends
upon

a red wheel
barrow

glazed with rain
water

beside the white
chickens.

The Yachts

contend in a sea which the land partly encloses
shielding them from the too-heavy blows
of an ungoverned ocean which when it chooses

tortures the biggest hulls, the best man knows
to pit against its beatings, and sinks them pitilessly.
Mothlike in mists, scintillant in the minute

brilliance of cloudless days, with broad bellying sails
they glide to the wind tossing green water
from their sharp prows while over them the crew crawls

ant-like, solicitously grooming them, releasing,
making fast as they turn, lean far over and having
caught the wind again, side by side, head for the mark.

In a well guarded arena of open water surrounded by
lesser and greater craft which, sycophant, lumbering
and flittering follow them, they appear youthful, rare

as the light of a happy eye, live with the grace
of all that in the mind is fleckless, free and
naturally to be desired. Now the sea which holds them

is moody, lapping their glossy sides, as if feeling
for some slightest flaw but fails completely.
Today no race. Then the wind comes again. The yachts

move, jockeying for a start, the signal is set and they
are off. Now the waves strike at them but they are too
well made, they slip through, though they take in canvas.

Arms with hands grasping seek to clutch at the prows.
Bodies thrown recklessly in the way are cut aside.
It is a sea of faces about them in agony, in despair

until the horror of the race dawns staggering the mind,
the whole sea become an entanglement of watery bodies
lost to the world bearing what they cannot hold. Broken,

beaten, desolate, reaching from the dead to be taken up
they cry out, failing, failing! their cries rising
in waves still as the skillful yachts pass over.

From *Asphodel, That Greeny Flower*

BOOK I

Of asphodel, that greeny flower,
            like a buttercup
                        upon its branching stem—
save that it's green and wooden—
            I come, my sweet,
                        to sing to you.
We lived long together
            a life filled,
                        if you will,
with flowers. So that
            I was cheered
                        when I came first to know
that there were flowers also
            in hell.
                        Today
I'm filled with the fading memory of those flowers
            that we both loved,
                        even to this poor
colorless thing—
            I saw it
                        when I was a child—
little prized among the living
            but the dead see,
                        asking among themselves:
What do I remember
            that was shaped
                        as this thing is shaped?
while our eyes fill
            with tears.
                        Of love, abiding love
it will be telling
            though too weak a wash of crimson
                        colors it

to make it wholly credible.
                    There is something
                                      something urgent
I have to say to you
                    and you alone
                                    but it must wait
while I drink in
                    the joy of your approach,
                                    perhaps for the last time.
And so
                    with fear in my heart
                                  I drag it out
and keep on talking
                    for I dare not stop.
                                  Listen while I talk on
against time.
                    It will not be
                                  for long.
I have forgot
                    and yet I see clearly enough
                                  something
central to the sky
                    which ranges round it.
                                  An odor
springs from it!
                    A sweetest odor!
                                  Honeysuckle! And now
there comes the buzzing of a bee!
                    and a whole flood
                                  of sister memories!
Only give me time,
                    time to recall them
                                before I shall speak out.
Give me time,
                    time.
When I was a boy
                    I kept a book
                                to which, from time
to time,
                    I added pressed flowers
                                until, after a time,
I had a good collection.
                    The asphodel,
                                forebodingly,

among them.
            I bring you,
                        reawakened,
a memory of those flowers.
            They were sweet
                        when I pressed them
and retained
            something of their sweetness
                        a long time.
It is a curious odor,
            a moral odor,
                        that brings me
near to you.
            The color
                        was the first to go.
There had come to me
            a challenge,
                        your dear self,
mortal as I was,
            the lily's throat
                        to the hummingbird!
Endless wealth,
            I thought,
                        held out its arms to me.
A thousand topics,
            in an apple blossom.
                        The generous earth itself
gave us lief.
            The whole world
                        became my garden!
But the sea
            which no one tends
                        is also a garden
when the sun strikes it
            and the waves
                        are wakened.
I have seen it
            and so have you
                        when it puts all flowers
to shame.
            Too, there are the starfish
                        stiffened by the sun
and other sea wrack
            and weeds. We knew that

                    along with the rest of it
for we were born by the sea,
              knew its rose hedges
                    to the very water's brink.
There the pink mallow grows
              and in their season
                    strawberries
and there, later,
              we went to gather
                    the wild plum.
I cannot say
              that I have gone to hell
                    for your love
but often
              found myself there
                    in your pursuit.
I do not like it
              and wanted to be
                    in heaven. Hear me out.
Do not turn away.

I have learned much in my life
              from books
                    and out of them
about love.
              Death
                    is not the end of it.
There is a hierarchy
              which can be attained,
                I think,
in its service.
              Its guerdon
                  is a fairy flower;
a cat of twenty lives.
              If no one came to try it
                the world
would be the loser.
              It has been
                  for you and me
as one who watches a storm
              come in over the water.
                  We have stood
from year to year

before the spectacle of our lives
        with joined hands.
The storm unfolds.
      Lightning
           plays about the edges of the clouds.
The sky to the north
      is placid,
          blue in the afterglow
as the storm piles up.
      It is a flower
         that will soon reach
the apex of its bloom.
      We danced,
         in our minds,
and read a book together.
      You remember?
         It was a serious book.
And so books
      entered our lives.
The sea! The sea!
      Always
         when I think of the sea
there comes to mind
      the *Iliad*
         and Helen's public fault
that bred it.
      Were it not for that
         there would have been
no poem but the world
      if we had remembered,
         those crimson petals
spilled among the stones,
      would have called it simply
         murder.
The sexual orchid that bloomed then
      sending so many
         disinterested
men to their graves
      has left its memory
         to a race of fools
or heroes
      if silence is a virtue.
         The sea alone
with its multiplicity

holds any hope.
                    The storm
has proven abortive
                    but we remain
                              after the thoughts it roused
to
                    re-cement our lives.
                              It is the mind
the mind
                    that must be cured
                              short of death's
intervention,
                    and the will becomes again
                              a garden. The poem
is complex and the place made
                    in our lives
                              for the poem.
Silence can be complex too,
                    but you do not get far
                              with silence.
Begin again.
                    It is like Homer's
                              catalogue of ships:
it fills up the time.
                    I speak in figures,
                              well enough, the dresses
you wear are figures also,
                    we could not meet
                              otherwise. When I speak
of flowers
                    it is to recall
                              that at one time
we were young.
                    All women are not Helen,
                              I know that,
but have Helen in their hearts.
                    My sweet,
                              you have it also, therefore
I love you
                    and could not love you otherwise.
                              Imagine you saw
a field made up of women
                    all silver-white.
                              What should you do

but love them?
>> The storm bursts
>>>> or fades! it is not
> the end of the world.
>> Love is something else,
>>> or so I thought it,
> a garden which expands,
>> though I knew you as a woman
>>> and never thought otherwise,
> until the whole sea
>> has been taken up
>>> and all its gardens.
> It was the love of love,
>> the love that swallows up all else,
>>> a grateful love,
> a love of nature, of people,
>> animals,
>>> a love engendering
> gentleness and goodness
>> that moved me
>>> and *that* I saw in you.
> I should have known
>> though I did not,
>>> that the lily-of-the-valley
> is a flower makes many ill
>> who whiff it.
>>> We had our children,
> rivals in the general onslaught.
>> I put them aside
>>> though I cared for them
> as well as any man
>> could care for his children
>>> according to my lights.
> You understand
>> I had to meet you
>>> after the event
> and have still to meet you.
>> Love
>>> to which you too shall bow
> along with me—
>> a flower
>>> a weakest flower
> shall be our trust
>> and not because

we are too feeble
to do otherwise
but because
at the height of my power
I risked what I had to do,
therefore to prove
that we love each other
while my very bones sweated
that I could not cry to you
in the act.
Of asphodel, that greeny flower,
I come, my sweet,
to sing to you!
My heart rouses
thinking to bring you news
of something
that concerns you
and concerns many men. Look at
what passes for the new.
You will not find it there but in
despised poems.
It is difficult
to get the news from poems
yet men die miserably every day
for lack
of what is found there.
Hear me out
for I too am concerned
and every man
who wants to die at peace in his bed
besides.

Sara Teasdale (1884–1933)

Sara Teasdale was born in St. Louis, Missouri. She contributed to magazines from an early age, moving to New York in 1916. Her poetry books include Sonnets to Duse and Other Poems *(1907),* Helen of Troy *(1911),* Rivers to the Sea *(1915),* Love Songs *(1917),* Flame and Shadow *(1920),* Dark of the Moon *(1926),* Stars To-night *(1930),* Strange Victory *(1933), and* Collected Poems *(1937). Among her honors was the 1918 Columbia University Poetry Society Prize (which would become the Pulitzer Prize in Poetry). Of fragile health all her life and suffering from chronic pneumonia, Sara Teasdale committed suicide in New York by drug overdose.*

Moonlight

It will not hurt me when I am old.
   A running tide where moonlight burned
      Will not sting me like silver snakes;
The years will make me sad and cold,
      It is the happy heart that breaks.

The heart asks more than life can give,
   When that is learned, then all is learned;
      The waves break fold on jewelled fold,
But beauty itself is fugitive,
      It will not hurt me when I am old.

There Will Come Soft Rains

(War Time)

There will come soft rains and the smell of the
      ground,
And swallows circling with their shimmering
      sound;

And frogs in the pools singing at night,
And wild plum-trees in tremulous white;

Robins will wear their feathery fire
Whistling their whims on a low fence-wire;

And not one will know of the war, not one
Will care at last when it is done.

Not one would mind, neither bird nor tree
If mankind perished utterly;

And Spring herself, when she woke at dawn,
Would scarcely know that we were gone.

Ezra (Weston Loomis) Pound (1885–1972)

Ezra Weston Loomis Pound was born in Hailey, Idaho. He attended the University of Pennsylvania and Hamilton College and traveled to Europe several times, eventually settling in London from 1908 to 1920. From 1921 to 1924 he lived in Paris, followed by twenty years in Italy. Arrested on treason charges because of his fascist propaganda radio broadcasts, he was declared mentally ill and confined to a psychiatric hospital in Washington, D.C. After his release in 1958, he returned to Italy. His many poetry books include A Lume Spento *(1908),* Exultations *(1909),* Personae *(1909),* Provença *(1910),* Canzoni *(1911),* Lustra and Other Poems *(1917),* Quia Pauper Amavi *(1919),* Umbra: Collected Poems *(1920),* Cantos I–XVI *(1925),* Cantos XVII–XXVII *(1928),* A Draft of XXX Cantos *(1930),* A Draft of Cantos XXXI–XLI *(1934),* Homage to Sextus Propertius *(1934),* The Fifth Decade of Cantos *(1937),* Cantos LII–LXXI *(1940),* The Pisan Cantos *(1948,* Bollingen Award*),* Patria Mia *(1950), and* The Cantos *(1972). Among his honors were the 1927 Dial Award and a 1963 Academy of American Poets Fellowship. Ezra Pound died in Venice, Italy.*

The Jewel Stairs' Grievance

The jewelled steps are already quite white with dew,
It is so late that the dew soaks my gauze stockings,
And I let down the crystal curtain
And watch the moon through the clear autumn.

By Rihaku

The River-Merchant's Wife: A Letter

While my hair was still cut straight across my forehead
Played I about the front gate, pulling flowers.
You came by on bamboo stilts, playing horse,
You walked about my seat, playing with blue plums.
And we went on living in the village of Chokan:
Two small people, without dislike or suspicion.

At fourteen I married My Lord you.
I never laughed, being bashful.
Lowering my head, I looked at the wall.
Called to, a thousand times, I never looked back.

At fifteen I stopped scowling,
I desired my dust to be mingled with yours
Forever and forever and forever.
Why should I climb the look out?

At sixteen you departed,
You went into far Ku-tō-en, by the river of swirling eddies,
And you have been gone five months.
The monkeys make sorrowful noise overhead.

You dragged your feet when you went out.
By the gate now, the moss is grown, the different mosses,
Too deep to clear them away!
The leaves fall early this autumn, in wind.
The paired butterflies are already yellow with August
Over the grass in the West garden;
They hurt me. I grow older.
If you are coming down through the narrows of the river Kiang,
Please let me know beforehand,
And I will come out to meet you
                    As far as Chō-fū-Sa.

                                        By Rihaku

In a Station of the Metro

The apparition of these faces in the crowd;
Petals on a wet, black bough.

Hugh Selwyn Mauberley

LIFE AND CONTACTS

> *"Vocat æstus in umbram"*
> NEMESIANUS EC. IV

E. P. Ode pour L'Election de Son Sepulchre

I

For three years, out of key with his time,
He strove to resuscitate the dead art
Of poetry; to maintain "the sublime"
In the old sense. Wrong from the start—

No, hardly, but seeing he had been born
In a half savage country, out of date;
Bent resolutely on wringing lilies from the acorn;
Capaneus; trout for factitious bait;

Ἴδμεν γάρ τοι πάνθ’, ὅσ’ ἐνὶ Τροίη
Caught in the unstopped ear;
Giving the rocks small lee-way
The chopped seas held him, therefore, that year.

His true Penelope was Flaubert,
He fished by obstinate isles;
Observed the elegance of Circe's hair
Rather than the mottoes on sun-dials.

Unaffected by "The march of events,"
He passed from men's memory *l'an trentuniesme*
De son eage; the case presents
No adjunct to the Muses' diadem.

II

The age demanded an image
Of its accelerated grimace,
Something for the modern stage,
Not, at any rate, an Attic grace;

Not, not certainly, the obscure reveries
Of the inward gaze;
Better mendacities
Than the classics in paraphrase!

The "age demanded" chiefly a mould in plaster,
Made with no loss of time,
A prose kinema, not, not assuredly, alabaster
Or the "sculpture" of rhyme.

III

The tea-rose tea-gown, etc.
Supplants the mousseline of Cos,
The pianola "replaces"
Sappho's barbitos.

Christ follows Dionysus,
Phallic and ambrosial
Made way for macerations;
Caliban casts out Ariel.

All things are a flowing,
Sage Heracleitus says;
But a tawdry cheapness
Shall outlast our days.

Even the Christian beauty
Defects—after Samothrace;
We see τὸ καλόν
Decreed in the market place.

Faun's flesh is not to us,
Nor the saint's vision.
We have the press for wafer;
Franchise for circumcision.

All men, in law, are equals.
Free of Pisistratus,
We choose a knave or an eunuch
To rule over us.

O bright Apollo,
τίν' ἄνδρα, τίν' ἥρωα, τίνα θεόν,
What god, man, or hero
Shall I place a tin wreath upon!

IV
These fought in any case,
and some believing,
                    pro domo, in any case . . .

Some quick to arm,
some for adventure,
some from fear of weakness,
some from fear of censure,
some for love of slaughter, in imagination,
learning later . . .
some in fear, learning love of slaughter;

Died some, pro patria,
                    non "dulce" non "et decor" . . .
walked eye-deep in hell
believing in old men's lies, then unbelieving
came home, home to a lie,

home to many deceits,
home to old lies and new infamy;
usury age-old and age-thick
and liars in public places.

Daring as never before, wastage as never before.
Young blood and high blood,
fair cheeks, and fine bodies;

fortitude as never before

frankness as never before,
disillusions as never told in the old days,
hysterias, trench confessions,
laughter out of dead bellies.

V

There died a myriad,
And of the best, among them,
For an old bitch gone in the teeth,
For a botched civilization,

Charm, smiling at the good mouth,
Quick eyes gone under earth's lid,

For two gross of broken statues,
For a few thousand battered books.

Yeux Glauques

Gladstone was still respected,
When John Ruskin produced
"Kings' Treasuries"; Swinburne
And Rossetti still abused.

Fœtid Buchanan lifted up his voice
When that faun's head of hers
Became a pastime for
Painters and adulterers.

The Burne-Jones cartons
Have preserved her eyes;
Still, at the Tate, they teach
Cophetua to rhapsodize;

Thin like brook-water,
With a vacant gaze.
The English Rubaiyat was still-born
In those days.

The thin, clear gaze, the same
Still darts out faun-like from the half-ruin'd face,
Questing and passive. . . .
"Ah, poor Jenny's case" . . .

Bewildered that a world
Shows no surprise
At her last maquero's
Adulteries.

"Siena Mi Fe'; Disfecemi Maremma"
Among the pickled fœtuses and bottled bones,
Engaged in perfecting the catalogue,
I found the last scion of the
Senatorial families of Strasbourg, Monsieur Verog.

For two hours he talked of Galliffet;
Of Dowson; of the Rhymers' Club;
Told me how Johnson (Lionel) died
By falling from a high stool in a pub . . .

But showed no trace of alcohol
At the autopsy, privately performed—
Tissue preserved—the pure mind
Arose toward Newman as the whiskey warmed.

Dowson found harlots cheaper than hotels;
Headlam for uplift; Image impartially imbued
With raptures for Bacchus, Terpsichore and the Church.
So spoke the author of "The Dorian Mood,"

M. Verog, out of step with the decade,
Detached from his contemporaries,
Neglected by the young,
Because of these reveries.

Brennbaum

The sky-like limpid eyes,
The circular infant's face,
The stiffness from spats to collar
Never relaxing into grace;

The heavy memories of Horeb, Sinai and the forty years,
Showed only when the daylight fell
Level across the face
Of Brennbaum "The Impeccable."

Mr. Nixon

In the cream gilded cabin of his steam yacht
Mr. Nixon advised me kindly, to advance with fewer
Dangers of delay. "Consider

       "Carefully the reviewer.

"I was as poor as you are;
"When I began I got, of course,
"Advance on royalties, fifty at first," said Mr. Nixon,
"Follow me, and take a column,
"Even if you have to work free.

"Butter reviewers. From fifty to three hundred
"I rose in eighteen months;
"The hardest nut I had to crack
"Was Dr. Dundas.

"I never mentioned a man but with the view
"Of selling my own works.
"The tip's a good one, as for literature
"It gives no man a sinecure.

"And no one knows, at sight, a masterpiece.
"And give up verse, my boy,
"There's nothing in it."

     .   .   .   .

Likewise a friend of Blougram's once advised me:
Don't kick against the pricks,
Accept opinion. The "Nineties" tried your game
And died, there's nothing in it.

X

Beneath the sagging roof
The stylist has taken shelter,
Unpaid, uncelebrated,
At last from the world's welter

Nature receives him;
With a placid and uneducated mistress
He exercises his talents
And the soil meets his distress.

The haven from sophistications and contentions
Leaks through its thatch;
He offers succulent cooking;
The door has a creaking latch.

XI

"Conservatrix of Milésien"
Habits of mind and feeling,
Possibly. But in Ealing
With the most bank-clerkly of Englishmen?

No, "Milésian" is an exaggeration.
No instinct has survived in her
Older than those her grandmother
Told her would fit her station.

XII

"Daphne with her thighs in bark
Stretches toward me her leafy hands,"—
Subjectively. In the stuffed-satin drawing-room
I await The Lady Valentine's commands,

Knowing my coat has never been
Of precisely the fashion
To stimulate, in her,
A durable passion;

Doubtful, somewhat, of the value
Of well-gowned approbation
Of literary effort,
But never of The Lady Valentine's vocation:

Poetry, her border of ideas,
The edge, uncertain but a means of blending
With other strata
Where the lower and higher have ending;

A book to catch the Lady Jane's attention,
A modulation toward the theatre,
Also, in the case of revolution,
A possible friend and comforter.

    •   •   •   •   •   •   •   •

Conduct, on the other hand, the soul
"Which the highest cultures have nourished"
To Fleet St. where
Dr. Johnson flourished;

Beside this thoroughfare
The sale of half-hose has
Long since superseded the cultivation
Of Pierian roses.

Envoi (1919)

Go, dumb-born book,
Tell her that sang me once that song of Lawes:
Hadst thou but song
As thou hast subjects known,
Then were there cause in thee that should condone
Even my faults that heavy upon me lie,
And build her glories their longevity.

Tell her that sheds
Such treasure in the air,
Recking naught else but that her graces give
Life to the moment,
I would bid them live
As roses might, in magic amber laid,
Red overwrought with orange and all made
One substance and one colour
Braving time.

Tell her that goes
With song upon her lips
But sings not out the song, nor knows

The maker of it, some other mouth,
May be as fair as hers,
Might, in new ages, gain her worshippers,
When our two dusts with Waller's shall be laid,
Siftings on siftings in oblivion,
Till change hath broken down
All things save Beauty alone.

From *Canto LXXXI*

Yet
Ere the season died a-cold
Borne upon a zephyr's shoulder
I rose through the aureaete sky
                    Lawes and Jenkyns guard thy rest
                    Dolmetsch ever be thy guest
Has he tempered the viol's wood
To enforce   both the grave   and the acute?
Has he curved us the bowl of the lute?
                    Lawes and Jenkyns guard thy rest
                    Dolmetsch ever be thy guest
Hast 'ou fashioned so airy a mood
        To draw up leaf from the root?
Has 'ou found   a cloud   so light
        As seemed neither mist nor shade?

                        Then resolve me, tell me aright
                        If Waller sang or Dowland played.

            Your eyen two wol sleye me sodenly
            I may the beauté of hem nat susteyne

And for 180 years almost nothing.

Ed ascoltando al leggier mormorio
        there came new subtlety of eyes into my tent,
whether of spirit or hypostasis,
        but what the blindfold hides
or at carneval
                    nor any pair showed anger
        Saw but the eyes and stance between the eyes,
colour, diastasis,
        careless or unaware it had not the

    whole tent's room
nor was place for the full Εἰδὼς
interpass, penetrate
      casting but shade beyond the other lights
        sky's clear
        night's sea
        green of the mountain pool
        shone from the unmasked eyes in half-mask's space.
What thou lovest well remains,
                the rest is dross
What thou lov'st well shall not be reft from thee
What thou lov'st well is thy true heritage
Whose world, or mine or theirs
           or is it of none?
First came the seen, then thus the palpable
    Elysium, though it were in the halls of hell,
What thou lovest well is thy true heritage

The ant's a centaur in his dragon world.
Pull down thy vanity, it is not man
Made courage, or made order, or made grace,
    Pull down thy vanity, I say pull down.
Learn of the green world what can be thy place
In scaled invention or true artistry,
Pull down thy vanity,
             Paquin pull down!
The green casque has outdone your elegance.

"Master thyself, then others shall thee beare"
    Pull down thy vanity
Thou are a beaten dog beneath the hail,
A swollen magpie in a fitful sun,
Half black half white
Nor knowst'ou wing from tail
Pull down thy vanity
       How mean thy hates
Fostered in falsity,
       Pull down thy vanity,
Rathe to destroy, niggard in charity,
Pull down thy vanity,
       I say pull down.

But to have done instead of not doing
    this is not vanity

To have, with decency, knocked
That a Blunt should open
      To have gathered from the air a live tradition
or from a fine old eye the unconquered flame
This is not vanity.
      Here error is all in the not done,
all in the diffidence that faltered . . .

Hilda Doolittle (H.D.) (1886–1961)

Hilda Doolittle was born in Bethlehem, Pennsylvania. She attended Bryn Mawr College before going to New York City for a short time, then moving to London in 1911. She later lived in Cornwall and Switzerland. Her poetry books include Sea Garden *(1916),* The God *(1917),* Hymen *(1921),* Heliodora and Other Poems *(1924),* Hippolytus Temporizes *(1927),* Red Roses for Bronze *(1931),* The Walls Do Not Fall *(1944),* Tribute to the Angels *(1945),* Trilogy *(1946),* Flowering of the Rod *(1946),* By Avon River *(1949),* Helen in Egypt *(1961), and* Hermetic Definition *(1972). Among her honors was the Award of Merit Medal for poetry from the National Institute and American Academy of Arts and Letters. H.D. died in Zurich, Switzerland.*

Sea Rose

Rose, harsh rose,
marred and with stint of petals,
meagre flower, thin,
sparse of leaf,

more precious
than a wet rose
single on a stem—
you are caught in the drift.

Stunted, with small leaf,
you are flung on the sand,
you are lifted
in the crisp sand
that drives in the wind.

Can the spice-rose
drip such acrid fragrance
hardened in a leaf?

Helen

All Greece hates
the still eyes in the white face,
the lustre as of olives
where she stands,
and the white hands.

All Greece reviles
the wan face when she smiles,
hating it deeper still
when it grows wan and white,
remembering past enchantments
and past ills.

Greece sees unmoved,
God's daughter, born of love,
the beauty of cool feet
and slenderest knees,
could love indeed the maid,
only if she were laid,
white ash amid funeral cypresses.

From *The Walls Do Not Fall*

To Bryher

for Karnak 1923
from London 1942

1.
An incident here and there,
and rails gone (for guns)
from your (and my) old town square:

mist and mist-grey, no colour,
still the Luxor bee, chick and hare
pursue unalterable purpose

in green, rose-red, lapis;
they continue to prophesy
from the stone papyrus:

there, as here, ruin opens
the tomb, the temple; enter,
there as here, there are no doors:

the shrine lies open to the sky,
the rain falls, here, there
sand drifts; eternity endures:

ruin everywhere, yet as the fallen roof
leaves the sealed room
open to the air,

so, through our desolation,
thoughts stir, inspiration stalks us
through gloom:

unaware, Spirit announces the Presence;
shivering overtakes us,
as of old, Samuel:

trembling at a known street-corner,
we know not nor are known;
the Pythian pronounces—we pass on

to another cellar, to another sliced wall
where poor utensils show
like rare objects in a museum;

Pompeii has nothing to teach us,
we know crack of volcanic fissure,
slow flow of terrible lava,

pressure on heart, lungs, the brain
about to burst its brittle case
(what the skull can endure!):

over us, Apocryphal fire,
under us, the earth sway, dip of a floor,
slope of a pavement

where men roll, drunk
with a new bewilderment,
sorcery, bedevilment:

the bone-frame was made for
no such shock knit within terror,
yet the skeleton stood up to it:

the flesh? it was melted away,
the heart burnt out, dead ember,
tendons, muscles shattered, outer husk dismembered,

yet the frame held:
we passed the flame: we wonder
what saved us? what for?

From *Hermetic Definition*

PART ONE

Red Rose and a Beggar

(August 17–September 24, 1960)

[1]
Why did you come
to trouble my decline?
I am old (I was old till you came);

the reddest rose unfolds,
(which is ridiculous
in this time, this place,

unseemly, impossible,
even slightly scandalous),
the reddest rose unfolds;

(nobody can stop that,
no immanent threat from the air,
not even the weather,

blighting our summer fruit),
the reddest rose unfolds,
(they've got to take that into account).

[2]
Take me anywhere, anywhere;
I walk into you,
Doge—Venice—

you are my whole estate;
I would hide in your mind
as a child hides in an attic,

what would I find there?
religion or majic—both? neither?
one or the other? together, matched,

mated, exactly the same,
equal in power, together yet separate,
your eyes' amber.

[5]

Venice—Venus?
this must he my stance,
my station: though you brushed aside

my verse,
I can't get away from it,
I've tried to;

true, it was "fascinating . . .
if you can stand its preciousness,"
you wrote of what I wrote;

why must I write?
you would not care for this,
but She draws the veil aside,

unbinds my eyes,
commands,
write, write or die.

Robinson Jeffers (1887–1962)

Robinson Jeffers was born in Pittsburgh, Pennsylvania. He attended Occidental College, the University of Southern California, and the University of Washington in Seattle before settling in Carmel, California. His poetry books include Flagons and Apples *(1912),* Californians *(1916),* Tamar *(1924),* The Women at Point Sur *(1927),* Cawdor *(1928),* Dear Judas *(1929),* Descent to the Dead *(1931),* Thurso's Landing *(1932),* Give Your Heart to the Hawks *(1933),* Solstice *(1935),* Such Counsels You Gave to Me *(1937),* Be Angry at the Sun *(1941),* The Double Axe *(1948),* Hungerfield *(1954), and* The Beginning and the End *(1963). Among his honors were a fellowship from the Book-of-the-Month Club and the Shelley Memorial Award. Robinson Jeffers died in Carmel, California.*

Gale in April

Intense and terrible beauty, how has our race with the frail naked nerves,
So little a craft swum down from its far launching?
Why now, only because the northwest blows and the headed grass billows,
Great seas jagging the west and on the granite
Blanching, the vessel is brimmed, this dancing play of the world is too
    much passion.
A gale in April so overfilling the spirit,
Though his ribs were thick as the earth's, arches of mountain, how shall one
    dare to live,
Though his blood were like the earth's rivers and his flesh iron,
How shall one dare to live? One is born strong, how do the weak endure it?
The strong lean upon death as on a rock.
After eighty years there is shelter and the naked nerves shall be covered
    with deep quietness.
O beauty of things go on, go on, O torture
Of intense joy I have lasted out my time, I have thanked God and finished,
Roots of millennial trees fold me in the darkness,
Northwest wind shake their tops, not to the root, not to the root, I have
    passed
From beauty to the other beauty, peace, the night splendor.

Shine, Perishing Republic

While this America settles in the mould of its vulgarity, heavily
    thickening to empire,
And protest, only a bubble in the molten mass, pops and sighs out, and the
    mass hardens,

I sadly smiling remember that the flower fades to make fruit, the fruit rots
    to make earth.
Out of the mother; and through the spring exultances, ripeness and
    decadence; and home to the mother.

You making haste haste on decay: not blameworthy; life is good, be it
    stubbornly long or suddenly
A mortal splendor: meteors are not needed less than mountains: shine,
    perishing republic.

But for my children, I would have them keep their distance from the
    thickening center; corruption
Never has been compulsory, when the cities lie at the monster's feet there
    are left the mountains.

And boys, be in nothing so moderate as in love of man, a clever servant,
    insufferable master.
There is the trap that catches noblest spirits, that caught—they say—God,
    when he walked on earth.

Clouds at Evening

Enormous cloud-mountains that form over Point Lobos and into the
    sunset,
Figures of fire on the walls of to-night's storm,
Foam of gold in gorges of fire, and the great file of warrior angels:
Dreams gathering in the curded brain of the earth,
The sky the brain-vault, on the threshold of sleep: poor earth, you like your
    children
By inordinate desires tortured make dreams?
Storms more enormous, wars nobler, more toppling mountains, more
    jewelled waters, more free
Fires on impossible headlands . . . as a poor girl
Wishing her lover taller and more desirous, and herself maned with gold,
Dreams the world right, in the cold bed, about dawn.
Dreams are beautiful; the slaves of form are beautiful also; I have grown to
    believe
A stone is a better pillow than many visions.

Credo

My friend from Asia has powers and magic, he plucks a blue leaf from
    the young blue-gum

And gazing upon it, gathering and quieting
The God in his mind, creates an ocean more real than the ocean, the salt,
    the actual
Appalling presence, the power of the waters.
He believes that nothing is real except as we make it. I humbler have found
    in my blood
Bred west of Caucasus a harder mysticism.
Multitude stands in my mind but I think that the ocean in the bone vault is
    only
The bone vault's ocean: out there is the ocean's;
The water is the water, the cliff is the rock, come shocks and flashes of
    reality. The mind
Passes, the eye closes, the spirit is a passage;
The beauty of things was born before eyes and sufficient to itself; the
    heart-breaking beauty
Will remain when there is no heart to break for it.

Marianne Moore (1887–1972)

Marianne Moore was born in Kirkwood, Missouri, and spent her youth in Carlisle, Pennsylvania. She attended Bryn Mawr and Carlisle Commercial colleges before working as a schoolteacher in Carlisle. After moving to New York City in 1918, she became a librarian and an editor. Her poetry books include Poems *(1921),* Observations *(1924),* Selected Poems *(1935),* What Are Years? *(1941),* Nevertheless *(1944),* Collected Poems *(1951, Pulitzer Prize, National Book Award),* Like a Bulwark, *(1956),* O to Be a Dragon *(1959),* A Marianne Moore Reader *(1961),* Tell Me, Tell Me *(1966), and* The Complete Poems *(1967). Among her honors were the 1924 Dial Award, the Shelley Memorial Award, a Guggenheim fellowship, and the Bollingen Prize; she also opened the 1968 baseball season at Yankee Stadium by tossing out the ball. Marianne Moore died in New York.*

The Fish

wade
through black jade.
    Of the crow-blue mussel shells, one keeps
    adjusting the ash heaps;
        opening and shutting itself like

an
injured fan.
    The barnacles which encrust the side
    of the wave, cannot hide
        there for the submerged shafts of the

sun,
split like spun
    glass, move themselves with spotlike swiftness
    into the crevices—
        in and out, illuminating

the
turquoise sea
    of bodies. The water drives a wedge
    of iron through the iron edge
        of the cliff, whereupon the stars,

pink
rice-grains, ink-
    bespattered jelly-fish, crabs like green
    lilies, and submarine
        toadstools, slide each on the other.

All
external
   marks of abuse are present on this
   defiant edifice—
      all the physical features of

ac-
cident—lack
   of cornice, dynamite grooves, burns, and
   hatchet strokes, these things stand
      out on it; the chasm-side is

dead.
Repeated
   evidence has proved that it can live
   on what can not revive
      its youth. The sea grows old in it.

Poetry

I, too, dislike it: there are things that are important beyond all this fiddle.
   Reading it, however, with a perfect contempt for it, one discovers that
      there is in
it after all, a place for the genuine.
   Hands that can grasp, eyes
   that can dilate, hair that can rise
      if it must, these things are important not because a

high sounding interpretation can be put upon them but because they are
   useful; when they become so derivative as to become unintelligible, the
   same thing may be said for all of us—that we
   do not admire what
   we cannot understand. The bat,
      holding on upside down or in quest of something to

eat, elephants pushing, a wild horse taking a roll, a tireless wolf under
   a tree, the immovable critic twinkling his skin like a horse that feels a flea,
      the base-
ball fan, the statistician—case after case
   could be cited did
   one wish it; nor is it valid
      to discriminate against "business documents and

school-books"; all these phenomena are important. One must make a
   distinction
   however: when dragged into prominence by half poets, the result is not
      poetry,
   nor till the autocrats among us can be
      "literalists of
      the imagination"—above
         insolence and triviality and can present

for inspection, imaginary gardens with real toads in them, shall we have
   it. In the meantime, if you demand on one hand, in defiance of their
      opinion—
   the raw material of poetry in
      all its rawness and
      that which is, on the other hand,
         genuine then you are interested in poetry.

Poetry

I, too, dislike it.
   Reading it, however, with a perfect contempt for it, one discovers in
   it, after all, a place for the genuine.

T. S. Eliot (1888–1965)

Thomas Stearns Eliot was born in St. Louis, Missouri. He attended Harvard University and the Sorbonne. In 1914 he settled in London, where he worked as a teacher, a banker, and eventually as an editor and publisher. He became a British citizen in 1927. His poetry books include Prufrock and Other Observations *(1917),* Poems *(1919),* The Waste Land *(1922, Dial Award),* Poems, 1909–1925 *(1925),* Ash Wednesday *(1930),* East Coker *(1940),* Burnt Norton *(1941),* The Dry Salvages *(1941),* Little Gidding *(1942),* Four Quartets *(1943),* Poems Written in Early Youth *(1950),* The Complete Poems and Plays *(1952), and* Collected Poems *(1962). The movie version of his verse drama* Murder in the Cathedral *(1935) won the Grand Prix at the 1951 Venice Film Festival. Among his numerous honors were the 1922 Dial Award, the 1948 Nobel Prize for Literature, and a 1950 Tony Award for* The Cocktail Party. *Eliot died in London, England.*

The Love Song of J. Alfred Prufrock

> *S'io credessi che mia risposta fosse*
> *a persona che mai tornasse al mondo,*
> *questa fiamma staria senza più scosse.*
> *Ma per ciò che giammai di questo fondo*
> *non tornò vivo alcun, s'i'odo il vero,*
> *senza tema d'infamia ti rispondo.*

Let us go then, you and I,
When the evening is spread out against the sky
Like a patient etherised upon a table;
Let us go, through certain half-deserted streets,
The muttering retreats
Of restless nights in one-night cheap hotels
And sawdust restaurants with oyster-shells:
Streets that follow like a tedious argument
Of insidious intent
To lead you to an overwhelming question . . .
Oh, do not ask, 'What is it?'
Let us go and make our visit.

In the room the women come and go
Talking of Michelangelo.

The yellow fog that rubs its back upon the window-panes,
The yellow smoke that rubs its muzzle on the window-panes,
Licked its tongue into the corners of the evening,
Lingered upon the pools that stand in drains,

Let fall upon its back the soot that falls from chimneys,
Slipped by the terrace, made a sudden leap,
And seeing that it was a soft October night,
Curled once about the house, and fell asleep.

And indeed there will be time
For the yellow smoke that slides along the street
Rubbing its back upon the window-panes;
There will be time, there will be time
To prepare a face to meet the faces that you meet;
There will be time to murder and create,
And time for all the works and days of hands
That lift and drop a question on your plate;
Time for you and time for me,
And time yet for a hundred indecisions,
And for a hundred visions and revisions,
Before the taking of a toast and tea.

In the room the women come and go
Talking of Michelangelo.

And indeed there will be time
To wonder, 'Do I dare?' and, 'Do I dare?'
Time to turn back and descend the stair,
With a bald spot in the middle of my hair—
(They will say: 'How his hair is growing thin!')
My morning coat, my collar mounting firmly to the chin,
My necktie rich and modest, but asserted by a simple pin—
(They will say; 'But how his arms and legs are thin!')
Do I dare
Disturb the universe?
In a minute there is time
For decisions and revisions which a minute will reverse.

For I have known them all already, known them all—
Have known the evenings, mornings, afternoons,
I have measured out my life with coffee spoons;
I know the voices dying with a dying fall
Beneath the music from a farther room.
    So how should I presume?

And I have known the eyes already, known them all—
The eyes that fix you in a formulated phrase,
And when I am formulated, sprawling on a pin,

When I am pinned and wriggling on the wall,
Then how should I begin
To spit out all the butt-ends of my days and ways?
    And how should I presume?

And I have known the arms already, known them all—
Arms that are braceleted and white and bare
(But in the lamplight, downed with light brown hair!)
Is it perfume from a dress
That makes me so digress?
Arms that lie along a table, or wrap about a shawl.
    And should I then presume?
    And how should I begin?

          .   .   .   .   .

Shall I say, I have gone at dusk through narrow streets
And watched the smoke that rises from the pipes
Of lonely men in shirt-sleeves, leaning out of windows? . . .

I should have been a pair of ragged claws
Scuttling across the floors of silent seas.

          .   .   .   .   .

And the afternoon, the evening, sleeps so peacefully!
Smoothed by long fingers,
Asleep . . . tired . . . or it malingers,
Stretched on the floor, here beside you and me.
Should I, after tea and cakes and ices,
Have the strength to force the moment to its crisis?
But though I have wept and fasted, wept and prayed,
Though I have seen my head (grown slightly bald) brought in upon a
        platter,
I am no prophet—and here's no great matter;
I have seen the moment of my greatness flicker,
And I have seen the eternal Footman hold my coat, and snicker,
And in short, I was afraid.

And would it have been worth it, after all,
After the cups, the marmalade, the tea,
Among the porcelain, among some talk of you and me,
Would it have been worth while,
To have bitten off the matter with a smile,
To have squeezed the universe into a ball

To roll it towards some overwhelming question,
To say: "I am Lazarus, come from the dead,
Come back to tell you all, I shall tell you all"—
If one, settling a pillow by her head,
    Should say: "That is not what I meant at all.
    That is not it, at all."

And would it have been worth it, after all,
Would it have been worth while,
After the sunsets and the dooryards and the sprinkled streets,
After the novels, after the teacups, after the skirts that trail along the floor—
And this, and so much more?—
It is impossible to say just what I mean!
But as if a magic lantern threw the nerves in patterns on a screen:
Would it have been worth while
If one, settling a pillow or throwing off a shawl,
And turning toward the window, should say:
    "That is not it at all,
    That is not what I meant, at all."

                •   •   •   •   •

No! I am not Prince Hamlet, nor was meant to be;
Am an attendant lord, one that will do
To swell a progress, start a scene or two,
Advise the prince; no doubt, an easy tool,
Deferential, glad to be of use,
Politic, cautious, and meticulous;
Full of high sentence, but a bit obtuse;
At times, indeed, almost ridiculous—
Almost, at times, the Fool.

I grow old . . . I grow old . . .
I shall wear the bottoms of my trousers rolled.

Shall I part my hair behind? Do I dare to eat a peach?
I shall wear white flannel trousers, and walk upon the beach.
I have heard the mermaids singing, each to each.

I do not think that they will sing to me.

I have seen them riding seaward on the waves
Combing the white hair of the waves blown back
When the wind blows the water white and black.

We have lingered in the chambers of the sea
By sea-girls wreathed with seaweed red and brown
Till human voices wake us, and we drown.

Preludes

I

The winter evening settles down
With smell of steaks in passageways.
Six o'clock.
The burnt-out ends of smoky days.
And now a gusty shower wraps
The grimy scraps
Of withered leaves about your feet
And newspapers from vacant lots;
The showers beat
On broken blinds and chimney-pots,
And at the corner of the street
A lonely cab-horse steams and stamps.
And then the lighting of the lamps.

II

The morning comes to consciousness
Of faint stale smells of beer
From the sawdust-trampled street
With all its muddy feet that press
To early coffee-stands.
With the other masquerades
That time resumes,
One thinks of all the hands
That are raising dingy shades
In a thousand furnished rooms.

III

You tossed a blanket from the bed,
You lay upon your back, and waited;
You dozed, and watched the night revealing
The thousand sordid images
Of which your soul was constituted;
They flickered against the ceiling.

And when all the world came back
And the light crept up between the shutters
And you heard the sparrows in the gutters,
You had such a vision of the street
As the street hardly understands;
Sitting along the bed's edge, where
You curled the papers from your hair,
Or clasped the yellow soles of feet
In the palms of both soiled hands.

IV

His soul stretched tight across the skies
That fade behind a city block,
Or trampled by insistent feet
At four and five and six o'clock;
And short square fingers stuffing pipes,
And evening newspapers, and eyes
Assured of certain certainties,
The conscience of a blackened street
Impatient to assume the world.

    I am moved by fancies that are curled
Around these images, and cling:
The notion of some infinitely gentle
Infinitely suffering thing.

    Wipe your hand across your mouth, and laugh;
The worlds revolve like ancient women
Gathering fuel in vacant lots.

The Waste Land

> 'Nam Sibyllam quidem Cumis ego ipse oculis meis vidi in ampulla
> pendere, et cum illi pueri dicerent: Σίβυλλα τί θέλεις respondebat illa:
> ἀποθανεῖν θέλω.'

> For Ezra Pound
> il miglior fabbro.

I. The Burial of the Dead

April is the cruellest month, breeding
Lilacs out of the dead land, mixing

Memory and desire, stirring
Dull roots with spring rain.
Winter kept us warm, covering
Earth in forgetful snow, feeding
A little life with dried tubers.
Summer surprised us, coming over the Starnbergersee
With a shower of rain; we stopped in the colonnade,
And went on in sunlight, into the Hofgarten,
And drank coffee, and talked for an hour.
Bin gar keine Russin, stamm' aus Litauen, echt deutsch.
And when we were children, staying at the arch-duke's,
My cousin's, he took me out on a sled,
And I was frightened. He said, Marie,
Marie, hold on tight. And down we went.
In the mountains, there you feel free.
I read, much of the night, and go south in the winter.

What are the roots that clutch, what branches grow
Out of this stony rubbish? Son of man,
You cannot say, or guess, for you know only
A heap of broken images, where the sun beats,
And the dead tree gives no shelter, the cricket no relief,
And the dry stone no sound of water. Only
There is shadow under this red rock,
(Come in under the shadow of this red rock),
And I will show you something different from either
Your shadow at morning striding behind you
Or your shadow at evening rising to meet you;
I will show you fear in a handful of dust.
              Frisch weht der Wind
              Der Heimat zu
              Mein Irisch Kind,
              Wo weilest du?
"You gave me hyacinths first a year ago;
"They called me the hyacinth girl."
—Yet when we came back, late from the hyacinth garden,
Your arms full, and your hair wet, I could not
Speak, and my eyes failed, I was neither
Living nor dead, and I knew nothing,
Looking into the heart of light, the silence.
Oed' und leer das Meer.

Madame Sosostris, famous clairvoyante,
Had a bad cold, nevertheless

Is known to be the wisest woman in Europe,
With a wicked pack of cards. Here, said she,
Is your card, the drowned Phoenician Sailor,
(Those are pearls that were his eyes. Look!)
Here is Belladonna, the Lady of the Rocks,
The lady of situations.
Here is the man with three staves, and here the Wheel,
And here is the one-eyed merchant, and this card,
Which is blank, is something he carries on his back,
Which I am forbidden to see. I do not find
The Hanged Man. Fear death by water.
I see crowds of people, walking round in a ring.
Thank you. If you see dear Mrs. Equitone,
Tell her I bring the horoscope myself:
One must be so careful these days.
Unreal City,
Under the brown fog of a winter dawn,
A crowd flowed over London Bridge, so many,
I had not thought death had undone so many.
Sighs, short and infrequent, were exhaled,
And each man fixed his eyes before his feet.
Flowed up the hill and down King William Street,
To where Saint Mary Woolnoth kept the hours
With a dead sound on the final stroke of nine.
There I saw one I knew, and stopped him, crying: "Stetson!
"You who were with me in the ships at Mylae!
"That corpse you planted last year in your garden,
"Has it begun to sprout? Will it bloom this year?
"Or has the sudden frost disturbed its bed?
"O keep the Dog far hence, that's friend to men,
"Or with his nails he'll dig it up again!
"You! hypocrite lecteur!—mon semblable,—mon frère!"

II. A Game of Chess

The Chair she sat in, like a burnished throne,
Glowed on the marble, where the glass
Held up by standards wrought with fruited vines
From which a golden Cupidon peeped out
(Another hid his eyes behind his wing)
Doubled the flames of sevenbranched candelabra
Reflecting light upon the table as
The glitter of her jewels rose to meet it,
From satin cases poured in rich profusion.

In vials of ivory and coloured glass
Unstoppered, lurked her strange synthetic perfumes,
Unguent, powdered, or liquid—troubled, confused
And drowned the sense in odours; stirred by the air
That freshened from the window, these ascended
In fattening the prolonged candle-flames,
Flung their smoke into the laquearia,
Stirring the pattern on the coffered ceiling.
Huge sea-wood fed with copper
Burned green and orange; framed by the coloured stone,
In which sad light a carvèd dolphin swam.
Above the antique mantel was displayed
As though a window gave upon the sylvan scene
The change of Philomel, by the barbarous king
So rudely forced; yet there the nightingale
Filled all the desert with inviolable voice
And still she cried, and still the world pursues,
"Jug Jug" to dirty ears.
And other withered stumps of time
Were told upon the walls; staring forms
Leaned out, leaning, hushing the room enclosed.
Footsteps shuffled on the stair.
Under the firelight, under the brush, her hair
Spread out in fiery points
Glowed into words, then would be savagely still.

"My nerves are bad to-night. Yes, bad. Stay with me.
"Speak to me. Why do you never speak. Speak.
     "What are you thinking of? What thinking? What?
"I never know what you are thinking. Think."

I think we are in rats' alley
Where the dead men lost their bones.

"What is that noise?"
                         The wind under the door.
"What is that noise now? What is the wind doing?"
                         Nothing again nothing.
                                                  "Do
"You know nothing? Do you see nothing? Do you remember
"Nothing?"

          I remember
Those are pearls that were his eyes.

"Are you alive, or not? Is there nothing in your head?"

                              But

O O O O that Shakespeherian Rag—
It's so elegant
So intelligent
"What shall I do now? What shall I do?"
"I shall rush out as I am, and walk the street
"With my hair down, so. What shall we do tomorrow?
"What shall we ever do?"

                          The hot water at ten.
And if it rains, a closed car at four.
And we shall play a game of chess,
Pressing lidless eyes and waiting for a knock upon the door.

When Lil's husband got demobbed, I said—
I didn't mince my words, I said to her myself,
HURRY UP PLEASE ITS TIME
Now Albert's coming back, make yourself a bit smart.
He'll want to know what you done with that money he gave you
To get yourself some teeth. He did, I was there.

You have them all out, Lil, and get a nice set,
He said, I swear, I can't bear to look at you.
And no more can't I, I said, and think of poor Albert,
He's been in the army four years, he wants a good time,
And if you don't give it him, there's others will, I said.
Oh is there, she said. Something o' that, I said.
Then I'll know who to thank, she said, and give me a straight look.
HURRY UP PLEASE ITS TIME
If you don't like it you can get on with it, I said.
Others can pick and choose if you can't.
But if Albert makes off, it won't be for lack of telling.
You ought to be ashamed, I said, to look so antique.
(And her only thirty-one.)
I can't help it, she said, pulling a long face,
It's them pills I took, to bring it off, she said.
(She's had five already, and nearly died of young George.)
The chemist said it would be all right, but I've never been the same.
You *are* a proper fool, I said.
Well, if Albert won't leave you alone, there it is, I said,
What you get married for if you don't want children?
HURRY UP PLEASE ITS TIME
Well, that Sunday Albert was home, they had a hot gammon
And they asked me in to dinner, to get the beauty of it hot—

HURRY UP PLEASE ITS TIME
HURRY UP PLEASE ITS TIME
Goonight Bill. Goonight Lou. Goonight May. Goonight.
Ta ta. Goonight. Goonight.
Good night, ladies, good night, sweet ladies, good night, good night.

III. The Fire Sermon

The river's tent is broken; the last fingers of leaf
Clutch and sink into the wet bank. The wind
Crosses the brown land, unheard. The nymphs are departed.
Sweet Thames, run softly, till I end my song.
The river bears no empty bottles, sandwich papers,
Silk handkerchiefs, cardboard boxes, cigarette ends
Or other testimony of summer nights. The nymphs are departed.
And their friends, the loitering heirs of City directors;
Departed, have left no addresses.
By the water of Leman I sat down and wept . . .
Sweet Thames, run softly till I end my song,
Sweet Thames, run softly, for I speak not loud or long.
But at my back in a cold blast I hear
The rattle of the bones, and chuckle spread from ear to ear.

A rat crept softly through the vegetation
Dragging its slimy belly on the bank
While I was fishing in the dull canal
On a winter evening round behind the gashouse
Musing upon the king my brother's wreck
And on the king my father's death before him.
White bodies naked on the low damp ground
And bones cast in a little low dry garret,
Rattled by the rat's foot only, year to year.
But at my back from time to time I hear
The sound of horns and motors, which shall bring
Sweeney to Mrs. Porter in the spring
O the moon shone bright on Mrs. Porter
And on her daughter
They wash their feet in soda water
Et O ces voix d'enfants, chantant dans la coupole!

Twit twit twit
Jug jug jug jug jug jug
So rudely forc'd.
Tereu

Unreal City
Under the brown fog of a winter noon
Mr. Eugenides, the Smyrna merchant
Unshaven, with a pocket full of currants
C.i.f. London: documents at sight,
Asked me in demotic French
To luncheon at the Cannon Street Hotel
Followed by a weekend at the Metropole.

At the violet hour, when the eyes and back
Turn upward from the desk, when the human engine waits
Like a taxi throbbing waiting,
I Tiresias, though blind, throbbing between two lives,
Old man with wrinkled female breasts, can see
At the violet hour, the evening hour that strives
Homeward, and brings the sailor home from sea,
The typist home at teatime, clears her breakfast, lights
Her stove, and lays out food in tins.
Out of the window perilously spread
Her drying combinations touched by the sun's last rays,
On the divan are piled (at night her bed)
Stockings, slippers, camisoles, and stays.
I Tiresias, old man with wrinkled dugs
Perceived the scene, and foretold the rest—
I too awaited the expected guest.
He, the young man carbuncular, arrives,
A small house agent's clerk, with one bold stare,
One of the low on whom assurance sits
As a silk hat on a Bradford millionaire.
The time is now propitious, as he guesses,
The meal is ended, she is bored and tired,
Endeavours to engage her in caresses
Which still are unreproved, if undesired.
Flushed and decided, he assaults at once;
Exploring hands encounter no defence;
His vanity requires no response,
And makes a welcome of indifference.
(And I Tiresias have foresuffered all
Enacted on this same divan or bed;
I who have sat by Thebes below the wall
And walked among the lowest of the dead.)
Bestows one final patronising kiss,
And gropes his way, finding the stairs unlit . . .

She turns and looks a moment in the glass,
Hardly aware of her departed lover;
Her brain allows one half-formed thought to pass:
"Well now that's done: and I'm glad it's over."
When lovely woman stoops to folly and
Paces about her room again, alone,
She smoothes her hair with automatic hand,
And puts a record on the gramophone.

"This music crept by me upon the waters"
And along the Strand, up Queen Victoria Street.
O City city, I can sometimes hear
Beside a public bar in Lower Thames Street,
The pleasant whining of a mandoline
And a clatter and a chatter from within
Where fishermen lounge at noon: where the walls
Of Magnus Martyr hold
Inexplicable splendour of Ionian white and gold.

   The river sweats
   Oil and tar
   The barges drift
   With the turning tide
   Red sails
   Wide
   To leeward, swing on the heavy spar.
   The barges wash
   Drifting logs
   Down Greenwich reach
   Past the Isle of Dogs.
      Weialala leia
      Wallala leialala

   Elizabeth and Leicester
   Beating oars
   The stern was formed
   A gilded shell
   Red and gold
   The brisk swell
   Rippled both shores
   Southwest wind
   Carried down stream
   The peal of bells
   White towers

> Weialala leia
> Wallala leialala

"Trams and dusty trees.
Highbury bore me. Richmond and Kew
Undid me. By Richmond I raised my knees
Supine on the floor of a narrow canoe."

"My feet are at Moorgate, and my heart
Under my feet. After the event
He wept. He promised 'a new start.'
I made no comment. What should I resent?"

"On Margate Sands.
I can connect
Nothing with nothing.
The broken fingernails of dirty hands.
My people humble people who expect
Nothing."
> > la la

To Carthage then I came

Burning burning burning burning
O Lord Thou pluckest me out
O Lord Thou pluckest

burning

IV. Death by Water

Phlebas the Phoenician, a fortnight dead,
Forgot the cry of gulls, and the deep sea swell
And the profit and loss.
> > A current under sea
Picked his bones in whispers. As he rose and fell
He passed the stages of his age and youth
Entering the whirlpool.

> > Gentile or Jew
O you who turn the wheel and look to windward,
Consider Phlebas, who was once handsome and
tall as you.

V. What the Thunder Said

After the torchlight red on sweaty faces
After the frosty silence in the gardens
After the agony in stony places
The shouting and the crying
Prison and palace and reverberation
Of thunder of spring over distant mountains
He who was living is now dead
We who were living are now dying
With a little patience

Here is no water but only rock
Rock and no water and the sandy road
The road winding above among the mountains
Which are mountains of rock without water
If there were water we should stop and drink
Amongst the rock one cannot stop or think
Sweat is dry and feet are in the sand
If there were only water amongst the rock
Dead mountain mouth of carious teeth that cannot spit
Here one can neither stand nor lie nor sit
There is not even silence in the mountains
But dry sterile thunder without rain
There is not even solitude in the mountains
But red sullen faces sneer and snarl
From doors of mudcracked houses
                              If there were water

        And no rock
        If there were rock
        And also water
        And water
        A spring
        A pool among the rock
        If there were the sound of water only
        Not the cicada
        And dry grass singing
        But sound of water over a rock
        Where the hermit-thrush sings in the pine trees
        Drip drop drip drop drop drop drop
        But there is no water

Who is the third who walks always beside you?
When I count, there are only you and I together

But when I look ahead up the white road
There is always another one walking beside you
Gliding wrapt in a brown mantle, hooded
I do not know whether a man or a woman
—But who is that on the other side of you?

What is that sound high in the air
Murmur of maternal lamentation
Who are those hooded hordes swarming
Over endless plains, stumbling in cracked earth
Ringed by the flat horizon only
What is the city over the mountains
Cracks and reforms and bursts in the violet air
Falling towers
Jerusalem Athens Alexandria
Vienna London
Unreal

A woman drew her long black hair out tight
And fiddled whisper music on those strings
And bats with baby faces in the violet light
Whistled, and beat their wings
And crawled head downward down a blackened wall
And upside down in air were towers
Tolling reminiscent bells, that kept the hours
And voices singing out of empty cisterns and exhausted wells

In this decayed hole among the mountains
In the faint moonlight, the grass is singing
Over the tumbled graves, above the chapel
There is the empty chapel, only the wind's home.
It has no windows, and the door swings,
Dry bones can harm no one.
Only a cock stood on the rooftree
Co co rico co co rico
In a flash of lightning. Then a damp gust
Bringing rain

Ganga was sunken, and the limp leaves
Waited for rain, while the black clouds
Gathered far distant, over Himavant.
The jungle crouched, humped in silence.
Then spoke the thunder
DA

Datta: what have we given?
My friend, blood shaking my heart
The awful daring of a moment's surrender
Which an age of prudence can never retract
By this, and this only, we have existed
Which is not to be found in our obituaries
Or in memories draped by the beneficent spider
Or under seals broken by the lean solicitor
In our empty rooms
DA
Dayadhvam: I have heard the key
Turn in the door once and turn once only
We think of the key, each in his prison
Thinking of the key, each confirms a prison
Only at nightfall, aethereal rumours
Revive for a moment a broken Coriolanus
DA
Damyata: The boat responded
Gaily, to the hand expert with sail and oar
The sea was calm, your heart would have responded
Gaily, when invited, beating obedient
To controlling hands

                         I sat upon the shore
Fishing, with the arid plain behind me
Shall I at least set my lands in order?
London Bridge is falling down falling down falling down
Poi s'ascose nel foco che gli affina
Quando fiam uti chelidon—O swallow swallow
Le Prince d'Aquitaine à la tour abolie
These fragments I have shored against my ruins
Why then Ile fit you. Hieronymo's mad againe.
Datta. Dayadhvam. Damyata.
                  Shantih   shantih   shantih

Claude McKay (1889–1948)

Festus Claudius McKay was born in Sunny Ville, Jamaica, where he apprenticed in cabinetmaking and worked as a police officer. In 1912 he came to the United States to attend Tuskegee Institute and then Kansas State University, before moving to New York in 1914, where he worked as a waiter and an editor. From 1919 to 1934 he lived in Europe; in 1934 he returned to New York, joined the Federal Writers Project, then worked at a shipyard. In 1943 he moved to Chicago. His poetry books include Songs of Jamaica *(1912),* Constab Ballads *(1912),* Spring in New Hampshire, and Other Poems *(1920),* Harlem Shadows *(1922), and* Selected Poems *(1953). In poor health and destitute, Claude McKay died in Chicago, Illinois.*

If We Must Die

If we must die, let it not be like hogs
Hunted and penned in an inglorious spot,
While round us bark the mad and hungry dogs,
Making their mock at our accursed lot.
If we must die, O let us nobly die,
So that our precious blood may not be shed
In vain; then even the monsters we defy
Shall be constrained to honor us though dead!
O kinsmen! we must meet the common foe!
Though far outnumbered let us show us brave,
And for their thousand blows deal one deathblow!
What though before us lies the open grave?
Like men we'll face the murderous, cowardly pack,
Pressed to the wall, dying, but fighting back!

The Harlem Dancer

Applauding youths laughed with young prostitutes
And watched her perfect, half-clothed body sway;
Her voice was like the sound of blended flutes
Blown by black players upon a picnic day.
She sang and danced on gracefully and calm,
The light gauze hanging loose about her form;
To me she seemed a proudly-swaying palm
Grown lovelier for passing through a storm.
Upon her swarthy neck black shiny curls

Luxuriant fell; and tossing coins in praise,
The wine-flushed, bold-eyed boys, and even the girls,
Devoured her shape with eager, passionate gaze;
But looking at her falsely-smiling face,
I knew her self was not in that strange place.

Archibald MacLeish (1892–1982)

Archibald McLeish was born in Glencoe, Illinois. He attended Yale University and Harvard Law School, interrupted by military service in World War I. After practicing law briefly, he lived in France (1923–28), then worked as a writer and magazine editor before becoming Librarian of Congress from 1939 to 1944. During the last year of World War II, he took over several other high-ranking government posts; afterward, he taught at Harvard and at Amherst College. His poetry books include Songs for a Summer's Day *(1915),* Tower of Ivory *(1917),* The Happy Marriage and Other Poems *(1924),* The Pot of Earth *(1925),* Streets in the Moon *(1926),* The Hamlet of A. MacLeish *(1928),* Before Match *(1932),* Conquistador *(1932, Pulitzer Prize),* Poems 1924–1933 *(1933),* Land of the Free *(1938),* America Was Promises *(1939),* Actfive and Other Poems *(1948),* Collected Poems 1917–52 *(1952, Pulitzer Prize, National Book Award),* Songs for Eve *(1954),* The Wild Old Wicked Man and Other Poems *(1968),* The Human Season *(1972), and* New and Collected Poems 1917–1976 *(1976). His honors include the Shelley Award, the Presidential Medal of Freedom, the 1959 Tony Award and 1959 Pulitzer Prize in drama, and the 1966 Oscar for best screenplay. Archibald MacLeish died in Boston, Massachusetts.*

Ars Poetica

A poem should be palpable and mute
As a globed fruit,

Dumb
As old medallions to the thumb,

Silent as the sleeve-worn stone
Of casement ledges where the moss has grown—

A poem should be wordless
As the flight of birds.

             *

A poem should be motionless in time
As the moon climbs,

Leaving, as the moon releases
Twig by twig the night-entangled trees,

Leaving, as the moon behind the winter leaves,
Memory by memory the mind—

A poem should be motionless in time
As the moon climbs.

*

A poem should be equal to:
Not true.

For all the history of grief
An empty doorway and a maple leaf.

For love
The leaning grasses and two lights above the sea—

A poem should not mean
But be.

Edna St. Vincent Millay (1892–1950)

Edna St. Vincent Millay was born in Rockland, Maine. She attended Vassar College and later lived in New York City and Austerlitz, New York. Her poetry books include Renascence, and Other Poems *(1917),* A Few Figs From Thistles *(1920),* Second April *(1921),* The Ballad of the Harp-Weaver *(1922, Pulitzer Prize),* Poems *(1923),* The Buck in the Snow, and Other Poems *(1928),* Fatal Interview *(1931),* Wine from These Grapes *(1934),* Conversation at Midnight *(1937),* Huntsman, What Quarry? *(1939).* There Are No Islands, Any More *(1940),* Make Bright the Arrows *(1940),* The Murder of Lidice *(1942), and* Collected Poems *(1950). She also wrote several successful plays and the libretto for the opera* The King's Henchman *(Metropolitan Opera, 1927). Edna St. Vincent Millay died in Austerlitz, New York, from injuries sustained in a fall.*

First Fig

My candle burns at both ends;
    It will not last the night;
But ah, my foes, and oh, my friends—
    It gives a lovely light!

Recuerdo

We were very tired, we were very merry—
We had gone back and forth all night on the ferry.
It was bare and bright, and smelled like a stable—
But we looked into a fire, we leaned across a table,
We lay on a hill-top underneath the moon;
And the whistles kept blowing, and the dawn came soon.

We were very tired, we were very merry—
We had gone back and forth all night on the ferry;
And you ate an apple, and I ate a pear,
From a dozen of each we had bought somewhere;
And the sky went wan, and the wind came cold,
And the sun rose dripping, a bucketful of gold.

We were very tired, we were very merry,
We had gone back and forth all night on the ferry.
We hailed, "Good morrow, mother!" to a shawl-covered head,
And bought a morning paper, which neither of us read;
And she wept, "God bless you!" for the apples and pears,
And we gave her all our money but our subway fares.

E. E. Cummings (1894–1962)

Edward Estlin Cummings was born in Cambridge, Massachusetts, and attended Harvard University. In World War I he volunteered as an ambulance driver in France and was imprisoned for expressing antiwar views. Later, while living in New York as a freelance writer, he returned to Paris frequently and traveled widely in Europe. His poetry books include Tulips and Chimneys *(1923),* XLI Poems *(1925),* is 5 *(1926),* ViVa *(1931),* No Thanks *(1935),* 1/20 *(1936),* Collected Poems *(1938),* 50 Poems *(1940),* 1 × 1 *(1944),* Xaipe *(1950),* Poems, 1923–1954 *(1954, National Book Award special citation),* 95 Poems *(1958),* 73 Poems *(1962), and* Complete Poems *(1991). Among his honors were the 1925 Dial Award, Guggenheim fellowships, the Shelley Memorial Award, and the Bollingen Prize. E. E. Cummings died in North Conway, New Hampshire.*

in Just-

in Just-
spring   when the world is mud-
luscious the little
lame balloonman

whistles   far   and wee

and eddieandbill come
running from marbles and
piracies and it's
spring

when the world is puddle-wonderful

the queer
old balloonman whistles
far   and   wee
and bettyandisbel come dancing

from hop-scotch and jump-rope and

it's
spring
and
    the

        goat-footed

balloonMan   whistles
far
and
wee

Buffalo Bill 's

Buffalo Bill 's
defunct
      who used to
      ride a watersmooth-silver
                stallion
and break onetwothreefourfive pigeonsjustlikethat
                       Jesus

he was a handsome man
               and what i want to know is
how do you like your blueeyed boy
Mister Death

the Cambridge ladies who live in furnished souls

the Cambridge ladies who live in furnished souls
are unbeautiful and have comfortable minds
(also, with the church's protestant blessings
daughters, unscented shapeless spirited)
they believe in Christ and Longfellow, both dead,
are invariably interested in so many things—
at the present writing one still finds
delighted fingers knitting for the is it Poles?
perhaps. While permanent faces coyly bandy
scandal of Mrs. N and Professor D
. . . . the Cambridge ladies do not care,above
Cambridge if sometimes in its box of
sky lavender and cornerless,the
moon rattles like a fragment of angry candy

next to of course god america i

"next to of course god america i
love you land of the pilgrims' and so forth oh

say can you see by the dawn's early my
country 'tis of centuries come and go
and are no more what of it we should worry
in every language even deafanddumb
thy sons acclaim your glorious name by gorry
by jingo by gee by gosh by gum
why talk of beauty what could be more beaut-
iful than these heroic happy dead
who rushed like lions to the roaring slaughter
they did not stop to think they died instead
then shall the voice of liberty be mute?"

He spoke.   And drank rapidly a glass of water.

somewhere i have never travelled,gladly beyond

somewhere i have never travelled,gladly beyond
any experience, your eyes have their silence:
in your most frail gesture are things which enclose me,
or which i cannot touch because they are too near

your slightest look easily will unclose me
though i have closed myself as fingers,
you open always petal by petal myself as Spring opens
(touching skilfully, mysteriously)her first rose

or if your wish be to close me,i and
my life will shut very beautifully,suddenly,
as when the heart of this flower imagines
the snow carefully everywhere descending;

nothing which we are to perceive in this world equals
the power of your intense fragility:whose texture
compels me with the colour of its countries,
rendering death and forever with each breathing

(i do not know what it is about you that closes
and opens; only something in me understands
the voice of your eyes is deeper than all roses)
nobody,not even the rain, has such small hands

r-p-o-p-h-e-s-s-a-g-r

                    r-p-o-p-h-e-s-s-a-g-r
          who
a)s w(e loo)k
upnowgath
        PPEGORHRASS
                  eringint(o-
a The):l
      eA
        !p:
S   a
          (r
rIvInG   .gRrEaPsPhOs)
                    to
rea(be)rran(com)gi(e)ngly
,grasshopper;

Jean Toomer (1894–1967)

Jean Toomer was born in Washington, D.C., and attended the University of Wisconsin, the University of Chicago, and New York University, among others, before working in a variety of jobs. He lived in New York and in France and finally moved to Doylestown, Pennsylvania, in 1940. Cane, his groundbreaking collage of prose sketches and poetry, appeared in 1923. The Collected Poems of Jean Toomer was published in 1988. Toomer died in Doylestown, Pennsylvania.

Reapers

Black reapers with the sound of steel on stones
Are sharpening scythes. I see them place the hones
In their hip-pockets as a thing that's done,
And start their silent swinging, one by one.
Black horses drive a mower through the weeds,
And there, a field rat, startled, squealing bleeds,
His belly close to ground. I see the blade,
Blood-stained, continue cutting weeds and shade.

November Cotton Flower

Boll-weevil's coming, and the winter's cold,
Made cotton-stalks look rusty, seasons old,
And cotton, scarce as any southern snow,
Was vanishing; the branch, so pinched and slow,
Failed in its function as the autumn rake;
Drouth fighting soil had caused the soil to take
All water from the streams; dead birds were found
In wells a hundred feet below the ground—
Such was the season when the flower bloomed.
Old folks were startled, and it soon assumed
Significance. Superstition saw
Something it had never seen before:
Brown eyes that loved without a trace of fear,
Beauty so sudden for that time of year.

Portrait in Georgia

Hair—braided chestnut,
    coiled like a lyncher's rope,

Eyes—fagots,
Lips—old scars, or the first red blisters,
Breath—the last sweet scent of cane,
And her slim body, white as the ash
      of black flesh after flame.

Louise Bogan (1897–1970)

Louise Bogan was born in Livermore Falls, Maine. She attended Boston University for one year and later lived in Vienna, Austria, and New York City, where she worked as an editor and book reviewer until 1969. Her poetry books include Body of This Death *(1923),* Dark Summer *(1929),* The Sleeping Fury *(1937),* Poems and New Poems *(1941),* Collected Poems, 1923–1953 *(1954, Bollingen Prize), and* The Blue Estuaries *(1968). Among her honors were Guggenheim and National Endowment for the Arts fellowships and the Harriet Monroe Award; in 1945–46 she served as Consultant in Poetry at the Library of Congress. Louise Bogan died from a heart attack in New York City.*

Medusa

I had come to the house, in a cave of trees,
Facing a sheer sky.
Everything moved,—a bell hung ready to strike,
Sun and reflection wheeled by.

When the bare eyes were before me
And the hissing hair,
Held up at a window, seen through a door.
The stiff bald eyes, the serpents on the forehead
Formed in the air.

This is a dead scene forever now.
Nothing will ever stir.
The end will never brighten it more than this,
Nor the rain blur.

The water will always fall, and will not fall,
And the tipped bell make no sound.
The grass will always be growing for hay
Deep on the ground.

And I shall stand here like a shadow
Under the great balanced day,
My eyes on the yellow dust, that was lifting in the wind,
And does not drift away.

New Moon

Cruel time-servers, here is the crescent moon,
Curved right to left in the sky, facing planets attendant.

Over the houses, leaned in the silent air,
Purest along the edge of darkness infinite.

Under it, men return from the office and factory,
From the little store at the corner of Eighty-eighth Street.

On the gnawed snow, or under the breezes of autumn,
With hope and fear in their hearts, and their arms full of groceries.
Above the trim suit, above the flesh starved or satiate,
Above the set hair, above the machines in the beauty shops;

Above the young men, thinking the popular song;
Above the children, who now in the dusk go wild.

Crescent, horn, cusp, above the clinics, the lodgings,
Sweet curve, sweet light, new thin moon, now purely at ease,

Above the old, going home to their deafness, their madness,
Their cancer, age, ugliness, pain, diabetes.

Melvin B. Tolson (1898–1966)

Melvin B. Tolson was born in Moberly, Missouri. He attended Fisk University, Lincoln University, and Columbia University before teaching at Wiley College in Texas, finally joining the faculty at Langston University in Oklahoma in 1947. His poetry books include Rendezvous with America *(1944),* Libretto for the Republic of Liberia *(1953),* Harlem Gallery: Book One, The Curator *(1965),* A Gallery of Harlem Portraits *(1979), and* Harlem Gallery, and Other Poems *(1999). Among his honors were the poet laureateship of Liberia (1947), the Bess Hokin Prize, the American Academy of Arts and Letters Award in Literature, and an appointment as Avalon Poet at Tuskegee Institute. Melvin B. Tolson died in Dallas, Texas, after cancer surgery.*

Dark Symphony

I

Allegro Moderato

Black Crispus Attucks taught
               Us how to die
Before white Patrick Henry's bugle breath
Uttered the vertical
               Transmitting cry:
"Yea, give me liberty, or give me death."

Waifs of the auction block,
               Men black and strong
The juggernauts of despotism withstood,
Loin-girt with faith that worms
               Equate the wrong
And dust is purged to create brotherhood.

No Banquo's ghost can rise
               Against us now,
Aver we hobnailed Man beneath the brute,
Squeezed down the thorns of greed
               On Labor's brow,
Garroted lands and carted off the loot.

II

Lento Grave

The centuries-old pathos in our voices
Saddens the great white world,
And the wizardry of our dusky rhythms
Conjures up shadow-shapes of ante-bellum years:

Black slaves singing *One More River to Cross*
In the torture tombs of slave-ships,
Black slaves singing *Steal Away to Jesus*
In jungle swamps,
Black slaves singing *The Crucifixion*
In slave-pens at midnight,
Black slaves singing *Swing Low, Sweet Chariot*
In cabins of death,
Black slaves singing *Go Down, Moses*
In the canebrakes of the Southern Pharaohs.

III

Andante Sostenuto

They tell us to forget
The Golgotha we tread . . .
We who are scourged with hate,
A price upon our head.
They who have shackled us
Require of us a song,
They who have wasted us
Bid us condone the wrong.

They tell us to forget
Democracy is spurned.
They tell us to forget
The Bill of Rights is burned.
Three hundred years we slaved,
We slave and suffer yet:
Though flesh and bone rebel,
They tell us to forget!

Oh, how can we forget
Our human rights denied?
Oh, how can we forget
Our manhood crucified?
When Justice is profaned
And plea with curse is met,
When Freedom's gates are barred,
Oh, how can we forget?

IV

Tempo Primo

The New Negro strides upon the continent
In seven-league boots . . .
The New Negro
Who sprang from the vigor-stout loins
Of Nat Turner, gallows-martyr for Freedom,
Of Joseph Cinquez, Black Moses of the Amistad Mutiny,
Of Frederick Douglass, oracle of the Catholic Man,
Of Sojourner Truth, eye and ear of Lincoln's legions,
Of Harriet Tubman, Saint Bernard of the Underground Railroad.

The New Negro
Breaks the icons of his detractors,
Wipes out the conspiracy of silence,
Speaks to *his* America:

"My history-moulding ancestors
Planted the first crops of wheat on these shores,
Built ships to conquer the seven seas,
Erected the Cotton Empire,
Flung railroads across a hemisphere,
Disemboweled the earth's iron and coal,
Tunneled the mountains and bridged rivers,
Harvested the grain and hewed forests,
Sentineled the Thirteen Colonies,
Unfurled Old Glory at the North Pole,
Fought a hundred battles for the Republic."

The New Negro:
His giant hands fling murals upon high chambers,
His drama teaches a world to laugh and weep,
His music leads continents captive,
His voice thunders the Brotherhood of Labor,
His science creates seven wonders,
His Republic of Letters challenges the Negro-baiters.

The New Negro,
Hard-muscled, Fascist-hating, Democracy-ensouled,
Strides in seven-league boots
Along the Highway of Today
Toward the Promised Land of Tomorrow!

V

Larghetto

None in the Land can say
To us black men Today:
You send the tractors on their bloody path,
And create Okies for *The Grapes of Wrath*.
You breed the slum that breeds a *Native Son*
To damn the good earth Pilgrim Fathers won.

None in the Land can say
To us black men Today:
You dupe the poor with rags-to-riches tales,
And leave the workers empty dinner pails.
You stuff the ballot box, and honest men
Are muzzled by your demagogic din.

None in the Land can say
To us black men Today:
You smash stock markets with your coined blitzkriegs,
And make a hundred million guinea pigs.
You counterfeit our Christianity,
And bring contempt upon Democracy.

None in the land can say
To us black men Today:
You prowl when citizens are fast asleep,
And hatch Fifth Column plots to blast the deep
Foundations of the State and leave the Land
A vast Sahara with a Fascist brand.

VI

Tempo Di Marcia

Out of abysses of Illiteracy,
Through labyrinths of Lies,
Across waste lands of Disease . . .
We advance!

Out of dead-ends of Poverty,
Through wildernesses of Superstition,
Across barricades of Jim Crowism . . .
We advance!

With the Peoples of the World . . .
We advance!

From *Harlem Gallery*

Psi

Black Boy,
let me get up from the white man's Table of Fifty Sounds
in the kitchen; let me gather the crumbs and cracklings
of this autobio-fragment,
before the curtain with the skull and bones descends.

Many a *t* in the ms.
I've left without a cross,
many an *i* without a dot.
A dusky Lot
with a third degree and a second wind and a seventh turn
of pitch-and-toss,
my psyche escaped the Sodom of Gylt
and the Big White Boss.

Black Boy,
you stand before your heritage,
naked and agape;
cheated like a mockingbird
pecking at a Zuexian grape,
pressed like an awl to do
duty as a screw-
driver, you
ask the American Dilemma in you:
"If the trying plane
of Demos fail,
what will the trowel
of Uncle Tom avail?"

Black Boy,
in this race, at this time, in this place,
to be a Negro artist is to be
a flower of the gods, whose growth
is dwarfed at an early stage—
a Brazilian owl moth,
a giant among his own in an acreage

dark with the darkman's designs,
where the milieu moves back downward like the sloth.

Black Boy,
true—you
have not
dined and wined
(*ignoti nulla cupido*)
in the El Dorado of aeried Art,
for unreasoned reasons;
and your artists, not so lucky as the Buteo,
find themselves without a
skyscape sanctuary
in the
season of seasons:
in contempt of the contemptible,
refuse the herb of grace, the rue
of Job's comforter;
take no
lie-tea in lieu
of Broken Orange Pekoe.
Doctor Nkomo said; "*What* is he who smacks
his lips when dewrot eats away the golden grain
of self-respect exposed like flax
to the rigors of sun and rain?"

Black Boy,
every culture,
every caste,
every people,
every class,
facing the barbarians
with lips hubris-curled,
believes its death rattle omens
the *Dies Irae* of the world.

Black Boy,
summon Boas and Dephino,
Blumenbach and Koelreuter,
from their posts
around the gravestone of Bilbo,
who, with cancer in his mouth,
orated until he quaked the magnolias of the South,
while the pocketbooks of his weeping black serfs

shriveled in the drouth;
summon the ghosts
of scholars with rams' horns from Jericho
and facies in letters from Jerusalem,
so
we may ask them:
"What is a Negro?"

Black Boy,
what's in a people's name that wries the brain
like the neck of a barley bird?
Can sounding brass create
an ecotype with a word?

Black Boy,
beware of the thin-bladed mercy
stroke, for one drop of Negro blood
(V. *The Black Act of the F. F. V.*)
opens the flood-
gates of the rising tide of color
and jettisons
the D. A. R. in the Heraclitean flux
with Uncle Tom and
Crispus Attucks.
The Black Belt White,
painstaking as a bedbug in
a tenant farmer's truckle bed,
rabbit-punched old Darrow
because
he quoted Darwin's sacred laws
(instead of the Lord God Almighty's)
and gabbled that the Catarrhine ape
(the C from a Canada goose nobody knows)
appears,
after X's of years,
in the vestigial shape
of the Nordic's thin lips, his aquiline nose,
his straight hair,
orangutanish on legs and chest and head.
Doctor Nkomo, a votary of touch-and-go,
who can stand the gaff
of Negrophobes and, like Aramis,
parry a thrust with a laugh,
said:

"In spite of the pig in the python's coils,
in spite of Blake's lamb in the jaws of the tiger,
Nature is kind, even in the raw: she toils
. . . aeons and aeons and aeons . . .
gives the African a fleecy canopy
to protect the seven faculties of the brain
from the burning convex lens of the sun;
she foils
whiteness
(without disdain)
to bless the African
(as Herodotus marvels)
with the birthright of a burnt skin for work or fun;
she roils
the Aryan
(as his eye and ear repose)
to give the African an accommodation nose
that cools the drying-up air;
she entangles the epidermis in broils
that keep the African's body free from lice-infested hair.
As man to man,
the Logos is
Nature is on the square
with the African.
If a black man circles the rim
of the Great White World, he will find
(even if Adamness has made him half blind)
the bitter waters of Marah *and*
the fresh fountains of Elim."
Although his transition
was a far cry
from Shakespeare to Sardou,
the old Africanist's byplay gave
no soothing feverfew
to the Dogs in the Zulu Club;
said he:
"A Hardyesque artistry
of circumstance
divides the Whites and Blacks in life,
like the bodies of the dead
eaten by vultures
in a Tower of Silence.
Let, then, the man with a maggot in his head
lean . . . lean . . . lean

on race or caste or class,
for the wingless worms of blowflies shall grub,
dry and clean,
the stinking skeletons of these,
when the face of the macabre weather-
cock turns to the torrid wind of misanthropy;
and later their bones shall be swept together
(like the Parsees')
in the Sepulchre of Anonymity."
A Zulu Wit cleared away his unsunned
mood with dark laughter;
but I sensed the thoughts of Doctor Nkomo
pacing nervously to and fro
like Asscher's, after
he'd cleaved the giant Cullinan Diamond.

Black Boy,
the vineyard is the fittest place
in which to booze (with Omar) and study
soil and time and integrity—
the telltale triad of grape and race.

Palates that can read the italics
of *salt* and *sugar* know
a grapevine
transplanted from Bordeaux
to Pleasant Valley
cannot give grapes that make a Bordeaux wine.

Like the sons of the lone mother of dead empires,
who boasted their ancestors,
page after page—
wines are peacocky
in their vintage and their age,
disdaining the dark ways of those engaging
in the profits
of chemical aging.
When the bluebirds sing
their perennial anthem
a capriccio, in the Spring,
the sap begins to move up the stem
of the vine, and the wine in the bed of the deep
cask stirs in its winter sleep.
Its bouquet

comes with the years, dry or wet;
so the connoisseurs say:
"The history of the wine
is repeated by the vine."

Black Boy,
beware of wine labels,
for the Republic does not guarantee
what the phrase "Château Bottled" means—
the estate, the proprietor, the quality.
This ignominy will baffle you, Black Boy,
because the white man's law
has raked your butt many a time
with fang and claw.
Beware of the waiter who wraps
a napkin around your Clos Saint Thierry,
if Chance takes you into high-hat places
open to all creeds and races
born to be or not to be.
Beware of the pop
of a champagne cork:
like the flatted fifth and octave jump in Bebop,
it is theatrical
in Vicksburg or New York.
Beware of the champagne cork
that does not swell up like your ma when she had you—*that*
comes out flat,
because the bottle of wine
is dead . . . dead
like Uncle Tom and the Jim Crow Sign.
Beware . . . yet
your dreams in the Great White World
shall be unthrottled
by pigmented and unpigmented lionhearts,
for we know *without no*
every people, by and by, produces its "Château Bottled."

White Boy,
as regards the ethnic origin
of Black Boy and me,
the *What* in Socrates' "*Tò tí?*"
is for the musk-ox habitat of anthropologists;
but there is another question,
dangerous as a moutaba tick,

secreted in the house
of every Anglo-Saxon sophist and hick:

Who is a Negro?
(I am a White in deah ole Norfolk.)
Who is a White?
(I am a Negro in little old New York.)
Since my mongrelization is invisible
and my Negroness a state of mind conjured up
by Stereotypus, I am a chameleon
on *that* side of the Mason-Dixon
that a white man's conscience
is not on.
My skin is as white
as a Roman's toga when he sought an office on the sly;
my hair is as blond
as xanthein;
my eyes are as blue
as the hawk's-eye.
At the Olympian powwow of curators,
when I revealed my Negroness,
my peers became shocked like virgins in a house
where satyrs tattooed on female thighs heralds of success.

White Boy,
counterfeit scholars have used
the newest brush-on Satinlac,
to make our ethnic identity
crystal clear for the lowest IQ
in every mansion and in every shack.
Therefore,
according to the myth that Negrophobes bequeath
to the Lost Gray Cause, since Black Boy is the color
of betel-stained teeth,
he and I
(from ocular proof
that cannot goof)
belong to races
whose dust-of-the-earth progenitors
the Lord God Almighty created
of different bloods,
in antipodal places.
However,
even the F. F. V. pate

is aware that laws defining a Negro
blackjack each other with*in* and with*out* a state.
The Great White World, White Boy, leaves you in a sweat
like a pitcher with three runners on the bases;
and, like Kant, you seldom get
your grammar straight—yet,
you are the wick that absorbs the oil in my lamp,
in all kinds of weather;
and we are teeth in the pitch wheel
that work together.

White Boy,
when I hear the word *Negro* defined,
why does it bring to mind
the chef, the gourmand, the belly-god,
the disease of kings, the culinary art
in alien lands, Black Mammy in a Dixie big house,
and the dietitian's chart?
Now, look at Black Boy scratch his head!
It's a stereotypic gesture of Uncle Tom,
a learned Gentleman of Color said
in his monumental tome,
The *Etiquette of the New Negro*,
which,
the publishers say,
by the way,
should be in every black man's home.

The Negro is a dish in the white man's kitchen—
a potpourri,
an ola-podrida,
a mixie-maxie,
a hotchpotch of lineal ingredients;
with UN guests at his table,
the host finds himself a Hamlet on the spot,
for, in spite of his catholic pose,
the Negro dish is a dish nobody knows:
to some . . . tasty,
like an exotic condiment—
to others . . . unsavory
and inelegant.

White Boy,
the Negro dish is a mix

like . . . and *un*like
pimiento brisque, chop suey,
eggs à la Goldenrod, and eggaroni;
tongue-and-corn casserole, mulligan stew,
baked fillets of halibut, and cheese fondue;
macaroni milanaise, egg-milk shake,
mullagatawny soup, and sour-milk cake.

Just as the Chinese lack
an ideogram for "to be,"
our lexicon has no definition
for an ethnic amalgam like Black Boy and me.

Behold a Gordian knot without
the *beau geste* of an Alexander's sword!
Water, O Modern Mariner, water, everywhere,
unfit for *vitro di trina* glass
or the old-oaken-bucket's gourd!

For dark hymens on the auction block,
the lord of the mansion knew the macabre score:
not a dog moved his tongue,
not a lamb lost a drop of blood to protect a door.
O
Xenos of Xanthos,
what midnight-to-dawn lecheries,
in cabin and big house,
produced these brown hybrids and yellow motleys?

White Boy,
Buchenwald is a melismatic song
whose single syllable is sung to blues notes
to dark wayfarers who listen for the gong
at the crack of doom along
. . . that Lonesome Road . . .
before they travel on.

A Pelagian with the *raison d'être* of a Negro,
I cannot say I have outwitted dread,
for I am conscious of the noiseless tread
of the Yazoo tiger's ball-like pads behind me
in the dark
as I trudge ahead,
up and up . . . that Lonesome Road . . . up and up.

In a Vision in a Dream,
from the frigid seaport of the proud Xanthochroid,
the good ship *Défineznegro*
sailed fine, under an unabridged moon,
to reach the archipelago
Nigeridentité.
In the Strait of Octoroon,
off black Scylla,
after the typhoon Phobos, out of the Stereotypus Sea,
had rived her hull and sail to a T,
the *Défineznegro* sank the rock
and disappeared in the abyss
(*Vanitas vanitatum!*)
of white Charybdis.

Hart Crane (1899–1932)

Hart Crane was born in Garrettsville, Ohio. He dropped out of high school and supported himself as a copywriter and factory worker while moving between Cleveland and New York and writing and publishing his poetry. His books include White Buildings *(1926),* The Bridge *(1930),* The Collected Poems *(1933), and* Ten Unpublished Poems *(1972). Among his honors were the Levinson Prize and a Guggenheim fellowship. Hart Crane committed suicide by jumping off a ship in the Gulf of Mexico.*

From *The Bridge*

> *From going to and fro in the earth,*
> *and from walking up and down in it.*
> —THE BOOK OF JOB

Proem: to Brooklyn Bridge

How many dawns, chill from his rippling rest
The seagull's wings shall dip and pivot him,
Shedding white rings of tumult, building high
Over the chained bay waters Liberty—

Then, with inviolate curve, forsake our eyes
As apparitional as sails that cross
Some page of figures to be filed away;
—Till elevators drop us from our day . . .

I think of cinemas, panoramic sleights
With multitudes bent toward some flashing scene
Never disclosed, but hastened to again,
Foretold to other eyes on the same screen;

And Thee, across the harbor, silver-paced
As though the sun took step of thee, yet left
Some motion ever unspent in thy stride,—
Implicitly thy freedom staying thee!

Out of some subway scuttle, cell or loft
A bedlamite speeds to thy parapets,
Tilting there momently, shrill shirt ballooning,
A jest falls from the speechless caravan.

Down Wall, from girder into street noon leaks,
A rip-tooth of the sky's acetylene;
All afternoon the cloud-flown derricks turn . . .
Thy cables breathe the North Atlantic still.

And obscure as that heaven of the Jews,
Thy guerdon . . . Accolade thou dost bestow
Of anonymity time cannot raise:
Vibrant reprieve and pardon thou dost show.

O harp and altar, of the fury fused,
(How could mere toil align thy choiring strings!)
Terrific threshold of the prophet's pledge,
Prayer of pariah, and the lover's cry,—

Again the traffic lights that skim thy swift
Unfractioned idiom, immaculate sigh of stars,
Beading thy path—condense eternity:
And we have seen night lifted in thine arms.

Under thy shadow by the piers I waited;
Only in darkness is thy shadow clear.
The City's fiery parcels all undone,
Already snow submerges an iron year . . .

O Sleepless as the river under thee,
Vaulting the sea, the prairies' dreaming sod,
Unto us lowliest sometime sweep, descend
And of the curveship lend a myth to God.

From *II. Powhatan's Daughter*

The River

Stick your patent name on a signboard
brother—all over—going west—young man
Tintex—Japalae—Certain-teed Overalls ads
and lands sakes! under the new playbill ripped
in the guaranteed corner—see Bert Williams what?
Minstrels when you steal a chicken just
save me the wing for if it isn't

*. . . and past
the din and
slogans of
the year—*

Erie it ain't for miles around a
Mazda—and the telegraphic night coming on Thomas

a Ediford—and whistling down the tracks
a headlight rushing with the sound—can you
imagine—while an Express makes time like
SCIENCE—COMMERCE and the HOLYGHOST
RADIO ROARS IN EVERY HOME WE HAVE THE NORTHPOLE
WALLSTREET AND VIRGINBIRTH WITHOUT STONES OR
WIRES OR EVEN RUNning brooks connecting ears
and no more sermons windows flashing roar
breathtaking—as you like it . . . eh?

                    So the 20th Century—so
whizzed the Limited—roared by and left
three men, still hungry on the tracks, ploddingly
watching the tail lights wizen and converge, slip-
ping gimleted and neatly out of sight.

    •   •   •   •   •   •   •

The last bear, shot drinking in the Dakotas
Loped under wires that span the mountain stream.
Keen instruments, strung to a vast precision
Bind town to town and dream to ticking dream.
But some men take their liquor slow—and count
—Though they'll confess no rosary nor clue—
The river's minute by the far brook's year.
Under a world of whistles, wires and steam
Caboose-like they go ruminating through
Ohio, Indiana—blind baggage—
To Cheyenne tagging . . . Maybe Kalamazoo.

to those
whose
addresses
are never near

Time's rendings, time's blendings they construe
As final reckonings of fire and snow;
Strange bird-wit, like the elemental gist
Of unwalled winds they offer, singing low
My Old Kentucky Home and *Casey Jones*,
Some Sunny Day. I heard a road-gang chanting so.
And afterwards, who had a colt's eyes—one said,
"Jesus! Oh I remember watermelon days!" And sped
High in a cloud of merriment, recalled
"—And when my Aunt Sally Simpson smiled," he drawled—
"It was almost Louisiana, long ago."
"There's no place like Booneville though, Buddy,"

One said, excising a last burr from his vest.
"—For early trouting." Then peering in the can,
"—But I kept on the tracks." Possessed, resigned,
He trod the fire down pensively and grinned,
Spreading dry shingles of a beard. . . .

                           Behind
My father's cannery works I used to see
Rail-squatters ranged in nomad raillery,
The ancient men—wifeless or runaway
Hobo-trekkers that forever search
An empire wilderness of freight and rails.
Each seemed a child, like me, on a loose perch,
Holding to childhood like some termless play.
John, Jake or Charley, hopping the slow freight
—Memphis to Tallahassee—riding the rods,
Blind fists of nothing, humpty-dumpty clods.

Yet they touch something like a key perhaps.
From pole to pole across the hills, the states
—They know a body under the wide rain;
Youngsters with eyes like fjords, old reprobates
With racetrack jargon,—dotting immensity
They lurk across her, knowing her yonder breast
Snow-silvered, sumac-stained or smoky blue—
Is past the valley-sleepers, south or west.
—As I have trod the rumorous midnights, too,

*but who have
touched her,
knowing her
without name*

And past the circuit of the lamp's thin flame
(O Nights that brought me to her body bare!)
Have dreamed beyond the print that bound her name.
Trains sounding the long blizzards out—I heard
Wail into distances I knew were hers.
Papooses crying on the wind's long mane
Screamed redskin dynasties that fled the brain,
—Dead echoes! But I knew her body there.
Time like a serpent down her shoulder, dark,
And space, an eaglet's wing, laid on her hair.

Under the Ozarks, domed by Iron Mountain,
The old gods of the rain lie wrapped in pools
Where eyeless fish curvet a sunken fountain
And re-descend with corn from querulous crows.
Such pilferings make up their timeless eatage,

*nor the
myths of her
fathers . . .*

Propitiate them for their timber torn
By iron, iron—always the iron dealt cleavage!
They doze now, below axe and powder horn.

And Pullman breakfasters glide glistening steel
From tunnel into field—iron strides the dew—
Straddles the hill, a dance of wheel on wheel.
You have a half-hour's wait at Siskiyou,
Or stay the night and take the next train through.
Southward, near Cairo passing, you can see
The Ohio merging,—borne down Tennessee;
And if it's summer and the sun's in dusk
Maybe the breeze will lift the River's musk
—As though the waters breathed that you might know
Memphis Johnny, Steamboat Bill, Missouri Joe.
Oh, lean from the window, if the train slows down,
As though you touched hands with some ancient clown,
—A little while gaze absently below
And hum *Deep River* with them while they go.

Yes, turn again and sniff once more—look see,
O Sheriff, Brakeman and Authority—
Hitch up your pants and crunch another quid,
For you, too, feed the River timelessly.
And few evade full measure of their fate;
Always they smile out eerily what they seem.
I could believe he joked at heaven's gate—
Dan Midland—jolted from the cold brake-beam.

Down, down—born pioneers in time's despite,
Grimed tributaries to an ancient flow—
They win no frontier by their wayward plight,
But drift in stillness, as from Jordan's brow.

You will not hear it as the sea; even stone
Is not more hushed by gravity . . . But slow,
As loth to take more tribute—sliding prone
Like one whose eyes were buried long ago

The River, spreading, flows—and spends your dream,
What are you, lost within this tideless spell?
You are your father's father, and the stream—
A liquid theme that floating niggers swell.

Damp tonnage and alluvial march of days—
Nights turbid, vascular with silted shale
And roots surrendered down of moraine clays:
The Mississippi drinks the farthest dale.

O quarrying passion, undertowed sunlight!
The basalt surface drags a jungle grace
Ochreous and lynx-barred in lengthening might;
Patience! and you shall reach the biding place!

Over De Soto's bones the freighted floors
Throb past the City storied of three thrones.
Down two more turns the Mississippi pours
(Anon tall ironsides up from salt lagoons)

And flows within itself, heaps itself free.
All fades but one thin skyline 'round . . . Ahead
No embrace opens but the stinging sea;
The River lifts itself from its long bed,

Poised wholly on its dream, a mustard glow
Tortured with history, its one will—flow!
—The Passion spreads in wide tongues, choked and slow,
Meeting the Gulf, hosannas silently below.

Robert Francis (1901–1987)

Robert Francis was born in Upland, Pennsylvania, and attended Harvard University. After a year teaching high school, he became a freelance writer in Amherst, Massachusetts. His poetry books include Stand with Me Here *(1936),* Valhalla and Other Poems *(1938),* The Sound I Listened For *(1944),* The Orb Weaver *(1960),* Come Out into the Sun *(1965),* The Satirical Rogue on Poetry *(1968),* Like Ghosts of Eagles *(1974),* Collected Poems, 1936–1976 *(1976),* Pot Shots at Poetry *(1980),* The Satirical Rogue on All Fronts *(1984), and* Late Fire, Late Snow *(1992). Among his honors were the Shelley Memorial Award and the Rome Prize. Robert Francis died in Northampton, Massachusetts.*

Silent Poem

backroad   leafmold   stonewall   chipmunk
underbrush   grapevine   woodchuck   shadblow

woodsmoke   cowbarn   honeysuckle   woodpile
sawhorse   bucksaw   outhouse   wellsweep

backdoor   flagstone   bulkhead   buttermilk
candlestick   ragrug   firedog   brownbread

hilltop   outcrop   cowbell   buttercup
whetstone   thunderstorm   pitchfork   steeplebrush

gristmill   millstone   cornmeal   waterwheel
watercress   buckwheat   firefly   jewelweed

gravestone   groundpine   windbreak   bedrock
weathercock   snowfall   starlight   cockcrow

Langston Hughes (1902–1967)

Langston Hughes was born in Joplin, Missouri, and spent his childhood and youth in Kansas, Illinois, Cleveland, Ohio, and Mexico City before moving to New York and attending Columbia University for a year. He then traveled in Europe, lived in Washington, D.C., working various jobs, and attended Lincoln University in Pennsylvania. From 1929 on, he lived mostly in Harlem, New York, as a writer and editor. His poetry books include The Weary Blues *(1926),* Fine Clothes to the Jew *(1927),* The Dream Keeper and Other Poems *(1932),* Lament for Dark Peoples and Other Poems *(1944),* Fields of Wonder *(1947),* One-Way Ticket *(1949),* Montage of a Dream Deferred *(1951),* Ask Your Mama: Twelve Moods for Jazz *(1961),* The Panther and the Lash: Poems of Our Times *(1967), and* The Collected Poems of Langston Hughes *(1994). Among his honors were the Harmon Gold Medal for Literature, Guggenheim and Rosenwald fellowships, the Anisfield-Wolf Book Award, and a Spingarn medal. Langston Hughes died in New York City.*

The Negro Speaks of Rivers

I've known rivers:
I've known rivers ancient as the world and older than the flow of human
    blood in human veins.

My soul has grown deep like the rivers.

I bathed in the Euphrates when dawns were young.
I built my hut near the Congo and it lulled me to sleep.
I looked upon the Nile and raised the pyramids above it.
I heard the singing of the Mississippi when Abe Lincoln went down to New
    Orleans, and I've seen its muddy bosom turn all golden in the sunset.

I've known rivers:
Ancient, dusky rivers.

My soul has grown deep like the rivers.

I, Too

I, too, sing America.

I am the darker brother.
They send me to eat in the kitchen
When company comes,
But I laugh,

And eat well,
And grow strong.

Tomorrow,
I'll be at the table
When company comes.
Nobody'll dare
Say to me,
"Eat in the kitchen,"
Then.

Besides,
They'll see how beautiful I am
And be ashamed—

I, too, am America.

Dream Boogie

Good morning, daddy!
Ain't you heard
The boogie-woogie rumble
Of a dream deferred?

Listen closely:
You'll hear their feet
Beating out and beating out a—

> *You think*
> *It's a happy beat?*

Listen to it closely:
Ain't you heard
something underneath
like a—

> *What did I say?*

Sure,
I'm happy!
Take it away!

Hey, pop!
Re-bop!
Mop!

Y-e-a-h!

Harlem

What happens to a dream deferred?

Does it dry up
like a raisin in the sun?
Or fester like a sore—
And then run?
Does it stink like rotten meat?
Or crust and sugar over—
like a syrupy sweet?

Maybe it just sags
like a heavy load.

Or does it explode?

Countee Cullen (1903–1946)

Countee Cullen was born in New York City. He attended New York University and Harvard University, worked as an editor and columnist, and traveled frequently to France from 1928 to 1934 before becoming a high school teacher of English, French, and creative writing. His poetry publications include Color *(1925),* Copper Sun *(1927),* The Ballad of the Brown Girl *(1928),* The Black Christ, and Other Poems *(1929),* The Medea, and Some Poems *(1935), and* On These I Stand: An Anthology of the Best Poems of Countee Cullen *(1947). Among his honors were the Witter Bynner Prize, the Spingarn Award, and a Guggenheim fellowship. Countee Cullen died of kidney failure in New York City.*

Incident

(For Eric Walrond)

Once riding in old Baltimore,
    Heart-filled, head-filled with glee,
I saw a Baltimorean
    Keep looking straight at me.

Now I was eight and very small,
    And he was no whit bigger,
And so I smiled, but he poked out
    His tongue, and called me, "Nigger."

I saw the whole of Baltimore
    From May until December;
Of all the things that happened there
    That's all that I remember.

To John Keats, Poet, at Spring Time*

(For Carl Van Vechten)†

I cannot hold my peace, John Keats;
There never was a spring like this;
It is an echo, that repeats

---

* Spring, 1924. [This footnote was in the original text.]

† Carl Van Vechten (1880–1964) was a noted novelist, photographer, and essayist who was one of the leading white promoters of the Harlem Renaissance. His 1926 novel *Nigger Heaven* was the center of much controversy. Among the several important collections Van Vechten established was the James Weldon Johnson Memorial Collection of Negro Arts and Letters at Yale University in 1941.

My last year's song and next year's bliss.
I know, in spite of all men say
Of Beauty, you have felt her most.
Yea, even in your grave her way
Is laid. Poor, troubled, lyric ghost,
Spring never was so fair and dear
As Beauty makes her seem this year.

I cannot hold my peace, John Keats,
I am as helpless in the toil
Of Spring as any lamb that bleats
To feel the solid earth recoil
Beneath his puny legs. Spring beats
Her tocsin call to those who love her,
And lo! the dogwood petals cover
Her breast with drifts of snow, and sleek
White gulls fly screaming to her, and hover
About her shoulders, and kiss her cheek,
While white and purple lilacs muster
A strength that bears them to a cluster
Of color and odor; for her sake
All things that slept are now awake.

And you and I, shall we lie still,
John Keats, while Beauty summons us?
Somehow I feel your sensitive will
Is pulsing up some tremulous
Sap road of a maple tree, whose leaves
Grow music as they grow, since your
Wild voice is in them, a harp that grieves
For life that opens death's dark door.
Though dust, your fingers still can push
The Vision Splendid to a birth,
Though now they work as grass in the hush
Of the night on the broad sweet page of the earth.

"John Keats is dead," they say, but I
Who hear your full insistent cry
In bud and blossom, leaf and tree,
Know John Keats still writes poetry.
And while my head is earthward bowed
To read new life sprung from your shroud,
Folks seeing me must think it strange
That merely spring should so derange

My mind. They do not know that you,
John Keats, keep revel with me, too.

Yet Do I Marvel

I doubt not God is good, well-meaning, kind,
And did He stoop to quibble could tell why
The little buried mole continues blind,
Why flesh that mirrors Him must some day die,
Make plain the reason tortured Tantalus
Is baited by the fickle fruit, declare
If merely brute caprice dooms Sisyphus
To struggle up a never-ending stair.
Inscrutable His ways are, and immune
To catechism by a mind too strewn
With petty cares to slightly understand
What awful brain compels His awful hand.
Yet do I marvel at this curious thing:
To make a poet black, and bid him sing!

From the Dark Tower

To Charles S. Johnson

We shall not always plant while others reap
The golden increment of bursting fruit,
Not always countenance, abject and mute,
That lesser men should hold their brothers cheap;
Not everlastingly while others sleep
Shall we beguile their limbs with mellow flute,
Not always bend to some more subtle brute;
We were not made eternally to weep.

The night whose sable breast relieves the stark,
White stars is no less lovely being dark,
And there are buds that cannot bloom at all
In light, but crumple, piteous, and fall;
So in the dark we hide the heart that bleeds,
And wait, and tend our agonizing seeds.

Stanley Kunitz (1905–2006)

Stanley Kunitz was born in Worcester, Massachusetts. He attended Harvard, then worked as a reporter and editor. After military service, he taught at Bennington College, the New School, and Columbia University, among other institutions. His poetry books include Intellectual Things *(1930),* Passport to the War *(1944),* Selected Poems, 1928–1958 *(1958, Pulitzer Prize),* The Testing-Tree *(1971),* The Terrible Threshold: Selected Poems, 1940–70 *(1974),* The Coat without a Seam: Sixty Poems, 1930–1972 *(1974),* The Lincoln Relics *(1978),* The Wellfleet Whale and Companion Poems *(1983),* Next-to-Last Things *(1985),* Passing Through *(1995, National Book Award), and* The Collected Poems *(2000). Among his honors were Guggenheim and National Endowment for the Arts fellowships, the Lenore Marshall Award, the Bollingen Prize, the National Medal of Arts, the Shelley Memorial Award, and the Frost Medal. Stanley Kunitz served as Consultant in Poetry at the Library of Congress from 1974 to 1976 and as U.S. poet laureate in 2000 and 2001. He died in New York City.*

Father and Son

Now in the suburbs and the falling light
I followed him, and now down sandy road
Whiter than bone-dust, through the sweet
Curdle of fields, where the plums
Dropped with their load of ripeness, one by one.
Mile after mile I followed, with skimming feet,
After the secret master of my blood,
Him, steeped in the odor of ponds, whose indomitable love
Kept me in chains. Strode years; stretched into bird;
Raced through the sleeping country where I was young,
The silence unrolling before me as I came,
The night nailed like an orange to my brow.

How should I tell him my fable and the fears,
How bridge the chasm in a casual tone,
Saying, "The house, the stucco one you built,
We lost. Sister married and went from home,
And nothing comes back, it's strange, from where she goes.
I lived on a hill that had too many rooms:
Light we could make, but not enough of warmth,
And when the light failed, I climbed under the hill.
The papers are delivered every day;
I am alone and never shed a tear."

At the water's edge, where the smothering ferns lifted
Their arms, "Father!" I cried, "Return! You know

The way. I'll wipe the mudstains from your clothes;
No trace, I promise, will remain. Instruct
Your son, whirling between two wars,
In the Gemara of your gentleness,
For I would be a child to those who mourn
And brother to the foundlings of the field
And friend of innocence and all bright eyes.
O teach me how to work and keep me kind."

Among the turtles and the lilies he turned to me
The white ignorant hollow of his face.

The Portrait

My mother never forgave my father
for killing himself,
especially at such an awkward time
and in a public park,
that spring
when I was waiting to be born.
She locked his name
in her deepest cabinet
and would not let him out,
though I could hear him thumping.
When I came down from the attic
with the pastel portrait in my hand
of a long-lipped stranger
with a brave moustache
and deep brown level eyes,
she ripped it into shreds
without a single word
and slapped me hard.
In my sixty-fourth year
I can feel my cheek
still burning.

Touch Me

Summer is late, my heart.
Words plucked out of the air
some forty years ago
when I was wild with love

and torn almost in two
scatter like leaves this night
of whistling wind and rain.
It is my heart that's late,
it is my song that's flown.
Outdoors all afternoon
under a gunmetal sky
staking my garden down,
I kneeled to the crickets trilling
underfoot as if about
to burst from their crusty shells;
and like a child again
marveled to hear so clear
and brave a music pour
from such a small machine.
What makes the engine go?
Desire, desire, desire.
The longing for the dance
stirs in the buried life.
One season only,
                                and it's done.
So let the battered old willow
thrash against the windowpanes
and the house timbers creak.
Darling, do you remember
the man you married? Touch me,
remind me who I am.

W. H. (Wystan Hugh) Auden (1907–1973)

Wystan Hugh Auden was born in York, England. He attended Oxford, worked as a schoolmaster, cofounded a theater, collaborated on films, and volunteered in the Spanish Civil War. He came to the United States in 1939 and became an American citizen in 1946. He taught at numerous colleges and universities before dividing his time between New York and Europe. From 1956 to 1961 he was professor of poetry at Oxford. His poetry books include Poems *(1928),* Look, Stranger! *(1936),* Selected Poems *(1938),* Another Time *(1940),* Some Poems *(1940),* The Double Man *(1941),* For the Time Being *(1944),* The Age of Anxiety *(1947, Pulitzer Prize),* The Shield of Achilles *(1955, National Book Award),* Homage to Clio *(1960),* About the House *(1965),* City without Walls *(1969),* Epistle to a Godson *(1972), and* Thank You, Fog: Last Poems *(1974). Among his honors were Guggenheim fellowships, the Feltrinelli Prize (Rome), and the Austrian State Prize for European Literature. W. H. Auden died in Vienna, Austria.*

Musée des Beaux Arts

About suffering they were never wrong,
The Old Masters: how well they understood
Its human position; how it takes place
While someone else is eating or opening a window or just walking dully
    along;
How, when the aged are reverently, passionately waiting
For the miraculous birth, there always must be
Children who did not specially want it to happen, skating
On a pond at the edge of the wood:
They never forgot
That even the dreadful martyrdom must run its course
Anyhow in a corner, some untidy spot
Where the dogs go on with their doggy life and the torturer's horse
Scratches its innocent behind on a tree.

In Breughel's *Icarus*, for instance: how everything turns away
Quite leisurely from the disaster; the ploughman may
Have heard the splash, the forsaken cry,
But for him it was not an important failure; the sun shone
As it had to on the white legs disappearing into the green
Water; and the expensive delicate ship that must have seen
Something amazing, a boy falling out of the sky,
Had somewhere to get to and sailed calmly on.

Epitaph on a Tyrant

Perfection, of a kind, was what he was after,
And the poetry he invented was easy to understand;
He knew human folly like the back of his hand,
And was greatly interested in armies and fleets;
When he laughed, respectable senators burst with laughter,
And when he cried the little children died in the streets.

Theodore Roethke (1908–1963)

Theodore Roethke was born in Saginaw, Michigan. He attended the University of Michigan at Ann Arbor and Harvard University before teaching at Lafayette College, Michigan State University, Pennsylvania State University, Bennington College, and the University of Washington. Among his books are Open House *(1941),* The Lost Son and Other Poems *(1948),* Praise to the End! *(1951),* The Waking: Poems 1933–1953 *(1953, Pulitzer Prize),* Words for the Wind *(1957, National Book Award, Bollingen Prize),* I Am! Says the Lamb *(1961),* Sequence, Sometimes Metaphysical *(1963), and* The Far Field *(1964, National Book Award). Other honors included Guggenheim fellowships, the Edna St. Vincent Millay Award, and the Shelley Memorial Award. Theodore Roethke died of a heart attack on Bainbridge Island, Washington.*

My Papa's Waltz

The whiskey on your breath
Could make a small boy dizzy;
But I hung on like death:
Such waltzing was not easy.

We romped until the pans
Slid from the kitchen shelf;
My mother's countenance
Could not unfrown itself.

The hand that held my wrist
Was battered on one knuckle;
At every step you missed
My right ear scraped a buckle.

You beat time on my head
With a palm caked hard by dirt,
Then waltzed me off to bed
Still clinging to your shirt.

The Waking

I wake to sleep, and take my waking slow.
I feel my fate in what I cannot fear.
I learn by going where I have to go.

We think by feeling. What is there to know?
I hear my being dance from ear to ear.
I wake to sleep, and take my waking slow.

Of those so close beside me, which are you?
God bless the Ground! I shall walk softly there,
And learn by going where I have to go.

Light takes the Tree; but who can tell us how?
The lowly worm climbs up a winding stair;
I wake to sleep, and take my waking slow.

Great Nature has another thing to do
To you and me; so take the lively air,
And, lovely, learn by going where to go.

This shaking keeps me steady. I should know.
What falls away is always. And is near.
I wake to sleep, and take my waking slow.
I learn by going where I have to go.

In a Dark Time

In a dark time, the eye begins to see,
I meet my shadow in the deepening shade;
I hear my echo in the echoing wood—
A lord of nature weeping to a tree.
I live between the heron and the wren,
Beasts of the hill and serpents of the den.

What's madness but nobility of soul
At odds with circumstances? The day's on fire!
I know the purity of pure despair,
My shadow pinned against a sweating wall.
That place among the rocks—is it a cave,
Or winding path? The edge is what I have.

A steady storm of correspondences!
A night flowing with birds, a ragged moon,
And in broad day the midnight come again!
A man goes far to find out what he is—

Death of the self in a long, tearless night;
All natural shapes blazing unnatural light.

Dark; dark my light, and darker my desire,
My soul, like some heat-maddened summer fly,
Keeps buzzing at the sill. Which I is *I*?
A fallen man, I climb out of my fear.
The mind enters itself, and God the mind,
And one is One, free in the tearing wind.

Charles Olson (1910–1970)

Charles Olson was born in Worcester, Massachusetts, and attended Wesleyan University and Harvard University. He worked in the Roosevelt administration during World War II and later became rector of Black Mountain College in North Carolina, also teaching at several other universities. His poetry books include In Cold Hell, in Thicket *(1953),* The Distances *(1960),* The Maximus Poems *(1960),* The Maximus Poems, IV, V, VI *(1968),* Archaeologist of Morning *(1970),* The Maximus Poems, Volume Three *(1975), and* The Collected Poems of Charles Olson *(1988, American Book Award). Among his honors were two Guggenheim fellowships. Charles Olson died from liver cancer in New York.*

From *The Maximus Poems*

I, Maximus of Gloucester, to You

> Off-shore, by islands hidden in the blood
> jewels & miracles, I, Maximus
> a metal hot from boiling water, tell you
> what is a lance, who obeys the figures of
> the present dance

1

the thing you're after
may lie around the bend
of the nest (second, time slain, the bird! the bird!

And there! (strong) thrust, the mast! flight

> (of the bird
> o kylix, o
> Antony of Padua
> sweep low, o bless

the roofs, the old ones, the gentle steep ones
on whose ridge-poles the gulls sit, from which they depart,

> And the flake-racks

of my city!

2

love is form, and cannot be without
important substance (the weight
say, 58 carats each one of us, perforce
our goldsmith's scale

feather to feather added
(and what is mineral, what
is curling hair, the string
you carry in your nervous beak, these

make bulk, these, in the end, are
the sum

(o my lady of good voyage
in whose arm, whose left arm rests
no boy but a carefully carved wood, a painted face, a schooner!
a delicate mast, as bow-sprit for

forwarding

3

the underpart is, though stemmed, uncertain
is, as sex is, as moneys are, facts!
facts, to be dealt with, as the sea is, the demand
that they be played by, that they only can be, that they must
be played by, said he, coldly, the
ear!

By ear, he sd.
But that which matters, that which insists, that which will last,
that! o my people, where shall you find it, how, where, where shall you listen
when all is become billboards, when, all, even silence, is spray-gunned?

when even our bird, my roofs,
cannot be heard

when even you, when sound itself is neoned in?

when, on the hill, over the water
where she who used to sing,
when the water glowed,
black, gold, the tide
outward, at evening

when bells came like boats
over the oil-slicks, milkweed
hulls

And a man slumped,
attentionless,
against pink shingles

o sea city)

4

one loves only form,
and form only comes
into existence when
the thing is born

>born of yourself, born
>of hay and cotton struts,
>of street-pickings, wharves, weeds
>you carry in, my bird

>>of a bone of a fish
>>of a straw, or will
>>of a color, of a bell
>>of yourself, torn

5

love is not easy
but how shall you know,
New England, now
that pejorocracy is here, how
that street-cars, o Oregon, twitter
in the afternoon, offend
a black-gold loin?

>how shall you strike,
>o swordsman, the blue-red black
>when, last night, your aim
>was mu-sick, mu-sick, mu-sick
>And not the cribbage game?

>>(o Gloucester-man,
>>weave
>>your birds and fingers
>>new, your roof-tops,
>>clean shit upon racks

sunned on
American
braid
with others like you, such
extricable surface
as faun and oral,
satyr lesbos vase

o kill kill kill kill kill
those
who advertise you
out)

6

in! in! the bow-sprit, bird, the beak
in, the bend is, in, goes in, the form
that which you make, what holds, which is
the law of object, strut after strut, what you are, what you must be, what
the force can throw up, can, right now hereinafter erect,
the mast, the mast, the tender
mast!

The nest, I say, to you, I Maximus, say
under the hand, as I see it, over the waters
from this place where I am, where I hear,
can still hear

from where I carry you a feather
as though, sharp, I picked up
in the afternoon delivered you
a jewel,
it flashing more than a wing,
than any old romantic thing,
than memory, than place,
than anything other than that which you carry

than that which is,
call it a nest, around the head of, call it
the next second

than that which you
can do!

The Distances

So the distances are Galatea
                       and one does fall in love and desires
mastery

           old Zeus—young Augustus

Love knows no distance, no place
                     is that far away or heat changes
Into signals, and control
           old Zeus—young Augustus

Death is a loving matter, then, a horror
                        we cannot bide, and avoid
by greedy life
          we think all living things are precious
          —Pygmalions

                        a German Inventor in Key West
who had a Cuban girl, and kept her, after her death
in his bed
                       after her family retrieved her
he stole the body again from the vault

Torso on torso in either direction,
         young Augustus
                     out via nothing where messages
are

     or in, down La Cluny's steps to the old man sitting
a god throned on torsoes,

         old Zeus

Sons go there hopefully as though there was a secret, the object
to undo distance?
                     They huddle there, at the bottom
of the shaft, against one young bum
               or two loving cheeks,

       Augustus?

You can teach the young nothing

all of them go away, Aphrodite

tricks it out,

old Zeus—young Augustus

You have love, and no object

or you have all pressed to your nose

which is too close,

old Zeus hiding in your chin your young
Galatea

the girl who makes you weep, and you keep the corpse live by all
your arts

whose cheek do you stroke when you stroke the stone face
of young Augustus, made for bed in a military camp,
o Caesar?

O love who places all where each is, as they are, for every moment,
yield

to this man

that the impossible distance

be healed,

that young Augustus
and old Zeus
be enclosed

"I wake you,
stone. Love this man."

Elizabeth Bishop (1911–1979)

Elizabeth Bishop was born in Worcester, Massachusetts. She grew up in Nova Scotia and Massachusetts and attended Vassar College. Independently wealthy, she was free to travel and dedicate herself to poetry. For several years, she lived in France, then in Key West, Florida, and later spent fifteen years in Brazil before teaching at Harvard. Her poetry books include North and South *(1946, Houghton Mifflin Poetry Award),* Poems: North and South—A Cold Spring *(1955, Pulitzer Prize),* Poems *(1956),* Questions of Travel *(1965, National Book Award),* The Ballad of the Burglar of Babylon *(1968),* The Complete Poems *(1969, National Book Award),* Poem *(1973),* Geography III *(1977, National Book Critics Circle Award and Neustadt International Prize for Literature),* The Complete Poems 1927–1979 *(1983), and* Edgar Allan Poe & The Juke-Box: Uncollected Poems, Drafts, and Fragments *(2006). Among her honors were also two Guggenheim fellowships. In 1949 and 1950 she served as Consultant in Poetry at the Library of Congress. Elizabeth Bishop died in Boston, Massachusetts.*

The Fish

I caught a tremendous fish
and held him beside the boat
half out of water, with my hook
fast in the corner of his mouth.
He didn't fight.
He hadn't fought at all.
He hung a grunting weight,
battered and venerable
and homely. Here and there
his brown skin hung in strips
like ancient wallpaper,
and its pattern of darker brown
was like wallpaper:
shapes like full-blown roses
stained and lost through age.
He was speckled with barnacles,
fine rosettes of lime,
and infested
with tiny white sea-lice,
and underneath two or three
rags of green weed hung down.
While his gills were breathing in
the terrible oxygen
—the frightening gills,
fresh and crisp with blood,
that can cut so badly—

I thought of the coarse white flesh
packed in like feathers,
the big bones and the little bones;
the dramatic reds and blacks
of his shiny entrails,
and the pink swim-bladder
like a big peony.
I looked into his eyes
which were far larger than mine
but shallower, and yellowed,
the irises backed and packed
with tarnished tinfoil
seen through the lenses
of old scratched isinglass.
They shifted a little, but not
to return my stare.
—It was more like the tipping
of an object toward the light.
I admired his sullen face,
the mechanism of his jaw,
and then I saw
that from his lower lip
—if you could call it a lip—
grim, wet, and weaponlike,
hung five old pieces of fish-line,
or four and a wire leader
with the swivel still attached,
with all their five big hooks
grown firmly in his mouth.
A green line, frayed at the end
where he broke it, two heavier lines,
and a fine black thread
still crimped from the strain and snap
when it broke and he got away.
Like medals with their ribbons
frayed and wavering,
a five-haired beard of wisdom,
trailing from his aching jaw.
I stared and stared
and victory filled up
the little rented boat,
from the pool of bilge
where oil had spread a rainbow
around the rusted engine

to the bailer rusted orange,
the sun-cracked thwarts,
the oarlocks on their strings,
the gunnels—until everything
was rainbow, rainbow, rainbow!
And I let the fish go.

Sestina

September rain falls on the house.
In the failing light, the old grandmother
sits in the kitchen with the child
beside the Little Marvel Stove,
reading the jokes from the almanac,
laughing and talking to hide her tears.

She thinks that her equinoctial tears
and the rain that beats on the roof of the house
were both foretold by the almanac,
but only known to a grandmother.
The iron kettle sings on the stove.
She cuts some bread and says to the child,

It's time for tea now; but the child
is watching the teakettle's small hard tears
dance like mad on the hot black stove,
the way the rain must dance on the house.
Tidying up, the old grandmother
hangs up the clever almanac

on its string. Birdlike, the almanac
hovers half open above the child,
hovers above the old grandmother
and her teacup full of dark brown tears.
She shivers and says she thinks the house
feels chilly, and puts more wood in the stove.

It was to be, says the Marvel Stove.
I know what I know, says the almanac.
With crayons the child draws a rigid house
and a winding pathway. Then the child
puts in a man with buttons like tears
and shows it proudly to the grandmother.

But secretly, while the grandmother
busies herself about the stove,
the little moons fall down like tears
from between the pages of the almanac
into the flower bed the child
has carefully placed in the front of the house.

Time to plant tears, says the almanac.
The grandmother sings to the marvellous stove
and the child draws another inscrutable house.

First Death in Nova Scotia

In the cold, cold parlor
my mother laid out Arthur
beneath the chromographs:
Edward, Prince of Wales,
with Princess Alexandra,
and King George with Queen Mary.
Below them on the table
stood a stuffed loon
shot and stuffed by Uncle
Arthur, Arthur's father.
Since Uncle Arthur fired
a bullet into him,
he hadn't said a word.
He kept his own counsel
on his white, frozen lake,
the marble-topped table.
His breast was deep and white,
cold and caressable;
his eyes were red glass,
much to be desired.

"Come," said my mother,
"Come and say good-bye
to your little cousin Arthur."
I was lifted up and given
one lily of the valley
to put in Arthur's hand.
Arthur's coffin was
a little frosted cake,

and the red-eyed loon eyed it
from his white, frozen lake.

Arthur was very small.
He was all white, like a doll
that hadn't been painted yet.
Jack Frost had started to paint him
the way he always painted
the Maple Leaf (Forever).
He had just begun on his hair,
a few red strokes, and then
Jack Frost had dropped the brush
and left him white, forever.

The gracious royal couples
were warm in red and ermine;
their feet were well wrapped up
in the ladies' ermine trains.
They invited Arthur to be
the smallest page at court.
But how could Arthur go,
clutching his tiny lily,
with his eyes shut up so tight
and the roads deep in snow?

Visits to St. Elizabeths

[1950]

This is the house of Bedlam.

This is the man
that lies in the house of Bedlam.

This is the time
of the tragic man
that lies in the house of Bedlam.

This is a wristwatch
telling the time
of the talkative man
that lies in the house of Bedlam.

This is a sailor
wearing the watch
that tells the time
of the honored man
that lies in the house of Bedlam.

This is the roadstead all of board
reached by the sailor
wearing the watch
that tells the time
of the old, brave man
that lies in the house of Bedlam.

These are the years and the walls of the ward,
the winds and clouds of the sea of board
sailed by the sailor
wearing the watch
that tells the time
of the cranky man
that lies in the house of Bedlam.

This is the Jew in a newspaper hat
that dances weeping down the ward
over the creaking sea of board
beyond the sailor
winding his watch
that tells the time
of the cruel man
that lies in the house of Bedlam.

This is a world of books gone flat.
This is a Jew in a newspaper hat
that dances weeping down the ward
over the creaking sea of board
of the batty sailor
that winds his watch
that tells the time
of the busy man
that lies in the house of Bedlam.

This is a boy that pats the floor
to see if the world is there, is flat,
for the widowed Jew in the newspaper hat

that dances weeping down the ward
waltzing the length of a weaving board
by the silent sailor
that hears his watch
that ticks the time
of the tedious man
that lies in the house of Bedlam.

These are the years and the walls and the door
that shut on a boy that pats the floor
to feel if the world is there and flat.
This is a Jew in a newspaper hat
that dances joyfully down the ward
into the parting seas of board
past the staring sailor
that shakes his watch
that tells the time
of the poet, the man
that lies in the house of Bedlam.

This is the soldier home from the war.
These are the years and the walls and the door
that shut on a boy that pats the floor
to see if the world is round or flat.
This is a Jew in a newspaper hat
that dances carefully down the ward,
walking the plank of a coffin board
with the crazy sailor
that shows his watch
that tells the time
of the wretched man
that lies in the house of Bedlam.

One Art

The art of losing isn't hard to master;
so many things seem filled with the intent
to be lost that their loss is no disaster.

Lose something every day. Accept the fluster
of lost door keys, the hour badly spent.
The art of losing isn't hard to master.

Then practice losing farther, losing faster:
places, and names, and where it was you meant
to travel. None of these will bring disaster.

I lost my mother's watch. And look! my last, or
next-to-last, of three loved houses went.
The art of losing isn't hard to master.

I lost two cities, lovely ones. And, vaster,
some realms I owned, two rivers, a continent.
I miss them, but it wasn't a disaster.

—Even losing you (the joking voice, a gesture
I love) I shan't have lied. It's evident
the art of losing's not too hard to master
though it may look like (*Write* it!) like disaster.

Robert Hayden (1913–1980)

Robert Hayden was born in Detroit, Michigan. He attended Wayne State University and worked for the Federal Writers' Project as a researcher before enrolling at the University of Michigan, Ann Arbor; he then taught at Fisk University for twenty-three years, returning to the University of Michigan in 1969 for the remainder of his life. His poetry books include Heart-Shape in the Dust *(1940),* Figure of Time *(1955),* A Ballad of Remembrance *(1962),* Selected Poems *(1966),* Words in the Mourning Time *(1970),* The Night-Blooming Cereus *(1972),* Angle of Ascent *(1975),* American Journal *(1982, National Book Award finalist), and* Collected Poems *(1985). Among his honors were the Hopwood Poetry Award and the World Festival of Negro Arts Grand Prize; he served as Consultant in Poetry at the Library of Congress from 1976 to 1978. Robert Hayden died in Ann Arbor, Michigan.*

Mourning Poem for the Queen of Sunday

Lord's lost Him His mockingbird,
His fancy warbler;
Satan sweet-talked her,
four bullets hushed her.
Who would have thought
she'd end that way?

Four bullets hushed her. And the world a-clang with evil.
Who's going to make old hardened sinner men tremble now
and the righteous rock?
Oh who and oh who will sing Jesus down
to help with struggling and doing without and being colored
all through blue Monday?
Till way next Sunday?

All those angels
in their cretonne clouds and finery
the true believer saw
when she rared back her head and sang,
all those angels are surely weeping.
Who would have thought
she'd end that way?

Four holes in her heart. The gold works wrecked.
But she looks so natural in her big bronze coffin
among the Broken Hearts and Gates-Ajar,
it's as if any moment she'd lift her head
from its pillow of chill gardenias

and turn this quiet into shouting Sunday
and make folks forget what she did on Monday.

Oh, Satan sweet-talked her,
and four bullets hushed her.
Lord's lost Him His diva,
His fancy warbler's gone.
Who would have thought,
who would have thought she'd end that way?

Those Winter Sundays

Sundays too my father got up early
and put his clothes on in the blueblack cold,
then with cracked hands that ached
from labor in the weekday weather made
banked fires blaze. No one ever thanked him.

I'd wake and hear the cold splintering, breaking.
When the rooms were warm, he'd call,
and slowly I would rise and dress,
fearing the chronic angers of that house,

Speaking indifferently to him,
who had driven out the cold
and polished my good shoes as well.
What did I know, what did I know
of love's austere and lonely offices?

Frederick Douglass

When it is finally ours, this freedom, this liberty, this beautiful
and terrible thing, needful to man as air,
usable as earth; when it belongs at last to all,
when it is truly instinct, brain matter, diastole, systole,
reflex action; when it is finally won; when it is more
than the gaudy mumbo jumbo of politicians:
this man, this Douglass, this former slave, this Negro
beaten to his knees, exiled, visioning a world
where none is lonely, none hunted, alien,
this man, superb in love and logic, this man

shall be remembered. Oh, not with statues' rhetoric,
not with legends and poems and wreaths of bronze alone,
but with the lives grown out of his life, the lives
fleshing his dream of the beautiful, needful thing.

Middle Passage

I

Jesús, Estrella, Esperanza, Mercy:

> Sails flashing to the wind like weapons,
> sharks following the moans the fever and the dying;
> horror the corposant and compass rose.

Middle Passage:
>> voyage through death
>>> to life upon these shores.

> "10 April 1800—
> Blacks rebellious. Crew uneasy. Our linguist says
> their moaning is a prayer for death,
> ours and their own. Some try to starve themselves.
> Lost three this morning leaped with crazy laughter
> to the waiting sharks, sang as they went under."

Desire, Adventure, Tartar, Ann:

> Standing to America, bringing home
> black gold, black ivory, black seed.

> *Deep in the festering hold thy father lies,*
> *of his bones New England pews are made,*
> *those are altar lights that were his eyes.*

Jesus   Saviour   Pilot   Me
Over   Life's   Tempestuous   Sea

We pray that Thou wilt grant, O Lord,
safe passage to our vessels bringing
heathen souls unto Thy chastening.

Jesus   Saviour

"8 bells. I cannot sleep, for I am sick
with fear, but writing eases fear a little
since still my eyes can see these words take shape
upon the page & so I write, as one
would turn to exorcism. 4 days scudding,
but now the sea is calm again. Misfortune
follows in our wake like sharks (our grinning
tutelary gods). Which one of us
has killed an albatross? A plague among
our blacks—Ophthalmia: blindness—& we
have jettisoned the blind to no avail.
It spreads, the terrifying sickness spreads.
Its claws have scratched sight from the Capt.'s eyes
& there is blindness in the fo'c'sle
& we must sail 3 weeks before we come
to port."

> *What port awaits us, Davy Jones'*
> *or home? I've heard of slavers drifting, drifting,*
> *playthings of wind and storm and chance, their crews*
> *gone blind, the jungle hatred*
> *crawling up on deck.*

Thou   Who   Walked   On   Galilee

"Deponent further sayeth *The Bella J*
left the Guinea Coast
with cargo of five hundred blacks and odd
for the barracoons of Florida:

"That there was hardly room 'tween-decks for half
the sweltering cattle stowed spoon-fashion there;
that some went mad of thirst and tore their flesh
and sucked the blood:

"That Crew and Captain lusted with the comeliest
of the savage girls kept naked in the cabins;
that there was one they called The Guinea Rose
and they cast lots and fought to lie with her:

"That when the Bo's 'n piped all hands, the flames
spreading from starboard already were beyond
control, the negroes howling and their chains
entangled with the flames:

"That the burning blacks could not be reached,
that the Crew abandoned ship,
leaving their shrieking negresses behind,
that the Captain perished drunken with the wenches:

"Further Deponent sayeth not."

Pilot   Oh   Pilot   Me

II

Aye, lad, and I have seen those factories,
Gambia, Rio Pongo, Calabar;
have watched the artful mongos baiting traps
of war wherein the victor and the vanquished

Were caught as prizes for our barracoons.
Have seen the nigger kings whose vanity
and greed turned wild black hides of Fellatah,
Mandingo, Ibo, Kru to gold for us.

And there was one—King Anthracite we named him—
fetish face beneath French parasols
of brass and orange velvet, impudent mouth
whose cups were carven skulls of enemies:

He'd honor us with drum and feast and conjo
and palm-oil-glistening wenches deft in love,
and for tin crowns that shone with paste,
red calico and German-silver trinkets

Would have the drums talk war and send
his warriors to burn the sleeping villages
and kill the sick and old and lead the young
in coffles to our factories.

Twenty years a trader, twenty years,
for there was wealth aplenty to be harvested
from those black fields, and I'd be trading still
but for the fevers melting down my bones.

III

Shuttles in the rocking loom of history,
the dark ships move, the dark ships move,
their bright ironical names

like jests of kindness on a murderer's mouth;
plough through thrashing glister toward
fata morgana's lucent melting shore,
weave toward New World littorals that are
mirage and myth and actual shore.

Voyage through death,
                  voyage whose chartings are unlove.
A charnel stench, effluvium of living death
spreads outward from the hold,
where the living and the dead, the horribly dying,
lie interlocked, lie foul with blood and excrement.

> *Deep in the festering hold thy father lies,*
> *the corpse of mercy rots with him,*
> *rats eat love's rotten gelid eyes.*

> *But, oh, the living look at you*
> *with human eyes whose suffering accuses you,*
> *whose hatred reaches through the swill of dark*
> *to strike you like a leper's claw.*

> *You cannot stare that hatred down*
> *or chain the fear that stalks the watches*
> *and breathes on you its fetid scorching breath;*
> *cannot kill the deep immortal human wish,*
> *the timeless will.*

>> "But for the storm that flung up barriers
>> of wind and wave, *The Amistad*, señores,
>> would have reached the port of Príncipe in two,
>> three days at most; but for the storm we should
>> have been prepared for what befell.
>> Swift as the puma's leap it came. There was
>> that interval of moonless calm filled only
>> with the water's and the rigging's usual sounds,
>> then sudden movement, blows and snarling cries
>> and they had fallen on us with machete
>> and marlinspike. It was as though the very
>> air, the night itself were striking us.
>> Exhausted by the rigors of the storm,
>> we were no match for them. Our men went down
>> before the murderous Africans. Our loyal
>> Celestino ran from below with gun
>> and lantern and I saw, before the cane-

knife's wounding flash, Cinquez,
that surly brute who calls himself a prince,
directing, urging on the ghastly work.
He hacked the poor mulatto down, and then
he turned on me. The decks were slippery
when daylight finally came. It sickens me
to think of what I saw, of how these apes
threw overboard the butchered bodies of
our men, true Christians all, like so much jetsam.
Enough, enough. The rest is quickly told:
Cinquez was forced to spare the two of us
you see to steer the ship to Africa,
and we like phantoms doomed to rove the sea
voyaged east by day and west by night,
deceiving them, hoping for rescue,
prisoners on our own vessel, till
at length we drifted to the shores of this
your land, America, where we were freed
from our unspeakable misery. Now we
demand, good sirs, the extradition of
Cinquez and his accomplices to La
Havana. And it distresses us to know
there are so many here who seem inclined
to justify the mutiny of these blacks.
We find it paradoxical indeed
that you whose wealth, whose tree of liberty
are rooted in the labor of your slaves
should suffer the august John Quincy Adams
to speak with so much passion of the right
of chattel slaves to kill their lawful masters
and with his Roman rhetoric weave a hero's
garland for Cinquez. I tell you that
we are determined to return to Cuba
with our slaves and there see justice done. Cinquez—
or let us say 'the Prince'—Cinquez shall die."

The deep immortal human wish,
the timeless will:

    Cinquez its deathless primaveral image,
    life that transfigures many lives.

Voyage through death
                 to life upon these shores.

Muriel Rukeyser (1913–1980)

Muriel Rukeyser was born in New York City and attended Vassar College and Columbia University. She worked as a social activist, teacher, biographer, screenwriter, dramatist, and translator and, after World War II, taught at Sarah Lawrence College. Her poetry books include Theory of Flight *(1935, Yale Younger Poets Prize),* A Turning Wind *(1939),* Wake Island *(1942),* Beast in View *(1944),* The Children's Orchard *(1947),* The Green Wave *(1948),* Elegies *(1949),* Orpheus *(1949),* Body of Waking *(1958),* Waterlily Fire: Poems 1932–1962 *(1962),* The Outer Banks *(1967),* The Speed of Darkness *(1968),* Breaking Open *(1973),* The Gates *(1976),* Out of Silence *(1992), and* The Collected Poems of Muriel Rukeyser *(2005). Among her honors were a Guggenheim fellowship, the Copernicus Award, and the Shelley Memorial Award. Muriel Rukeyser died in New York City.*

Effort at Speech Between Two People

  : Speak to me.   Take my hand.   What are you now?
I will tell you all.   I will conceal nothing.
When I was three, a little child read a story about a rabbit
who died, in the story, and I crawled under a chair   :
a pink rabbit   :   it was my birthday, and a candle
burnt a sore spot on my finger, and I was told to be happy.

  : Oh, grow to know me.   I am not happy.   I will be open:
Now I am thinking of white sails against a sky like music,
like glad horns blowing, and birds tilting, and an arm about me.
There was one I loved, who wanted to live, sailing.

  : Speak to me.   Take my hand.   What are you now?
When I was nine, I was fruitily sentimental,
fluid   :   and my widowed aunt played Chopin,
and I bent my head on the painted woodwork, and wept.
I want now to be close to you.   I would
link the minutes of my days close, somehow, to your days.

  : I am not happy.   I will be open.
I have liked lamps in evening corners, and quiet poems.
There has been fear in my life.   Sometimes I speculate
On what a tragedy his life was, really.

  : Take my hand.   Fist my mind in your hand.   What are
     you now?
When I was fourteen, I had dreams of suicide,

and I stood at a steep window, at sunset, hoping toward
    death:
if the light had not melted clouds and plains to beauty,
if light had not transformed that day, I would have leapt.
I am unhappy.   I am lonely.   Speak to me.

:   I will be open.   I think he never loved me:
he loved the bright beaches, the little lips of foam
that ride small waves, he loved the veer of gulls:
he said with a gay mouth: I love you.   Grow to know me.

:   What are you now?   If we could touch one another,
if these our separate entities could come to grips,
clenched like a Chinese puzzle . . . yesterday
I stood in a crowded street that was live with people,
and no one spoke a word, and the morning shone.
Everyone silent, moving. . . . Take my hand.   Speak to me.

Then I Saw What the Calling Was

All the voices of the wood called "Muriel!"
but it was soon solved;   it was nothing, it was not for me.
The words were a little like Mortal and More and Endure
and a word like Real, a sound like Health or Hell.
Then I saw what the calling was   :   it was the road I traveled,
    the clear
time and these colors of orchards, gold behind gold and the full
shadow behind each tree and behind each slope.   Not to me
the calling, but to anyone, and at last I saw   :   where
the road lay through sunlight and many voices and the marvel
orchards, not for me, not for me, not for me.
I came into my clear being;   uncalled, alive, and sure.
Nothing was speaking to me, but I offered and all was well.

And then I arrived at the powerful green hill.

The Poem as Mask

Orpheus

When I wrote of the women in their dances and wildness, it was a mask,
on their mountain, gold-hunting, singing, in orgy,
it was a mask; when I wrote of the god,

fragmented, exiled from himself, his life, the love gone down with song,
it was myself, split open, unable to speak, in exile from myself.

There is no mountain, there is no god, there is memory
of my torn life, myself split open in sleep, the rescued child
beside me among the doctors, and a word
of rescue from the great eyes.

No more masks! No more mythologies!

Now, for the first time, the god lifts his hand,
the fragments join in me with their own music.

Delmore Schwartz (1913–1966)

Delmore Schwartz was born in Brooklyn, New York. He attended the University of Wisconsin, New York University, and Harvard University, where he also taught for a number of years. He was editor of the Partisan Review *and poetry editor of the* New Republic, *lectured at a number of universities, and worked as a literary consultant. His poetry books include* In Dreams Begin Responsibilities *(1938),* Genesis, Book One *(1943),* Vaudeville for a Princess, and Other Poems *(1950), and* Summer Knowledge *(1959). Among his honors were Guggenheim fellowships, the Bollingen Prize, and the Shelley Memorial Award. Delmore Schwartz died in New York City.*

The Heavy Bear Who Goes with Me

"the withness of the body"

The heavy bear who goes with me,
A manifold honey to smear his face,
Clumsy and lumbering here and there,
The central ton of every place,
The hungry beating brutish one
In love with candy, anger, and sleep,
Crazy factotum, dishevelling all,
Climbs the building, kicks the football,
Boxes his brother in the hate-ridden city.

Breathing at my side; that heavy animal,
That heavy bear who sleeps with me,
Howls in his sleep for a world of sugar,
A sweetness intimate as the water's clasp,
Howls in his sleep because the tight-rope
Trembles and shows the darkness beneath.
—The strutting show-off is terrified,
Dressed in his dress-suit, bulging his pants,
Trembles to think that his quivering meat
Must finally wince to nothing at all.

That inescapable animal walks with me,
Has followed me since the black womb held,
Moves where I move, distorting my gesture,
A caricature, a swollen shadow,
A stupid clown of the spirit's motive,
Perplexes and affronts with his own darkness,
The secret life of belly and bone,

Opaque, too near, my private, yet unknown,
Stretches to embrace the very dear
With whom I would walk without him near,
Touches her grossly, although a word
Would bare my heart and make me clear,
Stumbles, flounders, and strives to be fed
Dragging me with him in his mouthing care,
Amid the hundred million of his kind,
The scrimmage of appetite everywhere.

John Berryman (1914–1972)

John Berryman was born in McAlester, Oklahoma, and attended Columbia University and Clare College at Cambridge University in England. He taught at Wayne State University, Harvard University, Princeton University, the University of Iowa, and the University of Minnesota. His poetry books include Poems *(1942),* The Dispossessed *(1948),* Homage to Mistress Bradstreet *(1956),* 77 Dream Songs *(1964, Pulitzer Prize),* Berryman's Sonnets *(1967),* His Toy, His Dream, His Rest *(1968, National Book Award),* Love and Fame *(1970), and* Delusions, Etc. *(1972). John Berryman committed suicide in Minneapolis, Minnesota.*

From *The Dream Songs*

4

Filling her compact & delicious body
with chicken páprika, she glanced at me
twice.
Fainting with interest, I hungered back
and only the fact of her husband & four other people
kept me from springing on her

or falling at her little feet and crying
'You are the hottest one for years of night
Henry's dazed eyes
have enjoyed, Brilliance.' I advanced upon
(despairing) my spumoni.—Sir Bones: is stuffed,
de world, wif feeding girls.

— Black hair, complexion Latin, jewelled eyes
downcast . . . The slob beside her   feasts . . . What wonders is
she sitting on, over there?
The restaurant buzzes. She might as well be on Mars.
Where did it all go wrong? There ought to be a law against Henry.
— Mr. Bones: there is.

14

Life, friends, is boring. We must not say so.
After all, the sky flashes, the great sea yearns,
we ourselves flash and yearn,
and moreover my mother told me as a boy
(repeatedly) 'Ever to confess you're bored
means you have no

Inner Resources.' I conclude now I have no
inner resources, because I am heavy bored.
Peoples bore me,
literature bores me, especially great literature,
Henry bores me, with his plights & gripes
as bad as achilles,

who loves people and valiant art, which bores me.
And the tranquil hills, & gin, look like a drag
and somehow a dog
has taken itself & its tail considerably away
into mountains or sea or sky, leaving
behind: me, wag.

29

There sat down, once, a thing on Henry's heart
só heavy, if he had a hundred years
& more, & weeping, sleepless, in all them time
Henry could not make good.
Starts again always in Henry's ears
the little cough somewhere, an odour, a chime.

And there is another thing he has in mind
like a grave Sienese face a thousand years
would fail to blur the still profiled reproach of. Ghastly,
with open eyes, he attends, blind.
All the bells say: too late. This is not for tears;
thinking.

But never did Henry, as he thought he did,
end anyone and hacks her body up
and hide the pieces, where they may be found.
He knows: he went over everyone, & nobody's missing.
Often he reckons, in the dawn, them up.
Nobody is ever missing.

149

This world is gradually becoming a place
where I do not care to be any more. Can Delmore die?
I don't suppose

in all them years a day went ever by
without a loving thought for him. Welladay.
In the brightness of his promise,

unstained, I saw him thro' the mist of the actual
blazing with insight, warm with gossip
thro' all our Harvard years
when both of us were just becoming known
I got him out of a police-station once, in Washington, the world is *tref*
and grief too astray for tears.

I imagine you have heard the terrible news,
that Delmore Schwartz is dead, miserably & alone,
in New York: he sang me a song
'I am the Brooklyn poet Delmore Schwartz
Harms & the child I sing, two parents' torts'
when he was young & gift-strong.

Henry's Understanding

He was reading late, at Richard's, down in Maine,
aged 32? Richard & Helen long in bed,
my good wife long in bed.
All I had to do was strip & get into my bed,
putting the marker in the book, & sleep,
& wake to a hot breakfast.

Off the coast was an island, P'tit Manaan,
the bluff from Richard's lawn was almost sheer.
A chill at four o'clock.
It only takes a few minutes to make a man.
A concentration upon now & here.
Suddenly, unlike Bach,

& horribly, unlike Bach, it occurred to me
that *one* night, instead of warm pajamas,
I'd take off all my clothes
& cross the damp cold lawn & down the bluff
into the terrible water & walk forever
under it out toward the island.

Randall Jarrell (1914–1965)

Randell Jarrell was born in Nashville, Tennessee, and attended Vanderbilt University. He served in the air force during World War II and taught at Kenyon College, the University of Texas at Austin, Sarah Lawrence College, Princeton University, and the University of North Carolina at Greensboro. His poetry books include Blood for a Stranger *(1942),* Little Friend, Little Friend *(1945),* Losses *(1948),* The Seven League Crutches *(1951),* Uncollected Poems *(1958),* The Woman at the Washington Zoo *(1960, National Book Award), and* The Lost World *(1965). Among his honors was a Guggenheim fellowship and an Ingram Merrill award; from 1956 to 1958 he served as Consultant in Poetry at the Library of Congress. Randall Jarrell died in a traffic accident in Chapel Hill, North Carolina.*

90 North

At home, in my flannel gown, like a bear to its floe,
I clambered to bed; up the globe's impossible sides
I sailed all night—till at last, with my black beard,
My furs and my dogs, I stood at the northern pole.

There in the childish night my companions lay frozen,
The stiff furs knocked at my starveling throat,
And I gave my great sigh: the flakes came huddling,
Were they really my end? In the darkness I turned to my rest.

—Here, the flag snaps in the glare and silence
Of the unbroken ice. I stand here,
The dogs bark, my beard is black, and I stare
At the North Pole . . .

                        And now what? Why, go back.

Turn as I please, my step is to the south.
The world—my world spins on this final point
Of cold and wretchedness: all lines, all winds
End in this whirlpool I at last discover.

And it is meaningless. In the child's bed
After the night's voyage, in that warm world
Where people work and suffer for the end
That crowns the pain—in that Cloud-Cuckoo-Land

I reached my North and it had meaning.
Here at the actual pole of my existence,
Where all that I have done is meaningless,
Where I die or live by accident alone—

Where, living or dying, I am still alone;
Here where North, the night, the berg of death
Crowd me out of the ignorant darkness,
I see at last that all the knowledge

I wrung from the darkness—that the darkness flung me—
Is worthless as ignorance: nothing comes from nothing,
The darkness from the darkness. Pain comes from the darkness
And we call it wisdom. It is pain.

The Death of the Ball Turret Gunner

From my mother's sleep I fell into the State,
And I hunched in its belly till my wet fur froze.
Six miles from earth, loosed from its dream of life,
I woke to black flak and the nightmare fighters.
When I died they washed me out of the turret with a hose.

The Woman at the Washington Zoo

The saris go by me from the embassies.

Cloth from the moon. Cloth from another planet.
They look back at the leopard like the leopard.

And I. . . .
                    this print of mine, that has kept its color
Alive through so many cleanings; this dull null
Navy I wear to work, and wear from work, and so
To my bed, so to my grave, with no
Complaints, no comment: neither from my chief,
The Deputy Chief Assistant, nor his chief—
Only I complain. . . . this serviceable
Body that no sunlight dyes, no hand suffuses
But, dome-shadowed, withering among columns,
Wavy beneath fountains—small, far-off, shining
In the eyes of animals, these beings trapped
As I am trapped but not, themselves, the trap,
Aging, but without knowledge of their age,
Kept safe here, knowing not of death, for death—
Oh, bars of my own body, open, open!

The world goes by my cage and never sees me.
And there come not to me, as come to these,
The wild beasts, sparrows pecking the llamas' grain,
Pigeons settling on the bears' bread, buzzards
Tearing the meat the flies have clouded. . . .

                               Vulture,
When you come for the white rat that the foxes left,
Take off the red helmet of your head, the black
Wings that have shadowed me, and step to me as man:
The wild brother at whose feet the white wolves fawn,
To whose hand of power the great lioness
Stalks, purring. . . .

                      You know what I was,
You see what I am: change me, change me!

Next Day

Moving from Cheer to Joy, from Joy to All,
I take a box
And add it to my wild rice, my Cornish game hens.
The slacked or shorted, basketed, identical
Food-gathering flocks
Are selves I overlook. Wisdom, said William James,

Is learning what to overlook. And I am wise
If that is wisdom.
Yet somehow, as I buy All from these shelves
And the boy takes it to my station wagon,
What I've become
Troubles me even if I shut my eyes.

When I was young and miserable and pretty
And poor, I'd wish
What all girls wish: to have a husband,
A house and children. Now that I'm old, my wish
Is womanish:
That the boy putting groceries in my car

See me. It bewilders me he doesn't see me.
For so many years
I was good enough to eat: the world looked at me
And its mouth watered. How often they have undressed me,

The eyes of strangers!
And, holding their flesh within my flesh, their vile

Imaginings within my imagining,
I too have taken
The chance of life. Now the boy pats my dog
And we start home. Now I am good.
The last mistaken,
Ecstatic, accidental bliss, the blind

Happiness that, bursting, leaves upon the palm
Some soap and water—
It was so long ago, back in some Gay
Twenties, Nineties, I don't know . . . Today I miss
My lovely daughter
Away at school, my sons away at school,

My husband away at work—I wish for them.
The dog, the maid,
And I go through the sure unvarying days
At home in them. As I look at my life,
I am afraid
Only that it will change, as I am changing:

I am afraid, this morning, of my face.
It looks at me
From the rear-view mirror, with the eyes I hate,
The smile I hate. Its plain, lined look
Of gray discovery
Repeats to me: "You're old." That's all, I'm old.

And yet I'm afraid, as I was at the funeral
I went to yesterday.
My friend's cold made-up face, granite among its flowers,
Her undressed, operated-on, dressed body
Were my face and body.
As I think of her I hear her telling me

How young I seem; I *am* exceptional;
I think of all I have.
But really no one is exceptional,
No one has anything, I'm anybody,
I stand beside my grave
Confused with my life, that is commonplace and solitary.

Weldon Kees (1914–1955)

Weldon Kees was born in Beatrice, Nebraska. He attended Doane College, the University of Missouri, and the University of Nebraska. He wrote for the Federal Writers' Project, worked as a librarian in Denver, Colorado, and as a journalist and visual artist in New York. In 1950 he moved to San Francisco as an experimental filmmaker, composer, and musician. His poetry books include The Last Man (1943), The Fall of the Magician (1947), Poems 1947–1954 (1954), and The Collected Poems of Weldon Kees (1960). On July 18, 1955, near the Golden Gate Bridge in San Francisco, Weldon Kees disappeared without a trace.

For My Daughter

Looking into my daughter's eyes I read
Beneath the innocence of morning flesh
Concealed, hintings of death she does not heed.
Coldest of winds have blown this hair, and mesh
Of seaweed snarled these miniatures of hands;
The night's slow poison, tolerant and bland,
Has moved her blood. Parched years that I have seen
That may be hers appear: foul, lingering
Death in certain war, the slim legs green.
Or, fed on hate, she relishes the sting
Of others' agony; perhaps the cruel
Bride of a syphilitic or a fool.
These speculations sour in the sun.
I have no daughter. I desire none.

Dudley Randall (1914–2000)

Dudley Randall was born in Washington, D.C. He attended Wayne State University, the University of Michigan, and, much later, the University of Ghana. He was a foundry worker and a mail carrier and clerk, and he worked as a librarian when he also became a publisher and editor. His poetry books include Cities Burning *(1968),* Love You *(1970),* More to Remember: Poems of Four Decades *(1971),* After the Killing *(1973), and* A Litany of Friends: New and Selected Poems *(1981). Among his honors were two National Endowment for the Arts fellowships, and he served as the first poet laureate of the City of Detroit. Dudley Randall died in Southfield, Michigan.*

A Different Image

The age
requires this task:
create
a different image;
re-animate
the mask.

Shatter the icons of slavery and fear.
Replace
the leer
of the minstrel's burnt-cork face
with a proud, serene
and classic bronze of Benin.

William Stafford (1914–1993)

William Stafford was born in Hutchinson, Kansas. He attended the University of Kansas and the University of Iowa. As a conscientious objector during World War II, he worked in Civilian Public Service camps in Arkansas, California, and Illinois. After the war, he taught mostly at Lewis & Clark College in Oregon. His poetry books include West of Your City *(1960),* Traveling through the Dark *(1962, National Book Award),* The Rescued Year *(1966),* Weather *(1969),* Allegiances *(1970),* Someday, Maybe *(1973, Melville Cane Award),* Stories That Could Be True: New and Collected Poems *(1977),* Things That Happen Where There Aren't Any People *(1980),* A Glass Face in the Rain *(1982),* An Oregon Message *(1987),* Passwords *(1991), and* Learning to Live in the World: Earth Poems *(1994). Among his honors were Yaddo, National Endowment for the Arts, and Guggenheim fellowships and the Shelley Memorial Award; he served as Consultant in Poetry at the Library of Congress in 1970. William Stafford died in Lake Oswego, Oregon, from a heart attack.*

Traveling through the Dark

Traveling through the dark I found a deer
dead on the edge of the Wilson River road.
It is usually best to roll them into the canyon:
that road is narrow; to swerve might make more dead.

By glow of the tail-light I stumbled back of the car
and stood by the heap, a doe, a recent killing;
she had stiffened already, almost cold.
I dragged her off; she was large in the belly.

My fingers touching her side brought me the reason—
her side was warm; her fawn lay there waiting,
alive, still, never to be born.
Beside that mountain road I hesitated.

The car aimed ahead its lowered parking lights;
under the hood purred the steady engine.
I stood in the glare of the warm exhaust turning red;
around our group I could hear the wilderness listen.

I thought hard for us all—my only swerving—,
then pushed her over the edge into the river.

At the Bomb Testing Site

At noon in the desert a panting lizard
waited for history, its elbows tense,
watching the curve of a particular road
as if something might happen.

It was looking for something farther off
than people could see, an important scene
acted in stone for little selves
at the flute end of consequences.

There was just a continent without much on it
under a sky that never cared less.
Ready for a change, the elbows waited.
The hands gripped hard on the desert.

Ruth Stone (1915–2011)

Ruth Stone was born in Roanoke, Virginia. She attended the University of Illinois and Harvard University, raised three daughters alone after her husband's death, and taught at numerous universities. In 1990 she became a faculty member at the State University of New York at Binghamton. Her poetry books include In an Iridescent Time *(1959),* Topography and Other Poems *(1971),* Cheap *(1975),* Second-Hand Coat *(1987),* Simplicity *(1995),* Ordinary Words *(1999, National Book Critics Circle Award),* In the Next Galaxy *(2002, National Book Award),* In the Dark *(2004), and* What Love Comes To *(2008). Among her honors are the Shelley Memorial Award, Guggenheim fellowships, the Delmore Schwartz Award, a Whiting award, and the 2002 Wallace Stevens Award. Ruth Stone died in Ripton, Vermont.*

Scars

Sometimes I am on a train
going to a strange city,
and you are outside the window
explaining your suicide,
nagging me like a sick child.
I have no unbroken rest.
Sometimes I cover you
with an alphabet
or the steers bellow your name
asking the impossible of me.
The chicory flowers speak for you.
They stare at the sky
as though I am invisible.
Often the distance from
here to the pond changes.
Last night a green fire
came down like a space ship,
and I remembered
those people in Argentina
who went inside one
where it burnt the grass,
and forgot their measures
like clabbered milk,
forgot who they meant to be
or suspected they might become,
and later showed the scars
on their foreheads
to everyone,
begging them to believe.

Margaret Walker (1915–1998)

Margaret Walker was born in Birmingham, Alabama. She attended Northwestern University and the University of Iowa before teaching at Livingstone College, West Virginia State College, and Jackson State College while raising four children. Her poetry books include For My People *(1942, Yale Younger Poets Prize),* Ballad of the Free *(1966),* Prophets for a New Day *(1970),* October Journey *(1973), and* This Is My Century *(1989). She also published the novel* Jubilee *(1966). Among her honors are Rosenthal, Ford, Fulbright, and National Endowment for the Humanities fellowships. Margaret Walker died of breast cancer in Chicago.*

For My People

For my people everywhere singing their slave songs repeatedly: their dirges
and their ditties and their blues and jubilees, praying their prayers
nightly to an unknown god, bending their knees humbly to an unseen
power;

For my people lending their strength to the years, to the gone years and the
now years and the maybe years, washing ironing cooking scrubbing
sewing mending hoeing plowing digging planting pruning patching
dragging along never gaining never reaping never knowing and never
understanding;

For my playmates in the clay and dust and sand of Alabama backyards
playing baptizing and preaching and doctor and jail and soldier and
school and mama and cooking and playhouse and concert and store
and hair and Miss Choomby and company;

For the cramped bewildered years we went to school to learn to know the
reasons why and the answers to and the people who and the places
where and the days when, in memory of the bitter hours when we
discovered we were black and poor and small and different and
nobody cared and nobody wondered and nobody understood;

For the boys and girls who grew in spite of these things to be man and
woman, to laugh and dance and sing and play and drink their wine
and religion and success, to marry their playmates and bear children
and then die of consumption and anemia and lynching;

For my people thronging 47th Street in Chicago and Lenox Avenue in
New York and Rampart Street in New Orleans, lost disinherited
dispossessed and happy people filling the cabarets and taverns and

other people's pockets needing bread and shoes and milk and land
and money and something—something all our own;

For my people walking blindly spreading joy, losing time being lazy, sleeping
when hungry, shouting when burdened, drinking when hopeless, tied
and shackled and tangled among ourselves by the unseen creatures
who tower over us omnisciently and laugh;

For my people blundering and groping and floundering in the dark of
churches and schools and clubs and societies, associations and
councils and committees and conventions, distressed and disturbed
and deceived and devoured by money-hungry glory-craving leeches,
preyed on by facile force of state and fad and novelty, by false prophet
and holy believer;

For my people standing staring trying to fashion a better way from confusion,
from hypocrisy and misunderstanding, trying to fashion a world that
will hold all the people, all the faces, all the adams and eves and their
countless generations;

Let a new earth rise. Let another world be born. Let a bloody peace be
written in the sky. Let a second generation full of courage issue forth;
let a people loving freedom come to growth. Let a beauty full of healing
and a strength of final clenching be the pulsing in our spirits and our
blood. Let the martial songs be written, let the dirges disappear. Let a
race of men now rise and take control.

Gwendolyn Brooks (1917–2000)

Gwendolyn Brooks was born in Topeka, Kansas. She attended Wilson Junior College before working for the National Association for the Advancement of Colored People (NAACP) in Chicago. Later she taught poetry at numerous colleges and universities, including Columbia College, Elmhurst College, Northeastern Illinois University, the University of Wisconsin at Madison, and Chicago State University. Her poetry books include A Street in Bronzeville *(1945),* Annie Allen *(1949, Pulitzer Prize),* The Bean Eaters *(1960),* Selected Poems *(1963),* In the Mecca *(1968, Anisfield-Wolf Book Award),* Riot *(1969),* Family Pictures *(1970),* Aloneness *(1971),* Aurora *(1972),* Beckonings *(1975),* Black Love *(1982),* The Near-Johannesburg Boy and Other Poems *(1987),* Gottschalk and the Grande Tarantelle *(1988),* Children Coming Home *(1991), and* In Montgomery and Other Poems *(2003). Among her honors were a place on* Mademoiselle *magazine's "ten women of the year" list for 1945, Guggenheim fellowships, the Shelley Memorial Award (1976), the Frost Medal, the National Endowment for the Arts Lifetime Achievement Award, and the National Book Foundation medal for lifetime achievement. In 1985 and 1986 Gwendolyn Brooks served as Consultant in Poetry at the Library of Congress. She died in Chicago.*

The Mother

Abortions will not let you forget.
You remember the children you got that you did not get,
The damp small pulps with a little or with no hair,
The singers and workers that never handled the air.
You will never neglect or beat
Them, or silence or buy with a sweet.
You will never wind up the sucking-thumb
Or scuttle off ghosts that come.
You will never leave them, controlling your luscious sigh,
Return for a snack of them, with gobbling mother-eye.

I have heard in the voices of the wind the voices of my dim
      killed children.
I have contracted. I have eased
My dim dears at the breasts they could never suck.
I have said, Sweets, if I sinned, if I seized
Your luck
And your lives from your unfinished reach,
If I stole your births and your names,
Your straight baby tears and your games,
Your stilted or lovely loves, your tumults, your marriages,
      aches, and your deaths,
If I poisoned the beginnings of your breaths,
Believe that even in my deliberateness I was not deliberate.

Though why should I whine,
Whine that the crime was other than mine?—
Since anyhow you are dead.
Or rather, or instead,
You were never made.
But that too, I am afraid,
Is faulty: oh, what shall I say, how is the truth to be said?
You were born, you had body, you died.
It is just that you never giggled or planned or cried.

Believe me, I loved you all.
Believe me, I knew you, though faintly, and I loved, I loved you
All.

A Song in the Front Yard

I've stayed in the front yard all my life.
I want to peek at the back
Where it's rough and untended and hungry weed grows.
A girl gets sick of a rose.

I want to go in the back yard now
And maybe down the alley,
To where the charity children play.
I want a good time today.

They do some wonderful things.
They have some wonderful fun.
My mother sneers, but I say it's fine
How they don't have to go in at quarter to nine.
My mother, she tells me that Johnnie Mae
Will grow up to be a bad woman.
That George'll be taken to Jail soon or late
(On account of last winter he sold our back gate).

But I say it's fine. Honest, I do.
And I'd like to be a bad woman, too,
And wear the brave stockings of night-black lace
And strut down the streets with paint on my face.

The Bean Eaters

They eat beans mostly, this old yellow pair.
Dinner is a casual affair.
Plain chipware on a plain and creaking wood,
Tin flatware.

Two who are Mostly Good.
Two who have lived their day,
But keep on putting on their clothes
And putting things away.

And remembering . . .
Remembering, with tinklings and twinges,
As they lean over the beans in their rented back room that is full of beads
      and receipts and dolls and cloths, tobacco crumbs, vases and fringes.

The Lovers of the Poor

                arrive. The Ladies from the Ladies' Betterment
                  League
Arrive in the afternoon, the late light slanting
In diluted gold bars across the boulevard brag
Of proud, seamed faces with mercy and murder hinting
Here, there, interrupting, all deep and debonair,
The pink paint on the innocence of fear;
Walk in a gingerly manner up the hall.
Cutting with knives served by their softest care,
Served by their love, so barbarously fair.
Whose mothers taught: You'd better not be cruel!
You had better not throw stones upon the wrens!
Herein they kiss and coddle and assault
Anew and dearly in the innocence
With which they baffle nature. Who are full,
Sleek, tender-clad, fit, fiftyish, a-glow, all
Sweetly abortive, hinting at fat fruit,
Judge it high time that fiftyish fingers felt
Beneath the lovelier planes of enterprise.
To resurrect. To moisten with milky chill.
To be a random hitching-post or plush.
To be, for wet eyes, random and handy hem.
              Their guild is giving money to the poor.
The worthy poor. The very very worthy
And beautiful poor. Perhaps just not too swarthy?
Perhaps just not too dirty nor too dim
Nor—passionate. In truth, what they could wish
Is—something less than derelict or dull.
Not staunch enough to stab, though, gaze for gaze!
God shield them sharply from the begger-bold!
The noxious needy ones whose battle's bald

Nonetheless for being voiceless, hits one down.
          But it's all so bad! and entirely too much for them.
The stench; the urine, cabbage, and dead beans,
Dead porridges of assorted dusty grains,
The old smoke, *heavy* diapers, and, they're told,
Something called chitterlings. The darkness. Drawn
Darkness, or dirty light. The soil that stirs.
The soil that looks the soil of centuries.
And for that matter the *general* oldness. Old
Wood. Old marble. Old tile. Old old old.
Not homekind Oldness! Not Lake Forest, Glencoe.
Nothing is sturdy, nothing is majestic,
There is no quiet drama, no rubbed glaze, no
Unkillable infirmity of such
A tasteful turn as lately they have left,
Glencoe, Lake Forest, and to which their cars
Must presently restore them. When they're done
With dullards and distortions of this fistic
Patience of the poor and put-upon.
          They've never seen such a make-do-ness as
Newspaper rugs before! In this, this "flat,"
Their hostess is gathering up the oozed, the rich
Rugs of the morning (tattered! the bespattered. . . .)
Readies to spread clean rugs for afternoon.
Here is a scene for you. The Ladies look,
In horror, behind a substantial citizeness
Whose trains clank out across her swollen heart.
Who, arms akimbo, almost fills a door.
All tumbling children, quilts dragged to the floor
And tortured thereover, potato peelings, soft-
Eyed kitten, hunched-up, haggard, to-be-hurt.
          Their League is allotting largesse to the Lost.
But to put their clean, their pretty money, to put
Their money collected from delicate rose-fingers
Tipped with their hundred flawless rose-nails seems . . .
          They own Spode, Lowestoft, candelabra,
Mantels, and hostess gowns, and sunburst clocks,
Turtle soup, Chippendale, red satin "hangings,"
Aubussons and Hattie Carnegie. They Winter
In Palm Beach; cross the Water in June; attend,
When suitable, the nice Art Institute;
Buy the right books in the best bindings; saunter
On Michigan, Easter mornings, in sun or wind.
Oh Squalor! This sick four-story hulk, this fibre

With fissures everywhere! Why, what are bringings
Of loathe-love largesse? What shall peril hungers
So old old, what shall flatter the desolate?
Tin can, blocked fire escape and chitterling
And swaggering seeking youth and the puzzled wreckage
Of the middle passage, and urine and stale shames
And, again, the porridges of the underslung
And children children children. Heavens! That
Was a rat, surely, off there, in the shadows? Long
And long-tailed? Gray? The Ladies from the Ladies'
Betterment League agree it will be better
To achieve the outer air that rights and steadies,
To hie to a house that does not holler, to ring
Bells elsetime, better presently to cater
To no more Possibilities, to get
Away. Perhaps the money can be posted.
Perhaps they two may choose another Slum!
Some serious sooty half-unhappy home!—
Where loathe-love likelier may be invested.
                    Keeping their scented bodies in the center
Of the hall as they walk down the hysterical hall,
They allow their lovely skirts to graze no wall,
Are off at what they manage of a canter,
And, resuming all the clues of what they were,
Try to avoid inhaling the laden air.

We Real Cool

THE POOL PLAYERS.
SEVEN AT THE GOLDEN SHOVEL.

We real cool. We
Left school. We

Lurk late. We
Strike straight. We

Sing sin. We
Thin gin. We

Jazz June. We
Die soon.

The Blackstone Rangers

I

AS SEEN BY DISCIPLINES

There they are.
Thirty at the corner.
Black, raw, ready.
Sores in the city
that do not want to heal.

II

THE LEADERS

Jeff. Gene. Geronimo. And Bop.
They cancel, cure and curry.
Hardly the dupes of the downtown thing
the cold bonbon,
the rhinestone thing. And hardly
in a hurry.
Hardly Belafonte, King,
Black Jesus, Stokely, Malcolm X or Rap.
Bungled trophies.
Their country is a Nation on no map.

Jeff, Gene, Geronimo and Bop
in the passionate noon,
in bewitching night
are the detailed men, the copious men.
They curry, cure,
they cancel, cancelled images whose Concerts
are not divine, vivacious; the different tins
are intense last entries; pagan argument;
translations of the night.

The Blackstone bitter bureaus
(bureaucracy is footloose) edit, fuse
unfashionable damnations and descent;
and exulting, monstrous hand on monstrous hand,
construct, strangely, a monstrous pearl or grace.

III

GANG GIRLS

A Rangerette

Gang Girls are sweet exotics.
Mary Ann
uses the nutrients of her orient,
but sometimes sighs for Cities of blue and jewel
beyond her Ranger rim of Cottage Grove.
(Bowery Boys, Disciples, Whip-Birds will
dissolve no margins, stop no savory sanctities.)

Mary is
a rose in a whiskey glass.

Mary's
Februaries shudder and are gone. Aprils
fret frankly, lilac hurries on.
Summer is a hard irregular ridge.
October looks away.
And that's the Year!
                    Save for her bugle-love.
Save for the bleat of not-obese devotion.

Save for Somebody Terribly Dying, under
the philanthropy of robins. Save for her Ranger
bringing
an amount of rainbow in a string-drawn bag.
"Where did you get the diamond?" Do not ask:
but swallow, straight, the spirals of his flask
and assist him at your zipper; pet his lips
and help him clutch you.

Love's another departure.
Will there be any arrivals, confirmations?
Will there be gleaning?

Mary, the Shakedancer's child
from the rooming-flat, pants carefully, peers at
her laboring lover. . . .
                    Mary! Mary Ann!
Settle for sandwiches! settle for stocking caps!
for sudden blood, aborted carnival,
the props and niceties of non-loneliness—
the rhymes of Leaning.

Robert Lowell (1917–1977)

Robert Lowell was born in Boston, Massachusetts. He attended Harvard University, Kenyon College, and Louisiana State University and worked as an editorial assistant in New York and as a visiting lecturer at numerous universities. His poetry books include Land of Unlikeness *(1944),* Lord Weary's Castle *(1946, Pulitzer Prize),* The Mills of the Kavanaughs *(1951),* Life Studies *(1959, National Book Award),* For the Union Dead *(1964),* Near the Ocean *(1967),* History *(1973),* For Lizzie and Harriet *(1973),* The Dolphin *(1973, Pulitzer Prize),* Selected Poems *(1976), and* Day by Day *(1977, National Book Critics Circle Award). He received a Guggenheim fellowship, an Obie for his play* The Old Glory, *and served as Consultant in Poetry at the Library of Congress in 1947 and 1948. Robert Lowell died from a heart attack in New York City.*

"To Speak of Woe That Is in Marriage"

> *It is the future generation that presses into being by means of these exuberant feelings and supersensible soap bubbles of ours.*
>
> —SCHOPENHAUER

"The hot night makes us keep our bedroom windows open.
Our magnolia blossoms. Life begins to happen.
My hopped up husband drops his home disputes,
and hits the streets to cruise for prostitutes,
free-lancing out along the razor's edge.
This screwball might kill his wife, then take the pledge.
Oh the monotonous meanness of his lust. . . .
It's the injustice . . . he is so unjust—
whiskey-blind, swaggering home at five.
My only thought is how to keep alive.
What makes him tick? Each night now I tie
ten dollars and his car key to my thigh. . . .
Gored by the climacteric of his want,
he stalls above me like an elephant."

Skunk Hour

(*For Elizabeth Bishop*)

Nautilus Island's hermit
heiress still lives through winter in her Spartan cottage;
her sheep still graze above the sea.

Her son's a bishop. Her farmer
is first selectman in our village;
she's in her dotage.

Thirsting for
the hierarchic privacy
of Queen Victoria's century,
she buys up all
the eyesores facing her shore,
and lets them fall.

The season's ill—
we've lost our summer millionaire,
who seemed to leap from an L. L. Bean
catalogue. His nine-knot yawl
was auctioned off to lobstermen.
A red fox stain covers Blue Hill.

And now our fairy
decorator brightens his shop for fall;
his fishnet's filled with orange cork,
orange, his cobbler's bench and awl;
there is no money in his work,
he'd rather marry.

One dark night,
my Tudor Ford climbed the hill's skull;
I watched for love-cars. Lights turned down,
they lay together, hull to hull,
where the graveyard shelves on the town. . . .
My mind's not right.

A car radio bleats,
"Love, O careless Love. . . ." I hear
my ill-spirit sob in each blood cell,
as if my hand were at its throat. . . .
I myself am hell;
nobody's here—

only skunks, that search
in the moonlight for a bite to eat.
They march on their soles up Main Street:
white stripes, moonstruck eyes' red fire

under the chalk-dry and spar spire
of the Trinitarian Church.

I stand on top
of our back steps and breathe the rich air—
a mother skunk with her column of kittens swills the garbage pail.
She jabs her wedge-head in a cup
of sour cream, drops her ostrich tail,
and will not scare.

For the Union Dead

"Relinquunt Omnia Servare Rem Publicam."

The old South Boston Aquarium stands
in a Sahara of snow now. Its broken windows are boarded.
The bronze weathervane cod has lost half its scales.
The airy tanks are dry.

Once my nose crawled like a snail on the glass;
my hand tingled
to burst the bubbles
drifting from the noses of the cowed, compliant fish.

My hand draws back. I often sigh still
for the dark downward and vegetating kingdom
of the fish and reptile. One morning last March,
I pressed against the new barbed and galvanized

fence on the Boston Common. Behind their cage,
yellow dinosaur steamshovels were grunting
as they cropped up tons of mush and grass
to gouge their underworld garage.

Parking spaces luxuriate like civic
sandpiles in the heart of Boston.
A girdle of orange, Puritan-pumpkin colored girders
braces the tingling Statehouse,

shaking over the excavations, as it faces Colonel Shaw
and his bell-cheeked Negro infantry
on St. Gaudens' shaking Civil War relief,
propped by a plank splint against the garage's earthquake.

Two months after marching through Boston,
half the regiment was dead;
at the dedication,
William James could almost hear the bronze Negroes breathe.

Their monument sticks like a fishbone
in the city's throat.
Its Colonel is as lean
as a compass-needle.

He has an angry wrenlike vigilance,
a greyhound's gentle tautness;
he seems to wince at pleasure,
and suffocate for privacy.

He is out of bounds now. He rejoices in man's lovely,
peculiar power to choose life and die—
when he leads his black soldiers to death,
he cannot bend his back.

On a thousand small town New England greens,
the old white churches hold their air
of sparse, sincere rebellion; frayed flags
quilt the graveyards of the Grand Army of the Republic.

The stone statues of the abstract Union Soldier
grow slimmer and younger each year—
wasp-wasted, they doze over muskets
and muse through their sideburns . . .

Shaw's father wanted no monument
except the ditch,
where his son's body was thrown
and lost with his "niggers."

The ditch is nearer.
There are no statues for the last war here;
on Boylston Street, a commercial photograph
shows Hiroshima boiling

over a Mosler Safe, the "Rock of Ages"
that survived the blast. Space is nearer.
When I crouch to my television set,
the drained faces of Negro school-children rise like balloons.

Colonel Shaw
is riding on his bubble,
he waits
for the blessèd break.

The Aquarium is gone. Everywhere,
giant finned cars nose forward like fish;
a savage servility
slides by on grease.

Robert Duncan (1919–1988)

Robert Duncan was born in Oakland, California. He attended the University of California at Berkeley and worked as an editor, administrator, and lecturer. His poetry books include Heavenly City, Earthly City *(1947),* Caesar's Gate: Poems, 1949–55 *(1956),* Selected Poems *(1959),* The Opening of the Field *(1960),* Roots and Branches *(1964),* The Years as Catches *(1966),* Bending the Bow *(1968),* The First Decade: Selected Poems, 1940–50 *(1968),* Derivations: Selected Poems, 1950–1956 *(1968),* Ground Work: Before the War *(1984, American Book Award), and* Ground Work II: In the Dark *(1987). Among his honors were Guggenheim and National Endowment for the Arts fellowships and the National Poetry Award for lifetime contribution to the art of poetry. He died in San Francisco.*

Often I Am Permitted to Return to a Meadow

as if it were a scene made-up by the mind,
that is not mine, but is a made place,

that is mine, it is so near to the heart,
an eternal pasture folded in all thought
so that there is a hall therein

that is a made place, created by light
wherefrom the shadows that are forms fall.

Wherefrom fall all architectures I am
I say are likenesses of the First Beloved
whose flowers are flames lit to the Lady.

She it is Queen Under The Hill
whose hosts are a disturbance of words within words
that is a field folded.

It is only a dream of the grass blowing
east against the source of the sun
in an hour before the sun's going down

whose secret we see in a children's game
of ring a round of roses told.

Often I am permitted to return to a meadow
as if it were a given property of the mind
that certain bounds hold against chaos,

that is a place of first permission,
everlasting omen of what is.

My Mother Would Be a Falconress

My mother would be a falconress,
and I, her gay falcon treading her wrist,
would fly to bring back
from the blue of the sky to her, bleeding, a prize,
where I dream in my little hood with many bells
jangling when I'd turn my head.

My mother would be a falconress,
and she sends me as far as her will goes.
She lets me ride to the end of her curb
where I fall back in anguish.
I dread that she will cast me away,
for I fall, I mis-take, I fail in her mission.

She would bring down the little birds.
And I would bring down the little birds.
When will she let me bring down the little birds,
pierced from their flight with their necks broken,
their heads like flowers limp from the stem?

I tread my mother's wrist and would draw blood.
Behind the little hood my eyes are hooded.
I have gone back into my hooded silence,
talking to myself and dropping off to sleep.

For she has muffled my dreams in the hood she has made me,
sewn round with bells, jangling when I move.
She rides with her little falcon upon her wrist.
She uses a barb that brings me to cower.
She sends me abroad to try my wings
and I come back to her.   I would bring down
the little birds to her
I may not tear into, I must bring back perfectly.

I tear at her wrist with my beak to draw blood,
and her eye holds me, anguisht, terrifying.

She draws a limit to my flight.
Never beyond my sight, she says.
She trains me to fetch and to limit myself in fetching.
She rewards me with meat for my dinner.
But I must never eat what she sends me to bring her.

Yet it would have been beautiful, if she would have carried me,
always, in a little hood with the bells ringing,
at her wrist, and her riding
to the great falcon hunt, and me
flying up to the curb of my heart from her heart
to bring down the skylark from the blue to her feet,
straining, and then released for the flight.

My mother would be a falconress,
and I her gerfalcon, raised at her will,
from her wrist sent flying, as if I were her own
pride, as if her pride
knew no limits, as if her mind
sought in me flight beyond the horizon.

Ah, but high, high in the air I flew.
And far, far beyond the curb of her will,
were the blue hills where the falcons nest.
And then I saw west to the dying sun—
it seemd my human soul went down in flames.

I tore at her wrist, at the hold she had for me,
until the blood ran hot and I heard her cry out,
far, far beyond the curb of her will

to horizons of stars beyond the ringing hills of the world where
    the falcons nest
I saw, and I tore at her wrist with my savage beak.
I flew, as if sight flew from the anguish in her eye beyond her sight,
sent from my striking loose, from the cruel strike at her wrist,
striking out from the blood to be free of her.

My mother would be a falconress,
and even now, years after this,
when the wounds I left her had surely heald,
and the woman is dead,

her fierce eyes closed, and if her heart
were broken, it is stilld

I would be a falcon and go free.
I tread her wrist and wear the hood,
talking to myself, and would draw blood.

Lawrence Ferlinghetti (1919–)

Lawrence Ferlinghetti was born in Yonkers, New York. During World War II, he spent four years in the U.S. Navy and commanded a ship during the Normandy invasion. He attended the University of North Carolina at Chapel Hill, Columbia University, and the Sorbonne, working as a journalist and French teacher before cofounding City Lights Books in San Francisco in 1953. Among his books are Pictures of the Gone World *(1955),* A Coney Island of the Mind *(1958),* An Eye on the World: Selected Poems *(1967),* The Secret Meaning of Things *(1969),* Back Roads to Far Places *(1971),* Open Eye, Open Heart *(1973),* Who Are We Now? *(1976),* Landscapes of Living and Dying *(1979),* Endless Life: Selected Poems *(1984),* Over All the Obscene Boundaries: European Poems and Transitions *(1985),* Wild Dreams of a New Beginning *(1988),* These Are My Rivers: New and Selected Poems, 1955–1993 *(1993),* A Far Rockaway of the Heart *(1997),* San Francisco Poems *(2001), and* How to Paint Sunlight *(2001). Honors include the poetry prize of the City of Rome, the Frost Medal, the inaugural Literarian Award from the National Book Foundation, and numerous lifetime achievement awards. In 2007 he was named Commandeur, French Order of Arts and Letters. Lawrence Ferlinghetti lives in San Francisco.*

Populist Manifesto

Poets, come out of your closets,
Open your windows, open your doors,
You have been holed-up too long
in your closed worlds.
Come down, come down
from your Russian Hills and Telegraph Hills,
your Beacon Hills and your Chapel Hills,
your Mount Analogues and Montparnasses,
down from your foot hills and mountains,
out of your tepees and domes.
The trees are still falling
and we'll to the woods no more.
No time now for sitting in them
As man burns down his own house
to roast his pig.
No more chanting Hare Krishna
while Rome burns.
San Francisco's burning,
Mayakovsky's Moscow's burning
the fossil-fuels of life.
Night & the Horse approaches
eating light, heat & power,
and the clouds have trousers.

No time now for the artist to hide
above, beyond, behind the scenes,
indifferent, paring his fingernails,
refining himself out of existence.
No time now for our little literary games,
no time now for our paranoias & hypochondrias,
no time now for fear & loathing,
time now only for light & love.
We have seen the best minds of our generation
destroyed by boredom at poetry readings.
Poetry isn't a secret society,
It isn't a temple either.
Secret words & chants won't do any longer.
The hour of *oming* is over,
the time for keening come,
time for keening & rejoicing
over the coming end
of industrial civilization
which is bad for earth & Man.
Time now to face outward
in the full lotus position
with eyes wide open,
Time now to open your mouths
with a new open speech,
time now to communicate with all sentient beings,
All you 'Poets of the Cities'
hung in museums, including myself,
All you poet's poets writing poetry
about poetry,
All you poetry workshop poets
in the boondock heart of America,
All you house-broken Ezra Pounds,
All you far-out freaked-out cut-up poets,
All you pre-stressed Concrete poets,
All you cunnilingual poets,
All you pay-toilet poets groaning with graffitti,
All you A-train swingers who never swing on birches,
All you masters of the sawmill haiku
in the Siberias of America,
All you eyeless unrealists,
All you self-occulting supersurrealists,
All you bedroom visionaries
and closet agitpropagators,
All you Groucho Marxist poets

and leisure-class Comrades
who lie around all day
and talk about the workingclass proletariat,
All you Catholic anarchists of poetry,
All you Black Mountaineers of poetry,
All you Boston Brahmins and Bolinas bucolics,
All you den mothers of poetry,
All you zen brothers of poetry,
All you suicide lovers of poetry,
All you hairy professors of poesie,
All you poetry reviewers
drinking the blood of the poet,
All you Poetry Police—
Where are Whitman's wild children,
where the great voices speaking out
with a sense of sweetness and sublimity,
where the great new vision,
the great world-view,
the high prophetic song
of the immense earth
and all that sings in it
And our relation to it—
Poets, descend
to the street of the world once more
And open your minds & eyes
with the old visual delight,
Clear your throat and speak up,
Poetry is dead, long live poetry
with terrible eyes and buffalo strength.
Don't wait for the Revolution
or it'll happen without you,
Stop mumbling and speak out
with a new wide-open poetry
with a new commonsensual 'public surface'
with other subjective levels
or other subversive levels,
a tuning fork in the inner ear
to strike below the surface.
Of your own sweet Self still sing
yet utter 'the word en-masse'—
Poetry the common carrier
for the transportation of the public
to higher places
than other wheels can carry it.

Poetry still falls from the skies
into our streets still open.
They haven't put up the barricades, yet,
the streets still alive with faces,
lovely men & women still walking there,
still lovely creatures everywhere,
in the eyes of all the secret of all
still buried there,
Whitman's wild children still sleeping there,
Awake and walk in the open air.

William Meredith (1919–2007)

William Meredith was born in New York City. He attended Princeton University, became a New York Times *reporter, and served in the U.S. Navy during World War II and the Korean War before taking teaching positions at Princeton, the University of Hawaii, and Connecticut College. His poetry books include* Love Letter from an Impossible Land *(1944, Yale Younger Poets Prize),* Ships and Other Figures *(1948),* The Open Sea and Other Poems *(1958),* The Wreck of the "Thresher" and Other Poems *(1964),* Earth Walk *(1970),* Hazard, the Painter *(1975),* The Cheer *(1980),* Partial Accounts *(1987, Pulitzer Prize), and* Effort at Speech *(1997, National Book Award). Among his honors were National Endowment for the Arts and Guggenheim fellowships. From 1978 to 1980 he served as Consultant in Poetry at the Library of Congress. William Meredith died in New London, Connecticut.*

Parents

For Vanessa Meredith and Samuel Wolf Gezari

What it must be like to be an angel
or a squirrel, we can imagine sooner.

The last time we go to bed good,
they are there, lying about darkness.

They dandle us once too often,
these friends who become our enemies.

Suddenly one day, their juniors
are as old as we yearn to be.

They get wrinkles where it is better
smooth, odd coughs, and smells.

It is grotesque how they go on
loving us, we go on loving them.

The effrontery, barely imaginable,
of having caused us. And of how.

Their lives: surely
we can do better than that.

This goes on for a long time. Everything
they do is wrong, and the worst thing,

they all do it, is to die,
taking with them the last explanation,

how we came out of the wet sea
or wherever they got us from,

taking the last link
of that chain with them.

Father, mother, we cry, wrinkling,
to our uncomprehending children and grandchildren.

Howard Nemerov (1920–1991)

Howard Nemerov was born in New York City. He attended Harvard University and served in the Royal Canadian Air Force during World War II, afterward teaching at Hamilton College, Bennington College, Brandeis University, and Washington University. His poetry books include The Image and the Law *(1947),* Guide to the Ruins *(1950),* The Salt Garden *(1955),* Mirrors and Windows *(1958),* New and Selected Poems *(1960),* The Next Room of the Dream *(1962),* The Blue Swallows *(1967, Theodore Roethke Award),* The Winter Lightning *(1968),* Gnomes and Occasions *(1973),* The Western Approaches *(1975),* The Collected Poems of Howard Nemerov *(1977, Pulitzer Prize, National Book Award),* Sentences *(1980),* Inside the Onion *(1984),* War Stories: Poems about Long Ago and Now *(1987), and* Trying Conclusions *(1991). Among his honors were National Endowment for the Arts and Guggenheim fellowships, the Frank O'Hara Prize, the Bollingen Prize, and the National Medal of the Arts. Howard Nemerov served as U.S. poet laureate from 1988 to 1990. He died of cancer in University City, Missouri.*

Because You Asked about the Line between Prose and Poetry

Sparrows were feeding in a freezing drizzle
That while you watched turned into pieces of snow
Riding a gradient invisible
From silver aslant to random, white, and slow.

There came a moment that you couldn't tell.
And then they clearly flew instead of fell.

Hayden Carruth (1921–2008)

Hayden Carruth was born in Waterbury, Connecticut. He attended the University of North Carolina at Chapel Hill and the University of Chicago and served in the air force in World War II. After years as a freelance writer and editor, he joined the Syracuse University faculty in 1979. His poetry books include The Crow and the Heart *(1959),* Journey to a Known Place *(1961),* The Norfolk Poems *(1962),* North Winter *(1964),* From Snow and Rock, From Chaos *(1973),* The Bloomingdale Papers *(1975),* Brothers, I Loved You All *(1978),* The Sleeping Beauty *(1982),* Asphalt Georgics *(1985),* Tell Me Again How the White Heron Rises and Flies Across the Nacreous River at Twilight Toward the Distant Islands *(1989),* Collected Shorter Poems, 1946–1991 *(1992, National Book Critics' Circle Award),* Collected Longer Poems *(1994),* Scrambled Eggs & Whiskey *(1996, Pulitzer Prize, National Book Award),* Doctor Jazz *(2001), and* Toward the Distant Islands *(2006). Among his honors were Bollingen, Guggenheim, and National Endowment for the Arts fellowships, the Lannan Award, the Lenore Marshall Award, a Whiting award, and the Ruth Lilly Prize. Hayden Carruth died in Munnsville, New York.*

The Hyacinth Garden in Brooklyn

A year ago friends
    took me walking
on the esplanade
    in Brooklyn. I've
no idea where it
    was, I could never
find it on my own.
    And as we walked,
looking out over
    the water, a sweet
aroma came to us,
    heavy and rich,
of a hyacinth
    garden set
on the landward side
    among apartment
houses, a quite large
    garden with flowers
of every size and color,
    and the famous
perfume filled the air.
    It surrounded me,

dazed me, as I stood
         by the rail looking
down. There vaguely
         among the blooms
I saw Hyacinthus,
         the lovely African
boy beloved by Apollo,
         lying there, dying,
the dark body already
         rotting, melting
among flowers, bleeding
         in Brooklyn, in
Paradise, struck down
         by the quoit thrown
by the grief-stricken god,
         an African boy
chosen for beauty, for love,
         for death, fragrance
beside the water
         on the esplanade
somewhere in Brooklyn,
         in Paradise.

August 1945

Sweating and greasy in the dovecote where one of them lived
         four young men drank "buzzy" from canteen cups, the drink
made from warm beer mixed half-and-half with colorless Italian
         distilled alcohol. A strange fierce taste like bees in the mouth.
Their faces gleamed in the light of a single candle. They were
         getting drunk, deliberately, for this was the only answer. They
sang songs of joy, they sang "Lili Marlene," they were silent,
         they broke into sobbing. They spoke of home, thousands
of miles away, of the years of filth and fear and loneliness,
         of war and war's ending, of the new bomb that had killed
hundreds of thousands at one blow in Japan. There near
         Manfredonia on the Adriatic coast, across from Ithaka where
Odysseus the Wise had once come home from war, in the huge
         disordered repple-depple where throngs of men had waited,
milling and shuffling, shuffling and milling, for shipment
         to the war in Asia, these four were delirious, dumbfounded.

Gratefully they slipped away, falling into the discontinuity
      and incoherence of drunkenness. In a tiny room perched high
on a wall over a courtyard, over a dark field where fires burned
      and cries resounded, the night so hot, the air so evil-smelling,
candlelight flickered on the slack faces of four young men,
      ravaged and stuporous, who knew that time had stopped
          and started again.

Richard Wilbur (1921–)

Richard Wilbur was born in New York City. He served in World War II and attended Amherst College and Harvard University, then taught at Harvard, Wellesley College, Wesleyan University, and Smith College. His poetry books include The Beautiful Changes and Other Poems *(1947),* Ceremony and Other Poems *(1950),* Things of This World *(1956, Pulitzer Prize, National Book Award),* Advice to a Prophet, and Other Poems *(1961),* Walking to Sleep *(1969, Bollingen Prize),* The Mind-Reader *(1976),* New and Collected Poems *(1988, Pulitzer Prize),* Mayflies *(2000),* Collected Poems: 1943–2004 *(2005), and* Anterooms *(2010). He has also published numerous plays, translations, and anthologies. Among his honors are Guggenheim fellowships, the Rome Prize, the Edna St. Vincent Millay Memorial Award, the Shelley Memorial Award, the National Medal of the Arts, the Frost Medal, the T. S. Eliot Award, and the Ruth Lilly Prize. In 1987 and 1988, Richard Wilbur served as U.S. poet laureate. He lives in Cummington, Massachusetts, and Key West, Florida.*

Love Calls Us to the Things of This World

The eyes open to a cry of pulleys,
And spirited from sleep, the astounded soul
Hangs for a moment bodiless and simple
As false dawn.
            Outside the open window
The morning air is all awash with angels.

Some are in bed-sheets, some are in blouses,
Some are in smocks: but truly there they are.
Now they are rising together in calm swells
Of halcyon feeling, filling whatever they wear
With the deep joy of their impersonal breathing;

Now they are flying in place, conveying
The terrible speed of their omnipresence, moving
And staying like white water; and now of a sudden
They swoon down into so rapt a quiet
That nobody seems to be there.
                        The soul shrinks

From all that it is about to remember,
From the punctual rape of every blessed day,
And cries,
        "Oh, let there be nothing on earth but laundry,
Nothing but rosy hands in the rising steam
And clear dances done in the sight of heaven."

Yet, as the sun acknowledges
With a warm look the world's hunks and colors,
The soul descends once more in bitter love
To accept the waking body, saying now
In a changed voice as the man yawns and rises,

"Bring them down from their ruddy gallows;
Let there be clean linen for the backs of thieves;
Let lovers go fresh and sweet to be undone.
And the heaviest nuns walk in a pure floating
Of dark habits,
                keeping their difficult balance."

Cottage Street, 1953

Framed in her phoenix fire-screen, Edna Ward
Bends to the tray of Canton, pouring tea
For frightened Mrs. Plath; then, turning toward
The pale, slumped daughter, and my wife, and me,

Asks if we would prefer it weak or strong.
Will we have milk or lemon, she enquires?
The visit seems already strained and long.
Each in his turn, we tell her our desires.

It is my office to exemplify
The published poet in his happiness,
Thus cheering Sylvia, who has wished to die;
But half-ashamed, and impotent to bless,

I am a stupid life-guard who has found,
Swept to his shallows by the tide, a girl
Who, far from shore, has been immensely drowned,
And stares through water now with eyes of pearl.

How large is her refusal; and how slight
That genteel chat whereby we recommend
Life, of a summer afternoon, despite
The brewing dusk which hints that it may end.

And Edna Ward shall die in fifteen years,
After her eight-and-eighty summers of
Such grace and courage as permit no tears,
The thin hand reaching out, the last word *love,*

Outliving Sylvia who, condemned to live,
Shall study for a decade, as she must,
To state at last her brilliant negative
In poems free and helpless and unjust.

The Writer

In her room at the prow of the house
Where light breaks, and the windows are tossed with linden,
My daughter is writing a story.

I pause in the stairwell, hearing
From her shut door a commotion of typewriter-keys
Like a chain hauled over a gunwale.

Young as she is, the stuff
Of her life is a great cargo, and some of it heavy:
I wish her a lucky passage.

But now it is she who pauses,
As if to reject my thought and its easy figure.
A stillness greatens, in which

The whole house seems to be thinking,
And then she is at it again with a bunched clamor
Of strokes, and again is silent.

I remember the dazed starling
Which was trapped in that very room, two years ago;
How we stole in, lifted a sash

And retreated, not to affright it;
And how for a helpless hour, through the crack of the door,
We watched the sleek, wild, dark

And iridescent creature
Batter against the brilliance, drop like a glove
To the hard floor, or the desk-top.

And wait then, humped and bloody,
For the wits to try it again; and how our spirits
Rose when, suddenly sure,

It lifted off from a chair-back,
Beating a smooth course for the right window
And clearing the sill of the world.

It is always a matter, my darling,
Of life or death, as I had forgotten. I wish
What I wished you before, but harder.

James Dickey (1923–1997)

James Lafayette Dickey was born in Buckhead, Georgia. He served in the air force in World War II and Korea, then attended Clemson College and Vanderbilt University before teaching at Rice University and the University of Florida; he also worked in advertising briefly before joining the University of South Carolina faculty in 1969. His poetry books include Into the Stone and Other Poems *(1960),* Drowning with Others *(1962),* Helmets *(1964),* Buckdancer's Choice *(1965, National Book Award),* Poems, 1957–1967 *(1968),* The Eye-Beaters, Blood, Victory, Madness, Buckhead, and Mercy *(1970),* The Zodiac *(1976),* The Strength of Fields *(1979),* Falling, May Day Sermon, and Other Poems *(1981),* Puella *(1982),* The Central Motion *(1983),* Of Prisons and Ideas *(1987),* The Eagle's Mile *(1990), and* The Whole Motion: Collected Poems, 1945–1992 *(1992). His bestselling novel* Deliverance *became a major motion picture. A Guggenheim Fellow, James Dickey served as Consultant in Poetry at the Library of Congress from 1966 to 1968. He died after a long illness in Columbia, South Carolina.*

The Sheep Child

Farm boys wild to couple
With anything   with soft-wooded trees
With mounds of earth   mounds
Of pinestraw   will keep themselves off
Animals by legends of their own:
In the hay-tunnel dark
And dung of barns, they will
Say   I have heard tell

That in a museum in Atlanta
Way back in a corner somewhere
There's this thing that's only half
Sheep   like a woolly baby
Pickled in alcohol   because
Those things can't live   his eyes
Are open   but you can't stand to look
I heard from somebody who . . .

But this is now almost all
Gone. The boys have taken
Their own true wives in the city,
The sheep are safe in the west hill
Pasture   but we who were born there
Still are not sure. Are we,
Because we remember, remembered
In the terrible dust of museums?

Merely with his eyes, the sheep-child may

Be saying   saying

> I am here, in my father's house.
> I who am half of your world, came deeply
> To my mother in the long grass
> Of the west pasture, where she stood like moonlight
> Listening for foxes. It was something like love
> From another world that seized her
> From behind, and she gave, not lifting her head
> Out of dew, without ever looking, her best
> Self to that great need. Turned loose, she dipped her face
> Farther into the chill of the earth, and in a sound
> Of sobbing   of something stumbling
> Away, began, as she must do,
> To carry me. I woke, dying,
>
> In the summer sun of the hillside, with my eyes
> Far more than human. I saw for a blazing moment
> The great grassy world from both sides,
> Man and beast in the round of their need,
> And the hill wind stirred in my wool,
> My hoof and my hand clasped each other,
> I ate my one meal
> Of milk, and died
> Staring. From dark grass I came straight
>
> To my father's house, whose dust
> Whirls up in the halls for no reason
> When no one comes   piling deep in a hellish mild corner,
> And, through my immortal waters,
> I meet the sun's grains eye
> To eye, and they fail at my closet of glass.
> Dead, I am most surely living
> In the minds of farm boys: I am he who drives
> Them like wolves from the hound bitch and calf
> And from the chaste ewe in the wind.
> They go into woods   into bean fields   they go
> Deep into their known right hands. Dreaming of me,
> They groan   they wait   they suffer
> Themselves, they marry, they raise their kind.

Alan Dugan (1923–2003)

Alan Dugan was born in Brooklyn, New York. He attended Queens College, Olivet College, and Mexico City College, served in World War II, and held jobs in advertising and publishing before teaching at Sarah Lawrence College, Bronxville, New York, and the Fine Arts Work Center in Provincetown, Massachusetts. His poetry books include Poems *(1961, Yale Younger Poets Prize, National Book Award, Pulitzer Prize),* Poems 2 *(1963),* Poems 3 *(1967),* Poems 4 *(1974),* New and Collected Poems *(1983),* Poems Six *(1989), and* Poems Seven *(2001, National Book Award). Among his honors were Rome and Guggenheim fellowships, the Shelley Memorial Award, and a Lannan Award. Alan Dugan died of pneumonia in Hyannis, Massachusetts.*

Love Song: I and Thou

Nothing is plumb, level, or square:
   the studs are bowed, the joists
are shaky by nature, no piece fits
   any other piece without a gap
or pinch, and bent nails
   dance all over the surfacing
like maggots. By Christ
   I am no carpenter. I built
the roof for myself, the walls
   for myself, the floors
for myself, and got
   hung up in it myself. I
danced with a purple thumb
   at this house-warming, drunk
with my prime whiskey: rage.
   Oh I spat rage's nails
into the frame-up of my work:
   it held. It settled plumb,
level, solid, square and true
   for that great moment. Then
it screamed and went on through,
   skewing as wrong the other way.
God damned it. This is hell,
   but I planned it, I sawed it,
I nailed it, and I
   will live in it until it kills me.

I can nail my left palm
    to the left-hand crosspiece but
I can't do everything myself.
    I need a hand to nail the right,
a help, a love, a you, a wife.

Anthony Hecht (1923–2004)

Anthony Hecht was born in New York, New York. He served in the U.S. Army during World War II and attended Bard College, Kenyon College, Columbia University, and the University of Iowa. He later taught at Bard, the University of Rochester, and George-town University. His poetry books include A Summoning of Stones *(1954),* The Hard Hours *(1967, Pulitzer Prize),* Millions of Strange Shadows *(1977),* The Venetian Vespers *(1977),* The Transparent Man *(1990),* Flight Among the Tombs *(1996), and* The Darkness and the Light *(2001). Among his honors were the Rome Prize, Guggenheim fellowships, the Bollingen Prize, the Ruth Lilly Prize, the Tanning Prize, and the National Medal of the Arts. From 1982 to 1984, he served as Consultant in Poetry at the Library of Congress. Anthony Hecht died in Washington, D.C.*

"More Light! More Light!"

For Heinrich Blücher and Hannah Arendt

Composed in the Tower before his execution
These moving verses, and being brought at that time
Painfully to the stake, submitted, declaring thus:
"I implore my God to witness that I have made no crime."

Nor was he forsaken of courage, but the death was horrible,
The sack of gunpowder failing to ignite.
His legs were blistered sticks on which the black sap
Bubbled and burst as he howled for the Kindly Light.

And that was but one, and by no means one of the worst;
Permitted at least his pitiful dignity;
And such as were by made prayers in the name of Christ,
That shall judge all men, for his soul's tranquility.

We move now to outside a German wood
Three men are there commanded to dig a hole
In which the two Jews are ordered to lie down
And be buried by the third, who is a Pole.

Not light from the shrine at Weimar beyond the hill
Nor light from heaven appeared. But he did refuse.
A Lüger settled back deeply in its glove.
He was ordered to change places with the Jews.

Much casual death had drained away their souls.
The thick dirt mounted toward the quivering chin.
When only the head was exposed the order came
To dig him out again and to get back in.

No light, no light in the blue Polish eye.
When he finished a riding boot packed down the earth.
The Lüger hovered lightly in its glove.
He was shot in the belly and in three hours bled to death.

No prayers or incense rose up in those hours
Which grew to be years, and every day came mute
Ghosts from the ovens, sifting through crisp air,
And settled upon his eyes in a black soot.

Richard Hugo (1923–1982)

Richard Hugo was born Richard Hogan in Seattle, Washington. After military service in World War II, he attended the University of Washington, then worked as a technical writer at Boeing for twelve years. From 1964 to 1982 he taught at the University of Montana in Missoula. His poetry books include A Run of Jacks *(1961),* Death of the Kapowsin Tavern *(1965),* Good Luck in Cracked Italian *(1969),* The Lady in Kicking Horse Reservoir *(1973),* Rain Five Days and I Love It *(1975),* What Thou Lovest Well, Remains American *(1975),* 31 Letters and 13 Dreams *(1977),* White Center *(1980),* The Right Madness on Skye *(1980),* Sea Lanes Out *(1983), and* Making Certain It Goes On *(1984). Among his honors were a Northwest Writers Award, a Guggenheim fellowship, and the Theodore Roethke Prize. Richard Hugo died of leukemia in Missoula, Montana.*

Degrees of Gray in Philipsburg

You might come here Sunday on a whim.
Say your life broke down. The last good kiss
you had was years ago. You walk these streets
laid out by the insane, past hotels
that didn't last, bars that did, the tortured try
of local drivers to accelerate their lives.
Only churches are kept up. The jail
turned 70 this year. The only prisoner
is always in, not knowing what he's done.

The principal supporting business now
is rage. Hatred of the various grays
the mountain sends, hatred of the mill,
The Silver Bill repeal, the best liked girls
who leave each year for Butte. One good
restaurant and bars can't wipe the boredom out.
The 1907 boom, eight going silver mines,
a dance floor built on springs—
all memory resolves itself in gaze,
in panoramic green you know the cattle eat
or two stacks high above the town,
two dead kilns, the huge mill in collapse
for fifty years that won't fall finally down.

Isn't this your life? That ancient kiss
still burning out your eyes? Isn't this defeat
so accurate, the church bell simply seems
a pure announcement: ring and no one comes?
Don't empty houses ring? Are magnesium

and scorn sufficient to support a town,
not just Philipsburg, but towns
of towering blondes, good jazz and booze
the world will never let you have
until the town you came from dies inside?

Say no to yourself. The old man, twenty
when the jail was built, still laughs,
although his lips collapse. Someday soon,
he says, I'll go to sleep and not wake up.
You tell him no. You're talking to yourself.
The car that brought you here still runs.
The money you buy lunch with,
no matter where it's mined, is silver
and the girl who serves your food
is slender and her red hair lights the wall.

The Freaks at Spurgin Road Field

The dim boy claps because the others clap.
The polite word, handicapped, is muttered in the stands.
Isn't it wrong, the way the mind moves back.

One whole day I sit, contrite, dirt, L.A.
Union Station, '46, sweating through last night.
The dim boy claps because the others clap.

Score, 5 to 3. Pitcher fading badly in the heat.
Isn't it wrong to be or not be spastic?
Isn't it wrong, the way the mind moves back.

I'm laughing at a neighbor girl beaten to scream
by a savage father and I'm ashamed to look.
The dim boy claps because the others clap.

The score is always close, the rally always short.
I've left more wreckage than a quake.
Isn't it wrong, the way the mind moves back.

The afflicted never cheer in unison.
Isn't it wrong, the way the mind moves back
to stammering pastures where the picnic should have worked.
The dim boy claps because the others clap.

Denise Levertov (1923–1997)

Denise Levertov was born in Ilford, Essex, England, and moved to the United States with her American husband in 1948. She worked as an editor, translator, and visiting lecturer at numerous universities before joining the faculties of, successively, Tufts, Brandeis, and Stanford universities. Her poetry books include The Double Image *(1946),* The Sharks *(1952),* Here and Now *(1956),* Overland to the Islands *(1958),* With Eyes at the Back of Our Heads *(1959),* The Jacob's Ladder *(1961),* O Taste and See *(1964),* The Sorrow Dance *(1967),* Relearning the Alphabet *(1970),* To Stay Alive *(1971),* Footprints *(1972),* The Freeing of the Dust *(1975),* Life in the Forest *(1978),* Collected Earlier Poems 1940–1960 *(1979),* Candles in Babylon *(1982),* Poems 1960–1967 *(1983),* Poems 1968–1972 *(1987),* Breathing the Water *(1987),* A Door in the Hive *(1989),* Evening Train *(1992),* The Sands of the Well *(1996),* The Life Around Us: Selected Poems on Nature *(1997),* The Stream & the Sapphire: Selected Poems on Religious Themes *(1997), and* This Great Unknowing: Last Poems *(2000). Among her honors were Guggenheim and National Endowment for the Arts fellowships, the Lenore Marshall Prize, a Shelley Memorial Award, the Frost Medal, and the Lannan Award. Denise Levertov died in Seattle.*

The Poem Unwritten

For weeks the poem of your body,
of my hands upon your body
     stroking, sweeping, in the rite of
     worship, going
     their way of wonder down
     from neck-pulse to breast-hair to level
     belly to cock—
for weeks that poem, that prayer,
unwritten.
          The poem unwritten, the act
left in the mind, undone. The years
a forest of giant stones, of fossil stumps,
blocking the altar.

Caedmon

All others talked as if
talk were a dance.
Clodhopper I, with clumsy feet
would break the gliding ring.
Early I learned to
hunch myself

close by the door:
then when the talk began
I'd wipe my
mouth and wend
unnoticed back to the barn
to be with the warm beasts,
dumb among body sounds
of the simple ones.
I'd see by a twist
of lit rush the motes
of gold moving
from shadow to shadow
slow in the wake
of deep untroubled sighs.
The cows
munched or stirred or were still. I
was at home and lonely,
both in good measure. Until
the sudden angel affrighted me—light effacing
my feeble beam,
a forest of torches, feathers of flame, sparks upflying:
but the cows as before
were calm, and nothing was burning,
      nothing but I, as that hand of fire
touched my lips and scorched my tongue
and pulled my voice
         into the ring of the dance.

Swan in Falling Snow

Upon the darkish, thin, half-broken ice
there seemed to lie a barrel-sized, heart-shaped snowball,
frozen hard, its white
identical with the untrodden white
of the lake shore. Closer, its somber face—
mask and beak—came clear, the neck's
long cylinder, and the splayed feet, balanced,
weary, immobile. Black water traced, behind it,
an abandoned gesture. Soft
in still air, snowflakes
fell and fell. Silence
deepened, deepened. The short day
suspended itself, endless.

Louis Simpson (1923–2012)

Louis Aston Marantz Simpson was born in Kingston, Jamaica, and came to the United States at the age of seventeen. His studies at Columbia University were interrupted by military service; after three years of World War II combat in Europe, he attended the University of Paris. He worked as an editor and taught at Columbia University, the New School, the University of California at Berkeley, and the State University of New York at Stony Brook. Among his poetry books are The Arrivistes *(1949),* Good News of Death *(1955),* A Dream of Governors *(1959),* At the End of the Open Road *(1963, Pulitzer Prize),* Adventures of the Letter I *(1971),* Searching for the Ox *(1976),* Armidale *(1979),* Out of Season *(1979),* Caviare at the Funeral *(1980),* The Best Hour of the Night *(1983),* People Live Here *(1983),* In the Room We Share *(1990),* There You Are *(1995), and* The Owner of the House *(2003, Griffin Prize). Among his honors are the Prix de Rome, the Edna St. Vincent Millay Memorial Award, and two Guggenheim fellowships. Louis Simpson died in Stony Brook, New York.*

American Poetry

Whatever it is, it must have
A stomach that can digest
Rubber, coal, uranium, moons, poems.

Like the shark, it contains a shoe.
It must swim for miles through the desert
Uttering cries that are almost human.

Carolyn Kizer (1925–)

Carolyn Kizer was born in Spokane, Washington, and attended Sarah Lawrence College, Columbia University, and the University of Washington. Founder and first editor of the magazine Poetry Northwest, *she was the inaugural director of the National Endowment for the Arts literature program and also taught as a guest lecturer at numerous universities. Her poetry books include* The Ungrateful Garden *(1961),* Knock upon Silence *(1965),* Midnight Was My Cry *(1971),* Mermaids in the Basement *(1984),* Yin *(1984, Pulitzer Prize),* The Nearness of You *(1986),* Harping On *(1996), and* Cool, Calm & Collected *(2000). Among her honors are the Frost Medal and the Theodore Roethke Memorial Foundation Award. Carolyn Kizer lives in Sonoma, California.*

A Muse of Water

We who must act as handmaidens
To our own goddess, turn too fast,
Trip on our hems, to glimpse the muse
Gliding below her lake or sea,
Are left, long-staring after her,
Narcissists by necessity;

Or water-carriers of our young
Till waters burst, and white streams flow
Artesian, from the lifted breast:
Cupbearers then, to tiny gods,
Imperious table-pounders, who
Are final arbiters of thirst.

Fasten the blouse, and mount the steps
From kitchen taps to Royal Barge,
Assume the trident, don the crown,
Command the Water Music now
That men bestow on Virgin Queens;
Or goddessing above the waist,

Appear as swan on Thames or Charles
Where iridescent foam conceals
The paddle-stroke beneath the glide:
Immortal feathers preened in poems!
Not our true, intimate nature, stained
By labor, and the casual tide.

Masters of civilization, you
Who moved to riverbank from cave,

Putting up tents, and deities,
Though every rivulet wander through
The final, unpolluted glades
To cinder-bank and culvert-lip,

And all the pretty chatterers
Still round the pebbles as they pass
Lightly over their watercourse,
And even the calm rivers flow,
We have, while springs and skies renew,
Dry wells, dead seas, and lingering drouth.

Water itself is not enough.
Harness her turbulence to work
For man: fill his reflecting pools.
Drained for his cofferdams, or stored
In reservoirs for his personal use:
Turn switches! Let the fountains play!

And yet these buccaneers still kneel
Trembling at the water's verge:
"Cool River-Goddess, sweet ravine,
Spirit of pool and shade, inspire!"
So he needs poultice for his flesh.
So he needs water for his fire.

We rose in mists and died in clouds
Or sank below the trammeled soil
To silent conduits underground,
Joining the blindfish, and the mole.
A gleam of silver in the shale:
Lost murmur! Subterranean moan!

So flows in dark caves, dries away,
What would have brimmed from bank to bank,
Kissing the fields you turned to stone,
Under the boughs your axes broke.
And you blame streams for thinning out,
plundered by man's insatiate want?

Rejoice when a faint music rises
Out of a brackish clump of weeds,
Out of the marsh at ocean-side,
Out of the oil-stained river's gleam,

By the long causeways and gray piers
Your civilizing lusts have made.

Discover the deserted beach
Where ghosts of curlews safely wade:
Here the warm shallows lave your feet
Like tawny hair of magdalens.
Here, if you care, and lie full-length,
Is water deep enough to drown.

Kenneth Koch (1925–2002)

Kenneth Koch was born in Cincinnati, Ohio. He served in the U.S. Army (1943–46) before attending Harvard University and Columbia University. He later taught at Rutgers University, Brooklyn College, Columbia University, and the New School. His poetry books include Poems *(1953),* Ko, or A Season on Earth *(1959),* Thank You and Other Poems *(1962),* The Pleasures of Peace and Other Poems *(1969),* The Art of Love *(1975),* The Duplications *(1977),* The Burning Mystery of Anna in 1951 *(1979),* Days and Nights *(1982),* On the Edge *(1986),* One Train *(1994),* Straits *(1998),* New Addresses *(2000),* Sun Out *(2002), and* A Possible World *(2002). Among his honors were Guggenheim, National Endowment for the Arts, and Ingram Merrill fellowships, the Frank O'Hara Prize, the Bollingen Prize, and the Bobbitt Prize. Kenneth Koch died of leukemia in New York.*

Fresh Air

1

At the Poem Society a black-haired man stands up to say
"You make me sick with all your talk about restraint and mature talent!
Haven't you ever looked out the window at a painting by Matisse,
Or did you always stay in hotels where there were too many spiders
      crawling on your visages?
Did you ever glance inside a bottle of sparkling pop,
Or see a citizen split in two by the lightning?
I am afraid you have never smiled at the hibernation
Of bear cubs except that you saw in it some deep relation
To human suffering and wishes, oh what a bunch of crackpots!"
The black-haired man sits down, and the others shoot arrows at him.
A blond man stands up and says,
"He is right! Why should we be organized to defend the kingdom
Of dullness? There are so many slimy people connected with poetry,
Too, and people who know nothing about it!
I am not recommending that poets like each other and organize to fight
      them,
But simply that lightning should strike them."
Then the assembled mediocrities shot arrows at the blond-haired man.
The chairman stood up on the platform, oh he was physically ugly!
He was small-limbed and -boned and thought he was quite seductive,
But he was bald with certain hideous black hairs,
And his voice had the sound of water leaving a vaseline bathtub,
And he said, "The subject for this evening's discussion is poetry
On the subject of love between swans." And everyone threw candy
      hearts

At the disgusting man, and they stuck to his bib and tucker,
And he danced up and down on the platform in terrific glee
And recited the poetry of his little friends—but the blond man stuck his
    head
Out of a cloud and recited poems about the east and thunder,
And the black-haired man moved through the stratosphere chanting
Poems of the relationships between terrific prehistoric charcoal whales,
And the slimy man with candy hearts sticking all over him
Wilted away like a cigarette paper on which the bumblebees have urinated,
And all the professors left the room to go back to their duty,
And all that were left in the room were five or six poets
And together they sang the new poem of the twentieth century
Which, though influenced by Mallarmé, Shelley, Byron, and Whitman,
Plus a million other poets, is still entirely original
And is so exciting that it cannot be here repeated.
You must go to the Poem Society and wait for it to happen.
Once you have heard this poem you will not love any other,
Once you have dreamed this dream you will be inconsolable,
Once you have loved this dream you will be as one dead,
Once you have visited the passages of this time's great art!

2

"Oh to be seventeen years old
Once again," sang the red-haired man, "and not know that poetry
Is ruled with the sceptre of the dumb, the deaf, and the creepy!"
And the shouting persons battered his immortal body with stones
And threw his primitive comedy into the sea
From which it sang forth poems irrevocably blue.

Who are the great poets of our time, and what are their names?
Yeats of the baleful influence, Auden of the baleful influence, Eliot of
    the baleful influence
(Is Eliot a great poet? no one knows), Hardy, Stevens, Williams (is
    Hardy of our time?),
Hopkins (is Hopkins of our time?), Rilke (is Rilke of our time?), Lorca
    (is Lorca of our time?), who is still of our time?
Mallarmé, Valéry, Apollinaire, Éluard, Reverdy, French poets are still of
    our time,
Pasternak and Mayakovsky, is Jouve of our time?

Where are the young poets in America, they are trembling in publishing
    houses and universities,
Above all they are trembling in universities, they are bathing the library
    steps with their spit,

They are gargling out innocuous (to whom?) poems about maple trees
    and their children,
Sometimes they brave a subject like the Villa d'Este or a lighthouse in
    Rhode Island,
Oh what worms they are! They wish to perfect their form.
Yet could not these young men, put in another profession,
Succeed admirably, say at sailing a ship? I do not doubt it, Sir, and I
    wish we could try them.
(A plane flies over the ship holding a bomb but perhaps it will not drop
    the bomb,
The young poets from the universities are staring anxiously at the skies,
Oh they are remembering their days on the campus when they looked
    up to watch birds excrete,
They are remembering the days they spent making their elegant poems.)

Is there no voice to cry out from the wind and say what it is like to be
    the wind,
To be roughed up by the trees and to bring music from the scattered
    houses
And the stones, and to be in such intimate relationship with the sea
That you cannot understand it? Is there no one who feels like a pair of
    pants?

3

Summer in the trees! "It is time to strangle several bad poets."
The yellow hobbyhorse rocks to and fro, and from the chimney
Drops the Strangler! The white and pink roses are slightly agitated by
    the struggle,
But afterwards beside the dead "poet" they cuddle up comfortingly
    against their vase. They are safer now, no one will compare them
    to the sea.

Here on the railroad train, one more time, is the Strangler.
He is going to get that one there, who is on his way to a poetry reading.

Agh! Biff! A body falls to the moving floor.

In the football stadium I also see him,
He leaps through the frosty air at the maker of comparisons
Between football and life and silently, silently strangles him!

Here is the Strangler dressed in a cowboy suit
Leaping from his horse to annihilate the students of myth!

The Strangler's ear is alert for the names of Orpheus,
Cuchulain, Gawain, and Odysseus,
And for poems addressed to Jane Austen, F. Scott Fitzgerald,
To Ezra Pound, and to personages no longer living
Even in anyone's thoughts—O Strangler the Strangler!

He lies on his back in the waves of the Pacific Ocean.

4

Supposing that one walks out into the air
On a fresh spring day and has the misfortune
To encounter an article on modern poetry
In *New World Writing*, or has the misfortune
To see some examples of some of the poetry
Written by the men with their eyes on the myth
And the Missus and the midterms, in the *Hudson Review*,
Or, if one is abroad, in *Botteghe Oscure*,
Or indeed in *Encounter*, what is one to do
With the rest of one's day that lies blasted to ruins
All bluely about one, what is one to do?
Oh, surely one cannot complain to the President,
Nor even to the deans of Columbia College,
Nor to T.S. Eliot, nor to Ezra Pound,
And supposing one writes to the Princess Caetani,
"Your poets are awful!" what good would it do?
And supposing one goes to the *Hudson Review*
With a package of matches and sets fire to the building?
One ends up in prison with trial subscriptions
To the *Partisan, Sewanee,* and *Kenyon Review*!

5

Sun out! perhaps there is a reason for the lack of poetry
In these ill-contented souls, perhaps they need air!

Blue air, fresh air, come in, I welcome you, you are an art student,
Take off your cap and gown and sit down on the chair.
Together we shall paint the poets—but no, air! perhaps you should go
        to them, quickly,
Give them a little inspiration, they need it, perhaps they are out of
        breath,
Give them a little inhuman company before they freeze the English
        language to death!

(And rust their typewriters a little, be sea air! be noxious! kill them, if
    you must, but stop their poetry!
I remember I saw you dancing on the surf on the Côte d'Azur,
And I stopped, taking my hat off, but you did not remember me,
Then afterwards you came to my room bearing a handful of orange
    flowers
And we were together all through the summer night!)

That we might go away together, it is so beautiful on the sea, there are
    a few white clouds in the sky!

But no, air! you must go . . . Ah, stay!

But she has departed and . . . Ugh! what poisonous fumes and clouds!
    what a suffocating atmosphere!
Cough! whose are these hideous faces I see, what is this rigor
Infecting the mind? where are the green Azores,
Fond memories of childhood, and the pleasant orange trolleys,
A girl's face, red-white, and her breasts and calves, blue eyes, brown
    eyes, green eyes, fahrenheit
Temperatures, dandelions, and trains, O blue?!
Wind, wind, what is happening? Wind! I can't see any bird but the gull,
    and I feel it should symbolize . . .
Oh, pardon me, there's a swan, one two three swans, a great white swan,
    hahaha how pretty they are! Smack!
Oh! stop! help! yes, I see—disrespect for my superiors—forgive me, dear
    Zeus, nice Zeus, parabolic bird, O feathered excellence! white!
There is Achilles too, and there's Ulysses, I've always wanted to see
    them,
And there is Helen of Troy, I suppose she is Zeus too, she's so terribly
    pretty—hello, Zeus, my you are beautiful, Bang!
One more mistake and I get thrown out of the Modern Poetry Association,
    help! Why aren't there any adjectives around?
Oh there are, there's practically nothing else—look, here's *grey, utter,*
    agonized, total, phenomenal, gracile, invidious, sundered, and
    fused,
Elegant, absolute, pyramidal, and . . . Scream! but what can I describe
    with these words? States!
States symbolized and divided by two, complex states, magic states,
    states of consciousness governed by an aroused sincerity, cockadoodle
    doo!
Another bird! is it morning? Help! where am I? am I in the barnyard?
    oink oink, scratch, moo! Splash!
My first lesson. "Look around you. What do you think and feel?" *Uhhh*

. . . "Quickly!" *This Connecticut landscape would have pleased*
   Vermeer. Wham! A-Plus. "Congratulations!" I am promoted.
OOOhhhhh I wish I were dead, what a headache! My second lesson:
   "Rewrite your first lesson line six hundred times. Try to make it
   into a magnetic field." I can do it too. But my poor line! What a
   nightmare! Here comes a tremendous horse.
Trojan, I presume. No, it's my third lesson. "Look, look! Watch him,
   see what he's doing? That's what we want you to do. Of course it
   won't be the same as his at first, but . . ." I demur. Is there no other
   way to fertilize minds?
Bang! I give in . . . Already I see my name in two or three anthologies,
   a serving girl comes into the barn bringing me the anthologies,
She is very pretty and I smile at her a little sadly, perhaps it is my last
   smile! Perhaps she will hit me! But no, she smiles in return, and she
   takes my hand.

My hand, my hand! what is this strange thing I feel in my hand, on my
   arm, on my chest, my face—can it be . . . ? it is! AIR!
Air, air, you've come back! Did you have any success? "What do you
   think?" I don't know, air. You are so strong, air.
And she breaks my chains of straw, and we walk down the road, behind
   us the hideous fumes!
Soon we reach the seaside, she is a young art student who places her
   head on my shoulder,
I kiss her warm red lips, and here is the Strangler, reading the *Kenyon
   Review*! Good luck to you, Strangler!
Goodbye, Helen! goodbye, fumes! goodbye, abstracted dried-up boys!
   goodbye, dead trees! goodbye, skunks!
Goodbye, manure! goodbye, critical manure! goodbye, you big fat men
   standing on the east coast as well as the west giving poems the test!
   farewell, Valéry's stern dictum!
Until tomorrow, then, scum floating on the surface of poetry! goodbye
   for a moment, refuse that happens to land in poetry's boundaries!
   adieu, stale eggs teaching imbeciles poetry to bolster up your egos!
   adios, boring anomalies of these same stale eggs!
Ah, but the scum is deep! Come, let me help you! and soon we pass
   into the clear blue water. Oh GOODBYE, castrati of poetry!
   farewell, stale pale skunky pentameters (the only honest English
   meter, gloop gloop!)! until tomorrow, horrors! oh, farewell!

Hello, sea! good morning, sea! hello, clarity and excitement, you great
   expanse of green—

O green, beneath which all of them shall drown!

Permanently

One day the Nouns were clustered in the street.
An Adjective walked by, with her dark beauty.
The Nouns were struck, moved, changed.
The next day a Verb drove up, and created the Sentence.

Each Sentence says one thing—for example, "Although it was a dark
    rainy day when the Adjective walked by, I shall remember the pure
    and sweet expression on her face until the day I perish from the
    green, effective earth."
Or, "Will you please close the window, Andrew?"
Or, for example, "Thank you, the pink pot of flowers on the window sill
    has changed color recently to a light yellow, due to the heat from the
    boiler factory which exists nearby."

In the springtime the Sentences and the Nouns lay silently on the grass.
A lonely Conjunction here and there would call, "And! But!"
But the Adjective did not emerge.

As the adjective is lost in the sentence,
So I am lost in your eyes, ears, nose, and throat—
You have enchanted me with a single kiss
Which can never be undone
Until the destruction of language.

Maxine Kumin (1925–)

Born Maxine Winokur in Philadelphia, Pennsylvania, Maxine Kumin attended Rad-cliffe College before taking a teaching position at Tufts University, followed by visiting lectureships at numerous colleges and universities. Her poetry books include Halfway *(1961),* The Privilege *(1965),* The Nightmare Factory *(1970),* Up Country *(1972, Pulitzer Prize),* House, Bridge, Fountain, Gate *(1975),* The Retrieval System *(1978),* Our Ground Time Here Will Be Brief *(1982),* The Long Approach *(1985),* Nurture *(1989),* Looking for Luck *(1992),* Connecting the Dots *(1996),* The Long Marriage *(2001),* Bringing Together: Uncollected Early Poems 1958–1988 *(2003),* Jack and Other New Poems *(2005),* Still to Mow *(2007), and* Where I Live *(2010). Among her honors are a National Endowment for the Arts fellowship, the Ruth Lilly Prize, and the Frost Medal; in 1981 and 1982 she served as Consultant in Poetry at the Library of Congress. Maxine Kumin lives in Warner, New Hampshire.*

Morning Swim

Into my empty head there come
a cotton beach, a dock wherefrom

I set out, oily and nude
through mist, in chilly solitude.

There was no line, no roof or floor
to tell the water from the air.

Night fog thick as terry cloth
closed me in its fuzzy growth.

I hung my bathrobe on two pegs.
I took the lake between my legs.

Invaded and invader, I
went overhand on that flat sky.

Fish twitched beneath me, quick and tame.
In their green zone they sang my name

and in the rhythm of the swim
I hummed a two-four-time slow hymn.

I hummed "Abide with Me." The beat
rose in the fine thrash of my feet,

rose in the bubbles I put out
slantwise, trailing through my mouth.

My bones drank water; water fell
through all my doors. I was the well

that fed the lake that met my sea
in which I sang "Abide with Me."

How It Is

Shall I say how it is in your clothes?
A month after your death I wear your blue jacket.
The dog at the center of my life recognizes
you've come to visit, he's ecstatic.
In the left pocket, a hole.
In the right, a parking ticket
delivered up last August on Bay State Road.
In my heart, a scatter like milkweed,
a flinging from the pods of the soul.
My skin presses your old outline.
It is hot and dry inside.

I think of the last day of your life,
old friend, how I would unwind it, paste
it together in a different collage,
back from the death car idling in the garage,
back up the stairs, your praying hands unlaced,
reassembling the bits of bread and tuna fish
into a ceremony of sandwich,
running the home movie backward to a space
we could be easy in, a kitchen place
with vodka and ice, our words like living meat.

Dear friend, you have excited crowds
with your example. They swell
like wine bags, straining at your seams.
I will be years gathering up our words,
fishing out letters, snapshots, stains,
leaning my ribs against this durable cloth
to put on the dumb blue blazer of your death.

Gerald Stern (1925–)

Gerald Stern was born in Pittsburgh, Pennsylvania. He attended the University of Pitts-burgh, Columbia University, and the University of Paris, France, before becoming a schoolteacher. He then taught at Temple University, Indiana University of Pennsylvania, Somerset County College, and the University of Iowa. His poetry books include Pineys *(1971),* Lucky Life *(1977, Lamont Poetry Prize),* The Red Coal *(1981),* Paradise Poems *(1984),* Lovesick *(1987),* New and Selected Poems *(1989),* Leaving An-other Kingdom *(1990),* Bread Without Sugar *(1992),* Odd Mercy *(1995),* This Time *(1998, National Book Award),* Last Blue *(2000),* American Sonnets *(2002),* Everything Is Burning *(2005), and* Save the Last Dance *(2008). Among his awards are National Endowment for the Arts and Guggenheim fellowships as well as the Wal-lace Stevens Award. Gerald Stern lives in Lambertville, New Jersey.*

Behaving Like a Jew

When I got there the dead opossum looked like
an enormous baby sleeping on the road.
It took me only a few seconds—just
seeing him there—with the hole in his back
and the wind blowing through his hair
to get back again into my animal sorrow.
I am sick of the country, the bloodstained
bumpers, the stiff hairs sticking out of the grilles,
the slimy highways, the heavy birds
refusing to move;
I am sick of the spirit of Lindbergh over everything,
that joy in death, that philosophical
understanding of carnage, that
concentration on the species.
—I am going to be unappeased at the opossum's death.
I am going to behave like a Jew
and touch his face, and stare into his eyes,
and pull him off the road.
I am not going to stand in a wet ditch
with the Toyotas and the Chevies passing over me
at sixty miles an hour
and praise the beauty and the balance
and lose myself in the immortal lifestream
when my hands are still a little shaky
from his stiffness and his bulk
and my eyes are still weak and misty
from his round belly and his curved fingers
and his black whiskers and his little dancing feet.

The Dancing

In all these rotten shops, in all this broken furniture
and wrinkled ties and baseball trophies and coffee pots
I have never seen a postwar Philco
with the automatic eye
nor heard Ravel's "Bolero" the way I did
in 1945 in that tiny living room
on Beechwood Boulevard, nor danced as I did
then, my knives all flashing, my hair all streaming,
my mother red with laughter, my father cupping
his left hand under his armpit, doing the dance
of old Ukraine, the sound of his skin half drum,
half fart, the world at last a meadow,
the three of us whirling and singing, the three of us
screaming and falling, as if we were dying,
as if we could never stop—in 1945—
in Pittsburgh, beautiful filthy Pittsburgh, home
of the evil Mellons, 5,000 miles away
from the other dancing—in Poland and Germany—
oh God of mercy, oh wild God.

Another Insane Devotion

This was gruesome—fighting over a ham sandwich
with one of the tiny cats of Rome, he leaped
on my arm and half hung on to the food and half
hung on to my shirt and coat. I tore it apart
and let him have his portion, I think I lifted him
down, sandwich and all, on the sidewalk and sat
with my own sandwich beside him, maybe I petted
his bony head and felt him shiver. I have
told this story over and over; some things
root in the mind; his boldness, of course, was frightening
and unexpected—his stubbornness—though hunger
drove him mad. It was the breaking of boundaries,
the sudden invasion, but not only that, it was
the sharing of food and the sharing of space; he didn't
run into an alley or into a cellar,
he sat beside me, eating, and I didn't run
into a trattoria, say, shaking,
with food on my lips and blood on my cheek, sobbing;
but not only that, I had gone there to eat

and wait for someone. I had maybe an hour
before she would come and I was full of hope
and excitement. I have resisted for years
interpreting this, but now I think I was given
a clue, or I was giving myself a clue,
across the street from the glass sandwich shop.
That was my last night with her, the next day
I would leave on the train for Paris and she would
meet her husband. Thirty-five years ago
I ate my sandwich and moaned in her arms, we were
dying together; we never met again
although she was pregnant when I left her—I have
a daughter or son somewhere, darling grandchildren
in Norwich, Connecticut, or Canton, Ohio.
Every five years I think about her again
and plan on looking her up. The last time
I was sitting in New Brunswick, New Jersey,
and heard that her husband was teaching at Princeton,
if she was still married, or still alive, and tried
calling. I went that far. We lived
in Florence and Rome. We rowed in the bay of Naples
and floated, naked, on the boards. I started
to think of her again today. I still
am horrified by the cat's hunger. I still
am puzzled by the connection. This is another
insane devotion, there must be hundreds, although
it isn't just that, there is no pain, and the thought
is fleeting and sweet. I think it's my own dumb boyhood,
walking around with Slavic cheeks and burning
stupid eyes. I think I gave the cat
half of my sandwich to buy my life, I think
I broke it in half as a decent sacrifice.
It was this I bought, the red coleus,
the split rocking chair, the silk lampshade.
Happiness. I watched him with pleasure.
I bought memory. I could have lost it.
How crazy it sounds. His face twisted with cunning.
The wind blowing through his hair. His jaws working.

A. R. Ammons (1926–2001)

Archie Randolph Ammons was born in Whiteville, North Carolina. After military service during World War II in the South Pacific, he attended Wake Forest University and the University of California at Berkeley, then worked ten years as a manufacturing executive before joining the faculty at Cornell University. His poetry books include Ommateum, with Doxology (1955), Expressions of Sea Level (1964), Corsons Inlet (1965), Tape for the Turn of the Year (1965), Northfield Poems (1966), Uplands (1970), Briefings (1971), Collected Poems, 1951–1971 (1972, National Book Award), Sphere: The Form of a Motion (1973), Diversifications (1975), The Snow Poems (1977), Selected Longer Poems (1980), A Coast of Trees (1981, National Book Critics Circle Award), Worldly Hopes (1982), Lake Effect Country (1982), Sumerian Vistas (1987), The Really Short Poems of A. R. Ammons (1990), Garbage (1993, National Book Award), Brink Road (1996), and Glare (1997). Among his honors were Guggenheim and MacArthur fellowships, the Bobbitt Prize, the Frost Medal, the Ruth Lilly Prize, and the Wallace Stevens Award. A. R. Ammons died in Ithaca, New York.

The City Limits

When you consider the radiance, that it does not withhold
itself but pours its abundance without selection into every
nook and cranny not overhung or hidden; when you consider

that birds' bones make no awful noise against the light but
lie low in the light as in a high testimony; when you consider
the radiance, that it will look into the guiltiest

swervings of the weaving heart and bear itself upon them,
not flinching into disguise or darkening; when you consider
the abundance of such resource as illuminates the glow-blue

bodies and gold-skeined wings of flies swarming the dumped
guts of a natural slaughter or the coil of shit and in no
way winces from its storms of generosity; when you consider

that air or vacuum, snow or shale, squid or wolf, rose or lichen,
each is accepted into as much light as it will take, then
the heart moves roomier, the man stands and looks about, the

leaf does not increase itself above the grass, and the dark
work of the deepest cells is of a tune with May bushes
and fear lit by the breadth of such calmly turns to praise.

Corsons Inlet

I went for a walk over the dunes again this morning
to the sea,
then turned right along
    the surf
                rounded a naked headland
                and returned

   along the inlet shore:

it was muggy sunny, the wind from the sea steady and high,
crisp in the running sand,
      some breakthroughs of sun
    but after a bit

continuous overcast:

the walk liberating, I was released from forms,
from the perpendiculars
      straight lines, blocks, boxes, binds
of thought
into the hues, shadings, rises, flowing bends and blends
        of sight:

                    I allow myself eddies of meaning:
yield to a direction of significance
running
like a stream through the geography of my work:
    you can find
in my sayings
              swerves of action
              like the inlet's cutting edge:
        there are dunes of motion,
organizations of grass, white sandy paths of remembrance
in the overall wandering of mirroring mind:

but Overall is beyond me: is the sum of these events
I cannot draw, the ledger I cannot keep, the accounting
beyond the account:

in nature there are few sharp lines: there are areas of
primrose
      more or less dispersed;

disorderly orders of bayberry; between the rows
of dunes,
irregular swamps of reeds,
though not reeds alone, but grass, bayberry, yarrow, all . . .
predominantly reeds:

I have reached no conclusions, have erected no boundaries,
shutting out and shutting in, separating inside
     from outside: I have
     drawn no lines:
     as

manifold events of sand
change the dune's shape that will not be the same shape
tomorrow,

so I am willing to go along, to accept
the becoming
thought, to stake off no beginnings or ends, establish
     no walls:

by transitions the land falls from grassy dunes to creek
to undercreek: but there are no lines, though
     change in that transition is clear
     as any sharpness: but "sharpness" spread out,
allowed to occur over a wider range
than mental lines can keep:

the moon was full last night: today, low tide was low:
black shoals of mussels exposed to the risk
of air
and, earlier, of sun,
waved in and out with the waterline, waterline inexact,
caught always in the event of change:
     a young mottled gull stood free on the shoals
     and ate
to vomiting: another gull, squawking possession, cracked a crab,
picked out the entrails, swallowed the soft-shelled legs, a ruddy
turnstone running in to snatch leftover bits:

risk is full: every living thing in
siege: the demand is life, to keep life: the small
white blacklegged egret, how beautiful, quietly stalks and spears
      the shallows, darts to shore

to stab—what? I couldn't
see against the black mudflats—a frightened
fiddler crab?

the news to my left over the dunes and
reeds and bayberry clumps was
fall: thousands of tree swallows
gathering for flight:
an order held
in constant change: a congregation
rich with entropy: nevertheless, separable, noticeable
as one event,
not chaos: preparations for
flight from winter,
cheet, cheet, cheet, cheet, wings rifling the green clumps,
beaks
at the bayberries
a perception full of wind, flight, curve,
sound:
the possibility of rule as the sum of rulelessness:
the "field" of action
with moving, incalculable center:

in the smaller view, order tight with shape:
blue tiny flowers on a leafless weed: carapace of crab:
snail shell:
pulsations of order
in the bellies of minnows: orders swallowed,
broken down, transferred through membranes
to strengthen larger orders: but in the large view, no
lines or changeless shapes: the working in and out, together
and against, of millions of events: this,
so that I make
no form of
formlessness:

orders as summaries, as outcomes of actions override
or in some way result, not predictably (seeing me gain
the top of a dune,
the swallows
could take flight—some other fields of bayberry
could enter fall
berryless) and there is serenity:

no arranged terror: no forcing of image, plan,
or thought:
no propaganda, no humbling of reality to precept:

terror pervades but is not arranged, all possibilities
of escape open: no route shut, except in
    the sudden loss of all routes:

    I see narrow orders, limited tightness, but will
not run to that easy victory:
        still around the looser, wider forces work:
        I will try
    to fasten into order enlarging grasps of disorder, widening
scope, but enjoying the freedom that
scope eludes my grasp, that there is no finality of vision,
that I have perceived nothing completely,
        that tomorrow a new walk is a new walk.

Robert Bly (1926–)

Robert Bly was born in Madison, Minnesota. He attended St. Olaf College, Harvard University, and the University of Iowa. He served in the U.S. Navy in World War II before becoming a translator, editor, and publisher. His poetry books include Silence in the Snowy Fields *(1962),* The Light Around the Body *(1967, National Book Award),* Sleepers Joining Hands *(1973),* Jumping out of Bed *(1973),* This Body Is Made of Camphor and Gopherwood *(1977),* This Tree Will Be Here for a Thousand Years *(1979),* The Man in the Black Coat Turns *(1981),* Selected Poems *(1986),* Loving a Woman in Two Worlds *(1987),* What Have I Ever Lost by Dying? *(1992),* Meditations on the Insatiable Soul *(1994),* Morning Poems *(1997),* Snowbanks North of the House *(1999),* The Night Abraham Called to the Stars *(2001), and* My Sentence Was a Thousand Years of Joy *(2005). Recipient of two Guggenheim fellowships, Robert Bly lives in Moose Lake, Minnesota.*

Snowfall in the Afternoon

I

The grass is half-covered with snow.
It was the sort of snowfall that starts in late afternoon,
And now the little houses of the grass are growing
    dark.

II

If I could reach down, near the earth,
I could take handfuls of darkness!
A darkness that was always there, which we never
    noticed.

III

As the snow grows heavier, the cornstalks fade farther
    away,
And the barn moves nearer to the house.
The barn moves all alone in the growing storm.

IV

The barn is full of corn, and moving toward us now,
Like a hulk blown toward us in a storm at sea;
All the sailors on deck have been blind for many
    years.

Driving to Town Late to Mail a Letter

It is a cold and snowy night. The main street is deserted.
The only things moving are swirls of snow.
As I lift the mailbox door, I feel its cold iron.
There is a privacy I love in this snowy night.
Driving around, I will waste more time.

Waking from Sleep

Inside the veins there are navies setting forth,
Tiny explosions at the waterlines,
And seagulls weaving in the wind of the salty blood.

It is the morning. The country has slept the whole
    winter.
Window seats are covered with fur skins, the yard is
    full
Of stiff dogs, and hands that clumsily hold heavy
    books.

Now we wake, and rise from bed, and eat
    breakfast!—
Shouts rise from the harbor of the blood,
Mist, and masts rising, the knocks of wooden tackle in
    the sunlight.

Now we sing, and do tiny dances on the kitchen floor.
Our whole body is like a harbor at dawn;
We know that our master has left us for the day.

Robert Creeley (1926–2005)

Robert Creeley was born in Arlington, Massachusetts. He attended Harvard University, Black Mountain College, and the University of New Mexico and taught at the University of New Mexico, the State University of New York at Buffalo, and Brown University. His poetry books include For Love: Poems, 1950–1960 *(1962),* Words *(1967),* The Finger *(1968),* The Charm *(1968),* Divisions and Other Early Poems *(1968),* Pieces *(1969),* Selected Poems *(1976),* Later *(1979),* The Collected Poems 1945–1975 *(1982),* Mirrors *(1983),* Memory Gardens *(1986),* Windows *(1990),* Echoes *(1994),* So There *(1998),* Just in Time *(2001),* If I Were Writing This *(2003), and* On Earth: Last Poems and an Essay *(2006). Among his honors were Guggenheim and National Endowment for the Arts fellowships, the Shelley Memorial Award, the Frost Medal, the Lila Wallace–Reader's Digest Writers' Award, the Bollingen Prize, and the Lannan Lifetime Achievement Award. He died in Odessa, Texas.*

The Flower

I think I grow tensions
like flowers
in a wood where
nobody goes.

Each wound is perfect,
encloses itself in a tiny
imperceptible blossom,
making pain.

Pain is a flower like that one,
like this one,
like that one,
like this one.

I Know a Man

As I sd to my
friend, because I am
always talking,—John, I

sd, which was not his
name, the darkness sur-
rounds us, what

can we do against
it, or else, shall we &
why not, buy a goddamn big car,

drive, he sd, for
christ's sake, look
out where yr going.

The Language

Locate *I*
love you some-
where in

teeth and
eyes, bite
it but

take care not
to hurt, you
want so

much so
little. Words
say everything,

I
love you
again,

then what
is emptiness
for. To

fill, fill.
I heard words
and words full

of holes
aching. Speech
is a mouth.

The Rain

All night the sound had
come back again,
and again falls
this quiet, persistent rain.

What am I to myself
that must be remembered,
insisted upon
so often? Is it

that never the ease,
even the hardness,
of rain falling
will have for me

something other than this,
something not so insistent—
am I to be locked in this
final uneasiness.

Love, if you love me,
lie next to me.
Be for me, like rain,
the getting out

of the tiredness, the fatuousness, the semi-
lust of intentional indifference.
Be wet
with a decent happiness.

Bresson's Movies

A movie of Robert
Bresson's showed a yacht,
at evening on the Seine,
all its lights on, watched

by two young, seemingly
poor people, on a bridge adjacent,
the classic boy and girl
of the story, any one

one cares to tell. So
years pass, of course, but
I identified with the young,
embittered Frenchman,

knew his almost complacent
anguish and the distance
he felt from his girl.
Yet another film

of Bresson's has the
aging Lancelot with his
awkward armor standing
in a woods, of small trees,

dazed, bleeding, both he
and his horse are
trying to get back to
the castle, itself of

no great size. It
moved me, that
life was after all
like that. You are

in love. You stand
in the woods, with
a horse, bleeding.
The story is true.

James Merrill (1926–1995)

James Merrill was born in New York City and attended Amherst College. Independently wealthy, he moved to Stonington, Connecticut, in 1955. For two decades, he spent part of each year in Athens, Greece, and also, after 1979, in Key West, Florida. His poetry books include The Black Swan *(1946),* First Poems *(1951),* The Country of a Thousand Years of Peace *(1959),* Water Street *(1962),* Nights and Days *(1966, National Book Award),* The Fire Screen *(1969),* Braving the Elements *(1972),* Divine Comedies *(1976, Pulitzer Prize),* Mirabell: Books of Number *(1978, National Book Award),* Scripts for the Pageant *(1980),* The Changing Light at Sandover *(1982, National Book Critics Circle Award),* Late Settings *(1985),* The Inner Room *(1988), and* A Scattering of Salts *(1995). Among his honors were the Bollingen Prize and the Bobbitt Prize. James Merrill died of a heart attack while vacationing in Tucson, Arizona.*

The Victor Dog

for Elizabeth Bishop

Bix to Buxtehude to Boulez,
The little white dog on the Victor label
Listens long and hard as he is able.
It's all in a day's work, whatever plays.

From judgment, it would seem, he has refrained.
He even listens earnestly to Bloch,
Then builds a church upon our acid rock.
He's man's—no—he's the Leiermann's best friend,

Or would be if hearing and listening were the same.
Does he hear? I fancy he rather smells
Those lemon-gold arpeggios in Ravel's
"Les jets d'eau du palais de ceux qui s'aiment."

He ponders the Schumann Concerto's tall willow hit
By lightning, and stays put. When he surmises
Through one of Bach's eternal boxwood mazes
The oboe pungent as a bitch in heat,

Or when the calypso decants its raw bay rum
Or the moon in *Wozzeck* reddens ripe for murder,
He doesn't sneeze or howl; just listens harder.
Adamant needles bear down on him from

Whirling of outer space, too black too near—
But he was taught as a puppy not to flinch,
Much less to imitate his bête noire Blanche
Who barked, fat foolish creature, at King Lear.

Still others fought in the road's filth over Jezebel,
Slavered on hearths of horned and pelted barons.
His forebears lacked, to say the least, forbearance.
Can nature change in him? Nothing's impossible.

The last chord fades. The night is cold and fine.
His master's voice rasps through the grooves' bare groves.
Obediently, in silence like the grave's
He sleeps there on the still-warm gramophone.

Only to dream he is at the première of a Handel
Opera long thought lost—*Il Cane Minore*.
Its allegorical subject is his story!
A little dog revolving round a spindle

Gives rise to harmonies beyond belief,
A cast of stars. . . . Is there in Victor's heart
No honey for the vanquished? Art is art.
The life it asks of us is a dog's life.

Frank O'Hara (1926–1966)

Francis Russell O'Hara was born in Baltimore, Maryland. He attended Harvard University and the University of Michigan at Ann Arbor before establishing himself as an art curator and critic in New York City. His poetry books include A City Winter, and Other Poems *(1952),* Second Avenue *(1960),* Lunch Poems *(1964),* Love Poems *(1965),* In Memory of My Feelings *(1967), and, posthumously,* The Collected Poems *(1971, National Book Award). On July 26, 1966, Frank O'Hara was severely injured by a speeding beach vehicle on Fire Island, New York; he died the next day.*

Steps

How funny you are today New York
like Ginger Rogers in *Swingtime*
and St. Bridget's steeple leaning a little to the left

here I have just jumped out of a bed full of V-days
(I got tired of D-days) and blue you there still
accepts me foolish and free
all I want is a room up there
and you in it
and even the traffic halt so thick is a way
for people to rub up against each other
and when their surgical appliances lock
they stay together
for the rest of the day (what a day)
I go by to check a slide and I say
that painting's not so blue

where's Lana Turner
she's out eating
and Garbo's backstage at the Met
everyone's taking their coat off
so they can show a rib-cage to the rib-watchers
and the park's full of dancers with their tights and shoes
in little bags
who are often mistaken for worker-outers at the West Side Y
why not
the Pittsburgh Pirates shout because they won
and in a sense we're all winning
we're alive

the apartment was vacated by a gay couple
who moved to the country for fun
they moved a day too soon
even the stabbings are helping the population explosion
though in the wrong country
and all those liars have left the UN
the Seagram Building's no longer rivalled in interest
not that we need liquor (we just like it)

and the little box is out on the sidewalk
next to the delicatessen
so the old man can sit on it and drink beer
and get knocked off it by his wife later in the day
while the sun is still shining

oh god it's wonderful
to get out of bed
and drink too much coffee
and smoke too many cigarettes
and love you so much

Poem

Lana Turner has collapsed!
I was trotting along and suddenly
it started raining and snowing
and you said it was hailing
but hailing hits you on the head
hard so it was really snowing and
raining and I was in such a hurry
to meet you but the traffic
was acting exactly like the sky
and suddenly I see a headline
LANA TURNER HAS COLLAPSED!
there is no snow in Hollywood
there is no rain in California
I have been to lots of parties
and acted perfectly disgraceful
but I never actually collapsed
oh Lana Turner we love you get up

The Day Lady Died

It is 12:20 in New York a Friday
three days after Bastille day, yes
it is 1959 and I go get a shoeshine
because I will get off the 4:19 in Easthampton
at 7:15 and then go straight to dinner
and I don't know the people who will feed me

I walk up the muggy street beginning to sun
and have a hamburger and a malted and buy
an ugly NEW WORLD WRITING to see what the poets
in Ghana are doing these days
                          I go on to the bank
and Miss Stillwagon (first name Linda I once heard)
doesn't even look up my balance for once in her life
and in the GOLDEN GRIFFIN I get a little Verlaine
for Patsy with drawings by Bonnard although I do
think of Hesiod, trans. Richmond Lattimore or
Brendan Behan's new play or *Le Balcon* or *Les Nègres*
of Genet, but I don't, I stick with Verlaine
after practically going to sleep with quandariness

and for Mike I just stroll into the PARK LANE
Liquor Store and ask for a bottle of Strega and
then I go back where I came from to 6th Avenue
and the tobacconist in the Ziegfeld Theatre and
casually ask for a carton of Gauloises and a carton
of Picayunes, and a NEW YORK POST with her face on it

and I am sweating a lot by now and thinking of
leaning on the john door in the 5 SPOT
while she whispered a song along the keyboard
to Mal Waldron and everyone and I stopped breathing

John Ashbery (1927–)

John Ashbery was born in Rochester, New York. He attended Harvard University, Columbia University, and New York University and worked as a librarian, copywriter, editor, and art critic before teaching at the City University of New York and Bard College. His poetry books include Some Trees *(1956, Yale Younger Poets Prize),* The Tennis Court Oath *(1962),* Rivers and Mountains *(1966),* The Double Dream of Spring *(1970),* Three Poems *(1972),* Self-Portrait in a Convex Mirror *(1975, Pulitzer Prize, National Book Award, National Book Critics Circle Award),* Houseboat Days *(1977),* As We Know *(1979),* Shadow Train *(1981),* A Wave *(1984),* April Galleons *(1987),* Flow Chart *(1991),* Hotel Lautréamont *(1992),* And the Stars Were Shining *(1994),* Can You Hear, Bird *(1995),* Wakefulness *(1998),* Girls on the Run *(1999),* Your Name Here *(2000),* Chinese Whispers *(2002),* Where Shall I Wander? *(2005),* A Worldly Country *(2007),* Notes from the Air *(2007, Griffin Prize), and* Planisphere *(2009). Among his honors are Ingram Merrill, Guggenheim, National Endowment for the Arts, and MacArthur fellowships, the Frank O'Hara Prize, the Ruth Lilly Prize, the Frost Medal, and the Wallace Stevens Award. He lives in New York City and Hudson, New York.*

Some Trees

These are amazing: each
Joining a neighbor, as though speech
Were a still performance.
Arranging by chance

To meet as far this morning
From the world as agreeing
With it, you and I
Are suddenly what the trees try

To tell us we are:
That their merely being there
Means something; that soon
We may touch, love, explain.

And glad not to have invented
Such comeliness, we are surrounded:
A silence already filled with noises,
A canvas on which emerges

A chorus of smiles, a winter morning.
Placed in a puzzling light, and moving,
Our days put on such reticence
These accents seem their own defense.

Self-Portrait in a Convex Mirror

As Parmigianino did it, the right hand
Bigger than the head, thrust at the viewer
And swerving easily away, as though to protect
What it advertises. A few leaded panes, old beams,
Fur, pleated muslin, a coral ring run together
In a movement supporting the face, which swims
Toward and away like the hand
Except that it is in repose. It is what is
Sequestered. Vasari says, "Francesco one day set himself
To take his own portrait, looking at himself for that purpose
In a convex mirror, such as is used by barbers . . .
He accordingly caused a ball of wood to be made
By a turner, and having divided it in half and
Brought it to the size of the mirror, he set himself
With great art to copy all that he saw in the glass,"
Chiefly his reflection, of which the portrait
Is the reflection once removed.
The glass chose to reflect only what he saw
Which was enough for his purpose: his image
Glazed, embalmed, projected at a 180-degree angle.
The time of day or the density of the light
Adhering to the face keeps it
Lively and intact in a recurring wave
Of arrival. The soul establishes itself.
But how far can it swim out through the eyes
And still return safely to its nest? The surface
Of the mirror being convex, the distance increases
Significantly; that is, enough to make the point
That the soul is a captive, treated humanely, kept
In suspension, unable to advance much farther
Than your look as it intercepts the picture.
Pope Clement and his court were "stupefied"
By it, according to Vasari, and promised a commission
That never materialized. The soul has to stay where it is,
Even though restless, hearing raindrops at the pane,
The sighing of autumn leaves thrashed by the wind,
Longing to be free, outside, but it must stay
Posing in this place. It must move
As little as possible. This is what the portrait says.
But there is in that gaze a combination
Of tenderness, amusement and regret, so powerful
In its restraint that one cannot look for long.

The secret is too plain. The pity of it smarts,
Makes hot tears spurt: that the soul is not a soul,
Has no secret, is small, and it fits
Its hollow perfectly: its room, our moment of attention.
That is the tune but there are no words.
The words are only speculation
(From the Latin *speculum*, mirror):
They seek and cannot find the meaning of the music.
We see only postures of the dream,
Riders of the motion that swings the face
Into view under evening skies, with no
False disarray as proof of authenticity.
But it is life englobed.
One would like to stick one's hand
Out of the globe, but its dimension,
What carries it, will not allow it.
No doubt it is this, not the reflex
To hide something, which makes the hand loom large
As it retreats slightly. There is no way
To build it flat like a section of wall:
It must join the segment of a circle,
Roving back to the body of which it seems
So unlikely a part, to fence in and shore up the face
On which the effort of this condition reads
Like a pinpoint of a smile, a spark
Or star one is not sure of having seen
As darkness resumes. A perverse light whose
Imperative of subtlety dooms in advance its
Conceit to light up: unimportant but meant.
Francesco, your hand is big enough
To wreck the sphere, and too big,
One would think, to weave delicate meshes
That only argue its further detention.
(Big, but not coarse, merely on another scale,
Like a dozing whale on the sea bottom
In relation to the tiny, self-important ship
On the surface.) But your eyes proclaim
That everything is surface. The surface is what's there
And nothing can exist except what's there.
There are no recesses in the room, only alcoves,
And the window doesn't matter much, or that
Sliver of window or mirror on the right, even
As a gauge of the weather, which in French is
Le temps, the word for time, and which

Follows a course wherein changes are merely
Features of the whole. The whole is stable within
Instability, a globe like ours, resting
On a pedestal of vacuum, a ping-pong ball
Secure on its jet of water.
And just as there are no words for the surface, that is,
No words to say what it really is, that it is not
Superficial but a visible core, then there is
No way out of the problem of pathos vs. experience.
You will stay on, restive, serene in
Your gesture which is neither embrace nor warning
But which holds something of both in pure
Affirmation that doesn't affirm anything.

The balloon pops, the attention
Turns dully away. Clouds
In the puddle stir up into sawtoothed fragments.
I think of the friends
Who came to see me, of what yesterday
Was like. A peculiar slant
Of memory that intrudes on the dreaming model
In the silence of the studio as he considers
Lifting the pencil to the self-portrait.
How many people came and stayed a certain time,
Uttered light or dark speech that became part of you
Like light behind windblown fog and sand,
Filtered and influenced by it, until no part
Remains that is surely you. Those voices in the dusk
Have told you all and still the tale goes on
In the form of memories deposited in irregular
Clumps of crystals. Whose curved hand controls,
Francesco, the turning seasons and the thoughts
That peel off and fly away at breathless speeds
Like the last stubborn leaves ripped
From wet branches? I see in this only the chaos
Of your round mirror which organizes everything
Around the polestar of your eyes which are empty,
Know nothing, dream but reveal nothing.
I feel the carousel starting slowly
And going faster and faster: desk, papers, books,
Photographs of friends, the window and the trees
Merging in one neutral band that surrounds
Me on all sides, everywhere I look.
And I cannot explain the action of leveling,

Why it should all boil down to one
Uniform substance, a magma of interiors.
My guide in these matters is your self,
Firm, oblique, accepting everything with the same
Wraith of a smile, and as time speeds up so that it is soon
Much later, I can know only the straight way out,
The distance between us. Long ago
The strewn evidence meant something,
The small accidents and pleasures
Of the day as it moved gracelessly on,
A housewife doing chores. Impossible now
To restore those properties in the silver blur that is
The record of what you accomplished by sitting down
"With great art to copy all that you saw in the glass"
So as to perfect and rule out the extraneous
Forever. In the circle of your intentions certain spars
Remain that perpetuate the enchantment of self with self:
Eyebeams, muslin, coral. It doesn't matter
Because these are things as they are today
Before one's shadow ever grew
Out of the field into thoughts of tomorrow.

Tomorrow is easy, but today is uncharted,
Desolate, reluctant as any landscape
To yield what are laws of perspective
After all only to the painter's deep
Mistrust, a weak instrument though
Necessary. Of course some things
Are possible, it knows, but it doesn't know
Which ones. Some day we will try
To do as many things as are possible
And perhaps we shall succeed at a handful
Of them, but this will not have anything
To do with what is promised today, our
Landscape sweeping out from us to disappear
On the horizon. Today enough of a cover burnishes
To keep the supposition of promises together
In one piece of surface, letting one ramble
Back home from them so that these
Even stronger possibilities can remain
Whole without being tested. Actually
The skin of the bubble-chamber's as tough as
Reptile eggs; everything gets "programmed" there
In due course: more keeps getting included

Without adding to the sum, and just as one
Gets accustomed to a noise that
Kept one awake but now no longer does,
So the room contains this flow like an hourglass
Without varying in climate or quality
(Except perhaps to brighten bleakly and almost
Invisibly, in a focus sharpening toward death—more
Of this later). What should be the vacuum of a dream
Becomes continually replete as the source of dreams
Is being tapped so that this one dream
May wax, flourish like a cabbage rose,
Defying sumptuary laws, leaving us
To awake and try to begin living in what
Has now become a slum. Sydney Freedberg in his
Parmigianino says of it: "Realism in this portrait
No longer produces an objective truth, but a *bizarria*. . . .
However its distortion does not create
A feeling of disharmony. . . . The forms retain
A strong measure of ideal beauty," because
Fed by our dreams, so inconsequential until one day
We notice the hole they left. Now their importance
If not their meaning is plain. They were to nourish
A dream which includes them all, as they are
Finally reversed in the accumulating mirror.
They seemed strange because we couldn't actually see them.
And we realize this only at a point where they lapse
Like a wave breaking on a rock, giving up
Its shape in a gesture which expresses that shape.
The forms retain a strong measure of ideal beauty
As they forage in secret on our idea of distortion.
Why be unhappy with this arrangement, since
Dreams prolong us as they are absorbed?
Something like living occurs, a movement
Out of the dream into its codification.

As I start to forget it
It presents its stereotype again
But it is an unfamiliar stereotype, the face
Riding at anchor, issued from hazards, soon
To accost others, "rather angel than man" (Vasari).
Perhaps an angel looks like everything
We have forgotten, I mean forgotten
Things that don't seem familiar when
We meet them again, lost beyond telling,

Which were ours once. This would be the point
Of invading the privacy of this man who
"Dabbled in alchemy, but whose wish
Here was not to examine the subtleties of art
In a detached, scientific spirit: he wished through them
To impart the sense of novelty and amazement to the spectator"
(Freedberg). Later portraits such as the Uffizi
"Gentleman," the Borghese "Young Prelate" and
The Naples "Antea" issue from Mannerist
Tensions, but here, as Freedberg points out,
The surprise, the tension are in the concept
Rather than its realization.
The consonance of the High Renaissance
Is present, though distorted by the mirror.
What is novel is the extreme care in rendering
The velleities of the rounded reflecting surface
(It is the first mirror portrait),
So that you could be fooled for a moment
Before you realize the reflection
Isn't yours. You feel then like one of those
Hoffmann characters who have been deprived
Of a reflection, except that the whole of me
Is seen to be supplanted by the strict
Otherness of the painter in his
Other room. We have surprised him
At work, but no, he has surprised us
As he works. The picture is almost finished,
The surprise almost over, as when one looks out,
Startled by a snowfall which even now is
Ending in specks and sparkles of snow.
It happened while you were inside, asleep,
And there is no reason why you should have
Been awake for it, except that the day
Is ending and it will be hard for you
To get to sleep tonight, at least until late.

The shadow of the city injects its own
Urgency: Rome where Francesco
Was at work during the Sack: his inventions
Amazed the soldiers who burst in on him;
They decided to spare his life, but he left soon after;
Vienna where the painting is today, where
I saw it with Pierre in the summer of 1959; New York
Where I am now, which is a logarithm

Of other cities. Our landscape
Is alive with filiations, shuttlings;
Business is carried on by look, gesture,
Hearsay. It is another life to the city,
The backing of the looking glass of the
Unidentified but precisely sketched studio. It wants
To siphon off the life of the studio, deflate
Its mapped space to enactments, island it.
That operation has been temporarily stalled
But something new is on the way, a new preciosity
In the wind. Can you stand it,
Francesco? Are you strong enough for it?
This wind brings what it knows not, is
Self-propelled, blind, has no notion
Of itself. It is inertia that once
Acknowledged saps all activity, secret or public:
Whispers of the word that can't be understood
But can be felt, a chill, a blight
Moving outward along the capes and peninsulas
Of your nervures and so to the archipelagoes
And to the bathed, aired secrecy of the open sea.
This is its negative side. Its positive side is
Making you notice life and the stresses
That only seemed to go away, but now,
As this new mode questions, are seen to be
Hastening out of style. If they are to become classics
They must decide which side they are on.
Their reticence has undermined
The urban scenery, made its ambiguities
Look willful and tired, the games of an old man.
What we need now is this unlikely
Challenger pounding on the gates of an amazed
Castle. Your argument, Francesco,
Had begun to grow stale as no answer
Or answers were forthcoming. If it dissolves now
Into dust, that only means its time had come
Some time ago, but look now, and listen:
It may be that another life is stocked there
In recesses no one knew of; that it,
Not we, are the change; that we are in fact it
If we could get back to it, relive some of the way
It looked, turn our faces to the globe as it sets
And still be coming out all right:
Nerves normal, breath normal. Since it is a metaphor

Made to include us, we are a part of it and
Can live in it as in fact we have done,
Only leaving our minds bare for questioning
We now see will not take place at random
But in an orderly way that means to menace
Nobody—the normal way things are done,
Like the concentric growing up of days
Around a life: correctly, if you think about it.

A breeze like the turning of a page
Brings back your face: the moment
Takes such a big bite out of the haze
Of pleasant intuition it comes after.
The locking into place is "death itself,"
As Berg said of a phrase in Mahler's Ninth;
Or, to quote Imogen in *Cymbeline,* "There cannot
Be a pinch in death more sharp than this," for,
Though only exercise or tactic, it carries
The momentum of a conviction that had been building.
Mere forgetfulness cannot remove it
Nor wishing bring it back, as long as it remains
The white precipitate of its dream
In the climate of sighs flung across our world,
A cloth over a birdcage. But it is certain that
What is beautiful seems so only in relation to a specific
Life, experienced or not, channeled into some form
Steeped in the nostalgia of a collective past.
The light sinks today with an enthusiasm
I have known elsewhere, and known why
It seemed meaningful, that others felt this way
Years ago. I go on consulting
This mirror that is no longer mine
For as much brisk vacancy as is to be
My portion this time. And the vase is always full
Because there is only just so much room
And it accommodates everything. The sample
One sees is not to be taken as
Merely that, but as everything as it
May be imagined outside time—not as a gesture
But as all, in the refined, assimilable state.
But what is this universe the porch of
As it veers in and out, back and forth,
Refusing to surround us and still the only
Thing we can see? Love once

Tipped the scales but now is shadowed, invisible,
Though mysteriously present, around somewhere.
But we know it cannot be sandwiched
Between two adjacent moments, that its windings
Lead nowhere except to further tributaries
And that these empty themselves into a vague
Sense of something that can never be known
Even though it seems likely that each of us
Knows what it is and is capable of
Communicating it to the other. But the look
Some wear as a sign makes one want to
Push forward ignoring the apparent
Naïveté of the attempt, not caring
That no one is listening, since the light
Has been lit once and for all in their eyes
And is present, unimpaired, a permanent anomaly,
Awake and silent. On the surface of it
There seems no special reason why that light
Should be focused by love, or why
The city falling with its beautiful suburbs
Into space always less clear, less defined,
Should read as the support of its progress,
The easel upon which the drama unfolded
To its own satisfaction and to the end
Of our dreaming, as we had never imagined
It would end, in worn daylight with the painted
Promise showing through as a gage, a bond.
This nondescript, never-to-be defined daytime is
The secret of where it takes place
And we can no longer return to the various
Conflicting statements gathered, lapses of memory
Of the principal witnesses. All we know
Is that we are a little early, that
Today has that special, lapidary
Todayness that the sunlight reproduces
Faithfully in casting twig-shadows on blithe
Sidewalks. No previous day would have been like this.
I used to think they were all alike,
That the present always looked the same to everybody
But this confusion drains away as one
Is always cresting into one's present.
Yet the "poetic," straw-colored space
Of the long corridor that leads back to the painting,
Its darkening opposite—is this

Some figment of "art," not to be imagined
As real, let alone special? Hasn't it too its lair
In the present we are always escaping from
And falling back into, as the waterwheel of days
Pursues its uneventful, even serene course?
I think it is trying to say it is today
And we must get out of it even as the public
Is pushing through the museum now so as to
Be out by closing time. You can't live there.
The gray glaze of the past attacks all know-how:
Secrets of wash and finish that took a lifetime
To learn and are reduced to the status of
Black-and-white illustrations in a book where colorplates
Are rare. That is, all time
Reduces to no special time. No one
Alludes to the change; to do so might
Involve calling attention to oneself
Which would augment the dread of not getting out
Before having seen the whole collection
(Except for the sculptures in the basement:
They are where they belong).
Our time gets to be veiled, compromised
By the portrait's will to endure. It hints at
Our own, which we were hoping to keep hidden.
We don't need paintings or
Doggerel written by mature poets when
The explosion is so precise, so fine.
Is there any point even in acknowledging
The existence of all that? Does it
Exist? Certainly the leisure to
Indulge stately pastimes doesn't,
Any more. Today has no margins, the event arrives
Flush with its edges, is of the same substance,
Indistinguishable. "Play" is something else;
It exists, in a society specifically
Organized as a demonstration of itself.
There is no other way, and those assholes
Who would confuse everything with their mirror games
Which seem to multiply stakes and possibilities, or
At least confuse issues by means of an investing
Aura that would corrode the architecture
Of the whole in a haze of suppressed mockery,
Are beside the point. They are out of the game,
Which doesn't exist until they are out of it.

It seems like a very hostile universe
But as the principle of each individual thing is
Hostile to, exists at the expense of all the others
As philosophers have often pointed out, at least
This thing, the mute, undivided present,
Has the justification of logic, which
In this instance isn't a bad thing
Or wouldn't be, if the way of telling
Didn't somehow intrude, twisting the end result
Into a caricature of itself. This always
Happens, as in the game where
A whispered phrase passed around the room
Ends up as something completely different.
It is the principle that makes works of art so unlike
What the artist intended. Often he finds
He has omitted the thing he started out to say
In the first place. Seduced by flowers,
Explicit pleasures, he blames himself (though
Secretly satisfied with the result), imagining
He had a say in the matter and exercised
An option of which he was hardly conscious,
Unaware that necessity circumvents such resolutions
So as to create something new
For itself, that there is no other way,
That the history of creation proceeds according to
Stringent laws, and that things
Do get done in this way, but never the things
We set out to accomplish and wanted so desperately
To see come into being. Parmigianino
Must have realized this as he worked at his
Life-obstructing task. One is forced to read
The perfectly plausible accomplishment of a purpose
Into the smooth, perhaps even bland (but so
Enigmatic) finish. Is there anything
To be serious about beyond this otherness
That gets included in the most ordinary
Forms of daily activity, changing everything
Slightly and profoundly, and tearing the matter
Of creation, any creation, not just artistic creation
Out of our hands, to install it on some monstrous, near
Peak, too close to ignore, too far
For one to intervene? This otherness, this
"Not-being-us" is all there is to look at
In the mirror, though no one can say

How it came to be this way. A ship
Flying unknown colors has entered the harbor.
You are allowing extraneous matters
To break up your day, cloud the focus
Of the crystal ball. Its scene drifts away
Like vapor scattered on the wind. The fertile
Thought-associations that until now came
So easily, appear no more, or rarely. Their
Colorings are less intense, washed out
By autumn rains and winds, spoiled, muddied,
Given back to you because they are worthless.
Yet we are such creatures of habit that their
Implications are still around *en permanence,* confusing
Issues. To be serious only about sex
Is perhaps one way, but the sands are hissing
As they approach the beginning of the big slide
Into what happened. This past
Is now here: the painter's
Reflected face, in which we linger, receiving
Dreams and inspirations on an unassigned
Frequency, but the hues have turned metallic,
The curves and edges are not so rich. Each person
Has one big theory to explain the universe
But it doesn't tell the whole story
And in the end it is what is outside him
That matters, to him and especially to us
Who have been given no help whatever
In decoding our own man-size quotient and must rely
On second-hand knowledge. Yet I know
That no one else's taste is going to be
Any help, and might as well be ignored.
Once it seemed so perfect—gloss on the fine
Freckled skin, lips moistened as though about to part
Releasing speech, and the familiar look
Of clothes and furniture that one forgets.
This could have been our paradise: exotic
Refuge within an exhausted world, but that wasn't
In the cards, because it couldn't have been
The point. Aping naturalness may be the first step
Toward achieving an inner calm
But it is the first step only, and often
Remains a frozen gesture of welcome etched
On the air materializing behind it,
A convention. And we have really

No time for these, except to use them
For kindling. The sooner they are burnt up
The better for the roles we have to play.
Therefore I beseech you, withdraw that hand,
Offer it no longer as shield or greeting,
The shield of a greeting, Francesco:
There is room for one bullet in the chamber:
Our looking through the wrong end
Of the telescope as you fall back at a speed
Faster than that of light to flatten ultimately
Among the features of the room, an invitation
Never mailed, the "it was all a dream"
Syndrome, though the "all" tells tersely
Enough how it wasn't. Its existence
Was real, though troubled, and the ache
Of this waking dream can never drown out
The diagram still sketched on the wind,
Chosen, meant for me and materialized
In the disguising radiance of my room.
We have seen the city; it is the gibbous
Mirrored eye of an insect. All things happen
On its balcony and are resumed within,
But the action is the cold, syrupy flow
Of a pageant. One feels too confined,
Sifting the April sunlight for clues,
In the mere stillness of the ease of its
Parameter. The hand holds no chalk
And each part of the whole falls off
And cannot know it knew, except
Here and there, in cold pockets
Of remembrance, whispers out of time.

What Is Poetry

The medieval town, with frieze
Of boy scouts from Nagoya? The snow

That came when we wanted it to snow?
Beautiful images? Trying to avoid

Ideas, as in this poem? But we
Go back to them as to a wife, leaving

The mistress we desire? Now they
Will have to believe it

As we believe it. In school
All the thought got combed out:

What was left was like a field.
Shut your eyes, and you can feel it for miles around.

Now open them on a thin vertical path.
It might give us—what?—some flowers soon?

Galway Kinnell (1927–)

Galway Kinnell was born in Providence, Rhode Island. He attended Princeton University and the University of Rochester and has taught at Alfred University, the University of Chicago, Columbia University, the University of Hawaii, New York University, and Sarah Lawrence College. His poetry books include What a Kingdom It Was *(1960),* Body Rags *(1968),* The Book of Nightmares *(1971),* The Avenue Bearing the Initial of Christ into the New World *(1974),* Mortal Acts, Mortal Words *(1980),* Selected Poems *(1982, Pulitzer Prize, National Book Award),* The Past *(1985, National Book Critics Circle Award),* When One Has Lived a Long Time Alone *(1990),* Imperfect Thirst *(1994),* Flower Herding on Mount Monadnock *(2002), and* Strong Is Your Hold *(2006). Among his honors are Guggenheim, National Endowment for the Arts, and MacArthur fellowships, the Frost Medal, and the Wallace Stevens Award. Galway Kinnell lives in Sheffield, Vermont.*

The Bear

1

In late winter
I sometimes glimpse bits of steam
coming up from
some fault in the old snow
and bend close and see it is lung-colored
and put down my nose
and know
the chilly, enduring odor of bear.

2

I take a wolf's rib and whittle
it sharp at both ends
and coil it up
and freeze it in blubber and place it out
on the fairway of the bears.

And when it has vanished
I move out on the bear tracks,
roaming in circles
until I come to the first, tentative, dark
splash on the earth.

And I set out
running, following the splashes
of blood wandering over the world.

At the cut, gashed resting places
I stop and rest,
at the crawl-marks
where he lay out on his belly
to overpass some stretch of bauchy ice
I lie out
dragging myself forward with bear-knives in my fists.

3

On the third day I begin to starve,
at nightfall I bend down as I knew I would
at a turd sopped in blood,
and hesitate, and pick it up,
and thrust it in my mouth, and gnash it down,
and rise
and go on running.

4

On the seventh day,
living by now on bear blood alone,
I can see his upturned carcass far out ahead, a scraggled,
steamy hulk,
the heavy fur riffling in the wind.

I come up to him
and stare at the narrow-spaced, petty eyes,
the dismayed
face laid back on the shoulder, the nostrils
flared, catching
perhaps the first taint of me as he
died.

I hack
a ravine in his thigh, and eat and drink,
and tear him down his whole length
and open him and climb in
and close him up after me, against the wind,
and sleep.

5

And dream
of lumbering flatfooted
over the tundra,

stabbed twice from within,
splattering a trail behind me,
splattering it out no matter which way I lurch,
no matter which parabola of bear-transcendence,
which dance of solitude I attempt,
which gravity-clutched leap,
which trudge, which groan.

6

Until one day I totter and fall—
fall on this
stomach that has tried so hard to keep up,
to digest the blood as it leaked in,
to break up
and digest the bone itself: and now the breeze
blows over me, blows off
the hideous belches of ill-digested bear blood
and rotted stomach
and the ordinary, wretched odor of bear,

blows across
my sore, lolled tongue a song
or screech, until I think I must rise up
and dance. And I lie still.

7

I awaken I think. Marshlights
reappear, geese
come trailing again up the flyway.
In her ravine under old snow the dam-bear
lies, licking
lumps of smeared fur
and drizzly eyes into shapes
with her tongue. And one
hairy-soled trudge stuck out before me,
the next groaned out,
the next,
the next,
the rest of my days I spend
wandering: wondering
what, anyway,
was that sticky infusion, that rank flavor of blood, that poetry, by which
  I lived?

After Making Love We Hear Footsteps

For I can snore like a bullhorn
or play loud music
or sit up talking with any reasonably sober Irishman
and Fergus will only sink deeper
into his dreamless sleep, which goes by all in one flash,
but let there be that heavy breathing
or a stifled come-cry anywhere in the house
and he will wrench himself awake
and make for it on the run—as now, we lie together,
after making love, quiet, touching along the length of our bodies,
familiar touch of the long-married,
and he appears—in his baseball pajamas, it happens,
the neck opening so small he has to screw them on—
and flops down between us and hugs us and snuggles himself to sleep,
his face gleaming with satisfaction at being this very child.

In the half darkness we look at each other
and smile
and touch arms across this little, startlingly muscled body—
this one whom habit of memory propels to the ground of his making,
sleeper only the mortal sounds can sing awake,
this blessing love gives again into our arms.

Saint Francis and the Sow

The bud
stands for all things,
even for those things that don't flower,
for everything flowers, from within, of self-blessing;
though sometimes it is necessary
to reteach a thing its loveliness,
to put a hand on its brow
of the flower
and retell it in words and in touch
it is lovely
until it flowers again from within, of self-blessing;
as Saint Francis
put his hand on the creased forehead
of the sow, and told her in words and in touch
blessings of earth on the sow, and the sow
began remembering all down her thick length,

from the earthen snout all the way
through the fodder and slops to the spiritual curl of the tail,
from the hard spininess spiked out from the spine
down through the great broken heart
to the sheer blue milken dreaminess spurting and shuddering
from the fourteen teats into the fourteen mouths sucking and blowing
    beneath them:
the long, perfect loveliness of sow.

W. S. Merwin (1927–)

William Stanley Merwin was born in New York City. He attended Princeton University before moving to Europe for a number of years. He has worked as a tutor, translator, and editor. His many poetry books include A Mask for Janus *(1952, Yale Younger Poets Prize),* The Dancing Bears *(1954),* Green with Beasts *(1956),* The Drunk in the Furnace *(1960),* The Moving Target *(1963),* Collected Poems *(1966),* The Lice *(1969),* The Carrier of Ladders *(1970, Pulitzer Prize),* Writings to an Unfinished Accompaniment *(1973),* The Compass Flower *(1977),* Opening the Hand *(1983),* The Rain in the Trees *(1988),* Travels *(1993, Lenore Marshall Prize),* The Vixen *(1996),* The Folding Cliffs *(verse novel, 1998),* The River Sound *(1999),* The Pupil *(2001),* Migration *(2005, National Book Award),* Present Company *(2005), and* The Shadow of Sirius *(2008, Pulitzer Prize). Among his other honors are Guggenheim and Lila Wallace–Reader's Digest Foundation fellowships, the Shelley Memorial Award, the Bollingen Prize, and the Tanning Prize. In 2010 Merwin was named U.S. poet laureate. He lives in Maui, Hawaii.*

Air

Naturally it is night.
Under the overturned lute with its
One string I am going my way
Which has a strange sound.

This way the dust, that way the dust.
I listen to both sides
But I keep right on.
I remember the leaves sitting in judgment
And then winter.

I remember the rain with its bundle of roads.
The rain taking all its roads.
Nowhere.

Young as I am, old as I am,

I forget tomorrow, the blind man.
I forget the life among the buried windows.
The eyes in the curtains.
The wall
Growing through the immortelles.
I forget silence
The owner of the smile.

This must be what I wanted to be doing,
Walking at night between the two deserts,
Singing.

For the Anniversary of My Death

Every year without knowing it I have passed the day
When the last fires will wave to me
And the silence will set out
Tireless traveller
Like the beam of a lightless star

Then I will no longer
Find myself in life as in a strange garment
Surprised at the earth
And the love of one woman
And the shamelessness of men
As today writing after three days of rain
Hearing the wren sing and the falling cease
And bowing not knowing to what

Yesterday

My friend says I was not a good son
you understand
I say yes I understand

he says I did not go
to see my parents very often you know
and I say yes I know

even when I was living in the same city he says
maybe I would go there once
a month or maybe even less
I say oh yes

he says the last time I went to see my father
I say the last time I saw my father

he says the last time I saw my father
he was asking me about my life

how I was making out and he
went into the next room
to get something to give me

oh I say
feeling again the cold
of my father's hand the last time

he says and my father turned
in the doorway and saw me
look at my wristwatch and he
said you know I would like you to stay
and talk with me

oh yes I say

but if you are busy he said
I don't want you to feel that you
have to
just because I'm here

I say nothing

he says my father
said maybe
you have important work you are doing
or maybe you should be seeing
somebody I don't want to keep you

I look out the window
my friend is older than I am
he says and I told my father it was so
and I got up and left him then
you know

though there was nowhere I had to go
and nothing I had to do

Chord

While Keats wrote they were cutting down the sandalwood forests
while he listened to the nightingale they heard their own axes
          echoing through the forests

while he sat in the walled garden on the hill outside the city they
　　　　thought of their gardens dying far away on the mountain
while the sound of the words clawed at him they thought of their wives
while the tip of his pen travelled the iron they had coveted was
　　　　hateful to them
while he thought of the Grecian woods they bled under red flowers
while he dreamed of wine the trees were falling from the trees
while he felt his heart they were hungry and their faith was sick
while the song broke over him they were in a secret place and they
　　　　were cutting it forever
while he coughed they carried the trunks to the hole in the forest
　　　　the size of a foreign ship
while he groaned on the voyage to Italy they fell on the trails and
　　　　were broken
when he lay with the odes behind him the wood was sold for cannons
when he lay watching the window they came home and lay down
and an age arrived when everything was explained in another language

James Wright (1927–1980)

James Wright was born in Martins Ferry, Ohio. He served in the U.S. military before attending Kenyon College and the University of Washington. He taught at the University of Minnesota, Macalester College, Hunter College, and the State University of New York at Buffalo. His poetry books include The Green Wall *(1957, Yale Younger Poets Prize),* Saint Judas *(1959, Ohioana Award),* The Branch Will Not Break *(1963),* Shall We Gather at the River *(1968),* Collected Poems *(1971, Pulitzer Prize),* Two Citizens *(1973),* To a Blossoming Pear Tree *(1978),* This Journey *(1982), and* Above the River *(1992). Among his honors were two Guggenheim fellowships. James Wright died in New York City.*

A Blessing

Just off the highway to Rochester, Minnesota,
Twilight bounds softly forth on the grass.
And the eyes of those two Indian ponies
Darken with kindness.
They have come gladly out of the willows
To welcome my friend and me.
We step over the barbed wire into the pasture
Where they have been grazing all day, alone.
They ripple tensely, they can hardly contain their happiness
That we have come.
They bow shyly as wet swans. They love each other.
There is no loneliness like theirs.
At home once more,
They begin munching the young tufts of spring in the darkness.
I would like to hold the slenderer one in my arms,
For she has walked over to me
And nuzzled my left hand.
She is black and white,
Her mane falls wild on her forehead,
And the light breeze moves me to caress her long ear
That is delicate as the skin over a girl's wrist.
Suddenly I realize
That if I stepped out of my body I would break
Into blossom.

Autumn Begins in Martins Ferry, Ohio

In the Shreve High football stadium,
I think of Polacks nursing long beers in Tiltonsville,

And gray faces of Negroes in the blast furnace at Benwood,
And the ruptured night watchman of Wheeling Steel,
Dreaming of heroes.

All the proud fathers are ashamed to go home.
Their women cluck like starved pullets,
Dying for love.

Therefore,
Their sons grow suicidally beautiful
At the beginning of October,
And gallop terribly against each other's bodies.

Lying in a Hammock at William Duffy's Farm in Pine Island, Minnesota

Over my head, I see the bronze butterfly,
Asleep on the black trunk,
Blowing like a leaf in green shadow.
Down the ravine behind the empty house,
The cowbells follow one another
Into the distances of the afternoon.
To my right,
In a field of sunlight between two pines,
The droppings of last year's horses
Blaze up into golden stones.
I lean back, as the evening darkens and comes on.
A chicken hawk floats over, looking for home.
I have wasted my life.

In Response to a Rumor That the Oldest Whorehouse in Wheeling, West Virginia, Has Been Condemned

I will grieve alone,
As I strolled alone, years ago, down along
The Ohio shore.
I hid in the hobo jungle weeds
Upstream from the sewer main,
Pondering, gazing.

I saw, down river,
At Twenty-third and Water Streets

By the vinegar works,
The doors open in early evening.
Swinging their purses, the women
Poured down the long street to the river
And into the river.

I do not know how it was
They could drown every evening.
What time near dawn did they climb up the other shore,
Drying their wings?

For the river at Wheeling, West Virginia,
Has only two shores:
The one in hell, the other
In Bridgeport, Ohio.

And nobody would commit suicide, only
To find beyond death
Bridgeport, Ohio.

Donald Hall (1928–)

Donald Hall was born in New Haven, Connecticut. He attended Harvard University, Oxford University, and Stanford University, taught at the University of Michigan–Ann Arbor, and has been a freelance writer since 1975. His poetry books include Exiles and Marriages *(1955, Lamont Poetry Prize),* The Dark Houses *(1958),* A Roof of Tiger Lilies *(1964),* The Alligator Bride *(1969),* The Yellow Room *(1971),* The Town of Hill *(1975),* Kicking the Leaves *(1978),* The Toy Bone *(1979),* The Happy Man *(1986, Lenore Marshall Prize),* The One Day *(1988, National Book Critics Circle Award),* Old and New Poems *(1990),* The Museum of Clear Ideas *(1993),* The Old Life *(1996),* Without *(1998),* The Painted Bed *(2002), and* White Apples and the Taste of Stone *(2006). Among his honors are the Frost Medal and the Ruth Lilly Prize; in 2006 and 2007 he served as U.S. poet laureate. Donald Hall lives in Danbury, New Hampshire.*

My Son My Executioner

My son, my executioner,
    I take you in my arms,
Quiet and small and just astir
    And whom my body warms.

Sweet death, small son, our instrument
    Of immortality,
Your cries and hungers document
    Our bodily decay.

We twenty-five and twenty-two,
    Who seemed to live forever,
Observe enduring life in you
    And start to die together.

Digging

One midnight, after a day when lilies
lift themselves out of the ground while you watch them,
and you come into the house at dark
your fingers grubby with digging, your eyes
vague with the pleasure of digging,

let a wind raised from the South
climb through your bedroom window, lift you in its arms
—you have become as small as a seed—

and carry you out of the house, over the black garden,
spinning and fluttering,

and drop you in cracked ground.
The dirt will be cool, rough to your clasped skin
like a man you have never known.
You will die into the ground
in a dead sleep, surrendered to water.

You will wake suffering
a widening pain in your side, a breach
gapped in your tight ribs
where a green shoot struggles to lift itself upwards
through the tomb of your dead flesh

to the sun, to the air of your garden
where you will blossom
in the shape of your own self, thoughtless
with flowers, speaking
to bees, in the language of green and yellow, white and red.

Philip Levine (1928–)

Philip Levine was born in Detroit, Michigan. He attended Wayne State University and the University of Iowa and has taught at California State University–Fresno, Tufts University, and New York University. His poetry books include Not This Pig *(1968),* They Feed They Lion *(1972),* 1933 *(1974),* The Names of the Lost *(1976, Lenore Marshall Award),* 7 Years from Somewhere *(1979),* Ashes *(1979, National Book Award and National Book Critics Circle Award),* One for the Rose *(1981),* Sweet Will *(1985),* A Walk with Tom Jefferson *(1988),* What Work Is *(1991, National Book Award),* The Simple Truth *(1994, Pulitzer Prize),* The Mercy *(1999),* Breath *(2004), and* News of the World *(2009). Among his honors are National Endowment for the Arts and Guggenheim fellowships, the Frank O'Hara Prize, and the Ruth Lilly Prize. In 2011/2012 he served as U.S. Poet Laureate. Philip Levine lives in Fresno, California, and New York City.*

Animals Are Passing from Our Lives

It's wonderful how I jog
on four honed-down ivory toes
my massive buttocks slipping
like oiled parts with each light step.

I'm to market. I can smell
the sour, grooved block, I can smell
the blade that opens the hole
and the pudgy white fingers

that shake out the intestines
like a hankie. In my dreams
the snouts drool on the marble,
suffering children, suffering flies,

suffering the consumers
who won't meet their steady eyes
for fear they could see. The boy
who drives me along believes

that any moment I'll fall
on my side and drum my toes
like a typewriter or squeal
and shit like a new housewife

discovering television,
or that I'll turn like a beast
cleverly to hook his teeth
with my teeth. No. Not this pig.

They Feed They Lion

Out of burlap sacks, out of bearing butter,
Out of black bean and wet slate bread,
Out of the acids of rage, the candor of tar,
Out of creosate, gasoline, drive shafts, wooden dollies,
They Lion grow.

            Out of the gray hills
Of industrial barns, out of rain, out of bus ride,
West Virginia to Kiss My Ass, out of buried aunties,
Mothers hardening like pounded stumps, out of stumps,
Out of the bones' need to sharpen and the muscles' to stretch,
They Lion grow.

            Earth is eating trees, fence posts,
Gutted cars, earth is calling her little ones,
"Come home, Come home!" From pig balls,
From the ferocity of pig driven to holiness,
From the furred ear and the full jowl come
The repose of the hung belly, from the purpose
They Lion grow.

            From the sweet glues of the trotters
Come the sweet kinks of the fist, from the full flower
Of the hams the thorax of caves,
From "Bow Down" come "Rise Up,"
Come they Lion from the reeds of shovels,
The grained arm that pulls the hands,
They Lion grow.

            From my five arms and all my hands,
From all my white sins forgiven, they feed,
From my car passing under the stars,
They Lion, from my children inherit,
From the oak turned to a wall, they Lion,

From they sack and they belly opened
And all that was hidden burning on the oil-stained earth
They feed they Lion and he comes.

You Can Have It

My brother comes home from work
and climbs the stairs to our room.
I can hear the bed groan and his shoes drop
one by one. You can have it, he says.

The moonlight streams in the window
and his unshaven face is whitened
like the face of the moon. He will sleep
long after noon and waken to find me gone.

Thirty years will pass before I remember
that moment when suddenly I knew each man
has one brother who dies when he sleeps
and sleeps when he rises to face this life,

and that together they are only one man
sharing a heart that always labors, hands
yellowed and cracked, a mouth that gasps
for breath and asks, Am I gonna make it?

All night at the ice plant he had fed
the chute its silvery blocks, and then I
stacked cases of orange soda for the children
of Kentucky, one gray boxcar at a time

with always two more waiting. We were twenty
for such a short time and always in
the wrong clothes, crusted with dirt
and sweat. I think now we were never twenty.

In 1948 in the city of Detroit, founded
by de la Mothe Cadillac for the distant purposes
of Henry Ford, no one wakened or died,
no one walked the streets or stoked a furnace,

for there was no such year, and now
that year has fallen off all the old newspapers,
calendars, doctors' appointments, bonds,
wedding certificates, drivers licenses.

The city slept. The snow turned to ice.
The ice to standing pools or rivers
racing in the gutters. Then bright grass rose
between the thousands of cracked squares,

and that grass died. I give you back 1948.
I give you all the years from then
to the coming one. Give me back the moon
with its frail light falling across a face.

Give me back my young brother, hard
and furious, with wide shoulders and a curse
for God and burning eyes that look upon
all creation and say, You can have it.

The Simple Truth

I bought a dollar and a half's worth of small red potatoes,
took them home, boiled them in their jackets
and ate them for dinner with a little butter and salt.
Then I walked through the dried fields
on the edge of town. In middle June the light
hung on in the dark furrows at my feet,
and in the mountain oaks overhead the birds
were gathering for the night, the jays and mockers
squawking back and forth, the finches still darting
into the dusty light. The woman who sold me
the potatoes was from Poland; she was someone
out of my childhood in a pink spangled sweater and sunglasses
praising the perfection of all her fruits and vegetables
at the road-side stand and urging me to taste
even the pale, raw sweet corn trucked all the way,
she swore, from New Jersey. "Eat, eat," she said,
"Even if you don't I'll say you did."
                                        Some things
you know all your life. They are so simple and true

they must be said without elegance, meter and rhyme,
they must be laid on the table beside the salt shaker,
the glass of water, the absence of light gathering
in the shadows of picture frames, they must be
naked and alone, they must stand for themselves.
My friend Henri and I arrived at this together in 1965
before I went away, before he began to kill himself,
and the two of us to betray our love. Can you taste
what I'm saying? It is onions or potatoes, a pinch
of simple salt, the wealth of melting butter, it is obvious,
it stays in the back of your throat like a truth
you never uttered because the time was always wrong,
it stays there for the rest of your life, unspoken,
made of that dirt we call earth, the metal we call salt,
in a form we have no words for, and you live on it.

Anne Sexton (1928–1974)

Anne Sexton was born in Newton, Massachusetts. She attended Garland Junior College in Boston and worked briefly as a fashion model and high school teacher before joining Boston University's creative writing faculty in 1970. Her poetry books include To Bedlam and Part Way Back *(1960),* All My Pretty Ones *(1962),* Live or Die *(1966, Pulitzer Prize),* Love Poems *(1969),* Transformations *(1971),* The Book of Folly *(1972),* The Death Notebooks *(1974), and* The Awful Rowing Toward God *(1975). Among her honors were the 1967 Shelley Memorial Award and a Guggenheim fellowship. Anne Sexton committed suicide in Weston, Massachusetts.*

Her Kind

I have gone out, a possessed witch,
haunting the black air, braver at night;
dreaming evil, I have done my hitch
over the plain houses, light by light:
lonely thing, twelve-fingered, out of mind.
A woman like that is not a woman, quite.
I have been her kind.

I have found the warm caves in the woods,
filled them with skillets, carvings, shelves,
closets, silks, innumerable goods;
fixed the suppers for the worms and the elves:
whining, rearranging the disaligned.
A woman like that is misunderstood.
I have been her kind.

I have ridden in your cart, driver,
waved my nude arms at villages going by,
learning the last bright routes, survivor
where your flames still bite my thigh
and my ribs crack where your wheels wind.
A woman like that is not ashamed to die.
I have been her kind.

The Abortion

Somebody who should have been born is gone.

Just as the earth puckered its mouth,
each bud puffing out from its knot,
I changed my shoes, and then drove south.

Up past the Blue Mountains, where
Pennsylvania humps on endlessly,
wearing, like a crayoned cat, its green hair,

its roads sunken in like a gray washboard;
where, in truth, the ground cracks evilly,
a dark socket from which the coal has poured,

Somebody who should have been born is gone.

the grass as bristly and stout as chives,
and me wondering when the ground would break,
and me wondering how anything fragile survives;

up in Pennsylvania, I met a little man,
not Rumpelstiltskin, at all, at all . . .
he took the fullness that love began.

Returning north, even the sky grew thin
like a high window looking nowhere.
The road was as flat as a sheet of tin.

Somebody who should have been born is gone.

Yes, woman, such logic will lead
to loss without death. Or say what you meant,
you coward . . . this baby that I bleed.

Wanting to Die

Since you ask, most days I cannot remember.
I walk in my clothing, unmarked by that voyage.
Then the almost unnameable lust returns.

Even then I have nothing against life.
I know well the grass blades you mention,
the furniture you have placed under the sun.

But suicides have a special language.
Like carpenters they want to know *which tools*.
They never ask *why build*.

Twice I have so simply declared myself,
have possessed the enemy, eaten the enemy,
have taken on his craft, his magic.

In this way, heavy and thoughtful,
warmer than oil or water,
I have rested, drooling at the mouth-hole.

I did not think of my body at needle point.
Even the cornea and the leftover urine were gone.
Suicides have already betrayed the body.

Still-born, they don't always die,
but dazzled, they can't forget a drug so sweet
that even children would look on and smile.

To thrust all that life under your tongue!—
that, all by itself, becomes a passion.
Death's a sad bone; bruised, you'd say,

and yet she waits for me, year after year,
to so delicately undo an old wound,
to empty my breath from its bad prison.

Balanced there, suicides sometimes meet,
raging at the fruit, a pumped-up moon,
leaving the bread they mistook for a kiss,

leaving the page of the book carelessly open,
something unsaid, the phone off the hook
and the love, whatever it was, an infection.

In Celebration of My Uterus

Everyone in me is a bird.
I am beating all my wings.
They wanted to cut you out
but they will not.
They said you were immeasurably empty
but you are not.
They said you were sick unto dying
but they were wrong.
You are singing like a school girl.
You are not torn.

Sweet weight,
in celebration of the woman I am
and of the soul of the woman I am
and of the central creature and its delight
I sing for you. I dare to live.
Hello, spirit. Hello, cup.
Fasten, cover. Cover that does contain.
Hello to the soil of the fields.
Welcome, roots.

Each cell has a life.
There is enough here to please a nation.
It is enough that the populace own these goods.
Any person, any commonwealth would say of it,
"It is good this year that we may plant again
and think forward to a harvest.
A blight had been forecast and has been cast out."
Many women are singing together of this:
one is in a shoe factory cursing the machine,
one is at the aquarium tending a seal,
one is dull at the wheel of her Ford,
one is at the toll gate collecting,
one is tying the cord of a calf in Arizona,
one is straddling a cello in Russia,
one is shifting pots on the stove in Egypt,
one is painting her bedroom walls moon color,
one is dying but remembering a breakfast,
one is stretching on her mat in Thailand,
one is wiping the ass of her child,
one is staring out the window of a train
in the middle of Wyoming and one is

anywhere and some are everywhere and all
seem to be singing, although some can not
sing a note.

Sweet weight,
in celebration of the woman I am
let me carry a ten-foot scarf,
let me drum for the nineteen-year-olds,
let me carry bowls for the offering
(if that is my part).
Let me study the cardiovascular tissue,
let me examine the angular distance of meteors,
let me suck on the stems of flowers
(if that is my part).
Let me make certain tribal figures
(if that is my part).
For this thing the body needs
let me sing
for the supper,
for the kissing,
for the correct
yes.

Rowing

A story, a story!
(Let it go. Let it come.)
I was stamped out like a Plymouth fender
into this world.
First came the crib
with its glacial bars.
Then dolls
and the devotion to their plastic mouths.
Then there was school,
the little straight rows of chairs,
blotting my name over and over,
but undersea all the time,
a stranger whose elbows wouldn't work.
Then there was life
with its cruel houses
and people who seldom touched—
though touch is all—
but I grew,

like a pig in a trenchcoat I grew,
and then there were many strange apparitions,
the nagging rain, the sun turning into poison
and all of that, saws working through my heart,
but I grew, I grew,
and God was there like an island I had not rowed to,
still ignorant of Him, my arms and my legs worked,
and I grew, I grew,
I wore rubies and bought tomatoes
and now, in my middle age,
about nineteen in the head I'd say,
I am rowing, I am rowing
though the oarlocks stick and are rusty
and the sea blinks and rolls
like a worried eyeball,
but I am rowing, I am rowing
though the wind pushes me back
and I know that that island will not be perfect,
it will have the flaws of life,
the absurdities of the dinner table,
but there will be a door
and I will open it
and I will get rid of the rat inside of me,
the gnawing pestilential rat.
God will take it with his two hands
and embrace it.

As the African says:
This is my tale which I have told,
if it be sweet, if it be not sweet,
take somewhere else and let some return to me.
This story ends with me still rowing.

Adrienne Rich (1929–)

Adrienne Rich was born in Baltimore, Maryland. Her first book, A Change of World, *was selected by W. H. Auden for the 1951 Yale Younger Poets Prize, and her numerous books since have earned her the National Book Award, two National Book Critics Circle Awards, the Ruth Lilly Prize, the Wallace Stevens Award, a MacArthur fellowship, and the National Book Foundation's Medal for Distinguished Contribution to American Letters, among many other honors. Her most recent books of poetry are* Tonight No Poetry Will Serve *(2011) and* Telephone Ringing in the Labyrinth *(2007). For the Library of America, she edited Muriel Rukeyser's* Selected Poems. *A Human Eye: Essays on Art in Society appeared in April 2009. She lives in California.*

Orion

Far back when I went zig-zagging
through tamarack pastures
you were my genius, you
my cast-iron Viking, my helmed
lion-heart king in prison.
Years later now you're young

my fierce half-brother, staring
down from that simplified west
your breast open, your belt dragged down
by an oldfashioned thing, a sword
the last bravado you won't give over
though it weighs you down as you stride

and the stars in it are dim
and maybe have stopped burning.
But you burn, and I know it;
as I throw back my head to take you in
an old transfusion happens again:
divine astronomy is nothing to it.

Indoors I bruise and blunder,
break faith, leave ill enough
alone, a dead child born in the dark.
Night cracks up over the chimney,
pieces of time, frozen geodes
come showering down in the grate.

A man reaches behind my eyes
and finds them empty
a woman's head turns away
from my head in the mirror
children are dying my death
and eating crumbs of my life.

Pity is not your forte.
Calmly you ache up there
pinned aloft in your crow's nest,
my speechless pirate!
You take it all for granted
and when I look you back

it's with a starlike eye
shooting its cold and egotistical spear
where it can do least damage.
Breathe deep! No hurt, no pardon
out here in the cold with you
you with your back to the wall.

Planetarium

Thinking of Caroline Herschel (1750–1848)
astronomer, sister of William; and others.

A woman in the shape of a monster
a monster in the shape of a woman
the skies are full of them

a woman   'in the snow
among the Clocks and instruments
or measuring the ground with poles'

in her 98 years to discover
8 comets

she whom the moon ruled
like us
levitating into the night sky
riding the polished lenses

Galaxies of women, there
doing penance for impetuousness
ribs chilled
in those spaces   of the mind

An eye,

            'virile, precise and absolutely certain'
            from the mad webs of Uranusborg

                                        encountering the NOVA

every impulse of light exploding
from the core
as life flies out of us

            Tycho whispering at last
            'Let me not seem to have lived in vain'

What we see, we see
and seeing is changing

the light that shrivels a mountain
and leaves a man alive

Heartbeat of the pulsar
heart sweating through my body

The radio impulse
pouring in from Taurus

            I am bombarded yet   I stand

I have been standing all my life in the
direct path of a battery of signals
the most accurately transmitted most
untranslateable language in the universe
I am a galactic cloud so deep   so invo-
luted that a light wave could take 15
years to travel through me   And has
taken   I am an instrument in the shape
of a woman trying to translate pulsations
into images   for the relief of the body
and the reconstruction of the mind.

A Valediction Forbidding Mourning

My swirling wants. Your frozen lips.
The grammar turned and attacked me.
Themes, written under duress.
Emptiness of the notations.

They gave me a drug that slowed the healing of wounds.

I want you to see this before I leave:
the experience of repetition as death
the failure of criticism to locate the pain
the poster in the bus that said:
my bleeding is under control

A red plant in a cemetery of plastic wreaths.

A last attempt: the language is a dialect called metaphor.
These images go unglossed: hair, glacier, flashlight.
When I think of a landscape I am thinking of a time.
When I talk of taking a trip I mean forever.
I could say: those mountains have a meaning
but further than that I could not say.

To do something very common, in my own way.

From *Twenty-One Love Poems*

XIII

The rules break like a thermometer,
quicksilver spills across the charted systems,
we're out in a country that has no language
no laws, we're chasing the raven and the wren
through gorges unexplored since dawn
whatever we do together is pure invention
the maps they gave us were out of date
by years . . . we're driving through the desert
wondering if the water will hold out
the hallucinations turn to simple villages

the music on the radio comes clear—
neither *Rosenkavalier* nor *Götterdämmerung*
but a woman's voice singing old songs
with new words, with a quiet bass, a flute
plucked and fingered by women outside the law.

Gregory Corso (1930–2001)

Gregory Nunzio Corso was born in New York City. He grew up under asocial circumstances and ran afoul of the law as a teenager. Self-educated in prison, he later worked in a variety of jobs, as well as teaching at the State University of New York at Buffalo. His poetry books include The Vestal Lady on Brattle and Other Poems *(1955),* Gasoline *(1958),* The Happy Birthday of Death *(1960),* Long Live Man *(1962),* There Is Yet Time to Run Back Through Life and Expiate All That's Been Sadly Done *(1965),* Elegiac Feelings American *(1970),* Herald of the Autochthonic Spirit *(1981), and* Mindfield *(1989). Gregory Corso died from cancer in Minneapolis, Minnesota.*

Marriage

Should I get married? Should I be good?
Astound the girl next door with my velvet suit and faustus hood?
Don't take her to movies but to cemeteries
tell all about werewolf bathtubs and forked clarinets
then desire her and kiss her and all the preliminaries
and she going just so far and I understanding why
not getting angry saying You must feel! It's beautiful to feel!
Instead take her in my arms lean against an old crooked tombstone
and woo her the entire night the constellations in the sky—

When she introduces me to her parents
back straightened, hair finally combed, strangled by a tie,
should I sit knees together on their 3rd degree sofa
and not ask Where's the bathroom?
How else to feel other than I am,
often thinking Flash Gordon soap—
O how terrible it must be for a young man
seated before a family and the family thinking
We never saw him before! He wants our Mary Lou!
After tea and homemade cookies they ask What do you do for a
                                         living?

Should I tell them: Would they like me then?
Say All right get married, we're losing a daughter
but we're gaining a son—
And should I then ask Where's the bathroom?

O God, and the wedding! All her family and her friends
and only a handful of mine all scroungy and bearded
just wait to get at the drinks and food—

And the priest! he looking at me as if I masturbated
asking me Do you take this woman for your lawful wedded wife?
And I trembling what to say say Pie Glue!
I kiss the bride all those corny men slapping me on the back
She's all yours, boy! Ha-ha-ha!
And in their eyes you could see some obscene honeymoon going

on—

Then all that absurd rice and clanky cans and shoes
Niagara Falls! Hordes of us! Husbands! Wives! Flowers!

Chocolates!

All streaming into cozy hotels
All going to do the same thing tonight
The indifferent clerk he knowing what was going to happen
The lobby zombies they knowing what
The whistling elevator man he knowing
The winking bellboy knowing
Everybody knowing! I'd be almost inclined not to do anything!
Stay up all night! Stare that hotel clerk in the eye!
Screaming: I deny honeymoon! I deny honeymoon!
running rampant into those almost climactic suites
yelling Radio belly! Cat shovel!
O I'd live in Niagara forever! in a dark cave beneath the Falls
I'd sit there the Mad Honeymooner
devising ways to break marriages, a scourge of bigamy
a saint of divorce—

But I should get married I should be good
How nice it'd be to come home to her
and sit by the fireplace and she in the kitchen
aproned young and lovely wanting my baby
and so happy about me she burns the roast beef
and comes crying to me and I get up from my big papa chair
saying Christmas teeth! Radiant brains! Apple deaf!
God what a husband I'd make! Yes, I should get married!
So much to do! like sneaking into Mr Jones' house late at night
and cover his golf clubs with 1920 Norwegian books
Like hanging a picture of Rimbaud on the lawnmower
like pasting Tannu Tuva postage stamps all over the picket fence
like when Mrs Kindhead comes to collect for the Community Chest
grab her and tell her There are unfavorable omens in the sky!
And when the mayor comes to get my vote tell him
When are you going to stop people killing whales!

And when the milkman comes leave him a note in the bottle
Penguin dust, bring me penguin dust, I want penguin dust—

Yet if I should get married and it's Connecticut and snow
and she gives birth to a child and I am sleepless, worn,
up for nights, head bowed against a quiet window, the past behind
              me,

finding myself in the most common of situations a trembling man
knowledged with responsibility not twig-smear nor Roman coin
              soup—

O what would that be like!
Surely I'd give it for a nipple a rubber Tacitus
For a rattle a bag of broken Bach records
Tack Della Francesca all over its crib
Sew the Greek alphabet on its bib
And build for its playpen a roofless Parthenon

No, I doubt I'd be that kind of father
not rural not snow no quiet window
but hot smelly tight New York City
seven flights up, roaches and rats in the walls
a fat Reichian wife screeching over potatoes Get a job!
And five nose running brats in love with Batman
And the neighbors all toothless and dry haired
like those hag masses of the 18th century
all wanting to come in and watch TV
The landlord wants his rent
Grocery store Blue Cross Gas & Electric Knights of Columbus
Impossible to lie back and dream Telephone snow, ghost parking—
No! I should not get married I should never get married!
But—imagine If I were married to a beautiful sophisticated woman
tall and pale wearing an elegant black dress and long black gloves
holding a cigarette holder in one hand and a highball in the other
and we lived high up in a penthouse with a huge window
from which we could see all of New York and ever farther on
              clearer days
No, can't imagine myself married to that pleasant prison dream—

O but what about love? I forget love
not that I am incapable of love
it's just that I see love as odd as wearing shoes—
I never wanted to marry a girl who was like my mother

And Ingrid Bergman was always impossible
And there's maybe a girl now but she's already married
And I don't like men and—
but there's got to be somebody!
Because what if I'm 60 years old and not married,
all alone in a furnished room with pee stains on my underwear
and everybody else is married! All the universe married but me!

Ah, yet well I know that were a woman possible as I am possible
then marriage would be possible—
Like SHE in her lonely alien gaud waiting her Egyptian lover
so I wait—bereft of 2,000 years and the bath of life.

Gary Snyder (1930–)

Gary Snyder was born in San Francisco and grew up in Washington and Oregon. He attended Reed College, Indiana University, and the University of California–Berkeley. He traveled extensively in the Far East and has taught at the University of California–Berkeley and the University of California–Davis. His numerous poetry books include Riprap *(1959),* The Back Country *(1968),* Regarding Wave *(1970),* Turtle Island *(1974, Pulitzer Prize),* Axe Handles *(1983, American Book Award),* Left Out in the Rain *(1986),* No Nature *(1993),* Mountains and Rivers Without End *(1996),* The Gary Snyder Reader *(1999), and* Danger on Peaks *(2004). Among his honors are Bollingen and Guggenheim fellowships, a Shelley Memorial Award, the American Academy of Arts and Letters Award, the Bess Hokin Prize, and the 2008 Ruth Lilly Prize. Gary Snyder lives in California.*

Hay for the Horses

He had driven half the night
From far down San Joaquin
Through Mariposa, up the
Dangerous mountain roads,
And pulled in at eight a.m.
With his big truckload of hay
    behind the barn.
With winch and ropes and hooks
We stacked the bales up clean
To splintery redwood rafters
High in the dark, flecks of alfalfa
Whirling through shingle-cracks of light,
Itch of haydust in the
    sweaty shirt and shoes.
At lunchtime under Black oak
Out in the hot corral,
—The old mare nosing lunchpails,
Grasshoppers crackling in the weeds—
"I'm sixty-eight" he said,
"I first bucked hay when I was seventeen.
I thought, that day I started,
I sure would hate to do this all my life.
And dammit, that's just what
I've gone and done."

Riprap

Lay down these words
Before your mind like rocks.
          placed solid, by hands
In choice of place, set
Before the body of the mind
          in space and time:
Solidity of bark, leaf, or wall
          riprap of things:
Cobble of milky way,
          straying planets,
These poems, people,
          lost ponies with
Dragging saddles—
          and rocky sure-foot trails.
The worlds like an endless
          four-dimensional
Game of *Go*.
          ants and pebbles
In the thin loam, each rock a word
          a creek-washed stone
Granite: ingrained
          with torment of fire and weight
Crystal and sediment linked hot
          all change, in thoughts,
As well as things.

Mid-August at Sourdough Mountain Lookout

Down valley a smoke haze
Three days heat, after five days rain
Pitch glows on the fir-cones
Across rocks and meadows
Swarms of new flies.

I cannot remember things I once read
A few friends, but they are in cities.
Drinking cold snow-water from a tin cup
Looking down for miles
Through high still air.

Derek Walcott (1930–)

Derek Walcott was born in Castries, St. Lucia, West Indies, where he attended St. Mary's College and the University of the West Indies in Kingston, Jamaica. He taught secondary school in Grenada and Jamaica, wrote for local newspapers, cofounded the St. Lucia Arts Guild, and founded the Trinidad Theatre Workshop. From 1981 to 2007 he taught at Boston University and is currently scholar in residence at the University of Alberta in Edmonton, Canada. His poetry books include In a Green Night *(1962),* Selected Poems *(1964),* The Gulf *(1970),* Another Life *(1973),* Sea Grapes *(1976),* The Star-Apple Kingdom *(1979),* The Fortunate Traveller *(1981),* Midsummer *(1984),* The Arkansas Testament *(1987),* Omeros *(1990),* The Bounty *(1997),* Tiepolo's Hound *(2000),* The Prodigal *(2004), and* White Egrets *(2010, T. S. Eliot Prize). Among his honors are Ingram Merrill, Guggenheim, and MacArthur fellowships; an Obie for his play* Dream on Monkey Mountain; *and the 1992 Nobel Prize for literature. Walcott lives in St. Lucia and New York.*

A Far Cry from Africa

A wind is ruffling the tawny pelt
Of Africa. Kikuyu, quick as flies,
Batten upon the bloodstreams of the veldt.
Corpses are scattered through a paradise.
Only the worm, colonel of carrion, cries:
"Waste no compassion on these separate dead!"
Statistics justify and scholars seize
The salients of colonial policy.
What is that to the white child hacked in bed?
To savages, expendable as Jews?

Threshed out by beaters, the long rushes break
In a white dust of ibises whose cries
Have wheeled since civilization's dawn
From the parched river or beast-teeming plain.
The violence of beast on beast is read
As natural law, but upright man
Seeks his divinity by inflicting pain.
Delirious as these worried beasts, his wars
Dance to the tightened carcass of a drum,
While he calls courage still that native dread
Of the white peace contracted by the dead.

Again brutish necessity wipes its hands
Upon the napkin of a dirty cause, again
A waste of our compassion, as with Spain,

The gorilla wrestles with the superman.
I who am poisoned with the blood of both,
Where shall I turn, divided to the vein?
I who have cursed
The drunken officer of British rule, how choose
Between this Africa and the English tongue I love?
Betray them both, or give back what they give?
How can I face such slaughter and be cool?
How can I turn from Africa and live?

Sea Grapes

That sail which leans on light,
tired of islands,
a schooner beating up the Caribbean

for home, could be Odysseus,
home-bound on the Aegean;
that father and husband's

longing, under gnarled sour grapes, is
like the adulterer hearing Nausicaa's name
in every gull's outcry.

This brings nobody peace. The ancient war
between obsession and responsibility
will never finish and has been the same

for the sea-wanderer or the one on shore
now wriggling on his sandals to walk home,
since Troy sighed its last flame,

and the blind giant's boulder heaved the trough
from whose groundswell the great hexameters come
to the conclusions of exhausted surf.

The classics can console. But not enough.

From *The Schooner* Flight

11. After the Storm

There's a fresh light that follows a storm
while the whole sea still havoc; in its bright wake
I saw the veiled face of Maria Concepcion
marrying the ocean, then drifting away
in the widening lace of her bridal train
with white gulls her bridesmaids, till she was gone.
I wanted nothing after that day.
Across my own face, like the face of the sun,
a light rain was falling, with the sea calm.

Fall gently, rain, on the sea's upturned face
like a girl showering; make these islands fresh
as Shabine once knew them! Let every trace,
every hot road, smell like clothes she just press
and sprinkle with drizzle. I finish dream;
whatever the rain wash and the sun iron:
the white clouds, the sea and sky with one seam,
is clothes enough for my nakedness.
Though my *Flight* never pass the incoming tide
of this inland sea beyond the loud reefs
of the final Bahamas, I am satisfied
if my hand gave voice to one people's grief.
Open the map. More islands there, man,
than peas on a tin plate, all different size,
one thousand in the Bahamas alone,
from mountains to low scrub with coral keys,
and from this bowsprit, I bless every town,
the blue smell of smoke in hills behind them,
and the one small road winding down them like twine
to the roofs below; I have only one theme:

The bowsprit, the arrow, the longing, the lunging heart—
the flight to a target whose aim we'll never know,
vain search for one island that heals with its harbour
and a guiltless horizon, where the almond's shadow
doesn't injure the sand. There are so many islands!
As many islands as the stars at night
on that branched tree from which meteors are shaken
like falling fruit around the schooner *Flight*.
But things must fall, and so it always was,

on one hand Venus, on the other Mars;
fall, and are one, just as this earth is one
island in archipelagoes of stars.
My first friend was the sea. Now, is my last.
I stop talking now. I work, then I read,
cotching under a lantern hooked to the mast.
I try to forget what happiness was,
and when that don't work, I study the stars.
Sometimes is just me, and the soft-scissored foam
as the deck turn white and the moon open
a cloud like a door, and the light over me
is a road in white moonlight taking me home.
Shabine sang to you from the depths of the sea.

The Light of the World

> *Kaya now, got to have kaya now,*
> *Got to have kaya now,*
> *For the rain is falling.*
> —BOB MARLEY

Marley was rocking on the transport's stereo
and the beauty was humming the choruses quietly.
I could see where the lights on the planes of her cheek
streaked and defined them; if this were a portrait
you'd leave the highlights for last, these lights
silkened her black skin; I'd have put in an earring,
something simple, in good gold, for contrast, but she
wore no jewelry. I imagined a powerful and sweet
odour coming from her, as from a still panther,
and the head was nothing else but heraldic.
When she looked at me, then away from me politely
because any staring at strangers is impolite,
it was like a statue, like a black Delacroix's
Liberty Leading the People, the gently bulging
whites of her eyes, the carved ebony mouth,
the heft of the torso solid, and a woman's,
but gradually even that was going in the dusk,
except the line of her profile, and the highlit cheek,
and I thought, O Beauty, you are the light of the world!

It was not the only time I would think of that phrase
in the sixteen-seater transport that hummed between

Gros Islet and the Market, with its grit of charcoal
and the litter of vegetables after Saturday's sales,
and the roaring rum-shops, outside whose bright doors
you saw drunk women on pavements, the saddest of all things,
winding up their week, winding down their week.
The Market, as it closed on this Saturday night,
remembered a childhood of wandering gas lanterns
hung on poles at street corners, and the old roar
of vendors and traffic, when the lamplighter climbed,
hooked the lantern on its pole, and moved on to another,
and the children turned their faces to its moth, their
eyes white as their nighties; the Market
itself was closed in its involved darkness
and the shadows quarrelled for bread in the shops,
or quarrelled for the formal custom of quarrelling
in the electric rum-shops. I remember the shadows.

The van was slowly filling in the darkening depot.
I sat in the front seat, I had no need for time.
I looked at two girls, one in a yellow bodice
and yellow shorts, with a flower in her hair,
and lusted in peace, the other less interesting.
That evening I had walked the streets of the town
where I was born and grew up, thinking of my mother
with her white hair tinted by the dyeing dusk,
and the tilting box houses that seemed perverse
in their cramp; I had peered into parlours
with half-closed jalousies, at the dim furniture,
Morris chairs, a centre table with wax flowers,
and the lithograph of *Christ of the Sacred Heart,*
vendors still selling to the empty streets—
sweets, nuts, sodden chocolates, nut cakes, mints.

An old woman with a straw hat over her headkerchief
hobbled towards us with a basket; somewhere,
some distance off, was a heavier basket
that she couldn't carry. She was in a panic.
She said to the driver: "*Pas quittez moi à terre,*"
which is, in her patois: "Don't leave me stranded,"
which is, in her history and that of her people:
"Don't leave me on earth," or, by a shift of stress:
"Don't leave me the earth" [for an inheritance];
"*Pas quittez moi à terre,* Heavenly transport,
Don't leave me on earth, I've had enough of it."

The bus filled in the dark with heavy shadows
that would not be left on earth; no, that would be left
on the earth, and would have to make out.
Abandonment was something they had grown used to.

And I had abandoned them, I knew that there
sitting in the transport, in the sea-quiet dusk,
with men hunched in canoes, and the orange lights
from the Vigie headland, black boats on the water;
I, who could never solidify my shadow
to be one of their shadows, had left them their earth,
their white rum quarrels, and their coal bags,
their hatred of corporals, of all authority.
I was deeply in love with the woman by the window.
I wanted to be going home with her this evening.
I wanted her to have the key to our small house
by the beach at Gros Islet; I wanted her to change
into a smooth white nightie that would pour like water
over the black rocks of her breasts, to lie
simply beside her by the ring of a brass lamp
with a kerosene wick, and tell her in silence
that her hair was like a hill forest at night,
that a trickle of rivers was in her armpits,
that I would buy her Benin if she wanted it,
and never leave her on earth. But the others, too.

Because I felt a great love that could bring me to tears,
and a pity that prickled my eyes like a nettle,
I was afraid I might suddenly start sobbing
on the public transport with the Marley going,
and a small boy peering over the shoulders
of the driver and me at the lights coming,
at the rush of the road in the country darkness,
with lamps in the houses on the small hills,
and thickets of stars; I had abandoned them,
I had left them on earth, I left them to sing
Marley's songs of a sadness as real as the smell
of rain on dry earth, or the smell of damp sand,
and the bus felt warm with their neighbourliness,
their consideration, and the polite partings
in the light of its headlamps. In the blare,
in the thud-sobbing music, the claiming scent
that came from their bodies. I wanted the transport
to continue forever, for no one to descend

and say a good night in the beams of the lamps
and take the crooked path up to the lit door,
guided by fireflies; I wanted her beauty
to come into the warmth of considerate wood,
to the relieved rattling of enamel plates
in the kitchen, and the tree in the yard,
but I came to my stop. Outside the Halcyon Hotel.
The lounge would be full of transients like myself.
Then I would walk with the surf up the beach.
I got off the van without saying good night.
Good night would be full of inexpressible love.
They went on in their transport, they left me on earth.

Then, a few yards ahead, the van stopped. A man
shouted my name from the transport window.
I walked up towards him. He held out something.
A pack of cigarettes had dropped from my pocket.
He gave it to me. I turned, hiding my tears.
There was nothing they wanted, nothing I could give them
but this thing I have called "The Light of the World."

From *Omeros,* Book VII

Chapter LXIV

I

I sang of quiet Achille, Afolabe's son,
who never ascended in an elevator,
who had no passport, since the horizon needs none,

never begged nor borrowed, was nobody's waiter,
whose end, when it comes, will be a death by water
(which is not for this book, which will remain unknown

and unread by him). I sang the only slaughter
that brought him delight, and that from necessity—
of fish, sang the channels of his back in the sun.

I sang our wide country, the Caribbean Sea.
Who hated shoes, whose soles were as cracked as a stone,
who was gentle with ropes, who had one suit alone,

whom no man dared insult and who insulted no one,
whose grin was a white breaker cresting, but whose frown
was a growing thunderhead, whose fist of iron

would do me a greater honour if it held on
to my casket's oarlocks than mine lifting his own
when both anchors are lowered in the one island,

but now the idyll dies, the goblet is broken,
and rainwater trickles down the brown cheek of a jar
from the clay of Choiseul. So much left unspoken

by my chirping nib! And my earth-door lies ajar.
I lie wrapped in a flour-sack sail. The clods thud
on my rope-lowered canoe. Rasping shovels scrape

a dry rain of dirt on its hold, but turn your head
when the sea-almond rattles or the rust-leaved grape
from the shells of my unpharaonic pyramid

towards paper shredded by the wind and scattered
like white gulls that separate their names from the foam
and nod to a fisherman with his khaki dog

that skitters from the wave-crash, then frown at his form
for one swift second. In its earth-trough, my pirogue
with its brass-handled oarlocks is sailing. Not from

but with them, with Hector, with Maud in the rhythm
of her beds trowelled over, with a swirling log
lifting its mossed head from the swell; let the deep hymn

of the Caribbean continue my epilogue;
may waves remove their shawls as my mourners walk home
to their rusted villages, good shoes in one hand,

passing a boy who walked through the ignorant foam,
and saw a sail going out or else coming in,
and watched asterisks of rain puckering the sand.

Miller Williams (1930–)

Miller Williams was born in Hoxie, Arkansas. He attended Arkansas State College and the University of Arkansas, teaching biology at a number of colleges before joining the English faculties at Louisiana State University, Loyola University, and (since 1971) the University of Arkansas. His poetry books include A Circle of Stone *(1964),* So Long at the Fair *(1968),* The Only World There Is *(1971),* Halfway from Hoxie *(1973),* Why God Permits Evil *(1977),* Distractions *(1981),* The Boys on Their Bony Mules *(1983),* Imperfect Love *(1986),* Living on the Surface *(1989),* Adjusting to the Light *(1992),* Points of Departure *(1995),* The Ways We Touch *(1997),* Some Jazz a While *(1999), and* Time and the Tilting Earth *(2008). Among his honors is the Rome Prize, and he read his poem "Of History and Hope" at President Clinton's second inauguration in 1997. Miller Williams lives in Fayetteville, Arkansas.*

Let Me Tell You

how to do it from the beginning.
First notice everything:
The stain on the wallpaper
of the vacant house,
the mothball smell
of a Greyhound toilet.
Miss nothing. Memorize it.
You cannot twist the fact you do not know.

Remember
the blond girl you saw in the bar.
Put a scar on her breast.
Say she left home to get away from her father.
Invent whatever will support your line.
Leave out the rest.

Use metaphors: The mayor is a pig
is a metaphor
which is not to suggest
it is not a fact.
Which is irrelevant.
Nothing is less important
than a fact.

Be suspicious of any word you learned
and were proud of learning.
It will go bad.
It will fall off the page.

When your father lies
in the last light
and your mother cries for him,
listen to the sound of her crying.
When your father dies
take notes
somewhere inside.

If there is a heaven
he will forgive you
if the line you found was a good one.

It does not have to be worth the dying.

Etheridge Knight (1931–1991)

Etheridge Knight was born in Corinth, Mississippi, and served in the U.S. Army as a medical technician. From 1960 to 1968 he was incarcerated for robbery at Indiana State Prison; after his release, he became writer-in-residence at the University of Pittsburgh, followed by similar positions at the University of Hartford, Connecticut, and Lincoln University, Missouri. His poetry books include Poems from Prison *(1968),* A Poem for Brother Man *(1972),* Belly Song and Other Poems *(1973),* Born of a Woman *(1980), and* The Essential Etheridge Knight *(1986, American Book Award). Among his honors were National Endowment for the Arts and Guggenheim fellowships. Etheridge Knight died from cancer in Indianapolis.*

The Idea of Ancestry

1

Taped to the wall of my cell are 47 pictures: 47 black
faces: my father, mother, grandmothers (1 dead), grand
fathers (both dead), brothers, sisters, uncles, aunts,
cousins (1st & 2nd), nieces, and nephews. They stare
across the space at me sprawling on my bunk. I know
their dark eyes, they know mine. I know their style,
they know mine. I am all of them, they are all of me;
they are farmers, I am a thief, I am me, they are thee.

I have at one time or another been in love with my mother,
1 grandmother, 2 sisters, 2 aunts (1 went to the asylum),
and 5 cousins. I am now in love with a 7 yr old niece
(she sends me letters written in large block print, and
her picture is the only one that smiles at me).

I have the same name as 1 grandfather, 3 cousins, 3 nephews,
and 1 uncle. The uncle disappeared when he was 15, just took
off and caught a freight (they say). He's discussed each year
when the family has a reunion, he causes uneasiness in
the clan, he is an empty space. My father's mother, who is 93
and who keeps the Family Bible with everybody's birth dates
(and death dates) in it, always mentions him. There is no
place in her Bible for "whereabouts unknown."

2

Each Fall the graves of my grandfathers call me, the brown
hills and red gullies of mississippi send out their electric
messages, galvanizing my genes. Last yr/like a salmon quitting

the cold ocean—leaping and bucking up his birthstream/I
hitchhiked my way from L.A. with 16 caps in my pocket and a
monkey on my back, and I almost kicked it with the kinfolks.
I walked barefooted in my grandmother's backyard/I smelled the old
land and the woods/I sipped cornwhiskey from fruit jars with the men/
I flirted with the women/I had a ball till the caps ran out
and my habit came down. That night I looked at my grandmother
and split/my guts were screaming for junk/but I was almost
contented/I had almost caught up with me.
(The next day in Memphis I cracked a croaker's crib for a fix.)

This yr there is a gray stone wall damming my stream, and when
the falling leaves stir my genes, I pace my cell or flop on my bunk
and stare at 47 black faces across the space. I am all of them,
they are all of me, I am me, they are thee, and I have no sons
to float in the space between.

Amiri Baraka (LeRoi Jones) (1934–)

Born Everett LeRoi Jones in Newark, New Jersey, Amiri Baraka attended Rutgers, Howard, and Columbia universities and served in the U.S. Air Force. He worked as an editor, publisher, theater director, and playwright and taught at the State University of New York at Stony Brook. His poetry books include Preface to a Twenty Volume Suicide Note *(1961),* The Dead Lecturer *(1964),* Black Magic *(1969),* It's Nation Time *(1970),* Spirit Reach *(1972),* Selected Poetry of Amiri Baraka/LeRoi Jones *(1979),* The LeRoi Jones–Amiri Baraka Reader *(1991),* Transbluesency *(1995),* Funk Lore *(1996), and* Somebody Blew Up America and Other Poems *(2004). Among his honors are Guggenheim and National Endowment for the Arts fellowships, an American Book Award, an Obie, and a PEN/Faulkner Award. Amiri Baraka lives in Newark, New Jersey.*

Preface to a Twenty Volume Suicide Note

(For Kellie Jones, born 16 May 1959)

Lately, I've become accustomed to the way
The ground opens up and envelops me
Each time I go out to walk the dog.
Or the broad edged silly music the wind
Makes when I run for a bus . . .

Things have come to that.

And now, each night I count the stars,
And each night I get the same number.
And when they will not come to be counted,
I count the holes they leave.

Nobody sings anymore.

And then last night, I tiptoed up
To my daughter's room and heard her
Talking to someone, and when I opened
The door, there was no one there . . .
Only she on her knees, peeking into

Her own clasped hands.

An Agony. As Now.

I am inside someone
who hates me. I look
out from his eyes. Smell
what fouled tunes come in
to his breath. Love his
wretched women.

Slits in the metal, for sun. Where
my eyes sit turning, at the cool air
the glance of light, or hard flesh
rubbed against me, a woman, a man,
without shadow, or voice, or meaning.

This is the enclosure (flesh,
where innocence is a weapon. An
abstraction. Touch. (Not mine.
Or yours, if you are the soul I had
and abandoned when I was blind and had
my enemies carry me as a dead man
(if he is beautiful, or pitied.

It can be pain. (As now, as all his
flesh hurts me.) It can be that. Or
pain. As when she ran from me into
that forest.
              Or pain, the mind
silver spiraled whirled against the
sun, higher than even old men thought
God would be. Or pain. And the other. The
yes. (Inside his books, his fingers. They
are withered yellow flowers and were never
beautiful.) The yes. You will, lost soul, say
'beauty.' Beauty, practiced, as the tree. The
slow river. A white sun in its wet sentences.

Or, the cold men in their gale. Ecstasy. Flesh
or soul. The yes. (Their robes blown. Their bowls
empty. They chant at my heels, not at yours.) Flesh
or soul, as corrupt. Where the answer moves too quickly.
Where the God is a self, after all.)

Cold air blown through narrow blind eyes. Flesh,
white hot metal. Glows as the day with its sun.
It is a human love, I live inside. A bony skeleton
you recognize as words or simple feeling.

But it has no feeling. As the metal, is hot, it is not,
given to love.

It burns the thing
inside it. And that thing
screams.

SOS

Calling black people
Calling all black people, man woman child
Wherever you are, calling you, urgent, come in
Black People, come in, wherever you are, urgent, calling
you, calling all black people
calling all black people, come in, black people, come
on in.

Black Art

Poems are bullshit unless they are
teeth or trees or lemons piled
on a step. Or black ladies dying
of men leaving nickel hearts
beating them down. Fuck poems
and they are useful, wd they shoot
come at you, love what you are,
breathe like wrestlers, or shudder
strangely after pissing. We want live
words of the hip world live flesh &
coursing blood. Hearts Brains
Souls splintering fire. We want poems
like fists beating niggers out of Jocks
or dagger poems in the slimy bellies
of the owner-jews. Black poems to
smear on girdlemamma mulatto bitches

whose brains are red jelly stuck
between 'lizabeth taylor's toes. Stinking
Whores! We want "poems that kill."
Assassin poems, Poems that shoot
guns. Poems that wrestle cops into alleys
and take their weapons leaving them dead
with tongues pulled out and sent to Ireland. Knockoff
poems for dope selling wops or slick halfwhite
politicians Airplane poems, rrrrrrrrrrrrrrr
rrrrrrrrrrrrrrr . . . tuhtuhtuhtuhtuhtuhtuhtuhtuh
. . . rrrrrrrrrrrrrrrr . . . Setting fire and death to
whities ass. Look at the Liberal
Spokesman for the jews clutch his throat
& puke himself into eternity . . . rrrrrrrr
There's a negroleader pinned to
a bar stool in Sardi's eyeballs melting
in hot flame Another negroleader
on the steps of the white house one
kneeling between the sheriff's thighs
negotiating cooly for his people.
Agggh . . . stumbles across the room . . .
Put it on him, poem. Strip him naked
to the world! Another bad poem cracking
steel knuckles in a jewlady's mouth
Poem scream poison gas on beasts in green berets
Clean out the world for virtue and love,
Let there be no love poems written
until love can exist freely and
cleanly. Let Black People understand
that they are the lovers and the sons
of lovers and warriors and sons
of warriors Are poems & poets &
all the loveliness here in the world

We want a black poem. And a
Black World.
Let the world be a Black Poem
And Let All Black People Speak This Poem
Silently
or LOUD

Ted Berrigan (1934–1983)

Edmund Joseph Michael Berrigan Jr. was born in Providence, Rhode Island. He attended Providence College and the University of Tulsa. After military service, he became an editor and publisher and taught at the University of Iowa, Yale University, the University of Michigan, the Naropa Institute, Northeastern Illinois University, and the City University of New York. His poetry books include The Sonnets *(1964, Poetry Foundation Award),* Living with Chris *(1966),* Many Happy Returns to Dick Gallup *(1967),* Train Ride *(1971),* The Drunken Boat *(1974),* A Feeling for Leaving *(1975),* Red Wagon *(1976),* Nothing for You *(1977),* Clear the Range *(1977),* So Going Around Cities *(1980),* In a Blue River *(1981),* A Certain Slant of Sunlight *(1988), and* The Collected Poems *(2005). Ted Berrigan died in New York from a liver ailment.*

Wrong Train

Here comes the man! He's talking a lot
I'm sitting, by myself. I've got
A ticket to ride. Outside is, "Out to Lunch."
It's no great pleasure, being on the make.
Well, who is? Or, well everyone is, tho.
"I'm laying there, & some guy comes up
& hits me with a billyclub!" A fat guy
Says. Shut up. & like that we cross a river
Into the Afterlife. Everything goes on as before
But never does any single experience make total use
Of you. You are always slightly ahead,
Slightly behind. It merely baffles, it doesn't hurt.
It's total pain & it breaks your heart
In a less than interesting way. Every day
Is payday. Never enough pay. A deja-vu
That lasts. It's no big thing, anyway.
A lukewarm greasy hamburger, ice-cold pepsi
            that hurts your teeth.

A Final Sonnet

> *for Chris*

How strange to be gone in a minute!   A man
Signs a shovel and so he digs   Everything
Turns into writing a name for a day

                        Someone
is having a birthday and someone is getting
married and someone is telling a joke   my dream
a white tree   I dream of the code of the west
But this rough magic I here abjure   and
When I have required some heavenly music   which even
      now
I do   to work mine end upon *their* senses
That this aery charm is for   I'll break
My staff   bury it certain fathoms in the earth
And deeper than did ever plummet sound
I'll drown my book.
It is 5:15 a.m.   Dear Chris, hello.

Audre Lorde (1934–1992)

Audre Lorde was born in New York, New York. She attended Hunter College and Co-lumbia University before working as a librarian. She then taught at several New York colleges, including Hunter College. Her poetry books include The First Cities *(1968),* From a Land Where Other People Live *(1973),* Coal *(1976),* The Black Unicorn *(1978),* Chosen Poems Old and New *(1982),* Our Dead Behind Us *(1986),* Un-dersong *(1992, Lambda Award),* The Marvelous Arithmetics of Distance *(1993, Lambda Award), and* The Collected Poems *(1997). Among her honors were National Endowment for the Arts fellowships and the American Book Award for her 1989 essay collection* A Burst of Light. *In 1991 she was named poet laureate of New York. Audre Lorde died from cancer in St. Croix, U.S. Virgin Islands.*

Power

The difference between poetry and rhetoric
is being ready to kill
yourself
instead of your children.

I am trapped on a desert of raw gunshot wounds
and a dead child dragging his shattered black
face off the edge of my sleep
blood from his punctured cheeks and shoulders
is the only liquid for miles
and my stomach
churns at the imagined taste while
my mouth splits into dry lips
without loyalty or reason
thirsting for the wetness of his blood
as it sinks into the whiteness
of the desert where I am lost
without imagery or magic
trying to make power out of hatred and destruction
trying to heal my dying son with kisses
only the sun will bleach his bones quicker.

A policeman who shot down a ten year old in Queens
stood over the boy with his cop shoes in childish blood
and a voice said "Die you little motherfucker" and
there are tapes to prove it. At his trial
this policeman said in his own defense
"I didn't notice the size nor nothing else

only the color." And
there are tapes to prove that, too.

Today that 37 year old white man
with 13 years of police forcing
was set free
by eleven white men who said they were satisfied
justice had been done
and one Black Woman who said
"They convinced me" meaning
they had dragged her 4′10″ Black Woman's frame
over the hot coals
of four centuries of white male approval
until she let go
the first real power she ever had
and lined her own womb with cement
to make a graveyard for our children.

I have not been able to touch the destruction
within me.
But unless I learn to use
the difference between poetry and rhetoric
my power too will run corrupt as poisonous mold
or lie limp and useless as an unconnected wire
and one day I will take my teenaged plug
and connect it to the nearest socket
raping an 85 year old white woman
who is somebody's mother
and as I beat her senseless and set a torch to her bed
a greek chorus will be singing in 3/4 time
"Poor thing. She never hurt a soul. What beasts they are."

Sonia Sanchez (1934–)

Born Wilsonia Benita Driver in Birmingham, Alabama, Sonia Sanchez attended Hunter College, New York University, and Wilberforce University. She taught at San Francisco State University, the University of Pittsburgh, Rutgers University, the City University of New York, Amherst College, the University of Pennsylvania, and Temple University. Her poetry books include Homecoming *(1969),* We a BaddDDD People *(1970),* Love Poems *(1973),* A Blues Book for Blue Black Magical Women *(1973),* I've Been a Woman *(1978),* Homegirls & Handgrenades *(1984, American Book Award),* Under a Soprano Sky *(1987),* Wounded in the House of a Friend *(1995),* Does Your House Have Lions? *(1997),* Like the Singing Coming off the Drums *(1998), and* Shake Loose My Skin *(1999). Among her honors are National Endowment for the Arts and Pew fellowships. She lives in Philadelphia, Pennsylvania.*

poem at thirty

it is midnight
no magical bewitching
hour for me
i know only that
i am here waiting
remembering that
once as a child
i walked two
miles in my sleep.
did i know
then where i
was going?
traveling. i'm
always traveling.
i want to tell
you about me
about nights on a
brown couch when
i wrapped my
bones in lint and
refused to move.
no one touches
me anymore.
father do not
send me out
among strangers.

you you black man
stretching scraping
the mold from your body.
here is my hand.
i am not afraid
of the night.

Mark Strand (1934–)

Mark Strand was born on Prince Edward Island, Canada. He attended Antioch College, Yale University, the University of Florence, Italy, and the University of Iowa Writers Workshop. He has taught at the University of Iowa, the University of Brazil in Rio de Janeiro, Mount Holyoke College, Columbia University, City University of New York, Princeton University, Brandeis University, the University of Utah, Johns Hopkins University, and Columbia University. His books include Reasons for Moving *(1968),* Darker *(1970),* The Story of Our Lives *(1973),* The Late Hour *(1978),* Selected Poems *(1980),* The Continuous Life *(1990),* Dark Harbor *(1993),* Blizzard of One *(1998, Pulitzer Prize), and* Man and Camel *(2005). Among his honors are Ingram Merrill, National Endowment for the Arts, Guggenheim, and MacArthur fellowships and the Wallace Stevens Award. Mark Strand served as U.S. poet laureate in 1991–92. He lives in New York City.*

The Prediction

That night the moon drifted over the pond,
turning the water to milk, and under
the boughs of the trees, the blue trees,
a young woman walked, and for an instant

the future came to her:
rain falling on her husband's grave, rain falling
on the lawns of her children, her own mouth
filling with cold air, strangers moving into her house,

a man in her room writing a poem, the moon drifting into it,
a woman strolling under its trees, thinking of death,
thinking of him thinking of her, and the wind rising
and taking the moon and leaving the paper dark.

The Night, the Porch

To stare at nothing is to learn by heart
What all of us will be swept into, and baring oneself
To the wind is feeling the ungraspable somewhere close by.
Trees can sway or be still. Day or night can be what they wish.
What we desire, more than a season or weather, is the comfort
Of being strangers, at least to ourselves. This is the crux

Of the matter, which is why even now we seem to be waiting
For something whose appearance would be its vanishing—
The sound, say, of a few leaves falling, or just one leaf,
Or less. There is no end to what we can learn. The book out there
Tells us as much, and was never written with us in mind.

Russell Edson (1935–)

Russell Edson was born in Connecticut. He attended the Art Students League, the New School, Columbia University, and Black Mountain College. His poetry books include The Childhood of an Equestrian *and* The Clam Theater *(both 1973),* The Intuitive Journey and Other Works *(1976),* The Reason Why the Closet-Man Is Never Sad *(1977),* With Sincerest Regrets *(1980),* The Wounded Breakfast *(1985),* The Tunnel *(1994),* The Tormented Mirror *(2001),* The Rooster's Wife *(2005), and* See Jack *(2009). Among his honors are Guggenheim and National Endowment for the Arts fellowships and a Whiting award. Russell Edson lives in Darien, Connecticut.*

A Stone Is Nobody's

A man ambushed a stone. Caught it. Made it a prisoner. Put it in a dark room and stood guard over it for the rest of his life.

His mother asked why.

He said, because it's held captive, because it is the captured.

Look, the stone is asleep, she said, it does not know whether it's in a garden or not. Eternity and the stone are mother and daughter; it is you who are getting old. The stone is only sleeping.

But I caught it, mother, it is mine by conquest, he said.

A stone is nobody's, not even its own. It is you who are conquered; you are minding the prisoner, which is yourself, because you are afraid to go out, she said.

Yes yes, I am afraid, because you have never loved me, he said.

Which is true, because you have always been to me as the stone is to you, she said.

Mary Oliver (1935–)

Mary Oliver was born in Maple Heights, Ohio. She briefly attended Ohio State University and Vassar College, then lived for a while in Edna St. Vincent Millay's house, helping sort through the literary estate, before teaching at a number of universities. Her poetry books include No Voyage *(1963),* The River Styx, Ohio *(1972),* Twelve Moons *(1978),* American Primitive *(1983, Pulitzer Prize),* Dream Work *(1986),* House of Light *(1990),* New and Selected Poems *(1992, National Book Award),* White Pine *(1994),* Blue Pastures *(1995),* West Wind *(1997),* Winter Hours *(1999),* The Leaf and the Cloud *(2000),* What Do We Know *(2002),* Blue Iris *(2004),* Why I Wake Early *(2005),* Owls and Other Fantasies *(2006),* Thirst *(2007),* Red Bird *(2009),* Evidence *(2009), and* Swan *(2010). Among her honors are the 1972 Shelley Memorial Award and the 1998 Lannan Award, as well as National Endowment for the Arts and Guggenheim fellowships. Mary Oliver lives in Provincetown, Massachusetts.*

Singapore

In Singapore, in the airport,
a darkness was ripped from my eyes.
In the women's restroom, one compartment stood open.
A woman knelt there, washing something
    in the white bowl.

Disgust argued in my stomach
and I felt, in my pocket, for my ticket.

A poem should always have birds in it.
Kingfishers, say, with their bold eyes and gaudy wings.
Rivers are pleasant, and of course trees.
A waterfall, or if that's not possible, a fountain
    rising and falling.
A person wants to stand in a happy place, in a poem.

When the woman turned I could not answer her face.
Her beauty and her embarrassment struggled together, and
    neither could win.
She smiled and I smiled. What kind of nonsense is this?
Everybody needs a job.

Yes, a person wants to stand in a happy place, in a poem.
But first we must watch her as she stares down at her labor,
    which is dull enough.
She is washing the tops of the airport ashtrays, as big as
    hubcaps, with a blue rag.

Her small hands turn the metal, scrubbing and rinsing.
She does not work slowly, nor quickly, but like a river.
Her dark hair is like the wing of a bird.

I don't doubt for a moment that she loves her life.
And I want her to rise up from the crust and the slop
    and fly down to the river.
This probably won't happen.
But maybe it will.
If the world were only pain and logic, who would want it?

Of course, it isn't.
Neither do I mean anything miraculous, but only
the light that can shine out of a life. I mean
the way she unfolded and refolded the blue cloth,
the way her smile was only for my sake; I mean
the way this poem is filled with trees, and birds.

The Summer Day

Who made the world?
Who made the swan, and the black bear?
Who made the grasshopper?
This grasshopper, I mean—
the one who has flung herself out of the grass,
the one who is eating sugar out of my hand,
who is moving her jaws back and forth instead of up and down—
who is gazing around with her enormous and complicated eyes.
Now she lifts her pale forearms and thoroughly washes her face.
Now she snaps her wings open, and floats away.
I don't know exactly what a prayer is.
I do know how to pay attention, how to fall down
into the grass, how to kneel down in the grass,
how to be idle and blessed, how to stroll through the fields,
which is what I have been doing all day.
Tell me, what else should I have done?
Doesn't everything die at last, and too soon?
Tell me, what is it you plan to do
with your one wild and precious life?

Charles Wright (1935–)

Charles Wright was born in Pickwick Dam, Tennessee. He attended Davidson College and the University of Iowa Writers Workshop, subsequently teaching at the University of California at Irvine and the University of Virginia. His poetry books include The Grave of the Right Hand *(1970),* Hard Freight *(1973),* Bloodlines *(1975),* China Trace *(1977),* The Southern Cross *(1981),* Country Music *(1982, National Book Award),* The Other Side of the River *(1984),* Zone Journals *(1988),* The World of the Ten Thousand Things *(1990),* Chickamauga *(1995),* Black Zodiac *(1997, Pulitzer Prize),* Appalachia *(1998),* Negative Blue *(2000),* A Short History of the Shadow *(2002),* Buffalo Yoga *(2004),* The Wrong End of the Rainbow *(2005),* Scar Tissue *(2006),* Littlefoot *(2007), and* Sestets *(2010). Among his honors are Guggenheim and Ingram Merrill fellowships and the 1993 Ruth Lilly Prize. He lives in Charlottesville, Virginia.*

Reunion

Already one day has detached itself from all the rest up ahead.
It has my photograph in its soft pocket.
It wants to carry my breath into the past in its bag of wind.

I write poems to untie myself, to do penance and disappear
Through the upper right-hand corner of things, to say grace.

Dead Color

I lie for a long time on my left side and my right side
And eat nothing,
                    but no voice comes on the wind
And no voice drops from the cloud.
Between the grey spiders and the orange spiders,
                         no voice comes on the wind . . .

Later, I sit for a long time by the waters of Har,
And no face appears on the face of the deep.

Meanwhile, the heavens assemble their dark map.
The traffic begins to thin.
Aphids munch on the sweet meat of the lemon trees.
The lawn sprinklers rise and fall . . .

And here's a line of brown ants cleaning a possum's skull.
And here's another, come from the opposite side.

Over my head, star-pieces dip in their yellow scarves toward their
                                                    black desire.

Windows, rapturous windows!

California Dreaming

We are not born yet, and everything's crystal under our feet.
We are not brethren, we are not underlings.
We are another nation,
                        living by voices that you will never hear,
Caught in the net of splendor
                        of time-to-come on the earth.
We shine in our distant chambers, we are golden.

                        ————————

Midmorning, and Darvon dustfall off the Pacific
Stuns us to ecstasy,
                    October sun
Stuck like a tack on the eastern drift of the sky,
The idea of God on the other,
                        body by body
Rinsed in the Sunday prayer-light, draining away
Into the undercoating and slow sparks of the west,
                        which is our solitude and our joy.

                        ————————

I've looked at this ridge of lights for six years now
                        and still don't like it,
Strung out like Good Friday along a cliff
That Easters down to the ocean,
A dark wing with ruffled feathers as far out as Catalina
Fallen from some sky,
                    ruffled and laid back by the wind,
Santa Ana that lisps its hot breath
                    on the neck of everything.

                        ————————

What if the soul indeed is outside the body,
                                a little rainfall of light
Moistening our every step, prismatic, apotheosizic?
What if inside the body another shape is waiting to come out,
White as a quilt, loose as a fever,
                                and sways in the easy tides there?
What other anagoge in this life but the self?
What other ladder to Paradise
                                but the smooth handholds of the rib cage?
High in the palm tree the orioles twitter and grieve.
We twitter and grieve, the spider twirls the honey bee.
Who twitters and grieves, around in her net,
                                then draws it by one leg
Up to the fishbone fern leaves inside the pepper tree
                                swaddled in silk
And turns it again and again until it is shining.

———

Some nights, when the rock-and-roll band next door has quit playing,
And the last helicopter has thwonked back to the Marine base,
And the dark lets all its weight down
                                to within a half inch of the ground,
I sit outside in the gold lamé of the moon
                                as the town sleeps and the country sleeps
Like flung confetti around me,
And wonder just what in the hell I'm doing out here
So many thousands of miles away from what I know best.
And what I know best
                                has nothing to do with Point Conception
And Avalon and the long erasure of ocean
Out there where the landscape ends.
What I know best is a little thing.
It sits on the far side of the simile,
                                the like that's like the like.

———

Today is sweet stuff on the tongue.
The question of how we should live our lives in this world
Will find no answer from us
                                this morning,
Sunflick, the ocean humping its back
Beneath us, shivering out

　　　　　　　　　　　　　wave after wave we fall from
And cut through in a white scar of healed waters,
Our wet suits glossed slick as seals,
　　　　　　　　　　　　　　　　　our boards grown sharp as cries.
We rise and fall like the sun.

————

Ghost of the Muse and her dogsbody
Suspended above the beach, November 25th,
Sun like a Valium disc, smog like rust in the trees.
White-hooded and friar-backed,
　　　　　　　　　　　　　a gull choir eyeballs the wave reach.
Invisibly pistoned, the sea keeps it up,
　　　　　　　　　　plunges and draws back, plunges and draws back,
Yesterday hung like a porcelain cup behind the eyes,
Sonorous valves, insistent extremities,
　　　　　　　　　　　the worm creeping out of the heart . . .

————

Who are these people we pretend to be,
　　　　　　　　　　　　　untouched by the setting sun?
They stand less stiffly than we do, and handsomer,
First on the left foot, and then the right.
Just for a moment we see ourselves inside them,
　　　　　　　　　　　　　　peering out,
And then they go their own way and we go ours,
Back to the window seat above the driveway,
Christmas lights in the pepper tree,
　　　　　　　　　　　black Madonna
Gazing out from the ailanthus.
Chalk eyes downcast, heavy with weeping and bitterness,
Her time has come round again.

————

Piece by small piece the world falls away from us like spores
From a milkweed pod,
　　　　　　　　　　and everything we have known,
And everyone we have known,
Is taken away by the wind to forgetfulness,
Somebody always humming,
　　　　　　　　　　California dreaming . . .

Lucille Clifton (1936–2010)

Lucille Clifton was born in Depew, New York. She attended Howard University and Fredonia State Teachers College. She taught at Coppin State College, George Washington University, and the University of California–Santa Cruz before settling at St. Mary's College of Maryland in 1989. Her poetry books include Good Times *(1969),* Good News About the Earth *(1972),* An Ordinary Woman *(1974),* Two-Headed Woman *(1980),* Good Woman *(1987),* Next *(1987),* Quilting *(1991),* The Book of Light *(1993),* The Terrible Stories *(1998),* Blessing the Boats *(2000, National Book Award),* Mercy *(2004), and* Voices *(2008). Among her honors were National Endowment for the Arts fellowships, Lannan and Lila Wallace–Reader's Digest awards, the Ruth Lilly Prize, and the Frost Medal. Lucille Clifton died in Baltimore, Maryland.*

homage to my hips

these hips are big hips
they need space to
move around in.
they don't fit into little
petty places. these hips
are free hips.
they don't like to be held back.
these hips have never been enslaved,
they go where they want to go
they do what they want to do.
these hips are mighty hips.
these hips are magic hips.
i have known them
to put a spell on a man and
spin him like a top!

[at last we killed the roaches]

at last we killed the roaches.
mama and me. she sprayed,
i swept the ceiling and they fell
dying onto our shoulders, in our hair
covering us with red. the tribe was broken,
the cooking pots were ours again
and we were glad, such cleanliness was grace

when i was twelve. only for a few nights,
and then not much, my dreams were blood
my hands were blades and it was murder murder
all over the place.

the death of fred clifton

11/10/84
age 49

i seemed to be drawn
to the center of myself
leaving the edges of me
in the hands of my wife
and i saw with the most amazing
clarity
so that i had not eyes but
sight,
and, rising and turning,
through my skin,
there was all around not the
shapes of things
but oh, at last, the things
themselves.

to my last period

well girl, goodbye,
after thirty-eight years.
thirty-eight years and you
never arrived
splendid in your red dress
without trouble for me
somewhere, somehow.

now it is done,
and i feel just like
the grandmothers who,
after the hussy has gone,
sit holding her photograph
and sighing, *wasn't she*
beautiful? wasn't she beautiful?

June Jordan (1936–2002)

June Jordan was born in New York City. She attended Barnard College and the University of Chicago, held a number of jobs in New York, and taught at City University of New York, Connecticut College, Sarah Lawrence College, and State University of New York at Stony Brook before moving to the University of California at Berkeley in 1989. Her poetry books include Some Changes *(1971),* New Days: Poems of Exile and Return *(1973),* Things That I Do in the Dark *(1977),* Passion *(1980),* Living Room *(1985),* Naming Our Destiny *(1989),* Haruko: Love Poems *(1994), and* Kissing God Goodbye *(1997). Among her honors were the PEN West Freedom to Write Award and a Lila Wallace–Reader's Digest Writers' Award, as well as Yaddo, MacDowell, and National Endowment for the Arts fellowships. June Jordan died of cancer in Berkeley, California.*

Poem About My Rights

Even tonight and I need to take a walk and clear
my head about this poem about why I can't
go out without changing my clothes my shoes
my body posture my gender identity my age
my status as a woman alone in the evening /
alone on the streets / alone not being the point /
the point being that I can't do what I want
to do with my own body because I am the wrong
sex the wrong age the wrong skin and
suppose it was not here in the city but down on the beach /
or far into the woods and I wanted to go
there by myself thinking about God / or thinking
about children or thinking about the world / all of it
disclosed by the stars and the silence:
I could not go and I could not think and I could not
stay there
alone
as I need to be
alone because I can't do what I want to do with my own
body and
who in the hell set things up
like this
and in France they say if the guy penetrates
but does not ejaculate then he did not rape me
and if after stabbing him if after screams if
after begging the bastard and if even after smashing
a hammer to his head if even after that if he

and his buddies fuck me after that
then I consented and there was
no rape because finally you understand finally
they fucked me over because I was wrong I was
wrong again to be me being me where I was / wrong
to be who I am
which is exactly like South Africa
penetrating into Namibia penetrating into
Angola and does that mean I mean how do you know if
Pretoria ejaculates what will the evidence look like the
proof of the monster jackboot ejaculation on Blackland
and if
after Namibia and if after Angola and if after Zimbabwe
and if after all of my kinsmen and women resist even to
self-immolation of the villages and if after that
we lose nevertheless what will the big boys say will they
claim my consent:
Do You Follow Me: We are the wrong people of
the wrong skin on the wrong continent and what
in the hell is everybody being reasonable about
and according to the *Times* this week
back in 1966 the C.I.A. decided that they had this problem
and the problem was a man named Nkrumah so they
killed him and before that it was Patrice Lumumba
and before that it was my father on the campus
of my Ivy League school and my father afraid
to walk into the cafeteria because he said he
was wrong the wrong age the wrong skin the wrong
gender identity and he was paying my tuition and
before that
it was my father saying I was wrong saying that
I should have been a boy because he wanted one / a
boy and that I should have been lighter skinned and
that I should have had straighter hair and that
I should not be so boy crazy but instead I should
just be one / a boy and before that
it was my mother pleading plastic surgery for
my nose and braces for my teeth and telling me
to let the books loose to let them loose in other
words
I am very familiar with the problems of the C.I.A.
and the problems of South Africa and the problems
of Exxon Corporation and the problems of white
America in general and the problems of the teachers

and the preachers and the F.B.I. and the social
workers and my particular Mom and Dad / I am very
familiar with the problems because the problems
turn out to be
me
I am the history of rape
I am the history of the rejection of who I am
I am the history of the terrorized incarceration of
my self
I am the history of battery assault and limitless
armies against whatever I want to do with my mind
and my body and my soul and
whether it's about walking out at night
or whether it's about the love that I feel or
whether it's about the sanctity of my vagina or
the sanctity of my national boundaries
or the sanctity of my leaders or the sanctity
of each and every desire
that I know from my personal and idiosyncratic
and indisputably single and singular heart
I have been raped
be-
cause I have been wrong the wrong sex the wrong age
the wrong skin the wrong nose the wrong hair the
wrong need the wrong dream the wrong geographic
the wrong sartorial I
I have been the meaning of rape
I have been the problem everyone seeks to
eliminate by forced
penetration with or without the evidence of slime and /
but let this be unmistakable this poem
is not consent I do not consent
to my mother to my father to the teachers to
the F.B.I. to South Africa to Bedford-Stuy
to Park Avenue to American Airlines to the hardon
idlers on the corners to the sneaky creeps in
cars
I am not wrong: Wrong is not my name
My name is my own my own my own
and I can't tell you who the hell set things up like this
but I can tell you that from now on my resistance
my simple and daily and nightly self-determination
may very well cost you your life

Frederick Seidel (1936–)

Frederick Seidel was born in St. Louis, Missouri, and attended Harvard University. Independently wealthy, he has eschewed teaching positions and public appearances. His poetry books include Final Solutions *(1963),* Sunrise *(1979, Lamont Poetry Prize),* These Days *(1989),* My Tokyo *(1993),* Going Fast *(1998),* The Cosmos Poems *(2000),* Life on Earth *(2001),* Area Code 212 *(2002),* The Cosmos Trilogy *(2003),* Ooga-Booga *(2006, L.A. Times Book Prize),* Evening Man *(2008), and* Poems 1959–2009 *(2009). He has been a finalist for several major awards. Frederick Seidel lives in New York City.*

1968

A football spirals through the oyster glow
Of dawn dope and fog in L.A.'s
Bel Air, punted perfectly. The foot
That punted it is absolutely stoned.

A rising starlet leans her head against the tire
Of a replica Cord,
A bonfire of red hair out of
Focus in the fog. Serenading her,
A boy plucks "God Bless America" from a guitar.
Vascular spasm has made the boy's hands blue
Even after hours of opium.

Fifty or so of the original
Four hundred
At the fundraiser,
Robert Kennedy for President, the remnants, lie
Exposed as snails around the swimming pool, stretched
Out on the paths, and in the gardens, and the drive.
Many dreams their famous bodies have filled.

The host, a rock superstar, has
A huge cake of opium,
Which he refers to as "King Kong,"
And which he serves on a silver salver
Under a glass bell to his close friends,
So called,
Which means all mankind apparently,

Except the fuzz,
Sticky as tar, the color of coffee,
A quarter of a million dollars going up in smoke.

This is Paradise painted
On the inside of an eggshell
With the light outside showing through,
Subtropical trees and flowers and lawns,
Clammy as albumen in the fog,
And smelling of fog. Backlit
And diffuse, the murdered
Voityck Frokowski, Abigail Folger and Sharon Tate
Sit together without faces.

This is the future.
Their future is the future. The future
Has been born,
The present is the afterbirth,
These bloodshot and blue acres of flowerbeds and stars.
Robert Kennedy will be killed.
It is '68, the campaign year—
And the beginning of a new day.

People are waiting.
When the chauffeur-bodyguard arrives
For work and walks
Into the ballroom, now recording studio, herds
Of breasts turn round, it seems in silence,
Like cattle turning to face a sound.
Like cattle lined up to face the dawn.
Shining eyes seeing all or nothing,
In the silence.

A stranger, and wearing a suit,
Has to be John the Baptist,
At least, come
To say someone else is coming.
He hikes up his shoulder holster
Self-consciously, meeting their gaze.
That is as sensitive as the future gets.

C. K. Williams (1936–)

Charles Kenneth Williams was born and grew up in New Jersey and attended the University of Pennsylvania. He taught at numerous universities before joining Princeton's faculty. His poetry books include Lies *(1969),* I Am the Bitter Name *(1972),* With Ignorance *(1977),* Tar *(1983),* Flesh and Blood *(1987, National Book Critics Circle Award),* Poems 1963–1983 *(1988),* A Dream of Mind *(1992),* The Vigil *(1996),* Repair *(1999, Pulitzer Prize),* The Singing *(2003, National Book Award), and* Wait *(2010). Among his honors are Guggenheim and National Endowment for the Arts fellowships as well as the Ruth Lilly Prize. C. K. Williams lives in Paris, France, and Princeton, New Jersey.*

From My Window

Spring: the first morning when that one true block of sweet, laminar, complex
    scent arrives
from somewhere west and I keep coming to lean on the sill, glorying in the
    end of the wretched winter.
The scabby-barked sycamores ringing the empty lot across the way are
    budded—I hadn't noticed—
and the thick spikes of the unlikely urban crocuses have already broken
    the gritty soil.
Up the street, some surveyors with tripods are waving each other left and
    right the way they do.
A girl in a gym suit jogged by a while ago, some kids passed, playing hooky,
    I imagine,
and now the paraplegic Vietnam vet who lives in a half-converted warehouse
    down the block
and the friend who stays with him and seems to help him out come weaving
    towards me,
their battered wheelchair lurching uncertainly from one edge of the sidewalk
    to the other.
I know where they're going—to the "Legion": once, when I was putting
    something out, they stopped,
both drunk that time, too, both reeking—it wasn't ten o'clock—and we
    chatted for a bit.
I don't know how they stay alive—on benefits most likely. I wonder if
    they're lovers?
They don't look it. Right now, in fact, they look a wreck, careening
    haphazardly along,
contriving, as they reach beneath me, to dip a wheel from the curb so that
    the chair skewers, teeters,

tips, and they both tumble, the one slowly, almost gracefully sliding in
stages from his seat,

his expression hardly marking it, the other staggering over him, spinning
heavily down,

to lie on the asphalt, his mouth working, his feet shoving weakly and
fruitlessly against the curb.

In the storefront office on the corner, Reed and Son, Real Estate, have come
to see the show.

Gazing through the golden letters of their name, they're not, at least, thank
god, laughing.

Now the buddy, grabbing at a hydrant, gets himself erect and stands there
for a moment, panting.

Now he has to lift the other one, who lies utterly still, a forearm shielding
his eyes from the sun.

He hauls him partly upright, then hefts him almost all the way into the chair,
but a dangling foot

catches a support-plate, jerking everything around so that he has to put him
down,

set the chair to rights, and hoist him again and as he does he jerks the grimy
jeans right off him.

No drawers, shrunken, blotchy thighs: under the thick, white coils of
belly blubber,

the poor, blunt pud, tiny, terrified, retracted, is almost invisible in the
sparse genital hair,

then his friend pulls his pants up, he slumps wholly back as though he
were, at last, to be let be,

and the friend leans against the cyclone fence, suddenly staring up at me
as though he'd known,

all along, that I was watching and I can't help wondering if he knows that
in the winter, too,

I watched, the night he went out to the lot and walked, paced rather, almost
ran, for how many hours.

It was snowing, the city in that holy silence, the last we have, when the
storm takes hold,

and he was making patterns that I thought at first were circles, then realized
made a figure eight,

what must have been to him a perfect symmetry but which, from where I
was, shivered, bent,

and lay on its side: a warped, unclear infinity, slowly, as the snow came
faster, going out.

Over and over again, his head lowered to the task, he slogged the path he'd
blazed,

but the race was lost, his prints were filling faster than he made them now
and I looked away,

up across the skeletal trees to the tall center city buildings, some, though it
      was midnight,
with all their offices still gleaming, their scarlet warning-beacons signaling
      erratically
against the thickening flakes, their smoldering auras softening portions of
      the dim, milky sky.
In the morning, nothing: every trace of him effaced, all the field pure white,
its surface glittering, the dawn, glancing from its glaze, oblique, relentless,
      unadorned.

Blades

When I was about eight, I once stabbed somebody, another kid, a little
      girl.
I'd been hanging around in front of the supermarket near our house
and when she walked by, I let her have it, right in the gap between her
      shirt and her shorts
with a piece of broken-off car antenna I used to carry around in my
      pocket.
It happened so fast I still don't know how I did it: I was as shocked as she
      was
except she squealed and started yelling as though I'd plunged a knife in
      her
and everybody in the neighborhood gathered around us, then they called
      the cops,
then the girl's mother came running out of the store saying "What
      happened? What happened?"
and the girl screamed, "He stabbed me!" and I screamed back, "I did
      not!" and she you did too
and me I didn't and we were both crying hysterically by that time.
Somebody pulled her shirt up and it was just a scratch but we went on
      and on
and the mother, standing between us, seemed to be absolutely terrified.
I still remember how she watched first one of us and then the other with
      a look of complete horror—
You did too! I did not!—as though we were both strangers, as though it
      was some natural disaster
she was beholding that was beyond any mode of comprehension so all
      she could do
was stare speechlessly at us, and then another expression came over her
      face,
one that I'd never seen before, that made me think she was going to cry
      herself

and sweep both of us, the girl and me, into her arms to hold us against
  her.
The police came just then, though, quieted everyone down, put the girl
  and the mother
into a squad-car to take to the hospital and me in another to take to jail
except they really only took me around the corner and let me go because
  the mother and daughter were black
and in those days you had to do something pretty terrible to get into trouble
  that way.

I don't understand how we twist these things or how we get them straight
  again
but I relived that day I don't know how many times before I realized I had
  it all wrong.
The boy wasn't me at all, he was another kid: I was just there.
And it wasn't the girl who was black, but him. The mother was real,
  though.
I really had thought she was going to embrace them both
and I had dreams about her for years afterwards: that I'd be being born
  again
and she'd be lifting me with that same wounded sorrow or she would
  suddenly appear out of nowhere,
blotting out everything but a single, blazing wing of holiness.
Who knows the rest? I can still remember how it felt the old way.
How I make my little thrust, how she crushes us against her, how I turn
  and snarl
at the cold circle of faces around us because something's torn in me,
some ancient cloak of terror we keep on ourselves because we'll do
  anything,
anything, not to know how silently we knell in the mouth of death
and not to obliterate the forgiveness and the lies we offer one another and
  call innocence.
This is innocence. I touch her, we kiss.
And this. I'm here or not here. I can't tell. I stab her. I stab her again. I
  still can't.

Diane Wakoski (1937–)

Diane Wakoski was born in Whittier, California, and attended the University of California at Berkeley. She held a number of jobs before joining Michigan State University's faculty in 1975. Her poetry books include The Collected Greed, Parts 1–13 *(1984),* Emerald Ice: Selected Poems 1962–1987 *(1988, William Carlos Williams Prize),* Medea the Sorceress *(1991),* Jason the Sailor *(1993),* The Emerald City of Las Vegas *(1995),* Argonaut Rose *(1998),* The Butcher's Apron *(2000), and* The Diamond Dog *(2010). Among her honors are Guggenheim and National Endowment for the Arts fellowships. Diane Wakoski lives in East Lansing, Michigan.*

The Mechanic

> *to T.W.*

Most men use
their eyes
like metronomes
clicking off the beats
of a woman's walk;
how her hips press
against the cloth, as figs just before
they split their purple skins
on the tree,
measuring how much of her walk
goes into bed at night,
the jar of the sky
being filled with the Milky Way
glittering for every time
she moves her lips

but of course
the secrets
are not the obvious beats
in the song
that even a bad drummer can play

hearing the speed of the motor
— it too made up of beats—
so fast,
subtle, I suppose,
they register
as continuous sound

or the heart which of course
beats without any fan belt to keep it
cool.
it is a test,
a rhythm,
they could not see
with those measuring eyes
though perhaps there are some
whose fingers and ears
are so close to the motors
with clean oil passing through their ears
and draining properly into the brain pan,
perhaps a few . . .

who can tell
what the secret bleeding of a woman
is all about

As a woman
with oily stars sticking
on all the tip points
of my skin
I could never
trust a man
who wasn't a mechanic,
a man who uses his
eyes,
his hands,
listens to
the
heart.

Michael S. Harper (1938–)

Michael Harper was born in Brooklyn, New York, and attended California State University at Los Angeles and the University of Iowa Writers Workshop. He taught at Contra Costa College, Lewis and Clark College, and California State University at Hayward, before settling at Brown University. Among his poetry books are Dear John, Dear Coltrane *(1970),* History Is Your Own Heartbeat *(1971),* Debridement *(1973),* Nightmare Begins Responsibility *(1974),* Images of Kin *(1977),* Healing Song for the Inner Ear *(1985),* Honorable Amendments *(1995), and* Songlines in Michaeltree *(2000). His honors include Guggenheim and National Endowment for the Arts fellowships, the Melville Cane Award, and the Robert Hayden Poetry Award. Michael Harper lives in Providence, Rhode Island.*

Dear John, Dear Coltrane

a love supreme, a love supreme
a love supreme, a love supreme

Sex fingers toes
in the marketplace
near your father's church
in Hamlet, North Carolina—
witness to this love
in this calm fallow
of these minds,
there is no substitute for pain:
genitals gone or going,
seed burned out,
you tuck the roots in the earth,
turn back, and move
by river through the swamps,
singing: *a love supreme, a love supreme;*
what does it all mean?
Loss, so great each black
woman expects your failure
in mute change, the seed gone.
You plod up into the electric city—
your song now crystal and
the blues. You pick up the horn
with some will and blow
into the freezing night:
a love supreme, a love supreme—

Dawn comes and you cook
up the thick sin 'tween
impotence and death, fuel
the tenor sax cannibal
heart, genitals and sweat
that makes you clean—
a love supreme, a love supreme—

Why you so black?
cause I am
why you so funky?
cause I am
why you so black?
cause I am
why you so sweet?
cause I am
why you so black?
cause I am
a love supreme, a love supreme:

So sick
you couldn't play *Naima,*
so flat we ached
for song you'd concealed
with your own blood,
your diseased liver gave
out its purity,
the inflated heart
pumps out, the tenor kiss,
tenor love:
a love supreme, a love supreme—
a love supreme, a love supreme—

Last Affair: Bessie's Blues Song

Disarticulated
arm torn out,
large veins cross
her shoulder intact,
her tourniquet
her blood in all-white big bands:

Can't you see
what love and heartache's done to me
I'm not the same as I used to be
this is my last affair

Mail truck or parked car
in the fast lane,
afloat at forty-three
on a Mississippi road,
two-hundred-pound muscle on her ham bone,
'nother nigger dead 'fore noon:

Can't you see
what love and heartache's done to me
I'm not the same as I used to be
this is my last affair

Fifty-dollar record
cut the vein in her neck,
fool about her money
toll her black train wreck,
white press missed her fun'ral
in the same stacked deck:

Can't you see
what love and heartache's done to me
I'm not the same as I used to be
this is my last affair

Loved a little blackbird
heard she could sing,
Martha in her vineyard
pestle in her spring,
Bessie had a bad mouth
made my chimes ring:

Can't you see
what love and heartache's done to me
I'm not the same as I used to be
this is my last affair

Grandfather

In 1915 my grandfather's
neighbours surrounded his house
near the dayline he ran
on the Hudson
in Catskill, N.Y.
and thought they'd burn
his family out
in a movie they'd just seen
and be rid of his kind:
the death of a lone black
family is *the Birth
of a Nation,*
or so they thought.
His 5′ 4″ waiter gait
quenched the white jacket smile
he'd brought back from watered
polish of my father
on the turning seats,
and he asked his neighbours
up on his thatched porch
for the first blossom of fire
that would bring him down.

They went away, his nation,
spittooning their torched necks
in the shadows of the riverboat
they'd seen, posse decomposing;
and I see him on Sutter
with white bag from your
restaurant, challenged by his first
grandson to a foot-race
he will win in white clothes.

I see him as he buys galoshes
for his railed yard near Mineo's
metal shop, where roses jump
as the el circles his house
toward Brooklyn, where his rain fell;
and I see cigar smoke in his eyes,
chocolate Madison Square Garden chews
he breaks on his set teeth,
stitched up after cancer,

the great white nation immovable
as his weight wilts
and he is on a porch
that won't hold my arms,
or the legs of the race run
forwards, or the film
played backwards on his grandson's eyes.

Nightmare Begins Responsibility

I place these numbed wrists to the pane
watching white uniforms whisk over
him in the tube-kept
prison
fear what they will do in experiment
watch my gloved stickshifting gasolined hands
breathe *boxcar-information-please* infirmary tubes
distrusting white-pink mending paperthin
silkened end hairs, distrusting tubes
shrunk in his *trunk-skincapped*
shaven head, in thighs
distrusting-white-hands-picking-baboon-light
on his son who will not make his second night
of this wardstrewn intensive airpocket
where his father's asthmatic
hymns of *night-train*, train done gone
his mother can only know that he has flown
up into essential calm unseen corridor
going boxscarred home, *mamaborn, sweetsonchild*
gonedowntown into *researchtestingwarehousebatteryacid*
mama-son-done-gone/me telling her 'nother
train tonight, no music, no breathstroked
heartbeat in my infinite distrust of them:

and of my distrusting self
white-doctor-who-breathed-for-him-all-night
say it for two sons gone,
say nightmare, say it loud
panebreaking heartmadness:
nightmare begins responsibility.

Charles Simic (1938–)

Charles Simic was born in Belgrade, Yugoslavia. He came to the United States in 1954, attended New York University, and taught at California State University–Hayward before settling at the University of New Hampshire. Among his poetry books are Dismantling the Silence *(1971),* Return to a Place Lit by a Glass of Milk *(1974),* Charon's Cosmology *(1977),* Classic Ballroom Dances *(1980),* Austerities *(1982),* Unending Blues *(1986),* The World Doesn't End *(1989, Pulitzer Prize),* The Book of Gods and Devils *(1990),* Hotel Insomnia *(1992),* A Wedding in Hell *(1994),* Walking the Black Cat *(1996),* Jackstraws *(1999),* Night Picnic *(2001),* The Voice at 3:00 A.M *(2003),* My Noiseless Entourage *(2005), and* That Little Something *(2008). His honors include Guggenheim, National Endowment for the Arts, Ingram Merrill, and MacArthur fellowships and the 2007 Wallace Stevens Award. In 2007–2008 he served as U.S. poet laureate. Simic lives in Strafford, New Hampshire.*

Stone

Go inside a stone
That would be my way.
Let somebody else become a dove
Or gnash with a tiger's tooth.
I am happy to be a stone.

From the outside the stone is a riddle:
No one knows how to answer it.
Yet within, it must be cool and quiet
Even though a cow steps on it full weight,
Even though a child throws it in a river;
The stone sinks, slow, unperturbed
To the river bottom
Where the fishes come to knock on it
And listen.

I have seen sparks fly out
When two stones are rubbed,
So perhaps it is not dark inside after all;
Perhaps there is a moon shining
From somewhere, as though behind a hill—
Just enough light to make out
The strange writings, the star-charts
On the inner walls.

Fork

This strange thing must have crept
Right out of hell.
It resembles a bird's foot
Worn around the cannibal's neck.

As you hold it in your hand,
As you stab with it into a piece of meat,
It is possible to imagine the rest of the bird:
Its head which like your fist
Is large, bald, beakless and blind.

Classic Ballroom Dances

Grandmothers who wring the necks
Of chickens; old nuns
With names like Theresa, Marianne,
Who pull schoolboys by the ear;

The intricate steps of pickpockets
Working the crowd of the curious
At the scene of an accident; the slow shuffle
Of the evangelist with a sandwich-board;

The hesitation of the early morning customer
Peeking through the window-grille
Of a pawnshop; the weave of a little kid
Who is walking to school with eyes closed;

And the ancient lovers, cheek to cheek,
On the dancefloor of the Union Hall,
Where they also hold charity raffles
On rainy Monday nights of an eternal November.

Paula Gunn Allen (1939–2008)

Paula Gunn Allen was born in New Mexico and grew up in Laguna Pueblo. She attended the University of Oregon and the University of New Mexico and taught at a number of universities before joining the University of California–Los Angeles in 1990. Her poetry books include The Blind Lion *(1974),* Coyote's Daylight Trip *(1978), A* Cannon Between My Knees *and* Star Child *(both 1981),* Shadow Country *(1982),* Wyrds *(1987),* Skins and Bones *(1988), and* Life Is a Fatal Disease *(1997). Among her honors were National Endowment for the Arts and Lannan Foundation fellowships. Paula Gunn Allen died in Fort Bragg, California.*

Grandmother

Out of her own body she pushed
silver thread, light, air
and carried it carefully on the dark, flying
where nothing moved.

Out of her body she extruded
shining wire, life, and wove the light
on the void.

From beyond time,
beyond oak trees and bright clear water flow,
she was given the work of weaving the strands
of her body, her pain, her vision
into creation, and the gift of having created,
to disappear.

After her,
the women and the men weave blankets into tales of life,
memories of light and ladders,
infinity-eyes, and rain.
After her I sit on my laddered rain-bearing rug
and mend the tear with string.

Frank Bidart (1939–)

*Frank Bidart was born in Bakersfield, California. He attended the University of California–
Riverside and Harvard University. He has taught at Wellesley College since 1972. Among
his poetry books are* Golden State *(1973),* The Book of the Body *(1977),* The Sacri-
fice *(1983),* In the Western Night *(1990),* Desire *(1997),* Music Like Dirt *(2002),*
Star Dust *(2005), and* Watching the Spring Festival *(2008). His honors include a Lila
Wallace–Reader's Digest Writers' Award, the Wallace Stevens Award, the Bobbitt Prize,
and the Bollingen Prize, as well as Guggenheim and Lannan fellowships. Frank Bidart
lives in Cambridge, Massachusetts.*

Ellen West

I love sweets,—
                 heaven
would be dying on a bed of vanilla ice cream . . .

But my true self
is thin, all profile

and effortless gestures, the sort of blond
elegant girl whose
                     body is the image of her soul.

—My doctors tell me I must give up
this ideal;
         but I
WILL NOT . . . cannot.

Only to my husband I'm not simply a "case."

But he is a fool. He married
meat, and thought it was a wife.

              •   •   •

Why am I a girl?

I ask my doctors, and they tell me they
don't know, that it is just "given."

But it has such
implications—;
                and sometimes,
I even feel like a girl.

. . .

Now, at the beginning of Ellen's thirty-second year, her physical condition
has deteriorated still further. Her use of laxatives increases beyond measure.
Every evening she takes sixty to seventy tablets of a laxative, with the result
that she suffers tortured vomiting at night and violent diarrhea by day,
often accompanied by a weakness of the heart. She has thinned down to a
skeleton, and weighs only 92 pounds.

. . .

About five years ago, I was in a restaurant,
eating alone
        with a book. I was
not married, and often did that . . .

—I'd turn down
dinner invitations, so I could eat alone;

I'd allow myself two pieces of bread, with
butter, at the beginning, and three scoops of
vanilla ice cream, at the end,—

                      sitting there alone
with a book, both in the book
and out of it, waited on, idly
watching people,—

            when an attractive young man
and woman, both elegantly dressed,
sat next to me.
        She was beautiful—;

with sharp, clear features, a good
bone structure—;
          if she took her make-up off
in front of you, rubbing cold cream
again and again across her skin, she still would be
beautiful—
       more beautiful.

And he,—
        I couldn't remember when I had seen a man
so attractive. I didn't know why. He was almost

a male version
　　　　　of her,—

I had the sudden, mad notion that I
wanted to be his lover . . .

—Were they married?
　　　　　　　　were *they* lovers?

They didn't wear wedding rings.

Their behavior was circumspect. They discussed
politics. They didn't touch . . .

—How could I discover?

　　　　　　　　Then, when the first course
arrived, I noticed the way

each held his fork out for the other

to taste what he had ordered . . .

　　　　　　　　They did this
again and again, with pleased looks, indulgent
smiles, for each course,
　　　　　　　　more than once for *each* dish—;
much too much for just friends . . .

—Their behavior somehow sickened me;

the way each *gladly*
put the *food* the other had offered *into his mouth*—;

I knew what they were. I knew they slept together.

An immense depression came over me . . .

—I knew I could never
with such ease allow another to put food into my mouth:

happily *myself* put food into another's mouth—;

I knew that to become a wife I would have to give up my ideal.

．　　　．　　　．

Even as a child,
I saw that the "natural" process of aging

is for one's middle to thicken—
one's skin to blotch;

as happened to my mother.
And her mother.
I loathed "Nature."

At twelve, pancakes
became the most terrible thought there is . . .

I shall *defeat* "Nature."

In the hospital, when they
weigh me, I wear weights secretly sewn into my belt.

．　　　．　　　．

January 16. The patient is allowed to eat in her room, but comes readily with her husband to afternoon coffee. Previously she had stoutly resisted this on the ground that she did not really eat but devoured like a wild animal. This she demonstrated with utmost realism. . . . Her physical examination showed nothing striking. Salivary glands are markedly enlarged on both sides.

    January 21. Has been reading *Faust* again. In her diary, writes that art is the "mutual permeation" of the "world of the body" and the "world of the spirit." Says that her own poems are "hospital poems . . . weak—without skill or perseverance; only managing to beat their wings softly."

    February 8. Agitation, quickly subsided again. Has attached herself to an elegant, very thin female patient. Homo-erotic component strikingly evident.

    February 15. Vexation, and torment. Says that her mind forces her always to think of eating. Feels herself degraded by this. Has entirely, for the first time in years, stopped writing poetry.

．　　　．　　　．

Callas is my favorite singer, but I've only
seen her once—;

I've never forgotten that night . . .
—It was in *Tosca*, she had long before

lost weight, her voice
had been, for years,

>   deteriorating, half itself . . .

When her career began, of course, she was fat,

enormous—; in the early photographs,
sometimes I almost don't recognize her . . .

The voice too then was enormous—

healthy; robust; subtle; but capable of
crude effects, even vulgar,

>   almost out of
high spirits, too much health . . .

But soon she felt that she must lose weight,—
that all she was trying to express

was obliterated by her body,
buried in flesh—;

>   abruptly, within
four months, she lost at least sixty pounds . . .

—The gossip in Milan was that Callas
had swallowed a tapeworm.

But of course she hadn't.

>   The *tapeworm*
was her *soul* . . .

—How her soul, uncompromising,
insatiable,

>   must have loved eating the flesh from her bones,

revealing this extraordinarily
mercurial; fragile; masterly creature . . .

—But irresistibly, nothing
stopped there; the huge voice

also began to change: at first, it simply diminished
in volume, in size,

              then the top notes became
shrill, unreliable—at last,
usually not there at all . . .

—No one knows *why*. Perhaps her mind,
ravenous, still insatiable, sensed

that to struggle with the *shreds* of a voice

must make her artistry subtler, more refined,
more capable of expressing humiliation,
rage, betrayal . . .

—Perhaps the opposite. Perhaps her spirit
loathed the unending struggle

to *embody* itself, to *manifest* itself, on a stage whose

mechanics, and suffocating customs,
seemed expressly designed to annihilate spirit . . .

—I know that in *Tosca*, in the second act,
when, humiliated, hounded by Scarpia,
she sang *Vissi d'arte*
                      —"I lived for art"—

and in torment, bewilderment, at the end she asks,
with a voice reaching
                  harrowingly for the notes,

"Art has *repaid* me LIKE THIS?"

                            I felt I was watching
autobiography—
              an art; skill;
virtuosity

miles distant from the usual soprano's
athleticism,—
              the usual musician's dream
of virtuosity *without* content . . .

—I wonder what she feels, now,
listening to her recordings.

For they have already, within a few years,
begun to date . . .

Whatever they express
they express through the style of a decade
and a half—;
        a style *she* helped create . . .

—She must know that now
she probably would *not* do a trill in
exactly that way,—
        that the whole sound, atmosphere,
dramaturgy of her recordings

have just slightly become those of the past . . .

—Is it bitter? Does her soul
tell her

that she was an *idiot* ever to think
anything
        material wholly could satisfy? . . .

—Perhaps it says: *The only way*
to escape
the History of Styles

is not to have a body.

            •   •   •

When I open my eyes in the morning, my great
mystery
        stands before me . . .
—I *know* that I am intelligent; therefore

the inability not to fear food
day-and-night; this unending hunger
ten minutes after I have eaten . . .
               a childish
dread of eating; hunger which can have no cause,—

half my mind says that all this
is *demeaning* . . .

    Bread
for days on end
drives all real thought from my brain . . .

—Then I think, No. The ideal of being thin

conceals the ideal
not to have a body—;
      which is NOT trivial . . .

This wish seems now as much a "given" of my existence

as the intolerable
fact that I am dark-complexioned; big-boned;
and once weighed
one hundred and sixty-five pounds . . .

—But then I think, *No.* That's too simple,—

without a body, who can
know himself at all?
     Only by
acting; choosing; rejecting; have I
made myself—
    discovered who and what *Ellen* can be . . .

—But then again I think, *NO.* This *I* is anterior
to name; gender; action;
fashion;
   MATTER ITSELF,—

. . . trying to stop my hunger with FOOD
is like trying to appease thirst
     with ink.

    • • •

March 30. Result of the consultation: Both gentlemen agree completely with my prognosis and doubt any therapeutic usefulness of commitment even more emphatically than I. All three of us are agreed that it is not a case of obsessional neurosis and not one of manic-depressive psychosis, and that no definitely reliable therapy is possible. We therefore resolved to give in to the patient's demand for discharge.

    • • •

The train-ride yesterday
was far *worse* than I expected . . .

                              In our compartment
were ordinary people: a student;
a woman; her child;—

they had ordinary bodies, pleasant faces;
                              but I thought
I was surrounded by creatures

with the pathetic, desperate
desire to be *not* what they were:—

the student was short,
and carried his body as if forcing
it to be taller—;

the woman showed her gums when she smiled,
and often held her
hand up to hide them—;

the child
seemed to cry simply because it was
small; a dwarf, and helpless . . .

—I was hungry. I had insisted that my husband
not bring food . . .

After about thirty minutes, the woman
peeled an orange

to quiet the child. She put a section
into its mouth—;
                         immediately it spit it out.

The piece fell to the floor.

—She pushed it with her foot through the dirt
toward me
several inches.

My husband saw me staring
down at the piece . . .

—I didn't move; how I wanted
to reach out,
              and as if invisible

shove it in my mouth—;

my body
became rigid. As I stared at him,
I could see him staring
at me,—
              then he looked at the student—; at the woman—; then
back to me . . .

I didn't move.

—At last, he bent down, and
casually
              threw it out the window.

He looked away.

—I got up to leave the compartment, then
saw his face,—

his eyes
were red;
              and I saw

—*I'm sure I saw*—

disappointment.

                    •   •   •

On the third day of being home she is as if transformed. At breakfast she
eats butter and sugar, at noon she eats so much that—for the first time in
thirteen years!—she is satisfied by her food and gets really full. At afternoon
coffee she eats chocolate creams and Easter eggs. She takes a walk with her
husband, reads poems, listens to recordings, is in a positively festive mood,
and all heaviness seems to have fallen away from her. She writes letters,
the last one a letter to the fellow patient here to whom she had become
so attached. In the evening she takes a lethal dose of poison, and on the
following morning she is dead. "She looked as she had never looked in
life—calm and happy and peaceful."

•   •   •

Dearest.—I remember how
at eighteen,
              on hikes with friends, when
they rested, sitting down to joke or talk,

I circled
around them, afraid to hike ahead alone,

yet afraid to rest
when I was not yet truly thin.

You and, yes, my husband,—
you and he

have by degrees drawn me within the circle;
forced me to sit down at last on the ground.

I am grateful.

But something in me *refuses* it.

—How eager I have been
to compromise, to kill this *refuser*,—

but each compromise, each attempt
to poison an ideal
which often seemed to *me* sterile and unreal,

heightens my hunger.

I am crippled. I disappoint you.

Will you greet with anger, or
happiness,

the news which might well reach you
before this letter?

              Your *Ellen*.

Carl Dennis (1939–)

Carl Dennis was born in St. Louis, Missouri, and attended Oberlin College, the University of Chicago, the University of Minnesota, and the University of California at Berkeley. He has taught at the State University of New York at Buffalo since 1966. His poetry books include House of My Own *(1974),* Climbing Down *(1976),* Signs and Wonders *(1979),* The Near World *(1985),* The Outskirts of Troy *(1988),* Meetings with Time *(1992),* Ranking the Wishes *(1997),* Practical Gods *(2001, Pulitzer Prize),* New and Selected Poems *(2004), and* Callings *(2010). Among his honors are Guggenheim and National Endowment for the Arts fellowships and the Ruth Lilly Prize. Carl Dennis lives in Buffalo, New York.*

Spring Letter

With the warmer days the shops on Elmwood
Stay open later, still busy long after sundown.
It looks like the neighborhood's coming back.
Gone are the boarded storefronts that you interpreted,
When you lived here, as an emblem of your private recession,
Your ship of state becalmed in the doldrums,
Your guiding stars obscured by fog. Now the cut-rate drugstore
Where you stocked your arsenal against migraine
Is an Asian emporium. Aisles of onyx, silk, and brass,
Of reed baskets so carefully woven and so inexpensive
Every house could have one, one work of art,
Though doubtless you'd refuse, brooding instead
On the weavers, their low wages and long hours,
The fruit of their labor stolen by middlemen.
Tomorrow I too may worry like that, but for now
I'm focusing on a mood of calm, a spirit of acceptance,
Loyal to my plan to keep my moods distinct
And do each justice, one by one.
The people in line for ice cream at the Sweet Tooth
Could be my aunts and uncles, nieces and nephews.
What ritual is more ancient or more peaceable?
Here are the old ones rewarding themselves
For making it to old age. Here are the children
Stunned into silence by the ten-foot list of flavors
From Mud Pie to Milky Way, a cosmic plenty.
And those neither young nor old, should they be loyal
To their favorite flavor or risk a new one?
It's a balmy night in western New York, in May,
Under the lights of Elmwood, which are too bright

For the stars to be visible as they pour down on my head
Their endless starry virtues. Nothing confines me.
Why you felt our town closing in, why here
You could never become whoever you wished to be,
Isn't easy to understand, but I'm trying.
Tomorrow I may ask myself again if my staying
Is a sign of greater enlightenment or smaller ambition.
But this evening, pausing by the window of Elmwood Liquors,
I want to applaud the prize-winning upstate Vouvray,
The equal of its kind in Europe, the sign says.
No time for a glass on your search
As you steer under stars too far to be friendly
Toward the island where True Beauty, the Princess,
Languishes as a prisoner. I can see you at the tiller
Squinting through spume, hoping your charts are accurate,
Hoping she can guess you're on your way.

Two or Three Wishes

Suppose Oedipus never discovers his ignorance
And remains king to the end,
Proud as he walks the streets of Thebes
To think of himself as his city's savior,
The fortunate husband of Queen Jocasta.
The blessed father of two dutiful daughters.
Would we call him happy, a man so unknowing?
If we did, we'd have to admit that happiness
Isn't all we ask for. We want some truth as well,
Whatever that means. We want our notions,
However beautiful and coherent,
Linked to something beyond themselves.
First, I want to dream I am in your thoughts.
Then I want that dream to be a picture
Faithful in flesh and spirit to what is the case.
First I imagine your heart as a city like Thebes
With me as the park you prefer to visit.
Then with my open eyes I want to see you
Resting again and again on one of the benches,
Gathering strength for the messenger
Who may be nearing the outskirts now
Wondering if you'll know how to take the news.

Stephen Dunn (1939–)

Stephen Dunn was born in Forest Hills, New York, and attended Hofstra University, the New School, and Syracuse University. He worked as a professional basketball player, copywriter, and editor, taught at Southwestern State University in Minnesota and Syracuse University, and settled at Richard Stockton College, Pomona, New Jersey, in 1974. His poetry books include Looking for Holes in the Ceiling *(1974),* Full of Lust and Good Usage *(1976),* A Circus of Needs *(1978),* Work and Love *(1981),* Not Dancing *(1984),* Local Time *(1986, National Poetry Series),* Between Angels *(1989),* Landscape at the End of the Century *(1991),* Loosestrife *(1996),* Different Hours *(2000, Pulitzer Prize),* Everything Else in the World *(2006),* What Goes On *(2010), and* Here and Now *(2011). Among his honors are National Endowment for the Arts, Yaddo, and Guggenheim fellowships. Stephen Dunn lives in Frostburg, Maryland.*

Allegory of the Cave

He climbed toward the blinding light
and when his eyes adjusted
he looked down and could see

his fellow prisoners captivated
by shadows; everything he had believed
was false. And he was suddenly

in the 20th century, in the sunlight
and violence of history, encumbered
by knowledge. Only a hero

would dare return with the truth.
So from the cave's upper reaches,
removed from harm, he called out

the disturbing news.
What lovely echoes, the prisoners said,
what a fine musical place to live.

He spelled it out, then, in clear prose
on paper scraps, which he floated down.
But in the semi-dark they read his words

with the indulgence of those who seldom read:
It's about my father's death, one of them said.
No, said the others, it's a joke.

By this time he no longer was sure
of what he'd seen. Wasn't sunlight a shadow too?
Wasn't there always a source

behind a source? He just stood there,
confused, a man who had moved
to larger errors, without a prayer.

Tucson

A man was dancing with the wrong woman
in the wrong bar, the wrong part of town.
He must have chosen the woman, the place,
as keenly as you choose what to wear
when you dress to kill.
And the woman, who could have said no,
must have made her choice years ago,
to look like the kind of trouble
certain men choose as their own.
I was there for no good reason myself,
with a friend looking for a friend,
but I'm not important.
They were dancing close
when a man from the bar decided
the dancing was wrong. I'd forgotten
how fragile the face is, how fists too
are just so many small bones.
The bouncer waited, then broke in.
Someone wiped up the blood.
The woman began to dance
with another woman, each in tight jeans.
The air pulsed. My hands
were fidgety, damp.
We were Mexicans, Indians, whites.
The woman was part this, part that.
My friend said nothing's wrong, stay put,
it's a good fighting bar, you won't get hurt
unless you need to get hurt.

Robert Pinsky (1940–)

Robert Pinsky was born in Long Branch, New Jersey. He attended Rutgers University and Stanford University before teaching at the University of Chicago, Wellesley College, the University of California–Berkeley, and since 1988, Boston University. His poetry books include Sadness and Happiness *(1975),* An Explanation of America *(1979),* History of My Heart *(1984),* The Want Bone *(1990),* The Figured Wheel *(1996),* Jersey Rain *(2000),* Samurai Song *(2001), and* Gulf Music *(2007). Robert Pinsky has published numerous anthologies, translations, and essays and is the poetry editor of* Slate *magazine. Among his honors are Guggenheim and National Endowment for the Arts fellowships, the Shelley Memorial Award, and the Lenore Marshall Prize. From 1997 to 2000, he served as U.S. poet laureate. He lives in Boston, Massachusetts.*

History of My Heart

I

One Christmastime Fats Waller in a fur coat
Rolled beaming from a taxicab with two pretty girls
Each at an arm as he led them in a thick downy snowfall

Across Thirty-fourth Street into the busy crowd
Shopping at Macy's: perfume, holly, snowflake displays.
Chimes rang for change. In Toys, where my mother worked

Over her school vacation, the crowd swelled and stood
Filling the aisles, whispered at the fringes, listening
To the sounds of the large, gorgeously dressed man,

His smile bemused and exalted, lips boom-booming a bold
Bass line as he improvised on an expensive, tinkly
Piano the size of a lady's jewel box or a wedding cake.

She put into my heart this scene from the romance of Joy,
Co-authored by her and the movies, like her others—
My father making the winning basket at the buzzer

And punching the enraged gambler who came onto the court—
The brilliant black and white of the movies, texture
Of wet snowy fur, the taxi's windshield, piano keys,

Reflections that slid over the thick brass baton
That worked the elevator. Happiness needs a setting:
Shepherds and shepherdesses in the grass, kids in a store,

The back room of Carly's parents' shop, record-player
And paper streamers twisted in two colors: what I felt
Dancing close one afternoon with a thin blond girl

Was my amazing good luck, the pleased erection
Stretching and stretching at the idea *She likes me,*
She likes it, the thought of legs under a woolen skirt,

To see eyes "melting" so I could think *This is it,*
They're melting! Mutual arousal of suddenly feeling
Desired: *This is it: "desire"!* When we came out

Into the street we saw it had begun, the firm flakes
Sticking, coating the tops of cars, melting on the wet
Black street that reflected storelights, soft

Separate crystals clinging intact on the nap of collar
And cuff, swarms of them stalling in the wind to plunge
Sideways and cluster in spangles on our hair and lashes,

Melting to a fresh glaze on the bloodwarm porcelain
Of our faces, Hey nonny-nonny boom-boom, the cold graceful
Manna, heartfelt, falling and gathering copious

As the air itself in the small-town main street
As it fell over my mother's imaginary and remembered
Macy's in New York years before I was even born,

II

And the little white piano, tinkling away like crazy—
My unconceived heart in a way waiting somewhere like
Wherever it goes in sleep. Later, my eyes opened

And I woke up glad to feel the sunlight warm
High up in the window, a brighter blue striping
Blue folds of curtain, and glad to hear the house

Was still sleeping. I didn't call, but climbed up
To balance my chest on the top rail, cheek
Pressed close where I had grooved the rail's varnish

With sets of double tooth-lines. Clinging
With both arms, I grunted, pulled one leg over
And stretched it as my weight started to slip down

With some panic till my toes found the bottom rail,
Then let my weight slide more till I was over—
Thrilled, half-scared, still hanging high up

With both hands from the spindles. Then lower
Slipping down until I could fall to the floor
With a thud but not hurt, and out, free in the house.

Then softly down the hall to the other bedroom
To push against the door; and when it came open
More light came in, opening out like a fan

So they woke up and laughed, as she lifted me
Up in between them under the dark red blanket,
We all three laughing there because I climbed out myself.

Earlier still, she held me curled in close
With everyone around saying my name, and hovering,
After my grandpa's cigarette burned me on the neck

As he held me up for the camera, and the pain buzzed
Scaring me because it twisted right inside me;
So when she took me and held me and I curled up, sucking,

It was as if she had put me back together again
So sweetly I was glad the hurt had torn me.
She wanted to have made the whole world up,

So that it could be hers to give. So she opened
A letter I wrote my sister, who was having trouble
Getting on with her, and read some things about herself

That made her go to the telephone and call me up:
"You shouldn't open other people's letters," I said
And she said "Yes—*who taught you that?*"

—As if she owned the copyright on good and bad,
Or having followed pain inside she owned her children
From the inside out, or made us when she named us,

III

Made me Robert. She took me with her to a print-shop
Where the man struck a slug: a five-inch strip of lead
With the twelve letters of my name, reversed,

Raised along one edge, that for her sake he made
For me, so I could take it home with me to keep
And hold the letters up close to a mirror

Or press their shapes into clay, or inked from a pad
Onto all kinds of paper surfaces, onto walls and shirts,
Lengthwise on a Band-Aid, or even on my own skin—

The little characters fading from my arm, the gift
Always ready to be used again. Gifts from the heart:
Her giving me her breast milk or my name, Waller

Showing off in a store, for free, giving them
A thrill as someone might give someone an erection,
For the thrill of it—or you come back salty from a swim:

Eighteen shucked fresh oysters and the cold bottle
Sweating in its ribbon, surprise, happy birthday!
So what if the giver also takes, is after something?

So what if with guile she strove to color
Everything she gave with herself, the lady's favor
A scarf or bit of sleeve of her favorite color

Fluttering on the horseman's bloodflecked armor
Just over the heart—how presume to forgive the breast
Or sudden jazz for becoming what we want? I want

Presents I can't picture until they come,
The generator flashlight Italo gave me one Christmas:
One squeeze and the gears visibly churning in the amber

Pistol-shaped handle hummed for half a minute
In my palm, the spare bulb in its chamber under my thumb,
Secret; or, the knife and basswood Ellen gave me to whittle.

And until the gift of desire, the heart is a titular,
Insane king who stares emptily at his counselors
For weeks, drools or babbles a little, as word spreads

In the taverns that he is dead, or an impostor. One day
A light concentrates in his eyes, he scowls, alert, and points
Without a word to one pass in the cold, grape-colored peaks—

Generals and courtiers groan, falling to work
With a frantic movement of farriers, cooks, builders,
The city thrown willing or unwilling like seed

(While the brain at the same time may be settling
Into the morning *Chronicle,* humming to itself,
Like a fat person eating M&Ms in the bathtub)

IV

Toward war, new forms of worship or migration.
I went out from my mother's kitchen, across the yard
Of the little two-family house, and into the Woods:

Guns, chevrons, swordplay, a scarf of sooty smoke
Rolled upwards from a little cratewood fire
Under the low tent of a Winesap fallen

With fingers rooting in the dirt, the old orchard
Smothered among the brush of wild cherry, sumac,
Sassafras and the stifling shade of oak

In the strip of overgrown terrain running
East from the train tracks to the ocean, woods
Of demarcation, where boys went like newly-converted

Christian kings with angels on helmet and breastplate,
Bent on blood or poaching. *There are a mountain and a woods
Between us*—a male covenant, longbows, headlocks. A pack

Of four stayed half-aware it was past dark
In a crude hut roasting meat stolen from the A&P
Until someone's annoyed father hailed us from the tracks

And scared us home to catch hell: We were worried,
Where have you been? In the Woods. With snakes and tramps.
An actual hobo knocked at our back door

One morning, declining food, to get hot water.
He shaved on our steps from an enamel basin with brush
And cut-throat razor, the gray hair on his chest

Armorial in the sunlight—then back to the woods,
And the otherlife of snakes, poison oak, boxcars.
Were the trees cleared first for the trains or the orchard?

Walking home by the street because it was dark,
That night, the smoke-smell in my clothes was like a bearskin.
Where the lone hunter and late bird have seen us

Pass and repass, the mountain and the woods seem
To stand darker than before—words of sexual nostalgia
In a song or poem seemed cloaked laments

For the woods when Indians made lodges from the skin
Of birch or deer. When the mysterious lighted room
Of a bus glided past in the mist, the faces

Passing me in the yellow light inside
Were a half-heard story or a song. And my heart
Moved, restless and empty as a scrap of something

Blowing in wide spirals on the wind carrying
The sound of breakers clearly to me through the pass
Between the blocks of houses. The horn of Roland

V

But what was it I was too young for? On moonless
Nights, water and sand are one shade of black,
And the creamy foam rising with moaning noises

Charges like a spectral army in a poem toward the bluffs
Before it subsides dreamily to gather again.
I thought of going down there to watch it a while,

Feeling as though it could turn me into fog,
Or that the wind would start to speak a language
And change me—as if I knocked where I saw a light

Burning in some certain misted window I passed,
A house or store or tap-room where the strangers inside
Would recognize me, locus of a new life like a woods

Or orchard that waxed and vanished into cloud
Like the moon, under a spell. Shrill flutes,
Oboes and cymbals of doom. My poor mother fell,

And after the accident loud noises and bright lights
Hurt her. And heights. She went down stairs backwards,
Sometimes with one arm on my small brother's shoulder.

Over the years, she got better. But I was lost in music;
The cold brazen bow of the saxophone, its weight
At thumb, neck and lip, came to a bloodwarm life

Like Italo's flashlight in the hand. In a white
Jacket and pants with a satin stripe I aspired
To the roughneck elegance of my Grandfather Dave.

Sometimes, playing in a bar or at a high school dance, I felt
My heart following after a capacious form,
Sexual and abstract, in the thunk, thrum,

Thrum, come-wallow and then a little screen
Of quicker notes goosing to a fifth higher, winging
To clang-whomp of a major seventh: listen to *me*

Listen to *me*, the heart says in reprise until sometimes
In the course of giving itself it flows out of itself
All the way across the air, in a music piercing

As the kids at the beach calling from the water *Look,*
Look at me, to their mothers, but out of itself, into
The listener the way feeling pretty or full of erotic revery

Makes the one who feels seem beautiful to the beholder
Witnessing the idea of the giving of desire—nothing more wanted
Than the little singing notes of wanting—the heart

Yearning further into giving itself into the air, breath
Strained into song emptying the golden bell it comes from,
The pure source poured altogether out and away.

The Questions

What about the people who came to my father's office
For hearing aids and glasses—chatting with him sometimes

A few extra minutes while I swept up in the back,
Addressed packages, cleaned the machines; if he was busy

I might sell them batteries, or tend to their questions:
The tall overloud old man with a tilted, ironic smirk

To cover the gaps in his hearing; a woman who hummed one
Prolonged note constantly, we called her "the hummer"—how

Could her white fat husband (he looked like Rev. Peale)
Bear hearing it day and night? And others: a coquettish old lady

In a bandeau, a European. She worked for refugees who ran
Gift shops or booths on the boardwalk in the summer;

She must have lived in winter on Social Security. One man
Always greeted my father in Masonic gestures and codes.

Why do I want them to be treated tenderly by the world, now
Long after they must have slipped from it one way or another,

While I was dawdling through school at that moment—or driving,
Reading, talking to Ellen. Why this new superfluous caring?

I want for them not to have died in awful pain, friendless.
Though many of the living are starving, I still pray for these,

Dead, mostly anonymous (but Mr. Monk, Mrs. Rose Vogel)
And barely remembered: that they had a little extra, something

For pleasure, a good meal, a book or a decent television set.
Of whom do I pray this rubbery, low-class charity? I saw

An expert today, a nun—wearing a regular skirt and blouse,
But the hood or headdress navy and white around her plain

Probably Irish face, older than me by five or ten years.
The Post Office clerk told her he couldn't break a twenty

So she got change next door and came back to send her package.
As I came out she was driving off—with an air, it seemed to me,

Of annoying, demure good cheer, as if the reasonableness
Of change, mail, cars, clothes was a pleasure in itself: veiled

And dumb like the girls I thought enjoyed the rules too much
In grade school. She might have been a grade school teacher;

But she reminded me of being there, aside from that—as a name
And person there, a Mary or John who learns that the janitor

Is Mr. Woodhouse; the principal is Mr. Ringleven; the secretary
In the office is Mrs. Apostolacos; the bus driver is Ray.

Samurai Song

When I had no roof I made
Audacity my roof. When I had
No supper my eyes dined.

When I had no eyes I listened.
When I had no ears I thought.
When I had no thought I waited.

When I had no father I made
Care my father. When I had
No mother I embraced order.

When I had no friend I made
Quiet my friend. When I had no
Enemy I opposed my body.

When I had no temple I made
My voice my temple. I have
No priest, my tongue is my choir.

When I have no means fortune
Is my means. When I have
Nothing, death will be my fortune.

Need is my tactic, detachment
Is my strategy. When I had
No lover I courted sleep.

James Welch (1940–2003)

James Welch was born in Browning, Montana, and educated at Indian reservation schools before attending the University of Montana and studying with Richard Hugo. Besides a number of novels and documentaries, he published one poetry collection—his first book—in 1971: Riding the Earthboy 40. *Among his honors are a National Endowment for the Arts grant, the Los Angeles Times Book Award for his 1986 novel* Fools Crow, *a 1991 Emmy Award (with Paul Stekler) for the PBS documentary* Last Stand at Little Bighorn, *and the French Chevalier de L'Ordre des Arts et des Lettres in 2000. James Welch died at his home in Missoula, Montana.*

Christmas Comes to Moccasin Flat

Christmas comes like this: Wise men
unhurried, candles bought on credit (poor price
for calves), warriors face down in wine sleep.
Winds cheat to pull heat from smoke.

Friends sit in chinked cabins, stare out
plastic windows and wait for commodities.
Charlie Blackbird, twenty miles from church
and bar, stabs his fire with flint.

When drunks drain radiators for love
or need, chiefs eat snow and talk of change,
an urge to laugh pounding their ribs.
Elk play games in high country.

Medicine Woman, clay pipe and twist tobacco,
calls each blizzard by name and predicts
five o'clock by spitting at her television.
Children lean into her breath to beg a story:

Something about honor and passion,
warriors back with meat and song,
a peculiar evening star, quick vision of birth.
Blackbird feeds his fire. Outside, a quick 30 below.

Billy Collins (1941–)

Billy Collins was born in New York City and attended the College of the Holy Cross and the University of California at Riverside. He has been teaching at Lehman College, City University of New York, since 1971. His poetry books include The Apple That Astonished Paris *(1988),* Questions About Angels *(1991, National Poetry Series),* The Art of Drowning *(1995),* Picnic, Lightning *(1998),* Sailing Alone Around the Room *(2001),* Nine Horses *(2002),* The Trouble with Poetry *(2005),* She Was Just Seventeen *(2006), and* Ballistics *(2008). Among his honors are the Mark Twain Award as well as National Endowment for the Arts and Guggenheim fellowships. He served as U.S. poet laureate from 2001 to 2003. Billy Collins lives in Somers, New York.*

Introduction to Poetry

I ask them to take a poem
and hold it up to the light
like a color slide

or press an ear against its hive.

I say drop a mouse into a poem
and watch him probe his way out,

or walk inside the poem's room
and feel the walls for a light switch.

I want them to waterski
across the surface of a poem
waving at the author's name on the shore.

But all they want to do
is tie the poem to a chair with rope
and torture a confession out of it.

They begin beating it with a hose
to find out what it really means.

The Dead

The dead are always looking down on us, they say,
while we are putting on our shoes or making a sandwich,
they are looking down through the glass-bottom boats of heaven
as they row themselves slowly through eternity.

They watch the tops of our heads moving below on earth,
and when we lie down in a field or on a couch,
drugged perhaps by the hum of a warm afternoon,
they think we are looking back at them,

which makes them lift their oars and fall silent
and wait, like parents, for us to close our eyes.

Toi Derricotte (1941–)

Toi Derricotte was born in Hamtramck, Michigan, and attended Wayne State University and New York University. She taught in secondary schools and at Old Dominion University before joining the University of Pittsburgh faculty. In 1996 she and Cornelius Eady founded Cave Canem, an organization fostering emerging African-American poets that has become an instrumental force in twenty-first-century American poetry. Her poetry books include The Empress of the Death House *(1978),* Natural Birth *(1983),* Captivity *(1989), and* Tender *(1997). Among her honors are MacDowell Colony, National Endowment for the Arts, and Guggenheim fellowships and the Anisfield-Wolf Book Award for nonfiction. Toi Derricotte lives in Pittsburgh, Pennsylvania.*

Allen Ginsberg

Once Allen Ginsberg stopped to pee at a bookstore
   in New Jersey,
but he looked like a bum—
not like the miracle-laden Christ with electric atom juice,
   not like the one whose brain is a river in which was plunked
   the stone of the world (the one bathing fluid to wash away
   25,000 year half-lives), he was dressed as a bum.
He had wobbled on a pee-heavy bladder
in search of a gas station,
a dime store with a quarter booth,
a Chinese restaurant,
when he came to that grocery store of dreams:
Chunks of Baudelaire's skin
glittered in plastic;
his eyes in sets, innocent
as the unhoused eyes of a butchered cow.
In a dark corner, Rimbaud's
genitals hung like jerky,
and the milk of Whitman's breasts
drifted in a carton, dry as talcum.
He wanted to pee and lay his head
on the cool stacks;
but the clerk took one look
and thought of the buttocks of clean businessmen squatting
   during lunch hour,
the thin flanks of pretty girls buying poetry for school.
Behind her, faintly,
the deodorized bathroom.
She was the one at the gate

protecting civilization.
He turned, walked to the gutter,
unzipped his pants, and peed.
Do you know who that was?
A man in the back came forth.
Soon she was known as
the woman in the store on Main
who said no to Allen Ginsberg;
and she is proud—
so proud she told this story
pointing to the spot outside, as if
still flowed that holy stream.

The Weakness

That time my grandmother dragged me
through the perfume aisles at Saks, she held me up
by my arm, hissing, "Stand up,"
through clenched teeth, her eyes
bright as a dog's
cornered in the light.
She said it over and over,
as if she were Jesus,
and I were dead. She had been
solid as a tree,
a fur around her neck, a
light-skinned matron whose car was parked, who walked on swirling
marble and passed through
brass openings—in 1945.
There was not even a black
elevator operator at Saks.
The saleswoman had brought velvet
leggings to lace me in, and cooed,
as if in the service of all grandmothers.
My grandmother had smiled, but not
hungrily, not like my mother
who hated them, but wanted to please,
and they had smiled back, as if
they were wearing wooden collars.
When my legs gave out, my grandmother
dragged me up and held me like God
holds saints by the
roots of the hair. I begged her

to believe I couldn't help it. Stumbling,
her face white
with sweat, she pushed me through the crowd, rushing
away from those eyes
that saw through
her clothes, under
her skin, all the way down
to the transparent
genes confessing.

Stephen Dobyns (1941–)

Stephen Dobyns was born in Orange, New Jersey, and grew up in Michigan, Virginia, and Pennsylvania. He attended Shimer College, Wayne State University, and the University of Iowa Writers Workshop, after which he taught at the State University of New York at Brockport before joining the Detroit News *as a reporter. Since 1971 he has worked as a freelance writer with numerous novels to his credit. His poetry books include* Concurring Beasts *(1972, Lamont Poetry Prize),* Griffon *(1976),* Heat Death *(1980),* The Balthus Poems *(1982),* Black Dog, Red Dog *(1984, National Poetry Series),* Cemetery Nights *(1987),* Body Traffic *(1990),* Velocities *(1994),* Common Carnage *(1996),* Pallbearers Envying the One Who Rides *(1999),* Mystery, So Long *(2005), and* Winter's Journey *(2010). Among his honors are MacDowell, Yaddo, National Endowment for the Arts, and Guggenheim fellowships.*

How to Like It

These are the first days of fall. The wind
at evening smells of roads still to be traveled,
while the sound of leaves blowing across the lawns
is like an unsettled feeling in the blood,
the desire to get in a car and just keep driving.
A man and a dog descend their front steps.
The dog says, Let's go downtown and get crazy drunk.
Let's tip over all the trash cans we can find.
This is how dogs deal with the prospect of change.
But in his sense of the season, the man is struck
by the oppressiveness of his past, how his memories
which were shifting and fluid have grown more solid
until it seems he can see remembered faces
caught up among the dark places in the trees.
The dog says, Let's pick up some girls and just
rip off their clothes. Let's dig holes everywhere.
Above his house, the man notices wisps of cloud
crossing the face of the moon. Like in a movie,
he says to himself, a movie about a person
leaving on a journey. He looks down the street
to the hills outside of town and finds the cut
where the road heads north. He thinks of driving
on that road and the dusty smell of the car
heater, which hasn't been used since last winter.
The dog says, Let's go down to the diner and sniff
people's legs. Let's stuff ourselves on burgers.
In the man's mind, the road is empty and dark.
Pine trees press down to the edge of the shoulder,

where the eyes of animals, fixed in his headlights,
shine like small cautions against the night.
Sometimes a passing truck makes his whole car shake.
The dog says, Let's go to sleep. Let's lie down
by the fire and put our tails over our noses.
But the man wants to drive all night, crossing
one state line after another, and never stop
until the sun creeps into his rearview mirror.
Then he'll pull over and rest awhile before
starting again, and at dusk he'll crest a hill
and there, filling a valley, will be the lights
of a city entirely new to him.
But the dog says, Let's just go back inside.
Let's not do anything tonight. So they
walk back up the sidewalk to the front steps.
How is it possible to want so many things
and still want nothing. The man wants to sleep
and wants to hit his head again and again
against a wall. Why is it all so difficult?
But the dog says, Let's go make a sandwich.
Let's make the tallest sandwich anyone's ever seen.
And that's what they do and that's where the man's
wife finds him, staring into the refrigerator
as if into the place where the answers are kept—
the ones telling why you get up in the morning
and how it is possible to sleep at night,
answers to what comes next and how to like it.

Lullaby

The zero of a yawn eclipses your face,
feeling drowsy, eyelids heavy:
goodnight, goodnight, blow out the light,
the century is going to sleep.
Goodnight, Adolf, you almost prevailed—
your dreams, little fellow, rose to fact
like a swamp beast from the muck, then
they settled back again: good luck for us,
bad luck for you, the century is going
to sleep. And Uncle Joe, your musings
tried to duplicate the density of concrete.
Should we add up the dead millions squeezed
like dry leaves to make your diamond?

But then, oh happy day, you passed away.
Dead brutes, dead bullies, the tyrants
totter past to forgottenhood, the century
is going to sleep. But also the heroes:
Babe Ruth, General MacArthur, Gypsy Rose Lee.
The stages you danced upon are compost now,
the newspapers headlining your exploits
pack the landfill. You imitate your shadows.
All the radio broadcasts have been silenced.
Hush! The century is going to sleep.
Ezra Pound, are you still grinding your teeth?
Robert Frost, is your bricklike heart
the only solid chunk left in your coffin?
Thelonious Monk, are you still bopping
someplace down below? Lady Day hums the tune:
lullabies, lullabies, the century
is going to sleep. And all the objects:
the Model T Fords, the 45-rpm records,
eight-track tape players—see them drowsing
in cobwebbed warehouses. Even the rats put a paw
to their lips. The century is going to sleep.
Maybe in another world John Kennedy was never shot,
maybe John Berryman lived a few years longer,
wrote a villanelle before downing Seconal.
And John Lennon, maybe in another world
the madman missed and more songs got made.
All the Johns, all the Janices, all the Sylvias—
blow out the light, the century is going to sleep.
Dead best-sellers, dead Nobel winners,
dead Academy Award winners, dead football
heroes, World Series champions, Kentucky
Derby winners: all tucked between warm sheets,
sweet dreams carouse across their brains.
My father, my grandparents, my cousins,
your faces slide away in the vapor. How
difficult to see you in memory anymore. You
are the frames from which a photo was stolen.
Or my friends, I have left behind too many—
their stories stopped before mine, their
straight lines banked up at black conclusions:
goodnight Ray, goodnight Betty, goodnight Dick,
the century is going to sleep. And those ideas,
the glad ones, the young ones—integration,
human rights. Goodnight, goodnight. The twelve-

tone scale, abstract expressionism. Sweet dreams,
sweet dreams. A chicken in every pot, two cars
in every garage, three TVs in every house.
Sleep tight, sleep tight. We are retreating
to books, electronic texts, some get paragraphs,
some sentences, some footnotes, most get silence.
Shouldn't we walk on tiptoe, shouldn't we whisper?
Do you have sand in your eyes, little fellow?
Let's take a breather. A baby's about to be born.
I won't see much of this one. Maybe a morsel,
if I'm lucky, of its infancy. This next one
belongs to my children and their children. What
Auschwitzes and Hiroshimas are already being
prepared? What will be the carnage of tomorrow?
What dumb ideas will be used to erase human breath?
But also the good stuff: what jokes, what
laughter, what kisses, will there still
be kisses? Better not know, better let it come,
like always, as a surprise. Feeling frightened?
Are you scared? Blow out the light, goodnight,
goodnight, the century is going to sleep.

for Stephen King

Robert Hass (1941–)

Robert Hass was born in San Francisco. He attended St. Mary's College of California and Stanford University. He has taught at the State University of New York at Buffalo, St. Mary's College, and since 1989, the University of California at Berkeley. His poetry books include Field Guide *(1973, Yale Younger Poets Award),* Praise *(1979),* Human Wishes *(1989),* Sun Under Wood *(1996, National Book Critics Circle Award),* Time and Materials *(2007, National Book Award, Pulitzer Prize), and* The Apple Trees at Olema *(2010). Other honors include MacArthur and Guggenheim fellowships. Robert Hass was U.S. poet laureate from 1995 to 1997. He lives in Berkeley, California.*

Song

Afternoon cooking in the fall sun—
who is more naked
                              than the man
yelling, "Hey, I'm home!"
                    to an empty house?
thinking because the bay is clear,
the hills in yellow heat,
& scrub oak red in gullies
          that great crowds of family
should tumble from the rooms
                    to throw their bodies on the Papa-body,
                              I-am-loved.

Cat sleeps in the windowgleam,
                    dust motes.
     On the oak table
     filets of sole
stewing in the juice of tangerines,
     slices of green pepper
          on a bone-white dish.

The Pornographer

He has finished a day's work.
Placing his pencil in a marmalade jar
which is colored the soft grey
of a crumbling Chinese wall
in a Sierra meadow, he walks

from his shed into the afternoon
where orioles rise aflame from the orchard.
He likes the sun and he is tired
of the art he has spent on the brown starfish
anus of his heroine, the wet duck's-feather tufts
of armpit and thigh, tender and roseate enfoldings
of labia within labia, the pressure and darkness
and long sudden falls from slippery stone
in the minds of the men with anonymous tongues
in his book. When he relaxes, old images
return. He is probably in Central Asia.
Once again he is marched to the wall.
All the faces are impassive. Now
he is blinded. There is a long silence
in which he images clearly the endless sky
and the horizon, swift with cloud scuds.
Each time, in imagination, he attempts
to stand as calmly as possible
in what is sometimes morning warmth,
sometimes evening chill.

The Return of Robinson Jeffers

1

He shuddered briefly and stared down the long valley
    where the headland rose
And the lean gum trees rattled in the wind above Point
    Sur;
Alive, he had littered the mind's coast
With ghosts of Indians and granite and the dead fleshed
Bodies of desire. That work was done
And, whether done well or not, it had occupied him
As the hawks and the sea were occupied.
Now he could not say what brought him back.
He had imagined resurrection once: the lover of a woman
Who lived lonely in a little ranch house up the ridge
Came back, dragged from the grave by her body's need
To feel under ashen cloud-skies and in the astonishments
Of sunrise some truth beyond the daily lie
Of feeding absolute hunger the way a young girl might
    trap meadow mice
To feed a red-tailed hawk she kept encaged. She
    wanted to die once

As the sun dies in pure fire on the farthest sea-swells.
She had had enough and more of nights when the brain
Flickered and dissolved its little constellations and
 the nerves
Performed their dumb show in the dark among the
 used human smells of bedsheets.
So she burned and he came, a ghost in khaki and
 stunned skin,
And she fled with him. He had imagined, though he
 had not written,
The later moment in the pasture, in moonlight like pale
 stone,
When she lay beside him with an after-tenderness in all
 her bones,
Having become entirely what she was, though aware
 that the thing
Beside her was, again, just so much cheese-soft flesh
And jellied eye rotting in the pools of bone.
Anguish afterwards perhaps, but he had not thought
 afterwards.
Human anguish made him cold.
He told himself the cries of men in war were no more
 conscious
Nor less savage than the shrill repetitions of the Steller's
 jay
Flashing through live oaks up Mal Paso Canyon
And that the oaks, rooted and growing toward their
 grace,
Were—as species go—
More beautiful.

2

He had given himself to stone gods.
I imagine him thinking of that woman
While a live cloud of gulls
Plumes the wind behind a trawler
Throbbing toward the last cannery at Monterey.
The pelicans are gone which had, wheeling,
Written Chinese poems on the sea. The grebes are gone
That feasted on the endless hunger of the flashing runs
Of salmon. And I imagine that he saw, finally,
That though rock stands, it does not breed.
He feels specific rage. Feels, obscurely, that his sex

Is his, not god-force only, but his own soft flesh grown
    thick
With inconsolable desire. The grebes are gone.
He feels a plain man's elegiac tenderness,
An awkward brotherhood with the world's numb poor
His poems had despised. Rage and tenderness are pain.
He feels pain as rounding at the hips, as breasts.
Pain blossoms in his belly like the first dark
Stirrings of a child, a surfeit of the love that he had
    bled to rock
And twisted into cypress haunts above the cliffs.
He knows he has come back to mourn,
To grieve, womanish, a hundred patient years
Along this fragile coast. I imagine the sky's arch,
Cloud-swift, lifts him then, all ache in sex and breasts,
Beyond the leached ashes of dead fire,
The small jeweled hunger in the seabird's eye.

Lyn Hejinian (1941–)

Lyn Hejinian was born in San Francisco. She attended Harvard University, worked as an editor, and has taught at the New College of California and the University of California at Berkeley. Her poetry books include A Thought Is the Bride of What Thinking *(1976),* A Mask of Motion *(1977),* Writing Is an Aid to Memory *(1978),* The Cell *(1992),* The Cold of Poetry *(1994),* Happily *(2000),* A Border Comedy *(2001),* My Life in the Nineties *(2003), and* Saga/Circus *(2008). Among her awards are National Endowment for the Arts and Academy of American Poets fellowships. Lyn Hejinian lives in Berkeley, California.*

From *My Life*

A name trimmed with colored ribbons

They are seated in the shadows husking corn, shelling peas. Houses of wood set in the ground. I try to find the spot at which the pattern on the floor repeats. Pink, and rosy, quartz. They wade in brackish water. The leaves outside the window tricked the eye, demanding that one see them, focus on them, making it impossible to look past them, and though holes were opened through the foliage, they were as useless as portholes underwater looking into a dark sea, which only reflects the room one seeks to look out from. Sometimes into benevolent and other times into ghastly shapes. It speaks of a few of the rather terrible blind. I grew stubborn until blue as the eyes overlooking the bay from the bridge scattered over its bowls through a fading light and backed by the protest of the bright breathless West. Each bit of jello had been molded in tiny doll dishes, each trembling orange bit a different shape, but all otherwise the same. I am urged out rummaging into the sunshine, and the depths increase of blue above. A paper hat afloat on a cone of water. The orange and gray bugs were linked from their mating but faced in opposite directions, and their scrambling amounted to nothing. This simply means that the imagination is more restless than the body. But, already, words. Can there be laughter without comparisons. The tongue lisps in its hilarious panic. If, for example, you say, "I always prefer being by myself," and, then, one afternoon, you want to telephone a friend, maybe you feel you have betrayed your ideals. We have poured into the sink the stale water in which the iris died. Life is hopelessly frayed, all loose ends. A pansy suddenly, a web, a trail remarkably's a snail's. It was an enormous egg, sitting in the vineyard—an enormous rock-shaped egg. On that still day my grandmother raked up the leaves beside a particular pelargonium. With a name like that there is a lot you can do. Children are not always inclined to choose such paths. You can tell by the eucalyptus tree, its shaggy branches scatter buttons. In the afternoons, when the shades were pulled for my nap, the light coming through was of a dark yellow, nearly orange, melancholy, as heavy as honey, and it made me thirsty. That doesn't say it all, nor even a greater part. Yet it seems even more incomplete when we were there in person. Half the day in half the room. The wool makes one itch and the scratching makes one warm. But herself that she obeyed she dressed. It talks. The baby is scrubbed everywhere, he is an apple. They are true kitchen stalwarts. The smell of breathing fish and breathing shells seems sad, a mystery, rapturous, then dead. A self-centered being, in this different world. A urinating doll, half-buried in sand. She is lying on her stomach with one eye closed, driving a toy truck along the road she has cleared with her fingers. I mean untroubled by the distortions. That was the fashion when she was a young woman and famed for her beauty, surrounded by beaux. Once it was circular and that shape can still be seen from the air. Protected by the dog. Protected by foghorns, frog honks, cricket circles on the brown hills. It was a message of happiness by which we were called into the room, as if to receive a birthday present given early, because it was too large to hide, or alive, a pony perhaps, his mane trimmed with colored ribbons.

B. H. Fairchild (1942–)

B. H. Fairchild was born in Houston, Texas, and attended the University of Kansas and the University of Tulsa. He has taught at the University of Nebraska–Kearney, the University of Tulsa, Southwest Texas State University, Texas Women's University, and since 1983, at California State University–San Bernardino. Among his poetry books are The Arrival of the Future *(1985),* The Art of the Lathe *(1998, Kingsley Tufts Award), *Early Occult Memory Systems of the Lower Midwest *(2003, National Book Critics Circle Award), and* Usher *(2009). Other honors include National Endowment for the Arts, MacDowell Colony, and Guggenheim fellowships and the Bobbitt Prize. B. H. Fairchild lives in Claremont, California.*

The Machinist, Teaching His Daughter to Play the Piano

The brown wrist and hand with its raw knuckles and blue nails
       packed with dirt and oil, pause in mid-air,
the fingers arched delicately,

and she mimics him, hand held just so, the wrist loose,
       then swooping down to the wrong chord.
She lifts her hand and tries again.

Drill collars rumble, hammering the nubbin-posts.
       The helper lifts one, turning it slowly,
then lugs it into the lathe's chuck.

The bit shears the dull iron into new metal, falling
       into the steady chant of lathe work,
and the machinist lights a cigarette, holding

in his upturned palms the polonaise he learned at ten,
       then later the easiest waltzes,
etudes, impossible counterpoint

like the voice of his daughter he overhears one night
       standing in the backyard. She is speaking
to herself but not herself, as in prayer,

the listener is some version of herself,
       and the names are pronounced carefully,
self-consciously: Chopin, Mozart,

Scarlatti, . . . these gestures of voice and hands
      suspended over the keyboard
that move like the lathe in its turning

toward music, the wind dragging the hoist chain, the ring
      of iron on iron in the holding rack.
His daughter speaks to him one night,

but not to him, rather someone created between them,
      a listener, there and not there,
a master of lathes, a student of music.

Haki R. Madhubuti (Don L. Lee) (1942–)

Born Donald Luther Lee in Little Rock, Arkansas, Haki R. Madhubuti attended Wilson Junior College, Roosevelt University, the University of Illinois at Chicago Circle, and the University of Iowa Writers Workshop. He has worked as a museum curator, publisher, and editor and taught at Chicago State University, where he was director of the Gwendolyn Brooks Center. His poetry books include Think Black *(1967),* Don't Cry, Scream *(1969),* We Walk the Way of the New World *(1970),* Directionscore *(1971),* Book of Life *(1973),* Killing Memory, Seeking Ancestors *(1987),* Groundwork *(1996),* Heart Love *(1998),* Run Toward Fear *(2004), and* Liberation Narratives *(2009). Among his honors are a 1991 American Book Award and a National Endowment for the Arts fellowship. Haki Madhubuti lives in Chicago.*

But He Was Cool

or: he even stopped for green lights

super-cool
ultrablack
a tan/purple
had a beautiful shade.

he had a double-natural
that wd put the sisters to shame.
his dashikis were tailor made
& his beads were imported sea shells
    (from some blk/country i never heard of)
he was triple-hip.

his tikis were hand carved
out of ivory
& came express from the motherland.
he would greet u in swahili
& say good-by in yoruba.
woooooooooooooo-jim he bes so cool & ill tel li gent
        cool-cool is so cool he was un-cooled by
            other niggers' cool
        cool-cool ultracool was bop-cool/ice box
            cool so cool cold cool
        his wine didn't have to be cooled, him was
            air conditioned cool
        cool-cool/real cool made me cool-now
            ain't that cool
        cool-cool so cool him nicknamed refrigerator.

cool-cool so cool
he didn't know,
after detroit, newark, chicago &c.,
we had to hip
   cool-cool/super-cool/real cool
  that
to be black
is
to be
very-hot.

A Poem to Complement Other Poems

change.
like if u were a match i wd light u into something beautiful.
 change.
change.
for the better into a realreal together thing. change, from
 a make believe
nothing on cornmeal and water. change.
change. from the last drop to the first, maxwellhouse
 did. change.
change was a programmer for ibm, thought him was a
 brown computer. change.
colored is something written on southern outhouses.
 change.
greyhound did, i mean they got restrooms on buses.
 change.
change.
change nigger.
saw a nigger hippy, him wanted to be different.
changed.
saw a nigger liberal, him wanted to be different.
 changed.
saw a nigger conservative, him wanted to be different.
 changed.
niggers don't u know that niggers are different. change.
a doublechange. nigger wanted a double zero in front of
 his name; a license to kill,
niggers are licensed to be killed. change. a negro: some
 thing pigs eat.
change. i say change into a realblack righteous aim. Like
 i don't play

saxophone but that doesn't mean i don't dig trane.
    change.

change.
hear u coming but yr/steps are too loud. change. even a
    lamppost changes nigger.
change, stop being an instant yes machine. change.
niggers don't change they just grow. that's a change;
    bigger & better niggers.
change, into a necessary blackself.
change, like a gas meter gets higher.
change, like a blues song talking about a righteous to-
    morrow.
change, like a tax bill getting higher.
change, like a good sister getting better.
change, like knowing wood will burn. change.
know the realenemy.
change,
change nigger: standing on the corner, thought him was
           cool. him still
              standing there. it's wintertime, him cool.
change,
know the realenemy.
change: him wanted to be a tv star. him is. ten o'clock
        news.
      wanted, wanted. nigger stole some lemon & lime
        popsicles,
      thought them were diamonds.
change nigger change.
know the realenemy.
change: is u is or is u aint. change. now now change. for
        the better change.
      read a change. live a change. read a blackpoem.
        change. be the realpeople.
      change. blackpoems
will change:

know the realenemy. change. know the realenemy. change
    yr/enemy change know the real
change know the realenemy change, change, know the
    realenemy, the realenemy, the real
realenemy change you're the enemies/change your change
    your change your enemy change

your enemy. know the realenemy, the world's enemy.
    know them know them know them the
realenemy change your enemy change your change
    change change your enemy change change
change change your change change change.
your
mind nigger.

William Matthews (1942–1997)

William Matthews was born in Cincinnati, Ohio. He attended Yale University and the University of North Carolina at Chapel Hill before teaching at Wells College, Cornell University, the University of Colorado, the University of Washington, and City College of New York. His poetry books include Ruining the New Road *(1970),* Sleek for the Long Flight *(1972),* Rising and Falling *(1979),* Flood *(1982),* A Happy Childhood *(1984),* Foreseeable Futures *(1987),* Blues If You Want *(1989),* Time & Money *(1995; National Book Critics Circle Award),* After All: Last Poems *(1998), and* Search Party: Collected Poems *(2005). Among his honors were National Endowment for the Arts, Guggenheim, Ingram Merrill, and Lila Wallace–Reader's Digest Foundation fellowships and the 1997 Ruth Lilly Poetry Prize. William Matthews died in New York City of a heart attack.*

In Memory of the Utah Stars

Each of them must have terrified
his parents by being so big, obsessive
and exact so young, already gone
and leaving, like a big tipper,
that huge changeling's body in his place.
The prince of bone spurs and bad knees.

The year I first saw them play
Malone was a high school freshman,
already too big for any bed,
14, a natural resource.
You have to learn not to
apologize, a form of vanity.
You flare up in the lane, exotic
anywhere else. You roll the ball
off fingers twice as long as your
girlfriend's. Great touch for a big man,
says some jerk. Now they're defunct
and Moses Malone, boy wonder at 19,
rises at 20 from the St. Louis bench,
his pet of a body grown sullen
as fast as it grew up.

Something in you remembers every
time the ball left your fingertips
wrong and nothing the ball
can do in the air will change that.
You watch it set, stupid moon,

the way you watch yourself
in a recurring dream.
You never lose your touch
or forget how taxed bodies
go at the same pace they owe,
how brutally well the universe
works to be beautiful,
how we metabolize loss
as fast as we have to.

The Accompanist

Don't play too much, don't play
too loud, don't play the melody.
You have to anticipate her
and to subdue yourself.
She used to give me her smoky
eye when I got boisterous,
so I learned to play on tip-
toe and to play the better half
of what I might. I don't like
to complain, though I notice
that I get around to it somehow.
We made a living and good music,
both, night after night, the blue
curlicues of smoke rubbing their
staling and wispy backs
against the ceilings, the flat
drinks and scarce taxis, the jazz life
we bitch about the way Army pals
complain about the food and then
re-up. Some people like to say
with smut in their voices how playing
the way we did at our best is partly
sexual. OK, I could tell them
a tale or two, and I've heard
the records Lester cut with Lady Day
and all that rap, and it's partly
sexual but it's mostly practice
and music. As for partly sexual,
I'll take wholly sexual any day,
but that's a duet and we're talking
accompaniment. Remember "Reckless

Blues"? Bessie Smith sings out "Daddy"
and Louis Armstrong plays back "Daddy"
as clear through his horn as if he'd
spoken it. But it's her daddy and her
story. When you play it you become
your part in it, one of her beautiful
troubles, and then, however much music
can do this, part of her consolation,
the way pain and joy eat off each other's
plates, but mostly you play to drunks,
to the night, to the way you judge
and pardon yourself, to all that goes
not unsung, but unrecorded.

Sharon Olds (1942–)

Sharon Olds was born in San Francisco. She attended Stanford University and Colum-
bia University, was lecturer-in-residence at the Theodor Herzl Institute in New York, and
has been teaching at New York University since 1983. Among her poetry books are Satan
Says (1980), The Dead and the Living (1984, Lamont Poetry Prize and National
Book Critics Circle Award), The Gold Cell (1987), The Father (1992), The Well-
spring (1996), Blood, Tin, Straw (1999), The Unswept Room (2002), and Strike
Sparks (2004), One Secret Thing (2008), and Stag's Leap (2012, Pulitzer Prize).
Her honors include Guggenheim, National Endowment for the Arts, Lila Wallace–
Reader's Digest Foundation, and Academy of American Poets fellowships and the 2004
Barnes & Noble Writers for Writers Award. Sharon Olds lives in New York.

The Language of the Brag

I have wanted excellence in the knife-throw,
I have wanted to use my exceptionally strong and accurate arms
and my straight posture and quick electric muscles
to achieve something at the center of a crowd,
the blade piercing the bark deep,
the haft slowly and heavily vibrating like the cock.

I have wanted some epic use for my excellent body,
some heroism, some American achievement
beyond the ordinary for my extraordinary self,
magnetic and tensile, I have stood by the sandlot
and watched the boys play.

I have wanted courage, I have thought about fire
and the crossing of the waterfalls, I have dragged around

my belly big with cowardice and safety,
my stool black with iron pills,
my huge breasts oozing mucus,
my legs swelling, my hands swelling,
my face swelling and darkening, my hair
falling out, my inner sex
stabbed again and again with terrible pain like a knife.
I have lain down.

I have lain down and sweated and shaken
and passed blood and feces and water and
slowly alone in the center of a circle I have

passed the new person out
and they have lifted the new person free of the act
and wiped the new person free of that
language of blood like praise all over the body.

I have done what you wanted to do, Walt Whitman,
Allen Ginsberg, I have done this thing,
I and the other women this exceptional
act with the exceptional heroic body,
this giving birth, this glistening verb,
and I am putting my proud American boast
right here with the others.

The Lifting

Suddenly my father lifted up his nightie, I
turned my head away but he cried out
Shar!, my nickname, so I turned and looked.
He was sitting in the high cranked-up hospital bed with the
gown up, around his neck,
to show me the weight he had lost. I looked
where his solid ruddy stomach had been
and I saw the skin fallen into loose
soft hairy rippled folds
lying in a pool of folds
down at the base of his abdomen,
the gaunt torso of a big man
who will die soon. Right away
I saw how much his hips are like mine,
the long, white angles, and then
how much his pelvis is shaped like my daughter's,
a chambered whelk-shell hollowed out,
I saw the folds of skin like something
poured, a thick batter, I saw
his rueful smile, the cast-up eyes as he
shows me his old body, he knows
I will be interested, he knows I will find him
appealing. If anyone had ever told me
I would sit by him and he would pull up his nightie
and I would look at him, at his naked body,
at the thick bud of his penis in all that
dark hair, look at him
in affection and uneasy wonder

I would not have believed it. But now I can still
see the tiny snowflakes, white and
night-blue, on the cotton of the gown as it
rises the way we were promised at death it would rise,
the veils would fall from our eyes, we would know everything.

Henry Taylor (1942–)

Henry Taylor was born in Loudoun County, Virginia. He attended the University of Virginia and Hollins College and has taught at Roanoke College, the University of Utah, and American University. His poetry books include The Horse Show at Midnight *(1966),* An Afternoon of Pocket Billiards *(1975),* The Flying Change *(1985, Pulitzer Prize),* Understanding Fiction *(1996),* Brief Candles: 101 Clerihews *(2000), and* Crooked Run *(2006). Among his honors are fellowships from the National Endowment of the Arts and the 1984 Witter Bynner Prize for poetry. Henry Taylor lives in Loudoun County, Virginia.*

Barbed Wire

One summer afternoon when nothing much
was happening, they were standing around
a tractor beside the barn while a horse
in the field poked his head between two strands
of the barbed-wire fence to get at the grass
along the lane, when it happened—something

they passed around the wood stove late at night
for years, but never could explain—someone
may have dropped a wrench into the toolbox
or made a sudden move, or merely thought
what might happen if the horse got scared, and
then he did get scared, jumped sideways and ran

down the fence line, leaving chunks of his throat
skin and hair on every barb for ten feet
before he pulled free and ran a short way
into the field, stopped and planted his hoofs
wide apart like a sawhorse, hung his head
down as if to watch his blood running out,

almost as if he were about to speak
to them, who almost thought he could regret
that he no longer had the strength to stand,
then shuddered to his knees, fell on his side,
and gave up breathing while the dripping wire
hummed like a bowstring in the splintered air.

Tess Gallagher (1943–)

Tess Gallagher was born in Port Angeles, Washington. She attended the University of Washington and the University of Iowa Writers Workshop. She has taught at a number of universities, most notably Syracuse University; since 1988, she has acted as executor of the estate of her deceased husband, Raymond Carver. Her poetry books include Instructions to the Double *(1976, Elliston Book Award),* Under Stars *(1978),* On Your Own *(1978),* Willingly *(1984),* Amplitude *(1987),* Moon Crossing Bridge *(1992),* My Black Horse *(1995),* Dear Ghosts *(2008), and* Midnight Lantern: New and Selected Poems *(2011). Among her honors are Guggenheim and National Endowment for the Arts fellowships. Tess Gallagher lives in Port Angeles, Washington.*

Black Silk

She was cleaning—there is always
that to do—when she found,
at the top of the closet, his old
silk vest. She called me
to look at it, unrolling it carefully
like something live
might fall out. Then we spread it
on the kitchen table and smoothed
the wrinkles down, making our hands
heavy until its shape against Formica
came back and the little tips
that would have pointed to his pockets
lay flat. The buttons were all there.
I held my arms out and she
looped the wide armholes over
them. "That's one thing I never
wanted to be," she said, "a man."
I went into the bathroom to see
how I looked in the sheen and
sadness. Wind chimes
off-key in the alcove. Then her
crying so I stood back in the sink-light
where the porcelain had been staring. Time
to go to her, I thought, with that
other mind, and stood still.

Under Stars

The sleep of this night deepens
because I have walked coatless from the house
carrying the white envelope.
All night it will say one name
in its little tin house by the roadside.

I have raised the metal flag
so its shadow under the roadlamp
leaves an imprint on the rain-heavy bushes.
Now I will walk back
thinking of the few lights still on
in the town a mile away.

In the yellowed light of a kitchen
the millworker has finished his coffee,
his wife has laid out the white slices of bread
on the counter. Now while the bed they have left
is still warm, I will think of you, you
who are so far away
you have caused me to look up at the stars.

Tonight they have not moved
from childhood, those games played after dark.
Again I walk into the wet grass
toward the starry voices. Again, I
am the found one, intimate, returned
by all I touch on the way.

Michael Palmer (1943–)

Michael Palmer was born in New York City and attended Harvard University. A free-lance writer and translator for much of his career, he has published the poetry books Blake's Newton *(1972),* The Circular Gates *(1974),* Without Music *(1977),* Notes for Echo Lake *(1981),* First Figure *(1984),* Sun *(1988),* At Passages *(1995),* The Lion Bridge *(1998),* The Promises of Glass *(2000),* Codes Appearing *(2001), and* Company of Moths *(2005). Among his honors are National Endowment for the Arts and Guggenheim Foundation fellowships as well as the 2001 Shelley Memorial Award and the 2006 Wallace Stevens Award. Michael Palmer lives in San Francisco.*

I Do Not

> *"Je ne sais pas l'anglais."*
> —GEORGES HUGNET

I do not know English.

I do not know English, and therefore I can have nothing to
    say about this latest war, flowering through a night-
    scope in the evening sky.

I do not know English and therefore, when hungry, can do no
    more than point repeatedly to my mouth.

Yet such a gesture might be taken to mean any number of
    things.

I do not know English and therefore cannot seek the requisite
    permissions, as outlined in the recent protocol.

Such as: May I utter a term of endearment; may I now proceed
    to put my arm or arms around you and apply gentle
    pressure; may I now kiss you directly on the lips; now
    on the left tendon of the neck; now on the nipple of
    each breast? And so on.

Would not in any case be able to decipher her response.

I do not know English. Therefore I have no way of
    communicating that I prefer this painting of nothing to
    that one of something.

No way to speak of my past or hopes for the future, of my
    glasses mysteriously shattered in Rotterdam, the statue
    of Eros and Psyche in the Summer Garden, the sudden,
    shrill cries in the streets of São Paulo, a watch
    abruptly stopping in Paris.

No way to tell the joke about the rabbi and the parrot, the
    bartender and the duck, the Pope and the porte-cochère.

You will understand why you have received no letters from me
    and why yours have gone unread.

Those, that is, where you write so precisely of the
    confluence of the visible universe with the invisible,
    and of the lens of dark matter.

No way to differentiate the hall of mirrors from the meadow
    of mullein, the beetlebung from the pinkletink, the
    kettlehole from the ventifact.

Nor can I utter the words science, seance, silence, language
    and languish.

Nor can I tell of the arboreal shadows elongated and shifting
    along the wall as the sun's angle approaches maximum
    hibernal declination.

Cannot tell of the almond-eyed face that peered from the
    well, the ship of stone whose sail was a tongue.

And I cannot report that this rose has twenty-four petals,
    one slightly cankered.

Cannot tell how I dismantled it myself at this desk.

Cannot ask the name of this rose.

I cannot repeat the words of the Recording Angel or those of
    the Angel of Erasure.

Can speak neither of things abounding nor of things
    disappearing.

Still the games continue. A muscular man waves a stick at a

ball. A woman in white, arms outstretched, carves a true
circle in space. A village turns to dust in the chalk
hills.

Because I do not know English I have been variously called
    Mr. Twisted, The One Undone, The Nonrespondent, The
    Truly Lost Boy, and Laughed-At-By-Horses.

The war is declared ended, almost before it has begun.

They have named it The Ultimate Combat between Nearness and
    Distance.

I do not know English.

James Tate (1943–)

James Tate was born in Kansas City, Missouri. He attended the University of Missouri, Kansas State College, and the University of Iowa Writers Workshop before teaching at Columbia University and, since 1971, at the University of Massachusetts at Amherst. Among his poetry books are The Lost Pilot *(1967, Yale Younger Poets Prize),* The Oblivion Ha-Ha *(1970),* Absences *(1972),* Viper Jazz *(1976),* Constant Defender *(1983),* Distance from Loved Ones *(1990),* Selected Poems *(1991, Pulitzer Prize),* Worshipful Company of Fletchers *(1994, National Book Award),* Shroud of the Gnome *(1997),* Memoir of the Hawk *(2001),* Return to the City of White Donkeys *(2004), and* The Ghost Soldiers *(2008). His honors include Guggenheim and National Endowment for the Arts fellowships, the 1995 Tanning Prize, and the 1996 Wallace Stevens Award. James Tate lives in Amherst, Massachusetts.*

The Lost Pilot

For my father, 1922–1944

Your face did not rot
like the others—the co-pilot,
for example, I saw him

yesterday. His face is corn-
mush: his wife and daughter,
the poor ignorant people, stare

as if he will compose soon.
He was more wronged than Job.
But your face did not rot

like the others—it grew dark,
and hard like ebony;
the features progressed in their

distinction. If I could cajole
you to come back for an evening,
down from your compulsive

orbiting, I would touch you,
read your face as Dallas,
your hoodlum gunner, now,

with the blistered eyes, reads
his braille editions. I would
touch your face as a disinterested

scholar touches an original page.
However frightening, I would
discover you, and I would not

turn you in; I would not make
you face your wife, or Dallas,
or the co-pilot, Jim. You

could return to your crazy
orbiting, and I would not try
to fully understand what

it means to you. All I know
is this: when I see you,
as I have seen you at least

once every year of my life,
spin across the wilds of the sky
like a tiny, African god,

I feel dead. I feel as if I were
the residue of a stranger's life,
that I should pursue you.

My head cocked toward the sky,
I cannot get off the ground,
and, you, passing over again,

fast, perfect, and unwilling
to tell me that you are doing
well, or that it was mistake

that placed you in that world,
and me in this; or that misfortune
placed these worlds in us.

Norman Dubie (1945–)

Norman Dubie was born in Barre, Vermont. He attended Goddard College and the University of Iowa Writers Workshop. He has taught at Ohio University and since 1975 at Arizona State University. Among his poetry books are Alehouse Sonnets *(1971),* Popham of the New Song *(1975),* In the Dead of the Night *(1975),* The Illustrations *(1977),* The City of the Olesha Fruit *(1979),* The Everlastings *(1980),* The Springhouse *(1986),* Groom Falconer *(1989),* Radio Sky *(1991),* The Mercy Seat *(2001),* Ordinary Mornings of a Coliseum *(2004),* The Insomniac Liar of Topo *(2007), and* The Volcano *(2010). His honors include Guggenheim, Ingram Merrill, and National Endowment for the Arts fellowships. Norman Dubie lives in Tempe, Arizona.*

Elizabeth's War with the Christmas Bear

> *For Paul Zimmer*

The bears are kept by hundreds within fences, are fed cracked
Eggs; the weakest are
Slaughtered and fed to the others after being scented
With the blood of deer brought to the pastures by Elizabeth's
Men—the blood spills from deep pails with bottoms of slate.

The balding Queen had bear gardens in London and in the country.
The bear is baited: the nostrils
Are blown full with pepper, the Irish wolf dogs
Are starved, then, emptied, made crazy with fermented barley:

And the bear's hind leg is chained to a stake, the bear
Is blinded and whipped, kneeling in his own blood and slaver, he is
Almost instantly worried by the dogs. At the very moment that
Elizabeth took Essex's head, a giant brown bear
Stood in the gardens with dogs hanging from his fur . . .
He took away the sun, took
A wolfhound in his mouth and tossed it into
The white lap of Elizabeth I—arrows and staves rained

On his chest, and standing, he, then, stood even taller, seeing
Into the Queen's private boxes—he grinned
Into her battered eggshell face.
Another volley of arrows and poles, and opening his mouth
He showered
Blood all over Elizabeth and her Privy Council.

The next evening, a cool evening, the Queen demanded
13 bears and the justice of 113 dogs: She slept

All that Sunday night and much of the next morning.
Some said she was guilty of *this* and *that*.
The Protestant Queen gave the defeated bear
A grave in a Catholic cemetery. The marker said:
Peter, a Solstice Bear, a gift of the Tsarevitch to Elizabeth.

After a long winter she had the grave opened. The bear's skeleton
Was cleaned with lye, she placed it at her bedside,
Put a candle inside behind the sockets of the eyes, and, then
She spoke to it:

You were a Christmas bear—behind your eyes
I see the walls of a snow cave where you are a cub still smelling
Of your mother's blood which has dried in your hair; you have
Troubled a Queen who was afraid
When seated in *shade* which, standing,
You had created! A Queen who often wakes with a dream
Of you at night—
Now, you'll stand by my bed in your long white bones; alone, you
Will frighten away at night all visions of bear, and all day
You will be in this cold room—your constant grin,
You'll stand in the long, white prodigy of your bones, and you are,

Every inch of you, a terrible vision, not bear, but virgin!

The Funeral

It felt like the zero in brook ice.
She was my youngest aunt; the summer before
We had stood naked
While she stiffened and giggled, letting the minnows
Nibble at her toes. I was almost four—
That evening she took me
To the springhouse where on the scoured planks
There were rows of butter in small bricks, a mold
Like ermine on the cheese,
And cut onions to rinse the air
Of the black, sickly-sweet meats of rotting pecans.

She said butter was colored with marigolds
Plucked down by the marsh
With its tall grass and miner's-candles.
We once carried the offal's pail beyond the barn
To where the fox could be caught in meditation.
Her bed linen smelled of camphor. We went

In late March for her burial. I heard the men talk.
I saw the minnows nibble at her toe.
And Uncle Peter, in a low voice, said
The cancer ate her like horse piss eats deep snow.

Carol Muske-Dukes (1945–)

Carol Muske-Dukes was born in St. Paul, Minnesota. She attended Creighton University and San Francisco State University. She taught at Columbia University and George Washington University before joining the faculty of the University of Southern California in 1985. Among her poetry books are Camouflage *(1975),* Skylight *(1981),* Wyndmere *(1985),* Applause *(1989),* Red Trousseau *(1993),* An Octave Above Thunder *(1997), and* Sparrow *(2003). She has also published novels and essays. Her honors include the Witter Bynner Award and Guggenheim, National Endowment for the Arts, and Ingram Merrill fellowships. Carol Muske-Dukes lives in Los Angeles.*

August, Los Angeles, Lullaby

The pure amnesia of her face,
newborn. I looked so far
into her that, for a while,

the visual held no memory.
Little by little, I returned
to myself, waking to nurse

those first nights in that
familiar room where all
the objects had been altered

imperceptibly: the gardenia
blooming in the dark
in the scarred water glass,

near the phone my handwriting
illegible, the patterned lamp-
shade angled downward and away

from the long mirror where
I stood and looked at
the woman holding her child.

Her face kept dissolving
into expressions resembling
my own, but the child's was pure

figurative, resembling no one.
We floated together in the space
a lullaby makes, head to head,

half-sleeping. *Save it,*
my mother would say, meaning
just the opposite. She didn't

want to hear my evidence
against her terrible optimism
for me. And though, despite her,

I can redeem, in a pawnshop
sense, almost any bad moment
from my childhood, I see now

what she must have intended
for me. I felt it for *her,*
watching her as she slept,

watching her suck as she
dreamed of sucking, lightheaded
with thirst as my blood flowed

suddenly into tissue that
changed it to milk. No matter
that we were alone, there's a

texture that moves between me
and whatever might have injured
us then. Like the curtain's sheer

opacity, it remains drawn
over what view we have of dawn
here in this onetime desert,

now green and replenished,
its perfect climate
unthreatened in memory—

though outside, as usual,
the wind blew, the bough bent,
under the eaves, the hummingbird

touched once the bloodcolored hourglass,
the feeder, then was gone.

Kay Ryan (1945–)

Kay Ryan was born in San Jose, California, and attended the University of California–Los Angeles. She has been a part-time teacher of remedial reading and English at the College of Marin in Kentfield, California, since the 1970s. Among her poetry books are Strangely Marked Metal *(1985),* Flamingo Watching *(1994),* Elephant Rocks *(1996),* Say Uncle *(2000),* The Niagara River *(2005), and* The Best of It *(2010). Her honors include Ingram Merrill, National Endowment for the Arts, and Guggenheim fellowships and the Ruth Lilly Prize. From 2008 to 2010 she served as U.S. poet laureate. Kay Ryan lives in Marin County, California.*

Turtle

Who would be a turtle who could help it?
A barely mobile hard roll, a four-oared helmet,
she can ill afford the chances she must take
in rowing toward the grasses that she eats.
Her track is graceless, like dragging
a packing-case places, and almost any slope
defeats her modest hopes. Even being practical,
she's often stuck up to the axle on her way
to something edible. With everything optimal,
she skirts the ditch which would convert
her shell into a serving dish. She lives
below luck-level, never imagining some lottery
will change her load of pottery to wings.
Her only levity is patience,
the sport of truly chastened things.

Bestiary

A bestiary catalogs
bests. The mediocres
both higher and lower
are suppressed in favor
of the singularly savage
or clever, the spectacularly
pincered, the archest
of the arch deceivers
who press their advantage
without quarter even after

they've won as of course they would.
Best is not to be confused with *good*—
a different creature altogether,
and treated of in the goodiary—
a text alas lost now for centuries.

Larry Levis (1946–1996)

Larry Levis was born in Fresno, California. He attended California State University–Fresno, Syracuse University, and the University of Iowa Writers Workshop before teaching at the University of Missouri, the University of Utah, and Virginia Commonwealth University. His poetry books include Wrecking Crew *(1972),* The Afterlife *(1977, Lamont Poetry Prize),* The Dollmaker's Ghost *(1981, National Poetry Series),* Winter Stars *(1985),* The Widening Spell of the Leaves *(1991), and* Elegy *(1997). Among his honors were National Endowment for the Arts, Guggenheim, and Fulbright fellowships. Larry Levis died from a heart attack in Richmond, Virginia.*

Childhood Ideogram

I lay my head sideways on the desk,
My fingers interlocked under my cheekbones,
My eyes closed. It was a three-room schoolhouse,
White, with a small bell tower, an oak tree.
From where I sat, on still days, I'd watch
The oak, the prisoner of that sky, or read
The desk carved with adults' names: Marietta
Martin, Truman Finnell, Marjorie Elm;
The wood hacked or lovingly hollowed, the flies
Settling on the obsolete & built-in inkwells.
I remember, tonight, only details, how
Mrs. Avery, now gone, was standing then
In her beige dress, its quiet, gazelle print
Still dark with lines of perspiration from
The day before; how Gracie Chin had just
Shown me how to draw, with chalk, a Chinese
Ideogram. Where did she go, white thigh
With one still freckle, lost in silk?
No one would say for sure, so that I'd know,
So that all shapes, for days after, seemed
Brushstrokes in Chinese: countries on maps
That shifted, changed colors, or disappeared:
Lithuania, Prussia, Bessarabia;
The numbers four & seven; the question mark.
That year, I ate almost nothing.
I thought my parents weren't my real parents,
I thought there'd been some terrible mistake.
At recess I would sit alone, seeing

In the print of each leaf shadow, an ideogram—
Still, indecipherable, beneath the green sound
The bell still made, even after it had faded,
When the dust-covered leaves of the oak tree
Quivered, slightly, if I looked up in time.
And my father, so distant in those days,
Where did he go, that autumn, when he chose
The chaste, faint ideogram of ash, & I had
To leave him there, white bones in a puzzle
By a plum tree, the sun rising over
The Sierras? It is not Chinese, but English—
When the past tense, when you first learn to use it
As a child, throws all the verbs in the language
Into the long, flat shade of houses you
Ride past, & into town. Your father's driving.
On winter evenings, the lights would come on earlier.
People would be shopping for Christmas. Each hand,
With the one whorl of its fingerprints, with twenty
Delicate bones inside it, reaching up
To touch some bolt of cloth, or choose a gift,
A little different from any other hand.
You know how the past tense turns a sentence dark,
But leaves names, lovers, places showing through:
Gracie Chin, my father, Lithuania;
A beige dress where dark gazelles hold still?
Outside, it's snowing, cold, & a New Year.
The trees & streets are turning white.
I always thought he would come back like this.
I always thought he wouldn't dare be seen.

Winter Stars

My father once broke a man's hand
Over the exhaust pipe of a John Deere tractor. The man,
Rubén Vásquez, wanted to kill his own father
With a sharpened fruit knife, & he held
The curved tip of it, lightly, between his first
Two fingers, so it could slash
Horizontally, & with surprising grace,
Across a throat. It was like a glinting beak in a hand,
And, for a moment, the light held still
On those vines. When it was over,
My father simply went in & ate lunch, & then, as always,

Lay alone in the dark, listening to music.
He never mentioned it.

I never understood how anyone could risk his life,
Then listen to Vivaldi.

Sometimes, I go out into this yard at night,
And stare through the wet branches of an oak
In winter, & realize I am looking at the stars
Again. A thin haze of them, shining
And persisting.

It used to make me feel lighter, looking up at them.
In California, that light was closer.
In a California no one will ever see again,
My father is beginning to die. Something
Inside him is slowly taking back
Every word it ever gave him.
Now, if we try to talk, I watch my father
Search for a lost syllable as if it might
Solve everything, & though he can't remember, now,
The word for it, he is ashamed. . . .
If you can think of the mind as a place continually
Visited, a whole city placed behind
The eyes, & shining, I can imagine, now, its end—
As when the lights go off, one by one,
In a hotel at night, until at last
All of the travelers will be asleep, or until
Even the thin glow from the lobby is a kind
Of sleep; & while the woman behind the desk
Is applying more lacquer to her nails,
You can almost believe that the elevator,
As it ascends, must open upon starlight.

I stand out on the street, & do not go in.
That was our agreement, at my birth.

And for years I believed
That what went unsaid between us became empty,
And pure, like starlight, & that it persisted.

I got it all wrong.
I wound up believing in words the way a scientist
Believes in carbon, after death.

Tonight, I'm talking to you, father, although
It is quiet here in the Midwest, where a small wind,
The size of a wrist, wakes the cold again—
Which may be all that's left of you & me.

When I left home at seventeen, I left for good.

That pale haze of stars goes on & on,
Like laughter that has found a final, silent shape
On a black sky. It means everything
It cannot say. Look, it's empty out there, & cold.
Cold enough to reconcile
Even a father, even a son.

Adrian C. Louis (1946–)

Adrian C. Louis was born in northern Nevada. He attended the University of Nevada–Reno and Brown University and taught at Oglala Lakota College in South Dakota before joining the Southwest Minnesota State University faculty in 1998. He also worked as a journalist and editor of tribal newspapers, including the Lakota Times, *and as managing editor of* Indian Country Today. *Among his poetry books are* The Indian Cheap Wine Seance *(1974),* Fire Water World *(1989),* Among the Dog Eaters *(1992),* Blood Thirsty Savages *(1994),* Vortex of Indian Fevers *(1995),* Ceremonies of the Damned *(1997),* Ancient Acid Flashes Back *(2000),* Bone and Juice *(2001),* Evil Corn *(2004), and* Logorrhea *(2006). His honors include National Endowment for the Arts and Lila Wallace–Reader's Digest Foundation fellowships. Adrian C. Louis lives in Marshall, Minnesota.*

Looking for Judas

Weathered gray, the wooden walls
of the old barn soak in the bright
sparkling blood of the five-point mule
deer I hang there in the moonlight.
Gutted, skinned, and shimmering in eternal
nakedness, the glint in its eyes could
be stolen from the dry hills of Jerusalem.
They say before the white man
brought us Jesus, we had honor.
They say when we killed the Deer People,
we told them their spirits
would live in our flesh.
We used bows of ash, no spotlights, no rifles,
and their holy blood became ours.
Or something like that.

Thomas Lux (1946–)

Thomas Lux was born in Northampton, Massachusetts. He attended Emerson College and the University of Iowa Writers Workshop and taught at Emerson College, Sarah Lawrence College, and a number of other universities before joining the Georgia Institute of Technology faculty. Among his poetry books are The Land Sighted *(1970),* Memory's Handgrenade *(1972),* Sunday *(1979),* Massachusetts *(1981),* Half Promised Land *(1986),* The Drowned River *(1990),* Split Horizon *(1994, Kingsley Tufts Award),* The Blind Swimmer *(1996),* New and Selected Poems *(1997),* Street of Clocks *(2001),* The Cradle Place *(2004), and* God Particles *(2008). His honors include MacDowell, Guggenheim, and National Endowment for the Arts fellowships. Thomas Lux lives in Atlanta, Georgia.*

The People of the Other Village

hate the people of this village
and would nail our hats
to our heads for refusing in their presence to remove them
or staple our hands to our foreheads
for refusing to salute them
if we did not hurt them first: mail them packages of rats,
mix their flour at night with broken glass.
We do this, they do that.
They peel the larynx from one of our brothers' throats.
We devein one of their sisters.
The quicksand pits they built were good.
Our amputation teams were better.
We trained some birds to steal their wheat.
They sent to us exploding ambassadors of peace.
They do this, we do that.
We canceled our sheep imports.
They no longer bought our blankets.
We mocked their greatest poet
and when that had no effect
we parodied the way they dance
which did cause pain, so they, in turn, said our God
was leprous, hairless.
We do this, they do that.
Ten thousand (10,000) years, ten thousand
(10,000) brutal, beautiful years.

Marilyn Nelson (1946–)

Marilyn Nelson was born in Cleveland, Ohio, and spent her youth on U.S. military bases. She attended the University of California–Davis, the University of Pennsylvania, and the University of Minnesota. She has taught at Saint Olaf College, the University of Connecticut–Storrs, and the University of Delaware. Among her poetry books are For the Body *(1978),* Mama's Promises *(1985),* The Homeplace *(1990, Anisfield-Wolf Book Award),* Magnificat *(1994),* The Fields of Praise *(1997),* Carver: A Life in Poems *(2001),* The Cachoeira Tales *(2005), and* Sweethearts of Rhythm *(2009). Her honors include National Endowment for the Arts and Guggenheim fellowships. Marilyn Nelson lives in Connecticut.*

The Ballad of Aunt Geneva

Geneva was the wild one.
Geneva was a tart.
Geneva met a blue-eyed boy
and gave away her heart.

Geneva ran a roadhouse.
Geneva wasn't sent
to college like the others:
Pomp's pride her punishment.

She cooked out on the river,
watching the shore slide by,
her lips pursed into hardness,
her deep-set brown eyes dry.

They say she killed a woman
over a good black man
by braining the jealous heifer
with an iron frying pan.

They say, when she was eighty,
she got up late at night
and sneaked her old, white lover in
to make love, and to fight.

First, they heard the tell-tale
singing of the springs,
then Geneva's voice rang out:
I need to buy some things,

So next time, bring more money.
And bring more moxie, too.
I ain't got no time to waste
on limp white mens like you.

Oh yeah? Well, Mister White Man,
it sure might be stone-white,
but my thing's white as it is.
And you know damn well I'm right.

Now listen: take your heart pills
and pay the doctor mind.
If you up and die on me,
I'll whip your white behind.

They tiptoed through the parlor
on heavy, time-slowed feet.
She watched him, from her front door,
walk down the dawnlit street.

Geneva was the wild one.
Geneva was a tart.
Geneva met a blue-eyed boy
and gave away her heart.

Star-Fix

for Melvin M. Nelson, Captain USAF (ret.) (1917–1966)

At his cramped desk
under the astrodome,
the navigator looks
thousands of light-years
everywhere but down.
He gets a celestial fix,
measuring head winds;
checking the log;
plotting wind-speed,
altitude, drift
in a circle of protractors,
slide-rules, and pencils.

He charts in his Howgozit
the points of no alternate
and of no return.
He keeps his eyes on the compass,
the two altimeters, the map.
He thinks, *Do we have enough fuel?*
What if my radio fails?

He's the only Negro in the crew.
The only black flier on the whole base,
for that matter. Not that it does:
this crew is a team.
Bob and Al, Les, Smitty, Nelson.

Smitty, who said once
after a poker game,
I love you, Nelson.
I never thought I could love
a colored man.
When we get out of this man's Air Force,
if you ever come down to Tuscaloosa,
look me up and come to dinner.
You can come in the front door, too;
hell, you can stay overnight!
Of course, as soon as you leave,
I'll have to burn down my house.
Because if I don't
my neighbors will.

The navigator knows where he is
because he knows where he's been
and where he's going.
At night, since he can't fly
by dead-reckoning,
he calculates his position
by shooting a star.

The octant tells him
the angle of a fixed star
over the artificial horizon.
His position in that angle
is absolute and true:
Where the hell are we, Nelson?

Alioth, in the Big Dipper.
Regulus. Antares, in Scorpio.

He plots their lines
of position on the chart,
gets his radio bearing,
corrects for lost time.

Bob, Al, Les, and Smitty
are counting on their navigator.
If he sleeps,
they all sleep.

If he fails,
they fall.

The navigator keeps watch
over the night and the instruments,
going hungry for five or six hours
to give his flight-lunch
to his two little girls.

Ron Silliman (1946–)

Ron Silliman was born in Pasco, Washington, and grew up in California's Bay Area. He attended Merritt College, San Francisco State University, and the University of California–Berkeley and has since worked as a community organizer, lecturer, public relations manager, and market analyst. His poetry books include Crow *(1971),* ABC *(1983),* Paradise *(1985),* What *(1988),* Xing *(1996),* Woundwood *(2004), and* The Alphabet *(2008). Among his honors are National Endowment for the Arts and Pew fellowships. Ron Silliman lives in Chester County, Pennsylvania.*

Albany

For Cliff Silliman

If the function of writing is to "express the world." My father withheld child support. forcing my mother to live with her parents. my brother and I to be raised together in a small room. Grandfather called them niggers. I can't afford an automobile. Far across the calm bay stood a complex of long yellow buildings, a prison. A line is the distance between. They circled the seafood restaurant, singing "We shall not be moved." My turn to cook. It was hard to adjust my sleeping to those hours when the sun was up. The event was nothing like their report of it. How concerned was I over her failure to have orgasms? Mondale's speech was drowned by jeers. Ye wretched. She introduces herself as a rape survivor. Yet his best friend was Hispanic. I decided not to escape to Canada. Revenue enhancement. Competition and spectacle. kinds of drugs. If it demonstrates form some people won't read it. Television unifies conversation. Died in action. If a man is a player, he will have no job. Becoming prepared to live with less space. Live ammunition. Secondary boycott. My crime is parole violation. Now that the piecards have control. Rubin feared McClure would read Ghost Tantras at the teach-in. This form is the study group. The sparts are impeccable, though filled with deceit. A benefit reading. He seduced me. AFT, local 1352. Enslavement is permitted as punishment for crime. Her husband broke both of her eardrums. I used my grant to fix my teeth. They speak in Farsi at the corner store. YPSL. The national question. I look forward to old age with some excitement. 42 years for Fibreboard Products. Food is a weapon. Yet the sight of people making love is deeply moving. Music is essential. The cops wear shields that serve as masks. Her lungs heavy with asbestos. Two weeks too old to collect orphan's benefits. A woman on the train asks Angela Davis for an autograph. You get read your Miranda. As if a correct line would somehow solve the future. They murdered his parents just to make the point. It's not easy if your audience doesn't identify as readers. Mastectomies are done by men. Our pets live at whim. Net income is down

13%. Those distant sirens down in the valley signal great hinges in the lives of strangers. A phone tree. The landlord's control of terror is implicit. Not just a party but a culture. Copayment. He held the Magnum with both hands and ordered me to stop. The garden is a luxury (a civilization of snail and spider). They call their clubs batons. They call their committees clubs. Her friendships with women are different. Talking so much is oppressive. Outplacement. A shadowy locked facility using drugs and double-celling (a rest home). That was the Sunday Henry's father murdered his wife on the front porch. If it demonstrates form they can't read it. If it demonstrates mercy they have something worse in mind. Twice, carelessness has led to abortion. To own a basement. Nor is the sky any less constructed. The design of a department store is intended to leave you fragmented, off-balance. A lit drop. They photograph Habermas to hide the harelip. The verb *to be* admits the assertion. The body is a prison. a garden. In kind. Client populations (cross the tundra). Off the books. The whole neighborhood is empty in the daytime. Children form lines at the end of each recess. Eminent domain. Rotating chair. The history of Poland in 90 seconds. Flaming pintos. There is no such place as the economy, the self. That bird demonstrates the sky. Our home, we were told, had been broken, but who were these people we lived with? Clubbed in the stomach, she miscarried. There were bayonets on campus. cows in India, people shoplifting books. I just want to make it to lunch time. Uncritical of nationalist movements in the Third World. Letting the dishes sit for a week. Macho culture of convicts. With a shotgun and "in defense" the officer shot him in the face. Here, for a moment, we are joined. The want-ads lie strewn on the table.

Ai (1947–2010)

Ai was born Florence Anthony in Albany, Texas, and grew up in Tucson, Arizona. She attended the University of Arizona and the University of California at Irvine before teaching at Wayne State University, George Mason University, Arizona State University, the University of Colorado, and Oklahoma State University. Her poetry books include Cruelty *(1973),* Killing Floor *(1979, Lamont Prize),* Sin *(1986, American Book Award),* Fate *(1991),* Greed *(1993),* Vice *(1999, National Book Award),* Dread *(2004), and* No Surrender *(2010). Among her honors were Guggenheim, Radcliffe, and National Endowment for the Arts fellowships, the 1983 Ingram Merrill award, and the 2009 United States Artists grant. Ai died in Stillwater, Oklahoma.*

Cuba, 1962

When the rooster jumps up on the windowsill
and spreads his red-gold wings,
I wake, thinking it is the sun
and call Juanita, hearing her answer,
but only in my mind.
I know she is already outside,
breaking the cane off at ground level,
using only her big hands.
I get the machete and walk among the cane,
until I see her, lying face-down in the dirt.

Juanita, dead in the morning like this.
I raise the machete—
what I take from the earth, I give back—
and cut off her feet.
I lift the body and carry it to the wagon,
where I load the cane to sell in the village.
Whoever tastes my woman in his candy, his cake,
tastes something sweeter than this sugar cane;
it is grief.
If you eat too much of it, you want more,
you can never get enough.

The Kid

My sister rubs the doll's face in mud,
then climbs through the truck window.
She ignores me as I walk around it,

hitting the flat tires with an iron rod.
The old man yells for me to help hitch the team,
but I keep walking around the truck, hitting harder,
until my mother calls.
I pick up a rock and throw it at the kitchen window,
but it falls short.
The old man's voice bounces off the air like a ball
I can't lift my leg over.

I stand beside him, waiting, but he doesn't look up
and I squeeze the rod, raise it, his skull splits open.
Mother runs toward us. I stand still,
get her across the spine as she bends over him.
I drop the rod and take the rifle from the house.
Roses are red, violets are blue,
one bullet for the black horse, two for the brown.
They're down quick. I spit, my tongue's bloody;
I've bitten it. I laugh, remember the one out back.
I catch her climbing from the truck, shoot.
The doll lands on the ground with her.
I pick it up, rock it in my arms.
Yeah. I'm Jack, Hogarth's son.
I'm nimble, I'm quick.
In the house, I put on the old man's best suit
and his patent leather shoes.
I pack my mother's satin nightgown
and my sister's doll in the suitcase.
Then I go outside and cross the fields to the highway.
I'm fourteen. I'm a wind from nowhere.
I can break your heart.

Finished

You force me to touch
the black, rubber flaps
of the garbage disposal
that is open like a mouth saying, ah.
You tell me it's the last thing I'll feel
before I go numb.
Is it my screaming that finally stops you,
or is it the fear
that even you are too near the edge
of this Niagara to come back from?

You jerk my hand out
and give me just enough room
to stagger around you.
I lean against the refrigerator,
not looking at you, or anything,
just staring at a space which you no longer inhabit,
that you've abandoned completely now
to footsteps receding
to the next feeding station,
where a woman will be eaten alive
after cocktails at five.
The flowers and chocolates, the kisses,
the swings and near misses of new love
will confuse her,
until you start to abuse her,
verbally at first.
As if trying to quench a thirst,
you'll drink her
in small outbursts of rage
then you'll whip out your semiautomatic,
make her undress, or listen to hours
of radio static as torture
for being amazed that the man of her dreams
is a nightmare, who only seems happy
when he's making her suffer.

The first time you hit me,
I left you, remember?
It was December. An icy rain was falling
and it froze on the roads,
so that driving was unsafe, but not as unsafe
as staying with you.
I ran outside in my nightgown,
while you yelled at me to come back.
When you came after me,
I was locked in the car.
You smashed the window with a crowbar,
but I drove off anyway.
I was back the next day
and we were on the bare mattress,
because you'd ripped up the sheets,
saying you'd teach me a lesson.
You wouldn't speak except
to tell me I needed discipline,

needed training in the fine art
of remaining still
when your fist slammed into my jaw.
You taught me how ropes could be tied
so I'd strangle myself,
how pressure could be applied to old wounds
until I cried for mercy,
until tonight, when those years
of our double exposure end
with shot after shot.

How strange it is to be unafraid.
When the police come,
I'm sitting at the table,
the cup of coffee
that I am unable to drink
as cold as your body.
I shot him, I say, he beat me.
I do not tell them how the emancipation from pain
leaves nothing in its place.

Yusef Komunyakaa (1947–)

Yusef Komunyakaa was born in Bogalusa, Louisiana. After U.S. Army service in Vietnam, he attended the University of Colorado, Colorado State University, and the University of California at Irvine. He held teaching positions at the University of New Orleans, Indiana University at Bloomington, and Princeton University before joining New York University's faculty. His poetry books include Dedications and Other Darkhorses *(1977),* Lost in the Bonewheel Factory *(1979),* Copacetic *(1984),* I Apologize for the Eyes in My Head *(1986),* Dien Cai Dau *(1988),* Magic City *(1992),* Neon Vernacular *(1993, Pulitzer Prize),* Thieves of Paradise *(1998),* Talking Dirty to the Gods *(2000),* Pleasure Dome *(2001),* Taboo: The Wishbone Trilogy, Part One *(2004), and* Warhorses *(2008). Among his honors are National Endowment for the Arts fellowships and the Kingsley Tufts Award. Yusef Komunyakaa lives in New York City.*

Thanks

Thanks for the tree
between me & a sniper's bullet.
I don't know what made the grass
sway seconds before the Viet Cong
raised his soundless rifle.
Some voice always followed,
telling me which foot
to put down first.
Thanks for deflecting the ricochet
against that anarchy of dusk.
I was back in San Francisco
wrapped up in a woman's wild colors,
causing some dark bird's love call
to be shattered by daylight
when my hands reached up
& pulled a branch away
from my face. Thanks
for the vague white flower
that pointed to the gleaming metal
reflecting how it is to be broken
like mist over the grass,
as we played some deadly
game for blind gods.
What made me spot the monarch
writhing on a single thread
tied to a farmer's gate,
holding the day together

like an unfingered guitar string,
is beyond me. Maybe the hills
grew weary & leaned a little in the heat.
Again, thanks for the dud
hand grenade tossed at my feet
outside Chu Lai. I'm still
falling through its silence.
I don't know why the intrepid
sun touched the bayonet,
but I know that something
stood among those lost trees
& moved only when I moved.

Tu Do Street

Music divides the evening.
I close my eyes & can see
men drawing lines in the dust.
America pushes through the membrane
of mist & smoke, & I'm a small boy
again in Bogalusa. *White Only*
signs & Hank Snow. But tonight
I walk into a place where bar girls
fade like tropical birds. When
I order a beer, the mama-san
behind the counter acts as if she
can't understand, while her eyes
skirt each white face, as Hank Williams
calls from the psychedelic jukebox.
We have played Judas where
only machine-gun fire brings us
together. Down the street
black GIs hold to their turf also.
An off-limits sign pulls me
deeper into alleys, as I look
for a softness behind these voices
wounded by their beauty & war.
Back in the bush at Dak To
& Khe Sanh, we fought
the brothers of these women
we now run to hold in our arms.
There's more than a nation
inside us, as black & white

soldiers touch the same lovers
minutes apart, tasting
each other's breath,
without knowing these rooms
run into each other like tunnels
leading to the underworld.

Facing It

My black face fades,
hiding inside the black granite.
I said I wouldn't,
dammit: No tears.
I'm stone. I'm flesh.
My clouded reflection eyes me
like a bird of prey, the profile of night
slanted against morning. I turn
this way—the stone lets me go.
I turn that way—I'm inside
the Vietnam Veterans Memorial
again, depending on the light
to make a difference.
I go down the 58,022 names,
half-expecting to find
my own in letters like smoke.
I touch the name Andrew Johnson;
I see the booby trap's white flash.
Names shimmer on a woman's blouse
but when she walks away
the names stay on the wall.
Brushstrokes flash, a red bird's
wings cutting across my stare.
The sky. A plane in the sky.
A white vet's image floats
closer to me, then his pale eyes
look through mine. I'm a window.
He's lost his right arm
inside the stone. In the black mirror
a woman's trying to erase names:
No, she's brushing a boy's hair.

Nude Interrogation

Did you kill anyone over there? Angelica shifts her gaze from the Janis Joplin poster to the Jimi Hendrix, lifting the pale muslin blouse over her head. The blacklight deepens the blues when the needle drops into the first groove of "All Along the Watchtower." I don't want to look at the floor. *Did you kill anyone? Did you dig a hole, crawl inside, and wait for your target?* Her miniskirt drops into a rainbow at her feet. Sandalwood incense hangs a slow comet of perfume over the room. I shake my head. She unhooks her bra and flings it against a bookcase made of plywood and cinderblocks. *Did you use an M-16, a handgrenade, a bayonet, or your own two strong hands, both thumbs pressed against that little bird in the throat?* She stands with her left thumb hooked into the elastic of her sky-blue panties. When she flicks off the blacklight, snowy hills rush up to the windows. *Did you kill anyone over there? Are you right-handed or left-handed? Did you drop your gun afterwards? Did you kneel beside the corpse and turn it over?* She's nude against the falling snow. Yes. The record spins like a bull's-eye on the far wall of Xanadu. *Yes, I say. I was scared of the silence. The night was too big. And afterwards, I couldn't stop looking up at the sky.*

Nathaniel Mackey (1947–)

Nathaniel Mackey was born in Miami, Florida. He attended Princeton and Stanford universities and taught at the University of Wisconsin–Madison and the University of Southern California–Los Angeles before joining the faculty of the University of California–Santa Cruz in 1979. Among his poetry books are Four for Trane *(1978),* Septet for the End of Time *(1983),* Eroding Witness *(1985, National Poetry Series), Outlantish *(1992),* School of Udhra *(1993),* Whatsaid Serif *(1998), and* Splay Anthem *(2006, National Book Award). Other honors include a Whiting award and a Guggenheim fellowship. Nathaniel Mackey lives in Santa Cruz, California.*

Song of the Andoumboulou: 21

Next a Brazilian cut came
on Sophia picked. Paulinho's
   voice lit our way for what
     seemed eternity,
                 minha
  primeira vez the one
               phrase
  we caught or could understand,
    no matter it ended
soon as it'd begun.
           Endless
  beginning. Endless goodbye.
    Always there if not ever all
there, staggered collapse, an
    accordion choir serenaded
                us,
loquat groves hurried by
   outside . . .

        It was a train
  in southern Spain we
    were on, notwithstanding
  Paulinho's "first" put one
    place atop another,
             brought
  Brazil in, air as much of
it as earth, even more, an ear
   we'd have called inner unexpectedly
    out . . . Neither all in our
heads nor was the world an array

                              less
random than we'd have
                    thought . . .
It was a train outside São
    Paulo on our way to Algeciras we
were on . . . Djbai came aboard.
    Bittabai followed . . .
                         A train
less of thought than of quantum
    solace, quantum locale. "Quantum
        strick, bend our way," we
begged, borne on by reflex, a
                              train
    gotten on in Miami, long since
    gone

                    •

    Lag was our true monument.
    It was an apse we strode under,
        made of air. There inasmuch
as we exacted it, aliquant amble,
                         crowds
        milling around on corners began
    to move, the great arrival day
        we'd heard so much about begun,
sown even if only dug up again.

    Call it loco, lock-kneed samba . . .
Multi-track train. Disenchanted
    feet . . .
            It was the book of
it sometimes going the wrong
    way we now read and wrote . . .
                              Split
    script. Polyrhythmic
remit

Gregory Orr (1947–)

Gregory Orr was born in Albany, New York. He attended Hamilton College, Antioch College, and Columbia University, and was a member of the University of Michigan Society of Fellows in Ann Arbor before joining the University of Virginia faculty in 1975. Among his poetry books are Burning the Empty Nests *(1973),* Gathering the Bones Together *(1975),* The Red House *(1980),* We Must Make a Kingdom of It *(1986),* New and Selected Poems *(1988),* City of Salt *(1995),* Orpheus and Eurydice *(2000),* The Caged Owl *(2003),* Concerning the Book that is the Body of the Beloved *(2005), and* How Beautiful the Beloved *(2009). His honors include Guggenheim and National Endowment for the Arts fellowships. Gregory Orr lives in Charlottesville, Virginia.*

Gathering the Bones Together

> *for Peter Orr*

> *When all the rooms of the house*
> *fill with smoke, it's not enough*
> *to say an angel is sleeping on the chimney.*

1. A NIGHT IN THE BARN

The deer carcass hangs from a rafter.
Wrapped in blankets, a boy keeps watch
from a pile of loose hay. Then he sleeps

and dreams about a death that is coming:
Inside him, there are small bones
scattered in a field among burdocks and dead grass.
He will spend his life walking there,
gathering the bones together.

Pigeons rustle in the eaves.
At his feet, the German shepherd
snaps its jaws in its sleep.

2

A father and his four sons
run down a slope toward
a deer they just killed.
The father and two sons carry
rifles. They laugh, jostle,

and chatter together.
A gun goes off
and the youngest brother
falls to the ground.
A boy with a rifle
stands beside him,
screaming.

3

I crouch in the corner of my room,
staring into the glass well
of my hands; far down
I see him drowning in air.

Outside, leaves shaped like mouths
make a black pool
under a tree. Snails glide
there, little death-swans.

4. SMOKE

Something has covered the chimney
and the whole house fills with smoke.
I go outside and look up at the roof,
but I can't see anything.
I go back inside. Everyone weeps,
walking from room to room.
Their eyes ache. This smoke
turns people into shadows.
Even after it is gone
and the tears are gone,
we will smell it in pillows
when we lie down to sleep.

5

He lives in a house of black glass.
Sometimes I visit him, and we talk.
My father says he is dead,
but what does that mean?
Last night I found a child
sleeping on a nest of bones.
He had a red, leaf-shaped
scar on his cheek.

I lifted him up
and carried him with me,
though I didn't know where I was going.

6. THE JOURNEY

Each night, I knelt on a marble slab
and scrubbed at the blood.
I scrubbed for years and still it was there.
But tonight the bones in my feet
begin to burn. I stand up
and start walking, and the slab
appears under my feet with each step,
a white road only as long as your body.

7. THE DISTANCE

The winter I was eight, a horse
slipped on the ice, breaking its leg.
Father took a rifle, a can of gasoline.
I stood by the road at dusk and watched
the carcass burning in the far pasture.

I was twelve when I killed him;
I felt my own bones wrench from my body.
Now I am twenty-seven and walk
beside this river, looking for them.
They have become a bridge
that arches toward the other shore.

Two Lines from the Brothers Grimm

for Larry and Judy Raab

Now we must get up quickly,
dress ourselves, and run away.
Because it surrounds us, because
they are coming with wolves on leashes,
because I stood just now at the window
and saw the wall of hills on fire.
They have taken our parents away.
Downstairs in the half dark, two strangers
move about, lighting the stove.

Origin of the Marble Forest

Childhood dotted with bodies.

Let them go, let them
be ghosts.

      No, I said,
make them stay, make them stone.

Roberta Hill Whiteman (1947–)

Roberta Hill Whiteman was born and grew up in Wisconsin, on the Oneida reservation and in Green Bay. She attended the University of Wisconsin, the University of Montana, and the University of Minnesota. Her poetry books include Star Quilt *(1984) and* Philadelphia Flowers *(1996). Among her honors are a Lila Wallace–Reader's Digest Writers' Award and a National Endowment for the Arts fellowship. Roberta Hill Whiteman teaches American literature at the University of Wisconsin–Eau Claire.*

Reaching Yellow River

"It isn't a game for girls,"
he said, grabbing a fifth
with his right hand,
the wind with his left.

"For six days
I raced Jack Daniels.
He cheated, told jokes.
Some weren't even funny.

That's how come he won.
It took a long time
to reach this Yellow River.
I'm not yet thirty,

or is it thirty-one?
Figured all my years
carried the same hard thaw.
Out here, houselights hid

deep inside the trees.
For awhile I believed this road
cut across to Spring Creek
and I was trucking home.

I could kid you now,
say I ran it clean,
gasping on one lung,
loaded by a knapsack

of distrust and hesitation.
I never got the tone
in all the talk of cure.
I sang Honor Songs, crawled

the railroad bridge to Canada.
Dizzy from the ties,
I hung between both worlds.
Clans of blackbirds circled

the nearby maple trees.
The dark heart of me said
no days more than these.
As sundown kindled the sumacs,

stunned by the river's smile,
I had no need for heat,
no need to feel ashamed.
Inside me then the sound

of burning leaves. Tell them
I tumbled through a gap on the horizon.
No, say I stumbled through a hummock
and fell in a pit of stars.

When rain weakened my stride,
I heard them singing
in a burl of white ash,
took a few more days to rave

at them in this wood.
Then their appaloosas nickered
in the dawn and they came
riding down a close ravine.

Though the bottle was empty,
I still hung on. Foxtails beat
the grimace from my brow
until I took off my pain

like a pair of old boots.
I became a hollow horn filled
with rain, reflecting everything.
The wind in my hand

burned cold as hoarfrost
when my grandfather nudged me
and called out
my Lakota name."

In memory of Mato Heholgeca's grandson

Albert Goldbarth (1948–)

Albert Goldbarth was born in Chicago, Illinois. He attended the University of Illinois at Chicago and the University of Iowa Writers Workshop and has taught at the University of Utah, Cornell University, the University of Texas at Austin, and since 1987 at Wichita State University. His poetry books include Jan. 31 *(1974),* Comings Back *(1976),* Original Light *(1983),* Popular Culture *(1990),* Heaven and Earth: A Cosmology *(1991, National Book Critics Circle Award),* Saving Lives *(2001, National Book Critics Circle Award),* The Kitchen Sink *(2007), and* To Be Read in 500 Years *(2009). Among his honors are National Endowment for the Arts fellowships and the 2008 Mark Twain Poetry Award. Albert Goldbarth lives in Wichita, Kansas.*

Away

We think a blink is tiny but
it's the size of all of our eyelashes, it's
the length of the drop of a meteor
that could rub out City Hall
and melt a mile circle of asphalt, so
like any of the body's several hundred taken-for-granted
accordion-pleatings, slinks, and spatula-flips, a blink
says a brachiate maze of human evolution going back
past protozoa, and also says, the way the shrilling voice
of a fallopian tube or the prostate will, that pain enough
to fell us like a hammer can fit on a pin.
If *that's* the standard, the eyelashes come to look
as large as a row of hussar swords uplifted in a toast.
If that's the standard, no wonder a blink is span aplenty
for the cockroach on the kitchen floor to vanish
without so much as even a hokey, magicianly poof
—to vanish, waving its own two perfect lashes that,
for all I know, detected the landing thump of Viking I on Mars
before it registered with NASA. Of course entire people disappear:
what genocide is all about; and also entire cities: Tikál,
Ixkún, Flores, Palenque, and the temple center of Copán,
all abandoned by the ancient Maya, given over
to jungle creeper and thorny furze
completely, like an origami metroplex undoing itself
not only back to paper but back
beyond that to the wild paper reeds. To the stones,
the god-faced Mayan stones, this
would have happened in the blink of an eye,
a stone's eye. But tonight I don't mean anything

that vast, I only mean my friend Dolores says
she turns these days to Eduardo in bed and sees
he's someone else—the man she married seven years ago
has been replaced by a figure of balsa and wax,
a *perfect* likeness, but a likeness none the less.
And the department of stats confirms this: each year,
thousands of wives and husbands put on parkas and go
inside of themselves, they say for a pack of cigarettes, and go
up in smoke. It happens. Who *hasn't*
lit the overheads suddenly onto some marriage and seen it
scuttle under the bed or behind the heirloom platter,
blasted out of the real world of community, into cockroach space?
The delights of Away are many. The grass of Away
is a deeper, sweeter, narcotic viridian than the lawns of Here
could ever be fertilized into. O write me c/o Vamoose,
Oblivion. When I was a child,
six or seven or so, and the day was six or seven thousand
consecutive terrors and humiliations, and everything spun
too fast to grasp exactly, including love, including self,
I'd curl in bed—the way I might now,
or my wife might now, although with the return half
of the ticket in our holding—and my lids would close
(those Roman galleys fitted out with oars),
would take me into the night, down the flow and the beat,
would row me away on the black sea
of that disappearing ink.

Heather McHugh (1948–)

Heather McHugh was born in San Diego, California, and grew up in Gloucester Point, Virginia. She attended Radcliffe College and the University of Denver and taught at the State University of New York at Binghamton before joining the University of Washington's faculty in 1983. Among her poetry books are Dangers *(1977),* A World of Difference *(1981),* To the Quick *(1987),* Shades *(1988),* Hinge and Sign *(1994),* The Father of the Predicaments *(1999),* Eyeshot *(2004), and* Upgraded to Serious *(2009). Her honors include MacDowell Colony, Yaddo, National Endowment for the Arts, and MacArthur fellowships, as well as a Lila Wallace–Reader's Digest Writers' Award. Heather McHugh lives in Seattle, Washington.*

Language Lesson 1976

When Americans say a man
takes liberties, they mean

he's gone too far. In Philadelphia today I saw
a kid on a leash look mom-ward

and announce his fondest wish: one
bicentennial burger, hold

the relish. Hold is forget,
in American.

On the courts of Philadelphia
the rich prepare

to serve, to fault. The language is a game as well,
in which love can mean nothing,

doubletalk mean lie. I'm saying
doubletalk with me. I'm saying

go so far the customs are untold.
Make nothing without words,

and let me be
the one you never hold.

What He Thought

for Fabbio Doplicher

We were supposed to do a job in Italy
and, full of our feeling for
ourselves (our sense of being
Poets from America) we went
from Rome to Fano, met
the mayor, mulled
a couple matters over (what's
cheap date, they asked us; what's
flat drink). Among Italian literati

we could recognize our counterparts:
the academic, the apologist,
the arrogant, the amorous,
the brazen and the glib—and there was one

administrator (the conservative), in suit
of regulation gray, who like a good tour guide
with measured pace and uninflected tone narrated
sights and histories the hired van hauled us past.
Of all, he was most politic and least poetic,
so it seemed. Our last few days in Rome
(when all but three of the New World Bards had flown)
I found a book of poems this
unprepossessing one had written: it was there
in the *pensione* room (a room he'd recommended)
where it must have been abandoned by
the German visitor (was there a bus of *them*?)
to whom he had inscribed and dated it a month before.
I couldn't read Italian, either, so I put the book
back in the wardrobe's dark. We last Americans

were due to leave tomorrow. For our parting evening then
our host chose something in a family restaurant, and there
we sat and chatted, sat and chewed,
till, sensible it was our last
big chance to be poetic, make
our mark, one of us asked
                              "What's poetry?
Is it the fruits and vegetables and

marketplace of Campo dei Fiori, or
the statue there?" Because I was

the glib one, I identified the answer
instantly, I didn't have to think—"The truth
is both, it's both," I blurted out. But that
was easy. That was easiest to say. What followed
taught me something about difficulty,
for our underestimated host spoke out,
all of a sudden, with a rising passion, and he said:

The statue represents Giordano Bruno,
brought to be burned in the public square
because of his offense against
authority, which is to say
the Church. His crime was his belief
the universe does not revolve around
the human being: God is no
fixed point or central government, but rather is
poured in waves through all things. All things
move. "If God is not the soul itself, He is
the soul of the soul of the world." Such was
his heresy. The day they brought him
forth to die, they feared he might
incite the crowd (the man was famous
for his eloquence). And so his captors
placed upon his face
an iron mask, in which

he could not speak. That's
how they burned him. That is how
he died: without a word, in front
of everyone.
        And poetry—
                    (we'd all
put down our forks by now, to listen to
the man in gray; he went on
softly)—
        poetry is what

he thought, but did not say.

Leslie Marmon Silko (1948–)

Leslie Marmon Silko was born in Albuquerque, New Mexico, and grew up on the nearby Laguna Pueblo. She attended the University of New Mexico and has taught at the University of Arizona. Her poetry books include Laguna Woman *(1974),* Voices Under One Sky *(1994),* Rain *(1996), and* Love Poem and Slim Canyon *(1996). She has also published numerous volumes of prose. Among her honors are National Endowment for the Arts and MacArthur fellowships; her novel* Ceremony *(1977) received the American Book Award. Leslie Marmon Silko lives near Tucson, Arizona.*

In Cold Storm Light

In cold storm light
I watch the sandrock
        canyon rim.

        The wind is wet
            with the smell of piñon.
        The wind is cold
            with the sound of juniper.
                And then
                    out of the thick ice sky
                        running swiftly
                        pounding
                        swirling above the treetops
                The snow elk come,
                Moving, moving
                        white song
                        storm wind in the branches.

And when the elk have passed
        behind them
                a crystal train of snowflakes
                strands of mist
                        tangled in rocks
                        and leaves.

Olga Broumas (1949–)

Olga Broumas was born on the Greek island of Syros and came to the United States as a Fulbright fellow at the University of Pennsylvania, then attended the University of Oregon before teaching at the University of Oregon, the University of Idaho, Goddard College, and Boston University. She founded the Freehand women writers and photographers community in Provincetown in 1982, and is poet-in-residence at Brandeis University. Among her books are Beginning with O *(1978, Yale Younger Poets Series),* Soie Sauvage *(1979),* Pastoral Jazz *(1983),* Perpetua *(1989), and* Rave *(1999, Lambda Literary Award). Her honors include Guggenheim and National Endowment for the Arts fellowships as well as a Wytter Bynner grant. Olga Broumas lives in Massachusetts.*

Calypso

I've gathered the women like talismans, one
by one. They first came for tarot card
gossip, mystified
by my hands, by offers
cut with escape. They came

undone in my studio, sailing long eyes, heavy
with smoke and wet
with the force of dream: a vagina
folding mandala-like
out of herself, in full bloom. I used them. I used

the significance
of each card to uphold the dream, soon
they came back with others. I let the bitch
twitch in my lap. I listened. I let the tea steep
till the pot was black. Soon

there was no need for cards. We would use
stills from our daily lives, every woman
a constellation of images, every
portrait each other's chart.
We came together

like months
in a lunar year, measured in nights, dividing
perfectly into female phases. Like women anywhere
living in groups we had synchronous menses. And had
no need of a wound, a puncture, to seal our bond.

Victor Hernández Cruz (1949–)

Victor Hernández Cruz was born in Aguas Buenas, Puerto Rico, and came to New York City in 1954. He cofounded the East Harlem Gut Theatre in 1968 and has been guest lecturer at a number of universities. His poetry books include Snaps *(1969),* Mainland *(1973),* Tropicalization *(poems and prose, 1976),* Rhythm, Content, and Flavor *(1989),* Red Beans *(1991),* Panoramas *(1997),* Maraca *(2001, Griffin Prize), and* The Mountain in the Sea *(2006). Among his honors are National Endowment for the Arts and Guggenheim fellowships. Victor Hernández Cruz lives in Puerto Rico and Morocco.*

Latin & Soul

> *for Joe Bataan*

1

some waves
        a wave of now
                a trombone speaking to you
a piano is trying to break a molecule
is trying to lift the stage into orbit
around the red spotlights

a shadow
the shadows   of dancers
dancers   they are dancing   falling
out that space   made for dancing

they should dance
on the tables   they should
dance inside of their drinks
they should dance on the
ceiling they should dance/dance

thru universes
leaning-moving
         we are traveling

where are we going
if we only knew

with this rhythm   with
this banging   with   fire

with this   all   this   O
my god i wonder   where are
we going
       sink into a room full of laughter
       full of happiness   full of life
       those dancers
       the dancers
            are clapping their hands
            stomping their feet

hold back them tears
            all those sentimental stories
cooked uptown   if you can   hold it for after

we are going
       away-away-away
       beyond these wooden tables
       beyond these red lights
       beyond these rugs & paper
       walls   beyond   way past
       i mean way past them clouds
       over the buildings   over the
       rivers   over towns   over cities
       like on rails   but faster   like
       a train   but smoother
       away past stars
       bursting with drums.

2

a sudden misunderstanding
            a cloud
            full of grayness
a body thru a store window
            a hand reaching
            into the back
            pocket
a scream
       a piano is talking to you
       thru all this
       why don't you answer it.

Jane Miller (1949–)

Jane Miller was born in New York City and attended Pennsylvania State University, Humboldt State University, and the University of Iowa Writers Workshop. She taught at the University of Iowa and Goddard College before joining the faculty of the University of Arizona. Among her poetry books are Many Junipers, Heartbeats *(1980),* Black Holes Black Stockings *(1983, with Olga Broumas),* American Odalisque *(1987),* August Zero *(1993),* Memory at These Speeds *(1996),* Wherever You Lay Your Head *(1999), and* A Palace of Pearls *(2005). Her honors include a Lila Wallace– Reader's Digest Writers' Award, Guggenheim and National Endowment for the Arts fellowships, and the 1993 Western States Book Award in poetry. Jane Miller lives in Tucson, Arizona.*

Miami Heart

In a long text, on live TV, in an amphitheater, in the soil,
after the post-moderns, after it is still proven
you can get a smile out of a pretty girl,
after the meta-ritual lectures,
after the flock to further awareness bends "south,"
and Heinz switches to plastic squeeze bottles,
as one flies into St. Louis listening to Lorca's "Luna, luna, luna . . . ,"
beyond Anacin time,
after, God help us, the dishwasher is emptied again,
and Miss America, Miss Mississippi, reveals she has entered 100 pageants
since age six,
Packer's ball, first down after a fumble,
the corn detassled,
the assembly of enthusiasms awakened,
and we meet in a car by the river
not not kissing, considering
making love, visiting Jerusalem, the awful daily knowledge
we have to die in a hospital on the sixth floor, in a lecture, on live TV,
or in an amphitheater at half-time,
at one's parents' condo, over pasta,
in a strange relative's arms, in debt, along the coast, staring
at a lighthouse, the heart bumping, bumping the old pebble up the old spine,
a squirrel scared up a sycamore by an infant,
along this stench of humility, along that highway of come,
charge card in hand,
I shall give my time freely
and the more I dissemble the more I resemble
and the more I order the more I reveal I hide,

the better, the faster
I sleep the more I remember
to go elsewhere,
a movie, excuse me, now I must whisper
not to disturb the patrons,
now I must drive, now park, tramp to the edge of the world,
roughness, ferocity, cannibalism,
bite, chew, transmogrify,
inside the lungs the little revolutionaries, between the thighs the reflex
it's too this, it's too that, it's not enough,
similarly, and more particularly, it's raw twice over,
it's the imagination draining its husks, left-handed,
because comparison is motive, which is why
one writes with one's desire.

David St. John (1949–)

David St. John was born and raised in Fresno, California. He attended California State University at Fresno and the University of Iowa Writers Workshop. He taught at Oberlin College and Johns Hopkins University before joining the University of Southern California's faculty in 1987. Among his poetry books are Hush *(1976),* The Shore *(1980),* No Heaven *(1985),* Study for the World's Body *(1994),* In the Pines: Lost Poems *(1999), and the verse novella* The Face *(2005). His honors include fellowships from the National Endowment for the Arts and the Guggenheim and Ingram Merrill foundations, a Prix de Rome fellowship, and the O. B. Hardison Jr. Prize in poetry. David St. John lives in Los Angeles.*

Iris

> *Vivian St. John (1891–1974)*

There is a train inside this iris:

You think I'm crazy, & like to say boyish
& outrageous things. No, there is

A train inside this iris.

It's a child's finger bearded in black banners.
A single window like a child's nail,

A darkened porthole lit by the white, angular face

Of an old woman, or perhaps the boy beside her in the stuffy,
Hot compartment. Her hair is silver, & sweeps

Back off her forehead, onto her cold & bruised shoulders.

The prairies fail along Chicago. Past the five
Lakes. Into the black woods of her New York; & as I bend

Close above the iris, I see the train

Drive deep into the damp heart of its stem, & the gravel
Of the garden path

Cracks under my feet as I walk this long corridor

Of elms, arched
Like the ceiling of a French railway pier where a boy

With pale curls holding

A fresh iris is waving goodbye to a grandmother, gazing
A long time

Into the flower, as if he were looking some great

Distance, or down an empty garden path & he believes a man
Is walking toward him, working

Dull shears in one hand; & now believe me: The train

Is gone. The old woman is dead, & the boy. The iris curls,
On its stalk, in the shade

Of those elms: Where something like the icy & bitter fragrance

In the wake of a woman who's just swept past you on her way
Home

& you remain.

C. D. Wright (1949–)

C. D. Wright was born in Mountain Home, Arkansas, and grew up in the Ozarks. She attended Memphis State University and the University of Arkansas and has taught at Brown University since 1983. Among her poetry books are Translation of the Gospel Back into Tongues *(1981),* Further Adventures with You *(1986),* String Light *(1991),* Just Whistle *(1993),* Tremble *(1996),* Deepstep Come Shining *(1998),* Steal Away *(2002),* Cooling Time: An American Poetry Vigil *(2005),* Rising, Falling, Hovering *(2008, Griffin Prize), and* One with Others *(2010). Her honors include National Endowment for the Arts, Guggenheim, Bunting, Lannan, and MacArthur fellowships, the Witter Bynner Poetry prize, and a Whiting award. C. D. Wright lives in Providence, Rhode Island.*

Why Ralph Refuses to Dance

He would have to put out his smoke.
  At this time of year the snakes are slow and sorry-acting
His ice would melt. He'd lose his seat.
  you don't take chances once in a while you still see
He does not feel the beat.
  a coontail tied to an aerial, but don't look
His pocket could be picked. His trousers rip.
  for signs keep your black shoes on the floor
He could break a major bone.
  burn every tick you pull off your head
He remembers the last time he stepped out on the floor.
  roll a set of steel balls around in your fist
Who do you think I am, she said, a broom.
  looking at the moon's punched-out face
No, he mumbled, saxophone.
  think about Lily coming down the staircase
At the tables they whispered about him.
  her crushed velvet chairs
He would begin to smell of baby shrimp.
  her pearled brown toes
The music could stop in the middle of his action.
  that time with the three of them in a boat
What would he do with his hands.
  and him throwing up in the river
The women his age are spoken for.
  as she stood up to skim his hat into the shallows
After sitting out so long, his heart could give out.
  and tomorrow would unleash another spell of spare-rib theology

People will be stepped on. A fight ensue.
     aw shuddup somebody clapped a hand on his shoulder
The cats in the band will lose respect.
     aw shuddup he was getting the heavy hand again
He will bring dishonor to his family name.
     are you going to dance or not, just say
good-night, no thanks, hallelujah yourself, go to hell.

Girl Friend Poem #3

She was white and flown
as a kleenex turning into a swan.
I lifted her veil; the face disappeared.
As if I had exposed some film
to sun. Twirling our skirts.
Laughing until the clouds sopped up
the light. And the peaches fell down around us.

    for sharon

Crescent

In recent months I have become intent on seizing happiness: to this end I applied various shades of blue: only the evening is outside us now propagating honeysuckle: I am trying to invent a new way of moving under my dress: the room squares off against this: watch the water glitter with excitement: when we cut below the silver skin of the surface the center retains its fluidity: do I still remind you of a locust clinging to a branch: I give you an idea of the damages: you would let edges be edges: believe me: when their eyes poured over your long body of poetry I also was there: when they lay their hands on your glass shade I also was there: when they put their whole trust in your grace I had to step outside to get away from my cravenness: we have done these things to one another without benefit of a mirror: unlike the honeysuckle goodness does not overtake us: yet the thigh keeps quiet under nylon: later beneath the blueness of trees the future falls out of place: something always happens: draw nearer my dear: never fear: the world spins nightly toward its brightness and we are on it

Carolyn Forché (1950–)

Carolyn Forché was born in Detroit, Michigan. She attended Michigan State University and Bowling Green State University and taught at San Diego State University, the University of Virginia, the University of Arkansas, New York University, Columbia University, George Mason University, and Skidmore College before joining Georgetown University's faculty. Among her poetry books are Gathering the Tribes *(1976, Yale Series of Younger Poets),* The Country Between Us *(1981, Lamont Poetry Prize),* The Angel of History *(1994, Los Angeles Times Book Award), and* Blue Hour *(2003, National Book Critics Circle Award). Her honors include National Endowment for the Arts, Guggenheim, and Lannan fellowships. Carolyn Forché lives in Maryland.*

Taking Off My Clothes

I take off my shirt, I show you.
I shaved the hair out under my arms.
I roll up my pants, I scraped off the hair
on my legs with a knife, getting white.

My hair is the color of chopped maples.
My eyes dark as beans cooked in the south.
(Coal fields in the moon on torn-up hills)

Skin polished as a Ming bowl
showing its blood cracks, its age, I have hundreds
of names for the snow, for this, all of them quiet.

In the night I come to you and it seems a shame
to waste my deepest shudders on a wall of a man.

You recognize strangers,
think you lived through destruction.
You can't explain this night, my face, your memory.

You want to know what I know?
Your own hands are lying.

Jorie Graham (1950–)

Jorie Graham was born in New York City and grew up in Italy and France. She attended New York University and the University of Iowa Writers Workshop before teaching at Murray State University, Humboldt State University, Columbia University, the University of Iowa, and Harvard University. Among her poetry books are Hybrids of Plants and of Ghosts *(1980),* Erosion *(1983),* The End of Beauty *(1987),* Region of Unlikeness *(1991),* Materialism *(1993),* The Dream of the Unified Field *(1995, Pulitzer Prize),* The Errancy *(1997),* Swarm *(2000),* Never *(2002),* Overlord *(2005), and* Sea Change *(2008). Her honors include Ingram Merrill, Guggenheim, National Endowment for the Arts, and MacArthur fellowships and a Whiting award.*

San Sepolcro

In this blue light
    I can take you there,
snow having made me
    a world of bone
seen through to. This
    is my house,

my section of Etruscan
    wall, my neighbor's
lemontrees, and, just below
    the lower church,
the airplane factory.
    A rooster

crows all day from mist
    outside the walls.
There's milk on the air,
    ice on the oily
lemonskins. How clean
    the mind is,

holy grave. It is this girl
    by Piero
della Francesca, unbuttoning
    her blue dress,
her mantle of weather,
    to go into

labor. Come, we can go in.
     It is before
the birth of god. No one
     has risen yet
to the museums, to the assembly
     line—bodies

and wings—to the open air
     market. This is
what the living do: go in.
     It's a long way.
And the dress keeps opening
     from eternity

to privacy, quickening.
     Inside, at the heart,
is tragedy, the present moment
     forever stillborn,
but going in, each breath
     is a button

coming undone, something terribly
     nimble-fingered
finding all of the stops.

Marie Howe (1950–)

Marie Howe was born and raised in Rochester, New York. She attended the University of Windsor and Columbia University and taught at several universities before joining the faculties of Sarah Lawrence College, Columbia University, and New York University. Among her poetry books are The Good Thief *(1988, National Poetry Series),* What the Living Do *(1997), and* The Kingdom of the Ordinary Time *(2008). Her honors include fellowships from the Provincetown Fine Arts Work Center, Radcliffe College's Bunting Institute, the National Endowment for the Arts, and the Guggenheim Foundation. Marie Howe lives in New York City.*

What the Living Do

Johnny, the kitchen sink has been clogged for days, some utensil probably
    fell down there.
And the Drano won't work but smells dangerous, and the crusty dishes
    have piled up

waiting for the plumber I still haven't called. This is the everyday we
    spoke of.
It's winter again: the sky's a deep headstrong blue, and the sunlight
    pours through

the open living room windows because the heat's on too high in here, and
    I can't turn it off.
For weeks now, driving, or dropping a bag of groceries in the street,
    the bag breaking,

I've been thinking: This is what the living do. And yesterday, hurrying
    along those
wobbly bricks in the Cambridge sidewalk, spilling my coffee down my
    wrist and sleeve,

I thought it again, and again later, when buying a hairbrush: This is it.
Parking. Slamming the car door shut in the cold. What you called
    that yearning.

What you finally gave up. We want the spring to come and the winter to
    pass. We want
whoever to call or not call, a letter, a kiss—we want more and more and
    then more of it.

But there are moments, walking, when I catch a glimpse of myself in the
    window glass,
say, the window of the corner video store, and I'm gripped by a cherishing
    so deep

for my own blowing hair, chapped face, and unbuttoned coat that I'm
    speechless:
I am living, I remember you.

Joy Harjo (1951–)

Joy Harjo was born in Tulsa, Oklahoma. She attended the University of New Mexico and the University of Iowa Writers Workshop and has taught at the Institute of American Indian Arts in Santa Fe, Arizona State University, the University of Colorado, the University of Arizona, and the University of New Mexico. Among her poetry books are She Had Some Horses *(1983),* Secrets from the Center of the World *(1989),* In Mad Love and War *(1990, American Book Award),* The Woman Who Fell from the Sky *(1994),* A Map to the Next World: Poetry and Tales *(2000), and* How We Became Human: New and Selected Poems *(2003, Oklahoma Book Award). Her honors include fellowships from the National Endowment for the Arts and the Witter Bynner Foundation. Joy Harjo lives in Albuquerque, New Mexico.*

She Had Some Horses

She had some horses.

She had horses who were bodies of sand.
She had horses who were maps drawn of blood.
She had horses who were skins of ocean water.
She had horses who were the blue air of sky.
She had horses who were fur and teeth.
She had horses who were clay and would break.
She had horses who were splintered red cliff.

She had some horses.

She had horses with eyes of trains.
She had horses with full, brown thighs.
She had horses who laughed too much.
She had horses who threw rocks at glass houses.
She had horses who licked razor blades.

She had some horses.

She had horses who danced in their mothers' arms.
She had horses who thought they were the sun and their
bodies shone and burned like stars.
She had horses who waltzed nightly on the moon.
She had horses who were much too shy, and kept quiet
in stalls of their own making.

She had some horses.

She had horses who liked Creek Stomp Dance songs.
She had horses who cried in their beer.
She had horses who spit at male queens who made
them afraid of themselves.
She had horses who said they weren't afraid.
She had horses who lied.
She had horses who told the truth, who were stripped
bare of their tongues.

She had some horses.

She had horses who called themselves, *horse*.
She had horses who called themselves, *spirit*, and kept
their voices secret and to themselves.
She had horses who had no names.
She had horses who had books of names.

She had some horses.

She had horses who whispered in the dark, who were afraid
to speak.
She had horses who screamed out of fear of the silence, who
carried knives to protect themselves from ghosts.
She had horses who waited for destruction.
She had horses who waited for resurrection.

She had some horses.

She had horses who got down on their knees for any saviour.
She had horses who thought their high price had saved them.
She had horses who tried to save her, who climbed in her
bed at night and prayed as they raped her.

She had some horses.

She had some horses she loved.
She had some horses she hated.

These were the same horses.

My House is the Red Earth

My house is the red earth; it could be the center of the world. I've heard New York, Paris, or Tokyo called the center of the world, but I say it is magnificently humble. You could drive by and miss it. Radio waves can obscure it. Words cannot construct it, for there are some sounds left to sacred wordless form. For instance, that fool crow, picking through trash near the corral, understands the center of the world as greasy strips of fat. Just ask him. He doesn't have to say that the earth has turned scarlet through fierce belief, after centuries of heartbreak and laughter—he perches on the blue bowl of the sky, and laughs.

Garrett Hongo (1951–)

Garrett Hongo was born in Volcano, Hawaii. He attended Pomona College, the University of Michigan, and the University of California–Irvine and taught at the University of Southern California and the University of Missouri before joining the faculty at the University of Oregon in 1989. His poetry books are Yellow Light *(1982),* The River of Heaven *(1988, Lamont Award), and* Coral Road *(2011). Hongo has also published drama and prose; his* Volcano: A Memoir of Hawaii *(1995) received the Oregon Book Award for Literary Nonfiction. Other honors include National Endowment for the Arts and Guggenheim fellowships. Garrett Hongo lives in Eugene, Oregon.*

The Legend

In Chicago, it is snowing softly
and a man has just done his wash for the week.
He steps into the twilight of early evening,
carrying a wrinkled shopping bag
full of neatly folded clothes,
and, for a moment, enjoys
the feel of warm laundry and crinkled paper,
flannellike against his gloveless hands.
There's a Rembrandt glow on his face,
a triangle of orange in the hollow of his cheek
as a last flash of sunset
blazes the storefronts and lit windows of the street.

He is Asian, Thai or Vietnamese,
and very skinny, dressed as one of the poor
in rumpled suit pants and a plaid mackinaw,
dingy and too large.
He negotiates the slick of ice
on the sidewalk by his car,
opens the Fairlane's back door,
leans to place the laundry in,
and turns, for an instant,
toward the flurry of footsteps
and cries of pedestrians
as a boy—that's all he was—
backs from the corner package store
shooting a pistol, firing it,
once, at the dumbfounded man
who falls forward,
grabbing at his chest.

A few sounds escape from his mouth,
a babbling no one understands
as people surround him
bewildered at his speech.
The noises he makes are nothing to them.
The boy has gone, lost
in the light array of foot traffic
dappling the snow with fresh prints.
Tonight, I read about Descartes'
grand courage to doubt everything
except his own miraculous existence
and I feel so distinct
from the wounded man lying on the concrete
I am ashamed.

Let the night sky cover him as he dies.
Let the weaver girl cross the bridge of heaven
and take up his cold hands.

In Memory of Jay Kashiwamura

Andrew Hudgins (1951–)

Andrew Hudgins was born in Killeen, Texas. He attended Huntingdon College in Alabama, the University of Alabama, and the University of Iowa Writers Workshop. He taught at Auburn University, Baylor University, and the University of Cincinnati before joining Ohio State University's faculty. His books include Saints and Strangers *(1985),* After the Lost War: A Narrative *(1988),* The Never-Ending *(1991),* The Glass Hammer: A Southern Childhood *(1994),* Babylon in a Jar *(1998),* Ecstatic in the Poison *(2003), and* American Rendering: New and Selected Poems *(2010). Among his honors are Wallace Stegner, Yaddo, MacDowell Colony, National Endowment for the Arts, and Fine Arts Work Center in Provincetown fellowships, an Ingram Merrill Foundation grant, and the Witter Bynner Foundation Prize. Andrew Hudgins lives near Columbus, Ohio.*

Begotten

I've never, as some children do,
looked at my folks and thought, I *must*
have come from someone else—
rich parents who'd misplaced me, but
who would, as in a myth or novel,
return and claim me. Hell, no. I saw
my face in cousins' faces, heard
my voice in their high drawls. And Sundays,
after the dinner plates were cleared,
I lingered, elbow propped on red
oilcloth, and studied great-uncles, aunts,
and cousins new to me. They squirmed.
I stared till I discerned the features
they'd gotten from the family larder:
eyes, nose, lips, hair? I stared until,
uncomfortable, they'd snap, "Hey, boy—
what are you looking at? At me?"
"No, sir," I'd lie. "No, ma'am." I'd count ten
and then continue staring at them.
I never had to ask, What am I?
I stared at my blood-kin, and thought,
So *this*, dear God, is what I am.

We Were Simply Talking

We were simply talking, probably work, or relatives
or even Christmas presents, when the car slid

and I corrected, fishtailed and I corrected, then we were gone,
sliding sideways, sliding backward on black ice
and staring into the grill of a diesel tractor, also sliding,
and in that instant I was ready to die.
I saw my wife and was overjoyed that I had married her,
though our marriage was already falling apart,
and I loved the car, a brown Toyota, loved
being warm in the car while it was white, cold, bitter
out in the world we'd lost control of. I loved
every molecule of breath I wasn't taking,
and for the moment I forgave myself every sin
and failure of my life, including this
ridiculous and undignified early death.
The car snapped backward into a frozen ditch.
I sat speechless, shaking, my wife speechless also,
and a man pulled up, a salesman: You folks okay?
Suddenly the radio roared, and by the car
a dog barked wildly and, yes, we were fine.
Fine. We were fine. But what was "fine," I wondered,
and why do we always, always have to speak?

Brigit Pegeen Kelly (1951–)

Brigit Pegeen Kelly was born in Palo Alto, California. She has taught at the University of California at Irvine, Purdue University, Warren Wilson College, and the University of Illinois at Urbana-Champaign. Her poetry books include To the Place of Trumpets *(1988, Yale Younger Poets Award),* Song *(1994, Lamont Poetry Prize), and* The Orchard *(2005). Among her honors are a Whiting award, the Discovery/The Nation Poetry Prize, and fellowships from the National Endowment for the Arts, the Guggenheim Foundation, and the Academy of American Poets.*

Imagining Their Own Hymns

What fools they are to believe the angels
in this window are in ecstasy. They
do not smile. Their eyes are rolled back in annoyance
not in bliss, as my mother's eyes roll back
when she finds us in the dirt with the cider—
flies and juice blackening our faces and hands.
When the sun comes up behind the angels
then even in their dun robes they are beautiful,
with their girlish hair and their mean lit faces,
but they do not love the light. As I
do not love it when I am made clean
for the ladies who bring my family money.
They stroke my face and smooth my hair. So sweet,
they say, so good, but I am not sweet or good.
I would take one of the possums we kill
in the dump by the woods where the rats slide
like dark boats into the dark stream and leave it
on the heavy woman's porch just to think
of her on her knees scrubbing and scrubbing
at a stain that will never come out.
And these angels that the women turn to
are not good either. They are sick of Jesus,
who never stops dying, hanging there white
and large, his shadow blue as pitch, and blue
the bruise on his chest, with spread petals,
like the hydrangea blooms I tear from
Mrs. Macht's bush and smash on the sidewalk.
One night they will get out of here. One night
when the weather is turning cold and a few
candles burn, they will leave St. Blase standing
under his canopy of glass lettuce

and together, as in a wedding march,
their pockets full of money from the boxes
for the sick poor, they will walk down the aisle,
imagining their own hymns, past the pews
and the water fonts in which small things float,
down the streets of our narrow town, while
the bells ring and the birds fly up in the fields
beyond—and they will never come back.

Song

Listen: there was a goat's head hanging by ropes in a tree.
All night it hung there and sang. And those who heard it
Felt a hurt in their hearts and thought they were hearing
The song of a night bird. They sat up in their beds, and then
They lay back down again. In the night wind, the goat's head
Swayed back and forth, and from far off it shone faintly
The way the moonlight shone on the train track miles away
Beside which the goat's headless body lay. Some boys
Had hacked its head off. It was harder work than they had imagined.
The goat cried like a man and struggled hard. But they
Finished the job. They hung the bleeding head by the school
And then ran off into the darkness that seems to hide everything.
The head hung in the tree. The body lay by the tracks.
The head called to the body. The body to the head.
They missed each other. The missing grew large between them,
Until it pulled the heart right out of the body, until
The drawn heart flew toward the head, flew as a bird flies
Back to its cage and the familiar perch from which it trills.
Then the heart sang in the head, softly at first and then louder,
Sang long and low until the morning light came up over
The school and over the tree, and then the singing stopped. . . .
The goat had belonged to a small girl. She named
The goat Broken Thorn Sweet Blackberry, named it after
The night's bush of stars, because the goat's silky hair
Was dark as well water, because it had eyes like wild fruit.
The girl lived near a high railroad track. At night
She heard the trains passing, the sweet sound of the train's horn
Pouring softly over her bed, and each morning she woke
To give the bleating goat his pail of warm milk. She sang
Him songs about girls with ropes and cooks in boats.
She brushed him with a stiff brush. She dreamed daily
That he grew bigger, and he did. She thought her dreaming

Made it so. But one night the girl didn't hear the train's horn,
And the next morning she woke to an empty yard. The goat
Was gone. Everything looked strange. It was as if a storm
Had passed through while she slept, wind and stones, rain
Stripping the branches of fruit. She knew that someone
Had stolen the goat and that he had come to harm. She called
To him. All morning and into the afternoon, she called
And called. She walked and walked. In her chest a bad feeling
Like the feeling of the stones gouging the soft undersides
Of her bare feet. Then somebody found the goat's body
By the high tracks, the flies already filling their soft bottles
At the goat's torn neck. Then somebody found the head
Hanging in a tree by the school. They hurried to take
These things away so that the girl would not see them.
They hurried to raise money to buy the girl another goat.
They hurried to find the boys who had done this, to hear
Them say it was a joke, a joke, it was nothing but a joke. . . .
But listen: here is the point. The boys thought to have
Their fun and be done with it. It was harder work than they
Had imagined, this silly sacrifice, but they finished the job,
Whistling as they washed their large hands in the dark.
What they didn't know was that the goat's head was already
Singing behind them in the tree. What they didn't know
Was that the goat's head would go on singing, just for them,
Long after the ropes were down, and that they would learn to listen,
Pail after pail, stroke after patient stroke. They would
Wake in the night thinking they heard the wind in the trees
Or a night bird, but their hearts beating harder. There
Would be a whistle, a hum, a high murmur, and, at last, a song,
The low song a lost boy sings remembering his mother's call.
Not a cruel song, no, no, not cruel at all. This song
Is sweet. It is sweet. The heart dies of this sweetness.

Paul Muldoon (1951–)

Paul Muldoon was born in County Armagh, Northern Ireland. He attended Queen's University (Belfast) before working as a radio and television producer for the BBC. Currently on the faculty at Princeton University and poetry editor of The New Yorker, *he has also been professor of poetry at Oxford. His poetry books include* New Weather *(1973),* Mules *(1977),* Why Brownlee Left *(1980),* Quoof *(1983),* Meeting the British *(1987),* Madoc: A Mystery *(1990),* The Annals of Chile *(1994),* Hay *(1998),* Poems 1968–1998 *(2001),* Moy Sand and Gravel *(2002, Pulitzer Prize, Griffin Prize),* Horse Latitudes *(2006), and* Maggot *(2010). Among his honors are the T. S. Eliot Prize, the Irish Times Poetry Prize, the 2004 Shakespeare Prize, the 2005 Aspen Prize for Poetry, and the 2006 European Prize for Poetry.*

Meeting the British

We met the British in the dead of winter.
The sky was lavender

and the snow lavender-blue.
I could hear, far below,

the sound of two streams coming together
(both were frozen over)

and, no less strange,
myself calling out in French

across that forest-
clearing. Neither General Jeffrey Amherst

nor Colonel Henry Bouquet
could stomach our willow-tobacco.

As for the unusual
scent when the Colonel shook out his hand-

kerchief: *C'est la lavande,
une fleur mauve comme le ciel.*

They gave us six fishhooks
and two blankets embroidered with smallpox.

Errata

For "Antrim" read "Armagh."
For "mother" read "other."
For "harm" read "farm."
For "feather" read "father."

For "Moncrieff" read "Monteith."
For "*Beal Fierste*" read "*Beal Feirste.*"
For "brave" read "grave."
For "revered" read "reversed."

For "married" read "marred."
For "pull" read "pall."
For "ban" read "bar."
For "smell" read "small."

For "spike" read "spoke."
For "lost" read "last."
For "Steinbeck" read "Steenbeck."
For "ludic" read "lucid."

For "religion" read "region."
For "ode" read "code."
For "Jane" read "Jean."
For "rod" read "road."

For "pharoah" read "pharaoh."
For "*Fíor-Gael*" read "*Fíor-Ghael.*"
For "Jeffrey" read "Jeffery."
For "vigil" read "Virgil."

For "flageolet" read "fava."
For "veto" read "vote."
Fur "Aiofe" read "Aoife."
For "anecdote" read "antidote."

For "Rosemont" read "Mount Rose."
For "plump" read "plumb."
For "hearse" read "hears."
For "loom" read "bloom."

The Throwback

Even I can't help but notice, my sweet,
that when you tuck your chin
into your chest, as if folding a sheet
while holding a clothespin

between your teeth, or when, a small detail,
you put your hands like so
on your little potbelly and twiddle
your thumbs like so, it's as if you're a throw-

back to the grandmother you never met,
the mother whom I sight
in this reddish patch of psoriasis

behind your ear that might
suddenly flare up into the helmet
she wore when she stood firm against Xerxes.

Judith Ortiz Cofer (1952–)

Judith Ortiz Cofer was born in Hormigueros, Puerto Rico; she grew up in Paterson, New Jersey, and Augusta, Georgia. She attended Augusta College and Florida Atlantic University and held a number of academic positions before joining the University of Georgia's faculty in 1994. Among her poetry books are Peregrina *(1986),* Terms of Survival *(1987),* The Latin Deli: Prose and Poetry *(1993, Anisfield-Wolf Award),* Reaching for the Mainland *(1996), and* A Love Story Beginning in Spanish *(2005). Cofer has also published fiction, essays, and drama. Her honors include grants from the Witter Bynner Foundation and a National Endowment for the Arts fellowship. She lives in Athens, Georgia.*

Quinceañera

My dolls have been put away like dead
children in a chest I will carry
with me when I marry.
I reach under my skirt to feel
a satin slip bought for this day. It is soft
as the inside of my thighs. My hair
has been nailed back with my mother's
black hairpins to my skull. Her hands
stretched my eyes open as she twisted
braids into a tight circle at the nape
of my neck. I am to wash my own clothes
and sheets from this day on, as if
the fluids of my body were poison, as if
the little trickle of blood I believe
travels from my heart to the world were
shameful. Is not the blood of saints and
men in battle beautiful? Do Christ's hands
not bleed into your eyes from His cross?
At night I hear myself growing and wake
to find my hands drifting of their own will
to soothe skin stretched tight
over my bones.
I am wound like the guts of a clock,
waiting for each hour to release me.

Rita Dove (1952–)

Rita Dove was born in Akron, Ohio, and attended Miami University (Ohio), Universität Tübingen (Germany), and the University of Iowa Writers Workshop. She taught at Arizona State University from 1981 to 1989 and has been at the University of Virginia since 1989. Her poetry books include The Yellow House on the Corner *(1980),* Museum *(1983),* Thomas and Beulah *(1986, Pulitzer Prize),* Grace Notes *(1989),* Selected Poems *(1993),* Mother Love *(1995),* On the Bus with Rosa Parks *(1999),* American Smooth *(2004), and* Sonata Mulattica *(2009). She has also published fiction and drama and served as U.S. poet laureate from 1993 to 1995. Among her honors are the NAACP Great American Artist Award, the Fulbright Lifetime Achievement Medal, and the National Medal of Arts. Rita Dove lives in Charlottesville, Virginia.*

Parsley

1. *The Cane Fields*

There is a parrot imitating spring
in the palace, its feathers parsley green.
Out of the swamp the cane appears

to haunt us, and we cut it down. El General
searches for a word; he is all the world
there is. Like a parrot imitating spring,

we lie down screaming as rain punches through
and we come up green. We cannot speak an R—
out of the swamp, the cane appears

and then the mountain we call in whispers *Katalina.*
The children gnaw their teeth to arrowheads.
There is a parrot imitating spring.

El General has found his word: *perejil.*
Who says it, lives. He laughs, teeth shining
out of the swamp. The cane appears

in our dreams, lashed by wind and streaming.
And we lie down. For every drop of blood
there is a parrot imitating spring.
Out of the swamp the cane appears.

2. *The Palace*

The word the general's chosen is parsley.
It is fall, when thoughts turn
to love and death; the general thinks
of his mother, how she died in the fall
and he planted her walking cane at the grave
and it flowered, each spring stolidly forming
four-star blossoms. The general

pulls on his boots, he stomps to
her room in the palace, the one without
curtains, the one with a parrot
in a brass ring. As he paces he wonders
Who can I kill today. And for a moment
the little knot of screams
is still. The parrot, who has traveled

all the way from Australia in an ivory
cage, is, coy as a widow, practicing
spring. Ever since the morning
his mother collapsed in the kitchen
while baking skull-shaped candies
for the Day of the Dead, the general
has hated sweets. He orders pastries
brought up for the bird; they arrive

dusted with sugar on a bed of lace.
The knot in his throat starts to twitch;
he sees his boots the first day in battle
splashed with mud and urine
as a soldier falls at his feet amazed—
how stupid he looked!— at the sound
of artillery. *I never thought it would sing*
the soldier said, and died. Now

the general sees the fields of sugar
cane, lashed by rain and streaming.
He sees his mother's smile, the teeth
gnawed to arrowheads. He hears
the Haitians sing without R's
as they swing the great machetes:
Katalina, they sing, *Katalina*,

mi madle, mi amol en muelte. God knows
his mother was no stupid woman; she
could roll an R like a queen. Even
a parrot can roll an R! In the bare room
the bright feathers arch in a parody
of greenery, as the last pale crumbs
disappear under the blackened tongue. Someone

calls out his name in a voice
so like his mother's, a startled tear
splashes the tip of his right boot.
My mother, my love in death.
The general remembers the tiny green sprigs
men of his village wore in their capes
to honor the birth of a son. He will
order many, this time, to be killed

for a single, beautiful word.

Daystar

She wanted a little room for thinking:
but she saw diapers steaming on the line,
a doll slumped behind the door.

So she lugged a chair behind the garage
to sit out the children's naps.

Sometimes there were things to watch—
the pinched armor of a vanished cricket,
a floating maple leaf. Other days
she stared until she was assured
when she closed her eyes
she'd see only her own vivid blood.

She had an hour, at best, before Liza appeared
pouting from the top of the stairs.
And just *what* was mother doing
out back with the field mice? Why,

building a palace. Later
that night when Thomas rolled over and

lurched into her, she would open her eyes
and think of the place that was hers
for an hour— where
she was nothing,
pure nothing, in the middle of the day.

After Reading *Mickey in the Night Kitchen* for the Third Time Before Bed

I'm in the milk and the milk's in me! . . . I'm Mickey!

My daughter spreads her legs
to find her vagina:
hairless, this mistaken
bit of nomenclature
is what a stranger cannot touch
without her yelling. She demands
to see mine and momentarily
we're a lopsided star
among the spilled toys,
my prodigious scallops
exposed to her neat cameo.

And yet the same glazed
tunnel, layered sequences.
She is three; that makes this
innocent. *We're pink!*
she shrieks, and bounds off.

Every month she wants
to know where it hurts
and what the wrinkled string means
between my legs. *This is good blood*
I say, but that's wrong, too.
How to tell her that it's what makes us—
black mother, cream child.
That we're in the pink
and the pink's in us.

Claudette Colvin Goes to Work

> *Another Negro woman has been arrested and thrown into jail*
> *because she refused to get up out of her seat on the bus and*
> *give it to a white person. This is the second time since the*
> *Claudette Colbert [sic] case. . . . This must be stopped.*
> —BOYCOTT FLIER, DECEMBER 5, 1955

Menial twilight sweeps the storefronts along Lexington
as the shadows arrive to take their places
among the scourge of the earth. Here and there
a fickle brilliance—lightbulbs coming on
in each narrow residence, the golden wattage
of bleak interiors announcing *Anyone home?*
or *I'm beat, bring me a beer.*

Mostly I say to myself *Still here.* Lay
my keys on the table, pack the perishables away
before flipping the switch. I like the sugary
look of things in bad light—one drop of sweat
is all it would take to dissolve an armchair pillow
into brocade residue. Sometimes I wait until
it's dark enough for my body to disappear;

then I know it's time to start out for work.
Along the Avenue, the cabs start up, heading
toward midtown; neon stutters into ecstasy
as the male integers light up their smokes and let loose
a stream of brave talk: "Hey Mama" souring quickly to
"Your Mama" when there's no answer—as if
the most injury they can do is insult the reason

you're here at all, walking in your whites
down to the stop so you can make a living.
So ugly, so fat, so dumb, so greasy—
What do we have to do to make God love us?
Mama was a maid; my daddy mowed lawns like a boy,
and I'm the crazy girl off the bus, the one
who wrote in class she was going to be President.

I take the Number 6 bus to the Lex Ave train
and then I'm there all night, adjusting the sheets,

emptying the pans. And I don't curse or spit
or kick and scratch like they say I did then.
I help those who can't help themselves,
I do what needs to be done . . . and I sleep
whenever sleep comes down on me.

Alice Fulton (1952–)

Alice Fulton was born in Troy, New York. She attended Cornell University and has taught at the University of Michigan and, since 2002, at Cornell University. Her poetry books include Dance Script with Electric Ballerina *(1983),* Palladium *(1986, National Poetry Series),* Powers of Congress *(1990),* Sensual Math *(1996),* Felt *(2001, Bobbitt Prize), and* Cascade Experiment *(2004). Among her honors are Guggenheim, National Endowment for the Arts, Ingram Merrill, and MacArthur fellowships. Alice Fulton lives in Ithaca, New York.*

Our Calling

To birth shape from the spill
>   *To silence is to kill*
To raise Cain from the matrix
>   Dislodge disperse dispatch—
lifting thoughts from nil
>   *the clean words for murder*
It's our conspiracy to see
>   Overlord's *a lord supreme*
the world one way
>   *and code name for the Allied*
empire by which we pledge
>   *invasion*
allegiance every time we speak
>   *of Northwest Europe A battle tactic*
a narrow anthem by which we zero in
>   *is called an* Operation
What's disarticulate doesn't exist
>   *after the knife the blood*
Nothing wakes in our head
>   *that makes us well*   ▼
unworded The unnamed stateless
>   *in clean surrounds*
sink into the winter page
>   *we call* the theater
unless we carve a clause of granite
>   *High drama's the standard!*
build snug
>   *Weapons etc.*
canons or grand rescue
>   are ordnance *from arranging making neat*
At best it's plenty

                    The enemy? Never
Its penultimate horizon says
                              let them choose their names
no zenith   no matter
                        Christen them Blemish Vegetative
how we reach
              Gook Kraut Cunt Zip Slit
At worst lies pit the mother tongue
                              Gossip *stands for tales*
like salt on roads
                  of birth epics
dry-rot the goddess
                    songs of war in short
The world waits for our orders
                              To man *is to make*
It haunts
          active To woman? *Fill in*
our heads the atomized
                        the blank
fuzz of gnats
                Those icons finding whys
barely there
            for war we call
visible only from uncertain
                          memorials
personal slants
                The preferences of men
except that from the swarm
                          we call our culture *Our end?*
we forge our terms
                  Will beings known as us know all-
except
        inclusive death? Oh yes
we call each shot
              We call it loss of personnel.

Barbara Hamby (1952–)

Barbara Hamby was born in New Orleans, Louisiana, and raised in Honolulu, Hawaii. She attended Florida State University and has taught there since 1999. Her poetry books include Delirium *(1994, Vassar Miller Prize),* The Alphabet of Desire *(named one of the 25 best books of 1999 by the New York Public Library),* Babel *(2004, Donald Hall Prize), and* All-Night Lingo Tango *(2009). Among her honors are National Endowment for the Arts and Guggenheim fellowships; her book of stories,* Lester Higata's 20th Century, *won a 2010 Iowa Short Fiction Award. Barbara Hamby lives in Tallahassee, Florida.*

Thinking of Galileo

When, during a weekend in Venice while standing
    with the dark sky above the Grand Canal
exploding in arcs of color and light,

a man behind me begins to explain
    the chemical composition of the fireworks
and how potassium-something-ate and sulfur catalyze

to make the gold waterfall of stars cascading
    in the moon-drunk sky, I begin to understand why
the Inquisition tortured Galileo

and see how it might be a good thing for people
    to think the sun revolves around the earth.
You don't have to know how anything works

to be bowled over by beauty,
    but with an attitude like mine we'd still be swimming
in a sea of smallpox and consumption,

not to mention plague, for these fireworks
    are in celebration of the Festival of the Redentore,
or Christ the Redeemer, whose church on the other side

of the canal was built after the great plague
    of 1575 to thank him for saving Venice,
though by that time 46,000 were dead,

and I suppose God had made his point if indeed he had one.
    The next morning, Sunday, we take the vaporetto
across the lagoon and walk along

the Fondamenta della Croce, littered
     with the tattered debris of spent rockets
and Roman candles, to visit the Church of the Redentore

by Palladio. The door is open for mass,
     and as I stand in the back, a miracle occurs:
after a year of what seems to be nearly futile study,

I am able to understand the Italian of the priest.
     He is saying how important it is
to live a virtuous life, to help one's neighbors,

be good to our families, and when we err
     to confess our sins and take communion.
He is speaking words I know: *vita, parlare, resurrezione.*

Later my professor tells me the holy fathers
     speak slowly and use uncomplicated constructions
so that even the simple can understand Christ's teachings.

The simple: well, that's me, as in one for whom
     even the most elementary transaction is difficult,
who must search for nouns the way a fisherman

throws his net into the wide sea, who must settle
     for the most humdrum verbs: I am, I have, I go, I speak,
and I see nothing is simple, even my desire to strangle

the man behind me or tell him that some things
     shouldn't be explained, even though they can be,
because most of the time it's as if we are wandering

lost in a desert, famished, delirious,
     set upon by wild lions, our minds blank with fear,
starving for a crumb, any morsel of light.

Hatred

Abracadabra, says Mephisto, the firefly
buddha of Rue Morgue, and the whole wide world

changes from a stumbling rick-rack machine
doing the rag time, the bag time, the I'm-on-the

edge-of-a-drag time to a tornado of unmitigated
fury. Yes sir, we are trampling out our vengeance,

grapes-of-wrath time is here again when I think about
Her Majesty, myself, all alone on her throne, tiara askew,

inconsistently worshipped, even by herself, and I could
just die to think how I betray myself in the great

Kabuki theater of my mind, the No Theater, so to speak, but
latitudinal issues aside, here I am starring in a

mystery play. Everyone's in place—cows, shepherds,
no-good-rotten Herod and his ridiculous Roman soldiers.

Only the savior's missing, so what's the point,
putti aside, of the whole big preposterous

Quattrocento mess, the fights, the plague, the frivolous
rococo results, postmodern la-di-da incarnate?

So what's a girl to do when stuck in the last vestiges of the
tawdry twentieth century—have a drink, a fling, say

Uncle? Oh, there's no loathing like self-loathing,
vox populi, vox dei or something like that. I'm rejecting

Western thought here, monotheism included, shuddering as
xenophobic clouds gather over the darkening earth, yeah,

yeah, everyone hates someone, me included, cowering in my
Zen bomb shelter, longing for a thermonuclear whack.

Mark Jarman (1952–)

Mark Jarman was born in Mount Sterling, Kentucky, and grew up in California and Scotland. He attended the University of California at Santa Cruz and the University of Iowa Writers Workshop before teaching at Indiana State University, the University of California at Irvine, Murray State University, and since 1983, Vanderbilt University. His poetry books include The Rote Walker *(1981),* Far and Away *(1985),* The Black Riviera *(1990),* Iris *(1992),* Questions for Ecclesiastes *(1997, Lenore Marshall Prize),* Unholy Sonnets *(2000),* To the Green Man *(2004),* Epistles *(2007), and* Bone Fires *(2011). Among his honors are Guggenheim and National Endowment for the Arts fellowships. Mark Jarman lives in Nashville, Tennessee.*

Unholy Sonnet 13

Drunk on the Umbrian hills at dusk and drunk
On one pink cloud that stood beside the moon,
Drunk on the moon, a marble smile, and drunk,
Two young Americans, on one another,
Far from home and wanting this forever—
Who needed God? We had our bodies, bread,
And glasses of a raw, green, local wine,
And watched our Godless perfect darkness breed
Enormous softly burning ancient stars.
Who needed God? And why do I ask now?
Because I'm older and I think God stirs
In details that keep bringing back that time,
Details that are just as vivid now—
Our bodies, bread, a sharp Umbrian wine.

Naomi Shihab Nye (1952–)

Naomi Shihab Nye was born in St. Louis, Missouri, and spent her adolescence in Palestine and San Antonio, Texas. She attended Trinity University in San Antonio and has been a freelance writer, editor, and speaker ever since, publishing numerous children's and young adult books across the genres. Her poetry books include Different Ways to Pray *(1980),* Hugging the Jukebox *(1982, National Poetry Series),* Yellow Glove *(1986),* Red Suitcase *(1994),* Fuel *(1998),* 19 Varieties of Gazelle: Poems of the Middle East *(2002), and* You and Yours *(2005). Among her many awards are Lannan, Guggenheim, and Witter Bynner fellowships. Naomi Shihab Nye lives in San Antonio.*

The Traveling Onion

> *It is believed that the onion originally came from India. In Egypt it was*
> *an object of worship—why I haven't been able to find out. From Egypt*
> *the onion entered Greece and on to Italy, thence into all of Europe.*
> —BETTER LIVING COOKBOOK

When I think how far the onion has traveled
just to enter my stew today, I could kneel and praise
all small forgotten miracles,
crackly paper peeling on the drainboard,
pearly layers in smooth agreement,
the way knife enters onion
and onion falls apart on the chopping block,
a history revealed.

And I would never scold the onion
for causing tears.
It is right that tears fall
for something small and forgotten.
How at meal, we sit to eat,
commenting on texture of meat or herbal aroma
but never on the translucence of onion,
now limp, now divided,
or its traditionally honorable career:
For the sake of others,
disappear.

Arabic

(Jordan, 1992)

The man with laughing eyes stopped smiling
to say, "Until you speak Arabic,
you will not understand pain."

Something to do with the back of the head,
an Arab carries sorrow in the back of the head
that only language cracks, the thrum of stones

weeping, grating hinge on an old metal gate.
"Once you know," he whispered, "you can enter the room
whenever you need to. Music you heard from a distance,

the slapped drum of a stranger's wedding,
wells up inside your skin, inside rain, a thousand
pulsing tongues. You are changed."

Outside, the snow had finally stopped.
In a land where snow rarely falls,
we had felt our days grow white and still.

I thought pain had no tongue. Or every tongue
at once, supreme translator, sieve. I admit my
shame. To live on the brink of Arabic, tugging

its rich threads without understanding
how to weave the rug . . . I have no gift.
The sound, but not the sense.

I kept looking over his shoulder for someone else
to talk to, recalling my dying friend who only scrawled
I can't write. What good would any grammar have been

to her then? I touched his arm, held it hard,
which sometimes you don't do in the Middle East,
and said, *I'll work on it,* feeling sad

for his good strict heart, but later in the slick street
hailed a taxi by shouting *Pain!* and it stopped
in every language and opened its doors.

Wedding Cake

Once on a plane
a woman asked me to hold her baby
and disappeared.
I figured it was safe,
our being on a plane and all.
How far could she go?

She returned one hour later,
having changed her clothes
and washed her hair.
I didn't recognize her.

By this time the baby
and I had examined
each other's necks.
We had cried a little.
I had a silver bracelet
and a watch.
Gold studs glittered
in the baby's ears.
She wore a tiny white dress
leafed with layers
like a wedding cake.

I did not want
to give her back.

The baby's curls coiled tightly
against her scalp,
another alphabet.
I read *new new new*.
My mother gets tired.
I'll chew your hand.

The baby left my skirt crumpled,
my lap aching.
Now I'm her secret guardian,
the little nub of dream
that rises slightly
but won't come clear.

As she grows,
as she feels ill at ease,
I'll bob my knee.

What will she forget?
Whom will she marry?
He'd better check with me.
I'll say once she flew
dressed like a cake
between two doilies of cloud.
She could slip the card into a pocket,
pull it out.
Already she knew the small finger
was funnier than the whole arm.

Alberto Ríos (1952–)

Alberto Ríos was born in Nogales, Arizona, and attended the University of Arizona in Tucson. He has taught at Arizona State University in Tempe since 1982. His poetry books include Whispering to Fool the Wind, *(2001, Walt Whitman Award)*, Five Indiscretions *(1985)*, The Lime Orchard Woman *(1988)*, Teodoro Luna's Two Kisses *(1990)*, The Smallest Muscle in the Human Body *(2002)*, The Theater of Night *(2007)*, and Dangerous Shirt *(2009)*. He has also published several books of fiction. Among his honors are National Endowment for the Arts and Guggenheim fellowships. Alberto Ríos lives in Chandler, Arizona.*

Nani

Sitting at her table, she serves
the sopa de arroz to me
instinctively, and I watch her,
the absolute *mamá*, and eat words
I might have had to say more
out of embarrassment. To speak,
now-foreign words I used to speak,
too, dribble down her mouth as she serves
me albondigas. No more
than a third are easy to me.
By the stove she does something with words
and looks at me only with her
back. I am full. I tell her
I taste the mint, and watch her speak
smiles at the stove. All my words
make her smile. Nani never serves
herself, she only watches me
with her skin, her hair. I ask for more.

I watch the *mamá* warming more
tortillas for me. I watch her
fingers in the flame for me.
Near her mouth, I see a wrinkle speak
of a man whose body serves
the ants like she serves me, then more words
from more wrinkles about children, words
about this and that, flowing more
easily from these other mouths. Each serves
as a tremendous string around her,
holding her together. They speak

nani was this and that to me
and I wonder just how much of me
will die with her, what were the words
I could have been, was. Her insides speak
through a hundred wrinkles, now, more
than she can bear, steel around her,
shouting, then, What is this thing she serves?

She asks me if I want more.
I own no words to stop her.
Even before I speak, she serves.

England Finally, Like My Mother Always Said We Would

The old dog and the old rabbit,
The old house and the cold
Air; the fog and the pigeons
Cooped up and warm as we watched:

I was there, finally—here;
Fake coal in the fireplace
Instead of fake wood, the habits
Of walking, and laughing.

Lanes instead of streets,
The taste of bitter in the pub,
Greenall's: lager was for
Shall we say, they said,

The women. All in sweaters
And pleats in their skirts,
Hands rubbing knees so hard
I expected flame.

The faces hurt here,
Laughing so hard.
So many wrinkles, lines
Like rivers they had not seen.

Laurie Sheck (1952–)

Laurie Sheck was born in New York City and attended the University of Iowa Writers Workshop. She has taught at Rutgers University, Princeton University, and the New School. Her poetry books include Amaranth *(1981),* Io at Night *(1990),* The Willow Grove *(1997),* Black Series *(2001), and* Captivity *(2007). In 2009 she published her genre-crossing literary hybrid* A Monster's Notes. *Among her honors are Guggenheim, Ingram Merrill Foundation, National Endowment for the Arts, and Radcliffe fellowships. Laurie Sheck lives in New York City.*

Nocturne: Blue Waves

There are times when the mind
knows no wholeness. It sees the moon broken
in the branches, the finch's shadow
as something terribly severed, black blood.
As if touch were annihilation.
As when a woman waits in her small room;
her lover enters,
raises his soft hand to her face. . . .
They lie down on the clean bed,
lie down on sweetness of pine,
feather pillows, polished wood;
but as he touches her
she pictures the shadow of a woman
burned into a wall, the others
who wandered in stunned silence
through the streets, their flesh
turned to rags in their hands.
She thinks of the woman's arms
outstretched though they held nothing,
though there was nothing to hold onto up ahead. . . .
She gets up from the bed.
It is dark now,
the man's throat
caged in shadows of branches as he sleeps.
Distance is the soul of the beautiful,
she had read, and she imagines an unknown planet
revolving in deep space, blue waves
in tender exile from the land.
Remorseless. Without witness.
If she could go there
she would possess nothing.

How beautiful the earth
might seem again from that distance.
How possible love.

The Unfinished

We were characters in a story
the writer couldn't bring himself to finish.
When he left us it was late, a child
was crying, newsprint smudged on our fingertips
as if to make of us a mechanism
by which the world would repeat itself, its story:
this happened—did you hear?—then that.
So many disparate versions. The terror
risen into words, shrouded there, hanging, so cold.
And the tenderness—how the words barely touched it,
as if to speak it were a further hurt.
It was night when he left us,
and the child who could not yet remember her dreams
woke saying, *where are the toys of the moon,
are we the moon's toys?* Outside, lines
of stiff trees stood like hieroglyphs,
the configuration of the one for dagger
so close to the one that stands for shrub,
so hard to understand the difference;
or the one for fear that also could mean
reverence, the one for medicine so similar
to entreaty and to prayer.
And in the distance the red tremor
of the radio tower, and the planes that passed above us
as we held to the earth and didn't understand the earth.

Gary Soto (1952–)

Gary Soto was born in Fresno, California, attended California State University and the University of California–Irvine, and taught at the University of California–Berkeley; he has been a freelance writer since 1993. His poetry books include The Elements of San Joaquin *(1977),* The Tale of Sunlight *(1978),* Where Sparrows Work Hard *(1981),* Black Hair *(1985),* Who Will Know Us? *(1990),* Home Course in Religion *(1991),* Neighborhood Odes *(1992),* New and Selected Poems *(1995),* A Simple Plan *(2007), and* Partly Cloudy: Poems of Love and Longing *(2009); he has also published numerous novels, memoirs, and books for young readers. Among his honors are the Bess Hokin Prize, Guggenheim and National Endowment for the Arts fellowships, and an American Book Award in fiction. Gary Soto lives in Berkeley and Fresno, California.*

Field Poem

When the foreman whistled
My brother and I
Shouldered our hoes,
Leaving the field.
We returned to the bus
Speaking
In broken English, in broken Spanish
The restaurant food,
The tickets to a dance
We wouldn't buy with our pay.

From the smashed bus window,
I saw the leaves of cotton plants
Like small hands waving good-bye.

Oranges

The first time I walked
With a girl, I was twelve,
Cold, and weighted down
With two oranges in my jacket.
December. Frost cracking
Beneath my steps, my breath
Before me, then gone,
As I walked toward
Her house, the one whose
Porch light burned yellow

Night and day, in any weather.
A dog barked at me, until
She came out pulling
At her gloves, face bright
With rouge. I smiled,
Touched her shoulder, and led
Her down the street, across
A used car lot and a line
Of newly planted trees,
Until we were breathing
Before a drugstore. We
Entered, the tiny bell
Bringing a saleslady
Down a narrow aisle of goods.
I turned to the candies
Tiered like bleachers,
And asked what she wanted—
Light in her eyes, a smile
Starting at the corners
Of her mouth. I fingered
A nickel in my pocket,
And when she lifted a chocolate
That cost a dime,
I didn't say anything.
I took the nickel from
My pocket, then an orange,
And set them quietly on
The counter. When I looked up,
The lady's eyes met mine,
And held them, knowing
Very well what it was all
About.

    Outside,
A few cars hissing past,
Fog hanging like old
Coats between the trees.
I took my girl's hand
In mine for two blocks,
Then released it to let
Her unwrap the chocolate.
I peeled my orange
That was so bright against
The gray of December

That, from some distance,
Someone might have thought
I was making a fire in my hands.

Black Hair

At eight I was brilliant with my body.
In July, that ring of heat
We all jumped through, I sat in the bleachers
Of Romain Playground, in the lengthening
Shade that rose from our dirty feet.
The game before us was more than baseball.
It was a figure—Hector Moreno
Quick and hard with turned muscles,
His crouch the one I assumed before an altar
Of worn baseball cards, in my room.

I came here because I was Mexican, a stick
Of brown light in love with those
Who could do it—the triple and hard slide,
The gloves eating balls into double plays.
What could I do with fifty pounds, my shyness,
My black torch of hair, about to go out?
Father was dead, his face no longer
Hanging over the table or our sleep,
And mother was the terror of mouths
Twisting hurt by butter knives.

In the bleachers I was brilliant with my body,
Waving players in and stomping my feet,
Growing sweaty in the presence of white shirts.
I chewed sunflower seeds. I drank water
And bit my arm through the late innings.
When Hector lined balls into deep
Center, in my mind I rounded the bases
With him, my face flared, my hair lifting
Beautifully, because we were coming home
To the arms of brown people.

Susan Stewart (1952–)

Susan Stewart was born in York, Pennsylvania, and attended Dickinson College, Johns Hopkins University, and the University of Pennsylvania. She taught at Temple University before joining the faculty at Princeton University. Among her poetry books are Yellow Stars and Ice (1981), The Hive (1987), The Forest (1995), and Columbarium (2003, National Book Critics Circle Award). Her honors include National Endowment for the Arts, Guggenheim, Pew, and MacArthur fellowships and the Lila Wallace–Reader's Digest Writers' Award. Her book of criticism, Poetry and the Fate of the Senses (2002), received the Christian Gauss Award and the Truman Capote Award.

Yellow Stars and Ice

I am as far as the deepest sky between clouds
and you are as far as the deepest root and wound,
and I am as far as a train at evening,
as far as a whistle you can't hear or remember.
You are as far as an unimagined animal
who, frightened by everything, never appears.
I am as far as cicadas and locusts
and you are as far as the cleanest arrow
that has sewn the wind to the light on
the birch trees. I am as far as the sleep of rivers
that stains the deepest sky between clouds,
you are as far as invention, and I am as far as memory.

You are as far as a red-marbled stream
where children cut their feet on the stones
and cry out. And I am as far as their happy
mothers, bleaching new linen on the grass
and singing, "You are as far as another life,
as far as another life are you."
And I am as far as an infinite alphabet
made from yellow stars and ice,
and you are as far as the nails of the dead man,
as far as a sailor can see at midnight
when he's drunk and the moon is an empty cup,
and I am as far as invention and you are as far as memory.

I am as far as the corners of a room where no one
has ever spoken, as far as the four lost corners
of the earth. And you are as far as the voices

of the dumb, as the broken limbs of saints
and soldiers, as the scarlet wing of the suicidal
blackbird, I am farther and farther away from you.
And you are as far as a horse without a rider
can run in six years, two months and five days.
I am as far as that rider, who rubs his eyes with
his blistered hands, who watches a ghost don his
jacket and boots and now stands naked in the road.
As far as the space between word and word,
as the heavy sleep of the perfectly loved
and the sirens of wars no one living can remember,
as far as this room, where no words have been spoken,
you are as far as invention, and I am as far as memory.

The Forest

You should lie down now and remember the forest,
for it is disappearing—
no, the truth is it is gone now
and so what details you can bring back
might have a kind of life.

Not the one you had hoped for, but a life
—you should lie down now and remember the forest—
nonetheless, you might call it "in the forest,"
no the truth is, it is gone now,
starting somewhere near the beginning, that edge,

Or instead the first layer, the place you remember
(not the one you had hoped for, but a life)
as if it were firm, underfoot, for that place is a sea,
nonetheless, you might call it "in the forest,"
which we can never drift above, we were there or we were not,

No surface, skimming. And blank in life, too,
or instead the first layer, the place you remember,
as layers fold in time, black humus there,
as if it were firm, underfoot, for that place is a sea,
like a light left hand descending, always on the same keys.

The flecked birds of the forest sing behind and before
no surface, skimming. And blank in life, too,

sing without a music where there cannot be an order,
as layers fold in time, black humus there,
where wide swatches of light slice between gray trunks,

Where the air has a texture of drying moss,
the flecked birds of the forest sing behind and before:
a musk from the mushrooms and scalloped molds.
They sing without a music where there cannot be an order,
though high in the dry leaves something does fall,

Nothing comes down to us here.
Where the air has a texture of drying moss,
(in that place where I was raised) the forest was tangled,
a musk from the mushrooms and scalloped molds,
tangled with brambles, soft-starred and moving, ferns

And the marred twines of cinquefoil, false strawberry, sumac—
nothing comes down to us here,
stained. A low branch swinging above a brook
in that place where I was raised, the forest was tangled,
and a cave just the width of shoulder blades.

You can understand what I am doing when I think of the entry—
and the marred twines of cinquefoil, false strawberry, sumac—
as a kind of limit. Sometimes I imagine us walking there
(. . . pokeberry, stained. A low branch swinging above a brook)
in a place that is something like a forest.

But perhaps the other kind, where the ground is covered
(you can understand what I am doing when I think of the entry)
by pliant green needles, there below the piney fronds,
a kind of limit. Sometimes I imagine us walking there.
And quickening below lie the sharp brown blades,

The disfiguring blackness, then the bulbed phosphorescence of the roots.
But perhaps the other kind, where the ground is covered,
so strangely alike and yet singular, too, below
the pliant green needles, the piney fronds.
Once we were lost in the forest, *so strangely alike and yet singular, too,*
but the truth is, it is, lost to us now.

Mark Doty (1953–)

Mark Doty was born in Maryville, Tennessee, and educated at Drake University and Goddard College. He taught at a number of universities before joining Rutgers University's faculty in 2009. Among his poetry books are Turtle, Swan *(1987),* Bethlehem in Broad Daylight *(1991),* My Alexandria *(1993, National Poetry Series, Los Angeles Times Book Award, National Book Critics Circle Award, T. S. Eliot Prize),* School of the Arts *(2005), and* Fire to Fire: New and Selected Poems *(2008, National Book Award). His honors include two Lambda Literary Awards as well as Guggenheim, National Endowment of the Arts, Whiting, Ingram Merrill, and Rockefeller fellowships. Mark Doty lives in New York City.*

Brilliance

Maggie's taking care of a man
who's dying; he's attended to everything,
said goodbye to his parents,

paid off his credit card.
She says *Why don't you just
run it up to the limit?*

but he wants everything
squared away, no balance owed,
though he misses the pets

he's already found a home for
—he can't be around dogs or cats,
too much risk. He says,

I can't have anything.
She says, *A bowl of goldfish?*
He says he doesn't want to start

with anything and then describes
the kind he'd maybe like,
how their tails would fan

to a gold flaring. They talk
about hot jewel tones,
gold lacquer, say maybe

they'll go pick some out
though he can't go much of anywhere and then
abruptly he says *I can't love*

anything I can't finish.
He says it like he's had enough
of the whole scintillant world,

though what he means is
he'll never be satisfied and therefore
has established this discipline,

a kind of severe rehearsal.
That's where they leave it,
him looking out the window,

her knitting as she does because
she needs to do something.
Later he leaves a message:

Yes to the bowl of goldfish.
Meaning: let me go, if I have to,
in brilliance. In a story I read,

a Zen master who'd perfected
his detachment from the things of the world
remembered, at the moment of dying,

a deer he used to feed in the park,
and wondered who might care for it,
and at that instant was reborn

in the stunned flesh of a fawn.
So, Maggie's friend—
is he going out

into the last loved object
of his attention?
Fanning the veined translucence

of an opulent tail,
undulant in some uncapturable curve,
is he bronze chrysanthemums,

copper leaf, hurried darting,
doubloons, icon-colored fins
troubling the water?

Esta Noche

In a dress with a black tulip's sheen
    la fabulosa Lola enters, late, mounts the stairs
to the plywood platform, and begs whoever runs
    the wobbling spot to turn the lights down

to something flattering. When they halo her
    with a petal-toned gel, she sets to haranguing,
shifting in and out of two languages like gowns
    or genders to please have a little respect

for the girls, flashing the one entrancing
    and unavoidable gap in the center of her upper teeth.
And when the cellophane drop goes black,
    a new spot coronas her in a wig

fit for the end of a century,
    and she tosses back her hair—risky gesture—
and raises her arms like a widow in a blood tragedy,
    all will and black lace, and lip-synchs "You and Me

Against the World." She's a man
    you wouldn't look twice at in street clothes,
two hundred pounds of hard living, the gap in her smile
    sadly narrative—but she's a monument,

in the mysterious permission of the dress.
    This is Esta Noche, a Latin drag bar in the Mission,
its black door a gap in the face
    of a battered wall. All over the neighborhood

storefront windows show all night
    shrined hats and gloves, wedding dresses,
First Communion's frothing lace:
    gowns of perfection and commencement,

fixed promises glowing. In the dress
    the color of the spaces between streetlamps
Lola stands unassailable, the dress
    in which she is in the largest sense

fabulous: a lesson, a criticism and colossus
    of gender, all fire and irony. Her spine's
perfectly erect, only her fluid hands moving
    and her head turned slightly to one side.

She hosts the pageant, Wednesdays and Saturdays,
    and men come in from the streets, the trains
and the repair shops, lean together to rank
    the artifice of the awkward or lovely

Lola welcomes onto her stage: Victoria, Elena,
    Francie, lamé pumps and stockings and always
the rippling night pulled down over broad shoulders
    and flounced around the hips, liquid,

the black silk of esta noche
    proving that perfection and beauty are so alien
they almost never touch. Tonight, she says,
    put it on. The costume is license

and calling. She says you could wear the whole damn
    black sky and all its spangles. It's the only night
we have to stand on. Put it on,
    it's the only thing we have to wear.

Bill's Story

When my sister came back from Africa,
we didn't know at first how everything
had changed. After a while Annie
bought men's and boys' clothes in all sizes,
and filled her closets with little
or huge things she could never wear.

Then she took to buying out
theatrical shops, rental places on the skids,

sweeping in and saying, *I'll take everything.*
Dementia was the first sign of something
we didn't even have a name for,
in 1978. She was just becoming stranger

—all those clothes, the way she'd dress me up
when I came to visit. It was like we could go back
to playing together again, and get it right.
She was a performance artist, and she did
her best work then, taking the clothes to clubs,
talking, putting them all on, talking.

It was years before she was in the hospital,
and my mother needed something
to hold onto, some way to be helpful,
so she read a book called *Deathing*:
(a cheap, ugly verb if ever I heard one)
and took its advice to heart;

she'd sit by the bed and say, *Annie,*
look for the light, look for the light.
It was plain that Anne did not wish
to be distracted by these instructions;
she came to, though she was nearly gone then,
and looked at our mother with what was almost certainly

annoyance. *It's a white light,*
Mom said, and this struck me
as incredibly presumptuous, as if the light
we'd all go into would be just the same.
Maybe she wanted to give herself up
to indigo, or red. If we can barely even speak

to each other, living so separately,
how can we all die the same?
I used to take the train to the hospital,
and sometimes the only empty seats
would be the ones that face backwards.
I'd sit there and watch where I'd been

waver and blur out, and finally
I liked it, seeing what you've left
get more beautiful, less specific.
Maybe her light was all that gabardine

and flannel, khaki and navy
and silks and stripes. If you take everything,

you've got to let everything go. Dying
must take more attention than I ever imagined.
Just when she'd compose herself
and seem fixed on the work before her,
Mother would fret, trying to help her
just one more time: *Look for the light,*

until I took her arm
and told her wherever I was in the world
I would come back, no matter how difficult
it was to reach her, if I heard her calling.
Shut up, mother, I said, and Annie died.

Harryette Mullen (1953–)

Harryette Mullen was born in Florence, Alabama, and grew up in Fort Worth, Texas. She attended the University of Texas–Austin and the University of California–Santa Cruz and currently teaches at the University of California–Los Angeles. Her poetry books include Tree Tall Woman *(1981),* Trimmings *(1991),* S*PeRM**K*T *(1992),* Muse and Drudge *(1995),* Blues Baby: Early Poems *(2002),* Sleeping with the Dictionary *(2002), and* Recylopedia *(2006). Among her honors are the 1994 Gertrude Stein Award in Innovative American Poetry, the 2009 Academy of American Poets Fellowship, and the 2010 Jackson Poetry Prize. Harryette Mullen lives in Los Angeles.*

Black Nikes

We need quarters like King Tut needed a boat. A slave could row him to heaven from his crypt in Egypt full of loot. We've lived quietly among the stars, knowing money isn't what matters. We only bring enough to tip the shuttle driver when we hitch a ride aboard a trailblazer of light. This comet could scour the planet. Make it sparkle like a fresh toilet swirling with blue. Or only come close enough to brush a few lost souls. Time is rotting as our bodies wait for now I lay me down to earth. Noiseless patient spiders paid with dirt when what we want is stardust. If nature abhors an expensive appliance, why does the planet suck ozone? This is a big-ticket item, a thickety ride. Please page our home and visit our sigh on the wide world's ebb. Just point and cluck at our new persuasion shoes. We're opening the gate that opens our containers for recycling. Time to throw down and take off on our launch. This flight will nail our proof of pudding. The thrill of victory is, we're exiting earth. We're leaving all this dirt.

Franz Wright (1953–)

Franz Wright—son of poet James Wright—was born in Vienna, Austria. He attended Oberlin College, the University of California at Irvine, and the University of Virginia. He has taught at many colleges and universities, including Emerson College, the University of Arkansas, and Brandeis University. His poetry books include Entry in an Unknown Hand *(1989),* The Night World and the Word Night *(1992),* Rorschach Test *(1995),* The Beforelife *(2001),* Walking to Martha's Vineyard *(2003, Pulitzer Prize),* God's Silence *(2006), and* Wheeling Motel *(2009). Among his honors are National Endowment for the Arts and Guggenheim fellowships, and a Whiting award. He lives in Waltham, Massachusetts.*

Alcohol

You do look a little ill.

But we can do something about that, now.

Can't we.

The fact is you're a shocking wreck.

Do you hear me.

You aren't all alone.

And you could use some help today, packing in the
dark, boarding buses north, putting the seat back and
grinning with terror flowing over your legs through
your fingers and hair . . .

I was always waiting, always here.

Know anyone else who can say that?

My advice to you is think of her for what she is: one
more name cut in the scar of your tongue.

What was it you said, "To rather be harmed than
harm is not abject."

Please.

Can we be leaving now.

We like bus trips, remember. Together

we could watch these winter fields slip past, and
never care again,

think of it.

I don't have to be anywhere.

Lorna Dee Cervantes (1954–)

Lorna Dee Cervantes was born in San Francisco. She attended San Jose State University and the University of California at Santa Cruz before teaching at the University of Colorado. She is also actively involved in the American Indian and Chicano movements. Her poetry books include Emplumada *(1981, American Book Award),* From the Cables of Genocide: Poems on Love and Hunger *(1991, Paterson Prize), and* Drive: The First Quartet *(2005). The recipient of two National Endowment for the Arts fellowships, Lorna Dee Cervantes lives in San Francisco.*

To My Brother

and for the lumpen bourgeoisie

We were so poor.
The air was a quiver
of thoughts we drew from

to poise, unsaid
in the ineffable
world we lived in.

Sun, scarcely a penny
in that dreary setting,
every night gave up

to a smog-strewn avalanche
of searchlights, crossing
the heavens, a bicker

to buy a new used car,
a four-door sedan, a six
month guarantee. I worked

the years through, thought
I could work my mind's way
out of there, out of needing

a dime bag of uppers for the next
buzzing shift. We paid our bills.
We were brilliant at wishing.

Our dreams wafted over the sullen skyline
like crazy meteors of flying embers:
a glow in the heart all night.

"Love of My Flesh, Living Death"

after García Lorca

Once I wasn't always so plain.
I was strewn feathers on a cross
of dune, an expanse of ocean
at my feet, garlands of gulls.

Sirens and gulls. They couldn't tame you.
You know as well as they: to be
a dove is to bear the falcon
at your breast, your nights, your seas.

My fear is simple, heart-faced
above a flare of etchings, a lineage
in letters, my sudden stare. It's you.

It's you! sang the heart upon its mantel
pelvis. Blush of my breath, catch
of my see—beautiful bird—It's you.

Sandra Cisneros (1954–)

Sandra Cisneros was born in Chicago and spent her childhood in Chicago and Mexico City. She attended Loyola University and the University of Iowa Writers Workshop. She is widely known for her prose (especially the novel The House on Mango Street, *1989, which won the American Book Award, and the short story collection* Woman Hollering Creek, *1991, which received the Anisfield-Wolf Award). Her poetry books include* My Wicked Wicked Ways *(1987) and* Loose Woman *(1994). Among her honors are National Endowment for the Arts, Lannan Foundation, and MacArthur fellowships. Sandra Cisneros lives in San Antonio, Texas.*

My Wicked Wicked Ways

This is my father.
See? He is young.
He looks like Errol Flynn.
He is wearing a hat
that tips over one eye,
a suit that fits him good,
and baggy pants.
He is also wearing
those awful shoes,
the two-toned ones
my mother hates.

Here is my mother.
She is not crying.
She cannot look into the lens
because the sun is bright.
The woman,
the one my father knows,
is not here.
She does not come till later.

My mother will get very mad.
Her face will turn red
and she will throw one shoe.
My father will say nothing.
After a while everyone
will forget it.
Years and years will pass.
My mother will stop mentioning it.

This is me she is carrying.
I am a baby.
She does not know
I will turn out bad.

Little Clown, My Heart

Little clown, my heart,
Spangled again and lopsided,
Handstands and Peking pirouettes,
Backflips snapping open like
A carpenter's hinged ruler,

Little gimp-footed hurray,
Paper parasol of pleasures,
Fleshy undertongue of sorrows,
Sweet potato plant of my addictions,

Acapulco cliff-diver *corazón*,
Fine as an obsidian dagger,
Alley-oop and here we go
Into the froth, my life,
Into the flames!

Cornelius Eady (1954–)

Cornelius Eady was born in Rochester, New York, attended Monroe Community College and Empire State College, and has taught at Sarah Lawrence College, New York University, City College of New York, the College of William and Mary, Sweet Briar College, the State University of New York at Stony Brook, the University of Missouri, and Notre Dame University. In 1996 he and Toi Derricotte founded Cave Canem, an organization fostering emerging African-American poets that has become an instrumental force in twenty-first-century American poetry. His poetry books include Kartunes *(1980),* Victims of the Latest Dance Craze *(1985, Lamont Poetry Prize),* Brutal Imagination *(2001), and* Hardheaded Weather *(2008). Cornelius Eady lives in South Bend, Indiana.*

Jack Johnson Does the Eagle Rock

Perhaps he left the newspaper stand that morning
    dazed, a few pennies lighter,
The illustration of the crippled ocean liner
    with the berth he had the money
But not the skin to buy
Engraving itself
On that portion of the mind reserved for
    lucky breaks.
Perhaps the newsboy, a figure too small to
    bring back,
Actually heard his laugh,
As the S.S. *Titanic*, sans one prize fighter,
Goes down again all over New York,
Watched his body dance
As his arms lift the ship, now a simple millimeter thick,
    above his head
In the bustling air, lift it up
As though it was meant to happen.

Crows in a Strong Wind

Off go the crows from the roof.
The crows can't hold on.
They might as well
Be perched on an oil slick.

Such an awkward dance,
These gentlemen
In their spottled-black coats.
Such a tipsy dance,

As if they didn't know where they were.
Such a humorous dance,
As they try to set things right,
As the wind reduces them.

Such a sorrowful dance.
How embarrassing is love
When it goes wrong

In front of everyone.

I'm a Fool to Love You

Some folks will tell you the blues is a woman,
Some type of supernatural creature.
My mother would tell you, if she could,
About her life with my father,
A strange and sometimes cruel gentleman.
She would tell you about the choices
A young black woman faces.
Is falling in love with some man
A deal with the devil
In blue terms, the tongue we use
When we don't want nuance
To get in the way,
When we need to talk straight?
My mother chooses my father
After choosing a man
Who was, as we sing it,
Of no account.
This man made my father look good,
That's how bad it was.
He made my father seem like an island
In the middle of a stormy sea,
He made my father look like a rock.
And is the blues the moment you realize
You exist in a stacked deck,
You look in a mirror at your young face,

The face my sister carries,
And you know it's the only leverage
You've got?
Does this create a hurt that whispers,
How you going to do?
Is the blues the moment
You shrug your shoulders
And agree, a girl without money
Is nothing, dust
To be pushed around by any old breeze?
Compared to this,
My father seems, briefly,
To be a fire escape.
This is the way the blues works
Its sorry wonders,
Makes trouble look like
A feather bed,
Makes the wrong man's kisses
A healing.

Louise Erdrich (1954–)

Louise Erdrich was born in Little Falls, Minnesota, and grew up in Wahpeton, North Dakota. Educated at Dartmouth College and Johns Hopkins University, she worked in a number of jobs before becoming a successful fiction writer and publisher. Her poetry books include Jacklight *(1984),* Baptism of Desire *(1989), and* Original Fire: New and Selected Poems *(2003). Among her numerous awards are MacDowell, Yaddo, Guggenheim, and National Endowment for the Arts fellowships; her fiction has received National Book Critics Circle and Los Angeles Times awards and the American Book Award. Louise Erdrich lives in Minneapolis.*

Indian Boarding School: The Runaways

Home's the place we head for in our sleep.
Boxcars stumbling north in dreams
don't wait for us. We catch them on the run.
The rails, old lacerations that we love,
shoot parallel across the face and break
just under Turtle Mountains. Riding scars
you can't get lost. Home is the place they cross.

The lame guard strikes a match and makes the dark
less tolerant. We watch through cracks in boards
as the land starts rolling, rolling till it hurts
to be here, cold in regulation clothes.
We know the sheriff's waiting at midrun
to take us back. His car is dumb and warm.
The highway doesn't rock, it only hums
like a wing of long insults. The worn-down welts
of ancient punishments lead back and forth.

All runaways wear dresses, long green ones,
the color you would think shame was. We scrub
the sidewalks down because it's shameful work.
Our brushes cut the stone in watered arcs
and in the soak frail outlines shiver clear
a moment, things us kids pressed on the dark
face before it hardened, pale, remembering
delicate old injuries, the spines of names and leaves.

David Mason (1954–)

David Mason was born in Bellingham, Washington. He attended Colorado College and the University of Rochester and taught at Moorhead State University in Minnesota; since 1998 he has been on the faculty of Colorado College. His poetry books include The Buried Houses *(1991, Nicholas Roerich Prize),* The Country I Remember *(1996, Alice Faye Di Castagnola Award),* Arrivals *(2004),* Ludlow *(2007), and* News from the Village *(2010). Mason has also edited several major poetry anthologies. He lives in Colorado Springs, Colorado.*

Spooning

After my grandfather died I went back
to help my mother sell his furniture:
the old chair he did his sitting on,
the kitchen things. Going through his boxes
I found letters, cancelled checks, the usual
old photographs of relatives I hardly knew
and grandmother, clutching an apron in both hands.
And *her*. There was an old publicity still
taken when she wore her hair like a helmet,
polished black. Posed before a cardboard shell
and painted waves, she seemed unattainable,
as she was meant to.

                  For years we thought he lied
about his knowing her when he was young,
but grandfather was a man who hated liars,
a man who worshipped all the tarnished virtues,
went daily to his shop at eight, until
the first of three strokes forced him to retire.

He liked talking. Somebody had to listen,
so I was the listener for hours after school
until my parents called me home for dinner.
We'd sit on his glassed-in porch where he kept a box
of apples wrapped in newsprint.

He told me about the time he lost a job
at the mill. Nooksack seemed to kill its young
with boredom even then, but he owned a car,
a '24 Ford. He drove it east to see
America, got as far as Spokane's desert,
sold the car and worked back on the railroad.

Sometimes he asked me what I liked to do.
I told him about the drive-in movies where
my brother, Billy, took me if I paid.
In small towns everyone goes to the movies.
Not grandfather. He said they made them better when
nobody talked, and faces told it all.
"I knew Lydia Truman Gates," he said,
"back when she was plain old Lydia Carter
down on Water Street. One time her old man
caught us spooning out to the railroad tracks.
Nearly tanned my hide. He was a fisherman—
that is, till she moved her folks to Hollywood."

I don't know why, but I simply couldn't ask
what spooning was. He seemed to talk then
more to his chair's abrasions on the floor,
more to the pale alders outside his window.
The way he said her name I couldn't ask
who was Lydia Truman Gates.

                        *

                "Nonsense,"
was all my mother said at dinner. "His mind
went haywire in the hospital. He's old.
He makes things up and can't tell the difference."

I think my father's smile embarrassed her
when he said, "The poor guy's disappointed.
Nothing went right for him, so he daydreams."

"Nonsense," my mother said. "And anyway
no Lydia Truman Gates ever came
from a town like this."

                "It's not so bad a place.
I make a pretty decent living here."

My mother huffed. While I stared past my plate
Billy asked, "Who is Lydia Truman Gates?"

                        *

It wasn't long before we all found out.
The papers ran a story on her. How
she was famous in the twenties for a while,

married the oil billionaire, Gates, and retired.
She was coming back home to Nooksack. The mayor
would give a big award and ask her help
to renovate our landmark theatre.

Our mother said we had better things to spend
our money on than some old movie house,
though she remembered how it used to look.
She said that people living in the past
wouldn't amount to much.
Billy and I pretended we didn't care.
We didn't tell our parents where we went
that night, riding our bikes in a warm wind
past the fishhouses on the Puget Sound,
and up Grant Street to the Hiawatha.

Inside, Billy held my hand, and showed me
faded paintings of Indians on the walls
and dark forest patterns in the worn carpet.
The place smelled stale like old decaying clothes
shut up in a trunk for twenty years,
but Nooksack's best were there, some in tuxes,
and women stuffed into their evening gowns.
We sat in the balcony looking down
on bald heads, high hair-dos and jewels.
Near the stage they had a twenty-piece band—
I still remember when the lights went out
the violins rose like a flock of birds
all at once. The drums sounded a shudder.

We saw *Morocco Gold, The Outlaw, Colonel Clay*
and the comic short, *A Bird in the Hand,*
flickering down to the screen
where Lydia Truman Gates arose in veils,
in something gossamer
astonishing even in 1965.
Lydia Truman Gates was like a dream
of lithe attention, her dark eyes laughing
at death, at poverty or a satin bed.
And when they brought her on the stage, applause
rising and falling like a tidal wave,
I had to stand up on my seat to see
a frail old woman assisted by two men,
tiny on that distant stage.

My brother
yanked me past what seemed like a hundred pairs
of knees for all the times I said, "Excuse us."
We ran out where the chauffeur
waited by her limousine, his face painted
green by the light from Heilman's Piano Store,
breathing smoke. "You guys keep your distance."

"Is she coming out?"

He crushed his cigarette:
"No, she's gonna die in there. What do you think?"

More people joined us, pacing in the alley,
watching the chauffeur smoke by the door propped
open with a cinderblock.
And then the door half-opened, sighed back,
opened at last on the forearm of a man.

Behind him, Lydia Truman Gates stepped out
with her cane—hardly the woman I had seen
enduring all the problems of the world
with such aplomb. She stared down at the pavement,
saying, "Thank you, I can see it clearly now."

"Mrs. Gates," Billy stuttered. "Mrs. Gates."

The chauffeur tried to block us, but she said,
"That's all right, Andrew. They're just kids. I'm safe."

"Our grandpa says hello," I blurted out.

She paused for half a beat, glanced at Billy,
then peered at me as if to study terror,
smiling. "Well I'll be damned. And who's he?"

"Don't listen to him," Billy said. "He's nuts."

"George McCracken," I said, "the one you spooned with
down by the railroad tracks."

"George McCracken."
She straightened, looked up at the strip of sky.
"Spooned. Well, that's one way to talk about it."

She laughed from deep down in her husky lungs.
"Old Georgie McCracken. Is he still alive?
Too scared to come downtown and say hello?"
She reached out from her furs and touched my hair.
"Thanks for the message, little man. I knew him.
I knew he'd never get out of this town.
You tell your grampa Hi from Liddy Carter."

The man at her elbow said they had to leave.
She nodded, handing her award and purse
to the chauffeur.

           Then flashbulbs started popping.
I saw her face lit up, then pale and caving
back into the darkness. "Christ," she whispered,
"get me out of here."

            I stumbled, or was pushed.
My eyes kept seeing her exploding at me,
a woman made entirely of light
beside the smaller figure who was real.
Two men tipped her into the limousine
and it slid off like a shark, parting the crowd.

          *

A picture ran in the next day's *Herald*—
the great actress touches a local boy.
For two weeks everybody talked about me,
but I kept thinking, "Is he still alive?
Too scared to come downtown and say hello?"

I thought of her decaying on a screen,
her ribs folding like a silk umbrella's rods,
while all the men who gathered around her
clutched at the remnants of her empty dress.

Marilyn Chin (1955–)

Marilyn Chin was born in Hong Kong and grew up in Portland, Oregon. She attended the University of Massachusetts, the University of Iowa Writers Workshop, and Stanford University as a Stegner Fellow. She teaches at San Diego State University. Her poetry books include Dwarf Bamboo *(1987),* The Phoenix Gone, The Terrace Empty *(1994), and* Rhapsody in Plain Yellow *(2002); she has also edited the anthology* Asian American Poetry: The Next Generation *(2004) and published a novel. Among her honors are National Endowment for the Arts, MacDowell Colony, Djerassi Foundation, Lannan Foundation, and Yaddo fellowships. Marilyn Chin lives in southern California.*

How I Got That Name

an essay on assimilation

I am Marilyn Mei Ling Chin.
Oh, how I love the resoluteness
of that first person singular
followed by that stalwart indicative
of "be," without the uncertain i-n-g
of "becoming." Of course,
the name had been changed
somewhere between Angel Island and the sea,
when my father the paper son
in the late 1950s
obsessed with some bombshell blonde
transliterated "Mei Ling" to "Marilyn."
And nobody dared question
his initial impulse—for we all know
lust drove men to greatness,
not goodness, not decency.
And there I was, a wayward pink baby,
named after some tragic
white woman, swollen with gin and Nembutal.
My mother couldn't pronounce the "r."
She dubbed me "Numba one female offshoot"
for brevity: henceforth, she will live and die
in sublime ignorance, flanked
by loving children and the "kitchen deity."
While my father dithers,
a tomcat in Hong Kong trash—
a gambler, a petty thug,
who bought a chain of chopsuey joints

in Piss River, Oregon,
with bootlegged Gucci cash.
Nobody dared question his integrity given
his nice, devout daughters
and his bright, industrious sons.
As if filial piety were the standard
with which all earthly men were measured.

*

Oh, how trustworthy our daughters,
how thrifty our sons!
How we've managed to fool the experts
in education, statistics and demography—
We're not very creative but not adverse to rote-learning.
Indeed, they can *use* us.
But the "Model Minority" is a tease.
We know you are watching now,
so we refuse to give you any!
Oh, bamboo shoots, bamboo shoots!
The further west we go, we'll hit east;
The deeper down we dig, we'll find China.
History has turned its stomach
on a black, polluted beach—
where life doesn't hinge
on that red, red wheelbarrow,
but whether or not our new lover
in the final episode of "Santa Barbara"
will lean over a scented candle
and call us a "bitch."
Oh God, where have we gone wrong?
We have no inner resources!

*

Then, one redolent spring morning
the Great Patriarch Chin
peered down from his kiosk in heaven
and saw that his descendants were ugly.
One had a squarish head and a nose without a bridge.
Another's profile—long and knobbed as a gourd.
A third, the sad, brutish one
may never, never marry.
And I, his least favorite—
"not quite boiled, not quite cooked,"
a plump pomfret simmering in my juices—

too listless to fight for my people's destiny.
"To kill without resistance is not slaughter"
says the proverb. So, I wait for imminent death.
The fact that this death is also metaphorical
is testament to my lethargy.

*

So, here lies Marilyn Mei Ling Chin,
married once, twice to so-and-so, a Lee and a Wong,
granddaughter of Jack "the patriarch" Chin
and the brooding Suilin Fong,
daughter of the virtuous Yuet Kuen Wong
and G.G. Chin the infamous,
sister of a dozen, cousin of a million,
survived by everybody and forgotten by all.
She was neither black nor white,
neither cherished nor vanquished,
just another squatter in her own bamboo grove
minding her poetry—
when one day heaven was unmerciful,
and a chasm opened where she then stood.
Like the jowls of a mighty white whale,
or the jaws of a metaphysical Godzilla,
it swallowed her whole.
She did not flinch nor writhe,
nor fret about the afterlife,
but stayed! Solid as wood, happily
a little gnawed, tattered, mesmerized
by all that was lavished upon her
and all that was taken away!

Composed Near the Bay Bridge

(after a wild party)

1)

Amerigo has his finger on the pulse of China.
He, Amerigo, is dressed profoundly punk:
Mohawk-pate, spiked dog collar, black leather thighs.
She, China, freshly hennaed and boaed, is intrigued
with the new diaspora and the sexual freedom
called bondage. "Isn't bondage, therefore,
a kind of freedom?" she asks, wanly.

2)

Thank God there was no war tonight.
Headbent, Amerigo plucks his bad guitar.
The Sleeping Giant snores with her mouth agape
while a lone nightingale trills on a tree.

Through the picture window, I watch the traffic
hone down to a quiver. Loneliness. Dawn.
A few geese winging south; minor officials return home.

The Survivor

Don't tap your chopsticks against your bowl.
Don't throw your teacup against the wall in anger.
Don't suck on your long black braid and weep.
Don't tarry around the big red sign that says "danger!"

All the tempests will render still; seas will calm,
horses will retreat, voices to surrender.

*

That you have bloomed this way and not that,
that your skin is yellow, not white, not black,
that you were born not a boychild but a girl,
that this world will be forever puce-pink are just as well.

Remember, the survivor is not the strongest or most clever;
merely, the survivor is almost always the youngest.
And you shall have to relinquish that title before long.

Cathy Song (1955–)

Cathy Song was born in Honolulu, Hawaii, and attended Wellesley College and Boston University. Her poetry books include Picture Bride *(1983, Yale Younger Poets Prize),* Frameless Windows, Squares of Light *(1988),* School Figures *(1994),* The Land of Bliss *(2001), and* Cloud Moving Hands *(2007). Among her many awards are the Shelley Memorial Award and the Hawaii Award for Literature, as well as a National Endowment for the Arts fellowship. Cathy Song lives in Hawaii.*

The Youngest Daughter

The sky has been dark
for many years.
My skin has become as damp
and pale as rice paper
and feels the way
mother's used to before the drying sun
parched it out there in the fields.

      Lately, when I touch my eyelids,
my hands react as if
I had just touched something
hot enough to burn.
My skin, aspirin colored,
tingles with migraine. Mother
has been massaging the left side of my face
especially in the evenings
when the pain flares up.

This morning
her breathing was graveled,
her voice gruff with affection
when I wheeled her into the bath.
She was in a good humor,
making jokes about her great breasts,
floating in the milky water
like two walruses,
flaccid and whiskered around the nipples.
I scrubbed them with a sour taste
in my mouth, thinking
six children and an old man
have sucked from these brown nipples.

I was almost tender
when I came to the blue bruises
that freckle her body,
places where she has been injecting insulin
for thirty years. I soaped her slowly,
she sighed deeply, her eyes closed.
It seems it has always
been like this: the two of us
in this sunless room,
the splashing of the bathwater.

In the afternoons
when she has rested,
she prepares our ritual of tea and rice,
garnished with a shred of gingered fish,
a slice of pickled turnip,
a token for my white body.
We eat in the familiar silence.
She knows I am not to be trusted,
even now planning my escape.
As I toast to her health
with the tea she has poured,
a thousand cranes curtain the window,
fly up in a sudden breeze.

Annie Finch (1956–)

Annie Finch grew up in New Rochelle, New York. She attended Yale University, the University of Houston, and Stanford University; since 2004 she has been teaching at the University of Southern Maine. Among her poetry books are The Encyclopedia of Scotland *(1982),* Eve *(1997),* Calendars *(2003),* Shadow-Bird *(2009), and* Among the Goddesses: An Epic Libretto in Seven Dreams *(2010). She has also written verse dramas and several textbooks on craft, particularly formal prosody. Her honors include a fellowship from the Black Earth Institute and the Robert Fitzgerald Prosody Award. Annie Finch lives in Maine.*

Another Reluctance

Chestnuts fell in the charred season,
Fell finally, finding room
In air to open their old cases
So they gleam out from the gold leaves,
In the dusk now, where they dropped down.

I go watch them, waiting for winter,
Their husks open and holding on.
Those rusted rims are rigid-hard
And cling clean to the clear brown,

And the fall sun sinks soon,
And the day draws to its dark end,
and the feet give up the gray walk,
no longer lingering, light gone,
and I am here and do not go home.

Hollow gifts to cold children:
The chestnuts they hid in small caches
Have gone hollow, their gleam gone,
Their grain gone, and the children are home.

Insect

That hour-glass-backed,
orchard-legged,
heavy-headed will,

paper-folded,
wedge-contorted,
savage—dense to kill—

pulls back on backward-moving,
arching
high legs still,

lowered through a deep, knees-reaching,
feathered down
green will,

antenna-honest,
thread-descending,
carpeted as if with skill,

a focus-changing,
sober-reaching,

tracing, killing will.

Li-Young Lee (1957–)

Li-Young Lee was born in Jakarta, Indonesia, and came to the United States in 1964. He attended the University of Pittsburgh, the University of Arizona, and the State University of New York at Brockport and has taught at Northwestern University, the University of Iowa, the University of Oregon, and the University of Texas at Austin. His poetry books include Rose *(1986, Delmore Schwartz Memorial Award),* The City in Which I Love You *(1990, Lamont Poetry Prize), and* Book of My Nights *(2002, William Carlos Williams Award). Among Lee's numerous other honors are National Endowment for the Arts fellowships, a Guggenheim fellowship, a Whiting award, and an American Book Award. Li-Young Lee lives in Chicago as a freelance writer.*

The Gift

To pull the metal splinter from my palm
my father recited a story in a low voice.
I watched his lovely face and not the blade.
Before the story ended, he'd removed
the iron sliver I thought I'd die from.

I can't remember the tale,
but hear his voice still, a well
of dark water, a prayer.
And I recall his hands,
two measures of tenderness
he laid against my face,
the flames of discipline
he raised above my head.

Had you entered that afternoon
you would have thought you saw a man
planting something in a boy's palm,
a silver tear, a tiny flame.
Had you followed that boy
you would have arrived here,
where I bend over my wife's right hand.

Look how I shave her thumbnail down
so carefully she feels no pain.
Watch as I lift the splinter out.
I was seven when my father
took my hand like this,
and I did not hold that shard

between my fingers and think,
Metal that will bury me,
christen it Little Assassin,
Ore Going Deep for My Heart.
And I did not lift up my wound and cry,
Death visited here!
I did what a child does
when he's given something to keep.
I kissed my father.

Eating Together

In the steamer is the trout
seasoned with slivers of ginger,
two sprigs of green onion, and sesame oil.
We shall eat it with rice for lunch,
brothers, sister, my mother who will
taste the sweetest meat of the head,
holding it between her fingers
deftly, the way my father did
weeks ago. Then he lay down
to sleep like a snow-covered road
winding through pines older than him,
without any travelers, and lonely for no one.

Carl Phillips (1959–)

Carl Phillips was born in Everett, Washington, and spent his high school years in Cape Cod, Massachusetts. He attended Harvard, the University of Massachusetts, and Boston University, was a high school Latin teacher for eight years, and has taught at Washington University since 1993. His poetry books include In the Blood *(1992),* Quiver of Arrows: Selected Poems 1986–2006 *(2007),* Speak Low *(2009), and* Double Shadow *(2011). A recipient of the Kingsley Tufts Award, Phillips serves as the current judge for the Yale Younger Poets Prize. He lives in St. Louis.*

Our Lady

In the final hour, our lady—Of
the electric rosary, Of the highway,
by then Of the snows mostly—was

the man he'd always been really,
though, yes, we'd sometimes forgotten.
Still, even while he lay fanning,

as one might any spent flame, where
it was hot, between his legs, and
saying it didn't much matter anymore

about dying, what came of having
come too often, perhaps, to what in
the end had fallen short of divine

always, he said that more than the
bare-chested dancers and all-conquering
bass-line that had marked his every

sudden, strobe-lit appearance, at
precisely the same moment, in all of
the city's best clubs; more than

the just-heated towels and the water
he'd called holy in those windowless,
too thinly-walled, now all but

abandoned bath-houses, he regretted
the fine gowns that he'd made, just
by wearing them, famous; and then,

half, it seemed, to remind us, half
himself, he recreated the old shrug,
slowly raising from his hospital

robe—not green, he insisted, but
two shades, maybe three, shy of
turquoise—one shoulder to show

the words still tattooed there:
Adore me; for a moment, it was
possible to see it, the once

extraordinary beauty, the heated
grace for which we'd all of us,
once, so eagerly sought him.

As from a Quiver of Arrows

What do we do with the body, do we
burn it, do we set it in dirt or in
stone, do we wrap it in balm, honey,
oil, and then gauze and tip it onto
and trust it to a raft and to water?

What will happen to the memory of his
body, if one of us doesn't hurry now
and write it down fast? Will it be
salt or late light that it melts like?
Floss, rubber gloves, a chewed cap

to a pen elsewhere—how are we to
regard his effects, do we throw them
or use them away, do we say they are
relics and so treat them like relics?
Does his soiled linen count? If so,

would we be wrong then, to wash it?
There are no instructions whether it
should go to where are those with no
linen, or whether by night we should
memorially wear it ourselves, by day

reflect upon it folded, shelved, empty.
Here, on the floor behind his bed is
a bent photo—why? Were the two of
them lovers? Does it mean, where we
found it, that he forgot it or lost it

or intended a safekeeping? Should we
attempt to make contact? What if this
other man too is dead? Or alive, but
doesn't want to remember, is human?
Is it okay to be human, and fall away

from oblation and memory, if we forget,
and can't sometimes help it and sometimes
it is all that we want? How long, in
dawns or new cocks, does that take?
What if it is rest and nothing else that

we want? Is it a findable thing, small?
In what hole is it hidden? Is it, maybe,
a country? Will a guide be required who
will say to us how? Do we fly? Do we
swim? What will I do now, with my hands?

Nick Flynn (1960–)

Nick Flynn was born in Scituate, Massachusetts. He worked in a number of jobs before attending the Fine Arts Work Center in Provincetown and New York University. He has since taught at Columbia University and the University of Houston. His poetry books include Some Ether *(2000, PEN/Joyce Osterweil Award , Larry Levis Prize) and* Blind Huber *(2002); he has also published two memoirs. Among his honors are Guggenheim and Witter Bynner fellowships. Nick Flynn lives in New York City.*

Bag of Mice

I dreamt your suicide note
was scrawled in pencil on a brown paperbag,
& in the bag were six baby mice. The bag
opened into darkness,
smoldering
from the top down. The mice,
huddled at the bottom, scurried the bag
across a shorn field. I stood over it
& as the burning reached each carbon letter
of what you'd written
your voice released into the night
like a song, & the mice
grew wilder.

Cartoon Physics, part 1

Children under, say, *ten*, shouldn't know
that the universe is ever-expanding,
inexorably pushing into the vacuum, galaxies

swallowed by galaxies, whole

solar systems collapsing, all of it
acted out in silence. At ten we are still learning

the rules of cartoon animation,

that if a man draws a door on a rock
only he can pass through it.
Anyone else who tries

will crash into the rock. Ten-year-olds
should stick with burning houses, car wrecks,
ships going down—earthbound, tangible

disasters, arenas

where they can be heroes. You can run
back into a burning house, sinking ships

have lifeboats, the trucks will come
with their ladders, if you jump

you will be saved. A child

places her hand on the roof of a schoolbus,
& drives across a city of sand. She knows

the exact spot it will skid, at which point
the bridge will give, who will swim to safety
& who will be pulled under by sharks. She will learn

that if a man runs off the edge of a cliff
he will not fall

until he notices his mistake.

Elizabeth Alexander (1962–)

Elizabeth Alexander was born in New York and grew up in Washington, D.C. She at-
tended Yale University, Boston University, and the University of Pennsylvania. After
teaching at the University of Chicago, she joined the Yale faculty in 2000 and currently
chairs its Department of African-American Studies. Her poetry books include The
Venus Hottentot *(1990),* Body of Life *(1996),* Antebellum Dream Book *(2001),*
American Sublime *(2005), and* Crave Radiance: New and Selected Poems *(2010).*
Among her honors is the 2010 Anisfield-Wolf Lifetime Achievement Award. Elizabeth
Alexander read her poem "Praise Song for the Day" at Barack Obama's 2009 Presiden-
tial Inauguration. She lives in New Haven, Connecticut.

The Venus Hottentot
(1825)

1. CUVIER

Science, science, science!
Everything is beautiful

blown up beneath my glass.
Colors dazzle insect wings.

A drop of water swirls
like marble. Ordinary

crumbs become stalactites
set in perfect angles

of geometry I'd thought
impossible. Few will

ever see what I see
through this microscope.

Cranial measurements
crowd my notebook pages,

and I am moving closer,
close to how these numbers

signify aspects of
national character.

Her genitalia
will float inside a labeled

pickling jar in the Musée
de l'Homme on a shelf

above Broca's brain:
"The Venus Hottentot."

Elegant facts await me.
Small things in this world are mine.

2.
There is unexpected sun today
in London, and the clouds that
most days sift into this cage
where I am working have dispersed.
I am a black cutout against
a captive blue sky, pivoting
nude so the paying audience
can view my naked buttocks.

I am called "Venus Hottentot."
I left Capetown with a promise
of revenue: half the profits
and my passage home: A boon!
Master's brother proposed the trip;
the magistrate granted me leave.
I would return to my family
a duchess, with watered-silk

dresses and money to grow food,
rouge and powders in glass pots,
silver scissors, a lorgnette,
voile and tulle instead of flax,
cerulean blue instead
of indigo. My brother would
devour sugar-studded non-
pareils, pale taffy, damask plums.

That was years ago. London's
circuses are florid and filthy,

swarming with cabbage-smelling
citizens who stare and query,
"Is it muscle? bone? or fat?"
My neighbor to the left is
The Sapient Pig, "The Only
Scholar of His Race." He plays

at cards, tells time and fortunes
by scraping his hooves. Behind
me is Prince Kar-mi, who arches
like a rubber tree and stares back
at the crowd from under the crook
of his knee. A professional
animal trainer shouts my cues.
There are singing mice here.

"The Ball of Duchess DuBarry":
In the engraving I lurch
toward the *belles dames*, mad-eyed, and
they swoon. Men in capes and pince-nez
shield them. Tassels dance at my hips.
In this newspaper lithograph
my buttocks are shown swollen
and luminous as a planet.

Monsieur Cuvier investigates
between my legs, poking, prodding,
sure of his hypothesis.
I half expect him to pull silk
scarves from inside me, paper poppies,
then a rabbit! He complains
at my scent and does not think
I comprehend, but I speak

English. I speak Dutch. I speak
a little French as well, and
languages Monsieur Cuvier
will never know have names.
Now I am bitter and now
I am sick. I eat brown bread,
drink rancid broth. I miss good sun,
miss Mother's *sadza*. My stomach

is frequently queasy from mutton
chops, pale potatoes, blood sausage.
I was certain that this would be
better than farm life. I am
the family entrepreneur!
But there are hours in every day
to conjur my imaginary
daughters, in banana skirts

and ostrich-feather fans.
Since my own genitals are public
I have made other parts private.
In my silence I possess
mouth, larynx, brain, in a single
gesture. I rub my hair
with lanolin, and pose in profile
like a painted Nubian

archer, imagining gold leaf
woven through my hair, and diamonds.
Observe the wordless Odalisque.
I have not forgotten my Xhosa
clicks. My flexible tongue
and healthy mouth bewilder
this man with his rotting teeth.
If he were to let me rise up

from this table, I'd spirit
his knives and cut out his black heart,
seal it with science fluid inside
a bell jar, place it on a low
shelf in a white man's museum
so the whole world could see
it was shriveled and hard,
geometric, deformed, unnatural.

Affirmative Action Blues (1993)

Right now two black people sit in a jury room
in Southern California trying to persuade
nine white people that what they saw when four white

police officers brought batons back like
they were smashing a beautiful piñata was
"a violation of Rodney King's civil rights,"
just as I am trying to convince my boss not ever
to use the word "niggardly" in my presence again.
He's a bit embarrassed, then asks, but don't you know
the word's etymology? as if that makes it
somehow not the word, as if a word can't batter.
Never again for as long as you live, I tell him,
and righteously. Then I dream of a meeting
with my colleagues where I scream so loud the inside
of my skull bleeds, and my face erupts in scabs.
In the dream I use an office which is overrun
with mice, rats, and round-headed baby otters
who peer at me from exposed water pipes (and somehow
I know these otters are Negroes), and my boss says,
Be grateful, your office is bigger than anyone
else's, and maybe if you kept it clean you wouldn't
have those rats. And meanwhile, black people are dying,
beautiful black men my age, from AIDS. It was amazing
when I learned the root of "venereal disease"
was "Venus," that there was such a thing as a disease
of love. And meanwhile, poor Rodney King can't think
    straight;
what was knocked into his head was some addled notion
of love his own people make fun of, "Can we all
get along? Please?" You can't hit a lick with a crooked
stick; a straight stick made Rodney King believe he was
not a piñata, that amor vincit omnia.
I know I have been changed by love.
I know that love is not a political agenda, it lacks sustained
analysis, and we can't dance our way out of our
    constrictions.
I know that the word "niggardly" is "of obscure etymology"
    but probably derived from the French Norman, and that
    Chaucer and Milton and Shakespeare used it. It means
    "stingy," and the root is not the same as "nigger," which
    derives from "negar," meaning black, but they are
    perhaps, perhaps, etymologically related. The two "g"s
    are two teeth gnawing; rodent is from the Latin "rodere"
    which means "to gnaw," as I have said elsewhere.
I know so many things, including the people who love me
    and the people who do not.

In Tourette's syndrome you say the very thing that you are
  thinking, and then a word is real.
These are words I have heard in the last 24 hours which
  fascinate me: "vermin," "screed," "carmine," and
  "niggardly."
I am not a piñata, Rodney King insists. Now can't we all get
  along?

Equinox

Now is the time of year when bees are wild
and eccentric. They fly fast and in cramped
loop-de-loops, dive-bomb clusters of conversants
in the bright, late-September out-of-doors.
I have found their dried husks in my clothes.

They are dervishes because they are dying,
one last sting, a warm place to squeeze
a drop of venom or of honey.
After the stroke we thought would be her last
my grandmother came back, reared back and slapped

a nurse across the face. Then she stood up,
walked outside, and lay down in the snow.
Two years later there is no other way
to say, we are waiting. She is silent, light
as an empty hive, and she is breathing.

Reetika Vazirani (1962–2003)

Reetika Vazirani was born in Punjab, India, and came to the United States in 1968. She grew up in Maryland and attended Wellesley College and the University of Virginia; she subsequently taught at the University of Oregon, Sweet Briar College, and William and Mary College. Her poetry books include White Elephants *(1995, Barnard New Women Poets Prize),* World Hotel *(2003, Anisfield-Wolf Book Award), and* Radha Says *(2009). Reetika Vazirani committed suicide in Washington, D.C.*

From *White Elephants*

[30]   A Million Balconies

I'm half Bengali, so I went to Calcutta
to find my half-Bengaliness. I scanned
the street for signs. I looked to the light
of the sky, and I sniffed the sooty air
for familiarity; but it smelt null
as home whenever I'd gone back. I took
the city tour to orient myself.
So many conquerors looted the state.
Was I supposed to think my house was robbed?
I was, and I was to be poor forever.
Then at a stop I fell out into the crowd.
It was like falling in love: I wasn't lost.
I saw a man waiting, a discreet shop
manager. I found a city on his face.

[42]   Train Windows
for Derek Walcott

Give me the summary, you said. What did
the journey come to? It came to this:
inheriting your richest lands, words:
moving through the framed spaces, square
train windows out of which I'd always look
for you in your khaki shirt. I'd pretend
the train was near a coast and listen for
your call, but hear myself, as if you were always
near like a rhyme or like one's native tongue;
later, like the sound of type, the click
of words—you let me hear them those days
in Boston. I felt at home again, or
calm among words, their clear panes through which views
peered back as greetings to a traveller.

Sherman Alexie (1966–)

Sherman Alexie was born on the Spokane Indian Reservation in Washington and educated at Gonzaga University in Spokane and Washington State University in Pullman before becoming a freelance writer. His poetry books include The Business of Fancy-dancing *(1991),* I Would Steal Horses *(1992),* First Indian on the Moon *(1993),* Dangerous Astronomy *(2005), and* Face *(2009). Among his honors are a National Endowment for the Arts fellowship, the 2007 National Book Award for young people's literature, and the 2010 PEN/Faulkner Award for fiction. Sherman Alexie lives in Seattle, Washington.*

What the Orphan Inherits

Language

I dreamed I was digging your grave
with my bare hands. I touched your face
and skin fell in thin strips to the ground

until only your tongue remained whole.
I hung it to smoke with the deer
for seven days. It tasted thick and greasy

sinew gripped my tongue tight. I rose
to walk naked through the fire. I spoke
English. I was not consumed.

Names

I do not have an Indian name.
The wind never spoke to my mother
when I was born. My heart was hidden

beneath the shells of walnuts switched
back and forth. I have to cheat to feel
the beating of drums in my chest.

Alcohol

"For bringing us the horse
we could almost forgive you
for bringing us whisky."

Time

We measure time leaning
out car windows shattering
beer bottles off road signs.

Tradition

Indian boys
sinewy and doe-eyed
frozen in headlights.

The Powwow at the End of the World

I am told by many of you that I must forgive and so I shall
after an Indian woman puts her shoulder to the Grand Coulee Dam
and topples it. I am told by many of you that I must forgive
and so I shall after the floodwaters burst each successive dam
downriver from the Grand Coulee. I am told by many of you
that I must forgive and so I shall after the floodwaters find
their way to the mouth of the Columbia River as it enters the Pacific
and causes all of it to rise. I am told by many of you that I must forgive
and so I shall after the first drop of floodwater is swallowed by that salmon
waiting in the Pacific. I am told by many of you that I must forgive and so I shall
after that salmon swims upstream, through the mouth of the Columbia
and then past the flooded cities, broken dams and abandoned reactors
of Hanford. I am told by many of you that I must forgive and so I shall
after that salmon swims through the mouth of the Spokane River
as it meets the Columbia, then upstream, until it arrives
in the shallows of a secret bay on the reservation where I wait alone.
I am told by many of you that I must forgive and so I shall after
that salmon leaps into the night air above the water, throws
a lightning bolt at the brush near my feet, and starts the fire
which will lead all of the lost Indians home. I am told
by many of you that I must forgive and so I shall
after we Indians have gathered around the fire with that salmon
who has three stories it must tell before sunrise: one story will teach us
how to pray; another story will make us laugh for hours;
the third story will give us reason to dance. I am told by many
of you that I must forgive and so I shall when I am dancing
with my tribe during the powwow at the end of the world.

Natasha Trethewey (1966–)

Natasha Trethewey was born in Gulfport, Mississippi, and attended the University of Georgia, Hollins College, and the University of Massachusetts. She has taught at Auburn University, the University of North Carolina at Chapel Hill, and Duke University, was a Bunting Fellow at Harvard, and currently teaches at Emory University. Her poetry books include Domestic Work *(1999, Cave Canem Prize),* Bellocq's Ophelia *(2002), and* Native Guard *(2006, Pulitzer Prize). Among her honors is a National Endowment of the Arts fellowship. In 2012 she was named U.S. Poet Laureate. Natasha Trethewey lives in Atlanta.*

Hot Combs

At the junk shop, I find an old pair,
black with grease, the teeth still pungent
as burning hair. One is small,
fine toothed as if for a child. Holding it,
I think of my mother's slender wrist,
the curve of her neck as she leaned
over the stove, her eyes shut as she pulled
the wooden handle and laid flat the wisps
at her temples. The heat in our kitchen
made her glow that morning I watched her
wincing, the hot comb singeing her brow,
sweat glistening above her lips,
her face made strangely beautiful
as only suffering can do.

Amateur Fighter

   —for my father

What's left is the tiny gold glove
hanging from his key chain. But,
before that, he had come to boxing,

as a boy, out of necessity—one more reason
to stay away from home, go late
to that cold house and dinner alone

in the dim kitchen. Perhaps he learned
just to box a stepfather, then turned
that anger into a prize at the Halifax gym.

Later, in New Orleans, there were the books
he couldn't stop reading. A scholar, his eyes
weakening. Fighting, then, a way to live

dangerously. He'd leave his front tooth out
for pictures so that I might understand
living meant suffering, loss. Really living

meant taking risks, so he swallowed
a cockroach in a bar on a dare, dreamt
of being a bullfighter. And at the gym

on Tchoupitoulas Street, he trained
his fists to pound into a bag
the fury contained in his gentle hands.

The red headgear, hiding his face,
could make me think he was someone else,
that my father was somewhere else, not here

holding his body up to pain.

Flounder

Here, she said, *put this on your head.*
She handed me a hat.
You 'bout as white as your dad,
and you gone stay like that.

Aunt Sugar rolled her nylons down
around each bony ankle,
and I rolled down my white knee socks
letting my thin legs dangle,

circling them just above water
and silver backs of minnows
flitting here then there between
the sun spots and the shadows.

This is how you hold the pole
to cast the line out straight.
Now put that worm on your hook,
throw it out and wait.

She sat spitting tobacco juice
into a coffee cup.
Hunkered down when she felt the bite,
jerked the pole straight up

reeling and tugging hard at the fish
that wriggled and tried to fight back.
A flounder, she said, *and you can tell*
'cause one of its sides is black.

The other side is white, she said.
It landed with a thump.
I stood there watching that fish flip-flop,
switch sides with every jump.

A. E. Stallings (1968–)

A. E. Stallings grew up in Decatur, Georgia. She studied classics at the University of Georgia and Oxford University in England and has lived in Athens, Greece, since 1999. Her poetry books include Archaic Smile *(1999, Richard Wilbur Award) and* Hapax *(2006, Poets' Prize). Penguin Classics issued her translation of Titus Lucretius Carus's* De rerum natura *(The Nature of Things) in 2007.*

The Tantrum

Struck with grief you were, though only four,
The day your mother cut her mermaid hair
And stood, a stranger, smiling at the door.

They frowned, tsk-tsked your willful, cruel despair,
When you slunk beneath the long piano strings
And sobbed until your lungs hiccupped for air,

Unbribable with curses, cake, playthings.
You mourned a mother now herself no more,
But brave and fashionable. The golden rings

That fringed her naked neck, whom were they for?
Not you, but for the world, now in your place,
A full eclipse. You wept down on the floor;

She wept up in her room. They told you this:
That she could grow it back, and just as long,
They told you, lying always about loss,

For you know she never did. And they were wrong.

Joanna Klink (1969–)

Joanna Klink was born in Iowa City, Iowa, and attended Carleton College in Minnesota, the University of Iowa Writers Workshop, and Johns Hopkins University. She has taught at the University of Montana since 2001 and has been the 2008–2011 Briggs-Copeland Poet at Harvard. Her poetry books include They Are Sleeping *(2000),* Circadian *(2007), and* Raptus *(2010). Among her honors is the 2003 Rona Jaffe Foundation Writers' Award.*

Spare

Shoulder me up. Drink careless down, for flinching

ask, break, call skimming, be slight then, be soon.

Would, wire air back to you, would. Would wind you

still, lift clear to you sitting. Sheeted around you

would care, could single you somehow, warm for floor-

weight down hurt to you, sinking. Though your arms hold:

just sun. I can't bring you. So tire to me quickly,

dumb solving cushions. Would spare wrists to you, skimming.

What sudden gives, what bent back look lifting (not my legs

here on me, nor the still sitting). For glass bowl bent over

caring. Keeps clear to tasting but warm to me, singing.

What serves then slips (orange, cold-orange, cannot spare

breaking). What wouldn't bend, what part offer, what fruit

sweet to flinching. Though cold cancels can sit can

reach. Does not know. But holds. But holds out, feeling.

Brenda Shaughnessy (1970–)

Brenda Shaughnessy was born in Okinawa, Japan. She attended the University of California at Santa Cruz and Columbia University before teaching at the New School and Princeton University. Her poetry books include Interior with Sudden Joy *(1999) and* Human Dark with Sugar *(2008, James Laughlin Award). Among her honors is also a Bunting Fellowship at Harvard. Brenda Shaughnessy lives in New York City.*

Postfeminism

There are two kinds of people, soldiers and women,
as Virginia Woolf said. Both for decoration only.

Now that is too kind. It's technical: virgins and wolves.
We have choices now. Two little girls walk into a bar,

one orders a shirley temple. Shirley Temple's pimp
comes over and says you won't be sorry. She's a fine

piece of work but she don't come cheap. Myself, I'm
in less fear of predators than of walking around

in my mother's body. That's sneaky, that's more
than naked. Let's even it up: you go on fuming in your

gray room. I am voracious alone. Blank and loose,
metallic lingerie. And rare black-tipped cigarettes

in a handmade basket case. Which of us weaves
the world together with a quicker blur of armed

seduction: your war-on-thugs, my body stockings.
Ascetic or carnivore. Men will crack your glaze

even if you leave them before morning. Pigs
ride the sirens in packs. Ah, flesh, technoflesh,

there are two kinds of people. Hot with mixed
light, drunk with insult. You and me.

Your One Good Dress

should never be light. That kind of thing feels
like a hundred shiny-headed waifs backlit
and skeletal, approaching. Dripping and in
unison, murmuring, "We *are* you."

No. And the red dress (think about it,
redress) is all neckhole. The brown
is a big wet beard with, of course, a backslit.
You're only as sick as your secrets.

There is an argument for the dull-chic,
the dirty olive and the Cinderelly. But those
who exhort it are only part of the conspiracy:
"Shimmer, shmimmer," they'll say. "Lush, shmush."

Do not listen. It's a part of the anti-obvious
movement and it's sheer matricide. Ask your mum.
It would kill her if you were ewe gee el why.
And is it a crime to wonder, am I. In the dark a dare,

Am I now. You put on your Niña, your Pinta, your
Santa María. Make it simple to last your whole
life long. Make it black. Glassy or deep.
Your body is opium and you are its only true smoker.

This black dress is your one good dress.
Bury your children in it. Visit your pokey
hometown friends in it. Go missing for days.
Taking it off never matters. That just wears you down.

Kevin Young (1970–)

Kevin Young was born in Lincoln, Nebraska. He attended Harvard, Stanford (as a Stegner Fellow), and Brown universities. He has taught at the University of Georgia, Indiana University, and Emory University. His poetry books include Most Way Home *(1995, National Poetry Series),* Jelly Roll: A Blues *(2003),* Black Maria *(2005),* For the Confederate Dead *(2007), and* Ardency: A Chronicle of the Amistad Rebels *(2011). Among his honors are National Endowment for the Arts and Guggenheim fellowships. Kevin Young lives in Boston and Atlanta.*

Quivira City Limits

For Thomas Fox Averill

Pull over. Your car with its slow
breathing. Somewhere outside Topeka

it suddenly all matters again,
those tractors blooming rust

in the fields only need a good coat
of paint. Red. You had to see

for yourself, didn't you; see that the world
never turned small, transportation

just got better; to learn
we can't say a town or a baseball

team without breathing in
a dead Indian. To discover why Coronado

pushed up here, following the guide
who said he knew fields of gold,

north, who led them past these plains,
past buffaloes dark as he was. Look.

Nothing but the wheat, waving them
sick, a sea. While they strangle

him blue as the sky above you
The Moor must also wonder

when will all this ever be enough?
this wide open they call discovery,

disappointment, this place my
thousand bones carry, now call home.

Everywhere Is Out of Town

for Maceo Parker & the JB Horns

Beanville. Tea
party. Five black cats
& a white boy. Chitlin
circuit. Gravy colored suits,
preacher stripes. Didn't
know you could buy
muttonchops these days.
Afros. Horns slung
round necks like giant
ladles. Dressing. Uptempo
blessing: *Good God*

everywhere! We bow our
heads before the band
lets loose. Drummer unknown
as a hymn's third verse.
Older woman pushes toward
the front, catching the spirit
like the crazy lady at church
six scotches later. Communion
breath. Hands waving. Sweaty
face rags, post-sermon
mop, suicidal white girls crying
like the newly baptized. All that
water. Play it. Swing
it. *Be suggestive.* Request
"Chicken" & "Pass the Peas"
like we used to say. Have mercy!
Thanksgiving's back in town

& we're all crammed in the club white
as the walls of a church basement. Feet
impatient as forks. Only ten bucks

a plate for this leftover band. Thigh,
drumsticks, neck. Dark meat.

Whatever You Want

for Arnold Kemp

This could be a good day. It starts
without you, as usual; you haven't seen
dawn in years. By noon it hits half-
boiling & the air breaks down. After lunch
even the fans turn lazy, not moving you
or wind. Is it the Negro in you that gets
in the car & just starts driving, keeps
the windows down, your music
bouncing off station wagons, power
windows? Whatever you want

to call it, it makes you feel you own
everything, even the creeping heat. Spin
the radio looking for summer, for love
songs with someone somewhere worse
off than you. Why doesn't anyone
advertise for rain? Instead the personalities
keep talking to prove they are indoors,
cool. By seven the temperature outsails
the price of gas, the movies are all sold out
& you can't get cool for the heavens.
So peel away, head for the edge
of town where the roads turn thin & alone,
speeding to prove you can summon death
like tortoises cracked open in the road
up ahead, the water stored in their shells
running free. Keep on trying to out-race
heat's red siren until radio sings out

Come home, come on home black boy
to your chimney full of birds, to this house
of flame. Evening, the heat holds you
with its aching, unavoidable fingers;
you sleep naked, dreamless to heat.
Windows thrown open as mouths, fan on,
it still feels like a ghost is baking sweet
potato pies through the night. Your favorite.

Terrance Hayes (1971–)

Terrance Hayes was born in Columbia, South Carolina. He attended Coker College in South Carolina and the University of Pittsburgh. His poetry books include Muscular Music *(1999, Kate Tufts Discovery Award),* Hip Logic *(2001, National Poetry Series),* Wind in a Box *(2006), and* Lighthead *(2010, National Book Award). Among his honors are a Whiting award as well as National Endowment for the Arts and Guggenheim fellowships. Terrance Hayes teaches at Carnegie-Mellon University in Pittsburgh.*

At Pegasus

They are like those crazy women
    who tore Orpheus
        when he refused to sing,

these men grinding
    in the strobe & black lights
        of Pegasus. All shadow & sound.

"I'm just here for the music,"
    I tell the man who asks me
        to the floor. But I have held

a boy on my back before.
    Curtis & I used to leap
        barefoot into the creek; dance

among maggots & piss,
    beer bottles & tadpoles
        slippery as sperm;

we used to pull off our shirts
    & slap music into our skin.
        He wouldn't know me now

at the edge of these lovers' gyre,
    glitter & steam, fire,
        bodies blurred sexless

by the music's spinning light.
    A young man slips his thumb
        into the mouth of an old one,

& I am not that far away.
   The whole scene raw & delicate
        as Curtis's foot gashed

on a sunken bottle shard.
   They press hip to hip,
        each breathless as a boy

carrying a friend on his back.
   The foot swelling green
        as the sewage in that creek.

We never went back.
   But I remember his weight
        better than I remember

my first kiss.
   These men know something
        I used to know.

How could I not find them
   beautiful, the way they dive & spill
        into each other,

the way the dance floor
   takes them,
        wet & holy in its mouth.

Lady Sings the Blues

Satin luscious, amber Beauty center-stage;
            gardenia in her hair. If flowers could sing
they'd sound like this. That legendary scene:
            the lady unpetals her song, the only light

in a room of smoke, nightclub tinkering
            with lovers in the dark, cigarette flares,
gin & tonic. This is where the heartache
            blooms. Forget the holes

zippered along her arms. Forget the booze.
            Center-stage, satin-tongue dispels a note.

Amber amaryllis, blue chanteuse, Amen.
            If flowers could sing they'd sound like this.

This should be Harlem, but it's not.
            It's Diana Ross with no *Supremes*.
Fox Theater, Nineteen Seventy-something.
            Ma and me; lovers crowded in the dark.

The only light breaks on the movie-screen.
            I'm a boy, but old enough to know *Heartache*.
We watch her rise and wither
            like a burnt-out cliche. You know the story:

Brutal lush. Jail-bird. Scag queen.
            In the asylum scene, the actress's eyes
are bruised; latticed with blood, but not quite sad
            enough. She's the star so her beauty persists.

Not like Billie: fucked-up satin, hair museless,
            heart ruined by the end.

The houselights wake and nobody's blue but Ma.
            Billie didn't sound like that, she says
as we walk hand in hand to the street.
            Nineteen Seventy-something,

My lady hums, *Good Morning Heartache,*
            My father's in a distant place.

Credits

Index

Authors *Titles* First Lines

A

A bestiary catalogs, 421
Abortion, The, 288
Abortions will not let you forget, 181
About suffering they were never wrong, 136
Abracadabra, says Mephisto, the firefly, 495
Accompanist, The, 403
Affirmative Action Blues (1993), 552
A football spirals through the oyster glow, 340
After Making Love We Hear Footsteps, 271
After my grandfather died I went back, 529
Afternoon cooking in the fall sun, 390
After Reading Mickey in the Night Kitchen for the Third Time Before Bed, 489
After the Storm, 306
Agony. As Now, An, 317
Ai, 435
Air, 273
A large box is handily made of what is necessary to replace any substance, 26
Albany, 433
Alcohol, 519
Alexander, Elizabeth, 549
Alexie, Sherman, 556
Allegory of the Cave, 369
Allen, Paula Gunn, 355
Allen Ginsberg, 383

All Greece hates, 65
All others talked as if, 219
All night the sound had, 246
All the voices of the wood called "Muriel!" 163
Already one day has detached itself from all the rest up ahead, 331
A man ambushed a stone. Caught it. Made it a prisoner. Put it in a dark, 328
A man was dancing with the wrong woman, 370
Amateur Fighter, 558
American Poetry, 221
Amerigo has his finger on the pulse of China, 536
Ammons, A. R., 237
Among twenty snowy mountains, 34
A movie of Robert, 246
And God stepped out on space, 7
Anecdote of the Jar, 36
Animals Are Passing from Our Lives, 282
An incident here and there, 66
An occasion for a plate, an occasional resource is in buying and how, 27
Another Insane Devotion, 235
Another Reluctance, 540
A poem should be palpable and mute, 95
Applauding youths laughed with young prostitutes, 93
April is the cruelest month, breeding, 81
Arabic, 499
arrive. The Ladies from the Ladies' Betterment, 183

Ars Poetica, 95

As from a Quiver of Arrows, 545

Ashbery, John, 253

as if it were a scene made-up by the
  mind, 193

As I sd to my, 244

As Parmigianino did it, the right hand,
  254

Asphodel, That Greeny Flower, from, 43
  Book I, 43

A story, a story! 291

At eight I was brilliant with my body,
  508

At his cramped desk, 430

At home, in my flannel gown, like a bear
  to its floe, 170

at last we killed the roaches, 335

[at last we killed the roaches], 335

At noon in the desert a panting lizard,
  177

At Pegasus, 568

At the Bomb Testing Site, 177

At the junk shop, I find an old pair, 558

At the Poem Society a black-haired man
  stands up to say, 225

Auden, W. H. (Wystan Hugh), 136

August, Los Angeles, Lullaby, 419

August 1945, 205

Autumn Begins in Martins Ferry, Ohio,
  277

Away, 452

A wind is ruffling the tawny pelt, 304

A woman in the shape of a monster,
  294

A year ago friends, 204

B
_____

Back out of all this now too much for
  us, 21

Backroad leafmold stonewall
  chipmunk, 126

Bag of Mice, 547

Ballad of Aunt Geneva, The, 429

Baraka, Amiri, (LeRoi Jones), 316

Barbed Wire, 408

Bean Eaters, The, 182

Beanville. Tea/party. Five black cats,
  566

Bear, The, 268

Because You Asked about the Line
  between Prose and Poetry, 203

Begotten, 477

Behaving Like a Jew, 234

Berrigan, Ted, 320

Berryman, John, 167

Bestiary, 421

Bidart, Frank, 356

Bill's Story, 515

Birches, 18

Bishop, Elizabeth, 147

Bix to Buxtehude to Boulez, 248

Black Art, 318

Black Boy/let me get up from the
  white man's Table of Fifty
  Sounds, 110

Black Crispus Attucks taught, 106

Black Hair, 508

Black Nikes, 518

Black reapers with the sound of steel on
  stones, 102

Black Silk, 409

Blackstone Rangers, The, 186

Blades, 344

Blessing, A, 277

Bly, Robert, 242

Bogan, Louise, 104

Boll-weevil's coming, and the winter's
  cold, 102

Box, A, 26

Bresson's Movies, 246

Bridge, The, from, 120
  From II: Powhatan's Daughter: The
    River, 121
  Proem: To Brooklyn Bridge, 120

Brillance, 512

Brooks, Gwendolyn, 181

Broumas, Olga, 458

Buffalo Bill 's, 99

Buffalo Bill 's/defunct, 99

But He Was Cool or: he even stopped for
  green lights, 398

C

Caedmon, 219
Cahoots, 29
California Dreaming, 332
Calling black people, 318
Call the roller of big cigars, 36
Calypso, 458
Cambridge ladies who live in furnished souls, the, 99
Canto LXXXI, from, 62
    Yet/ Ere the season died a-cold, 62
Carruth, Hayden, 204
Cartoon Physics, part I, 547
Cervantes, Lorna Dee, 521
change./like if u were a match i wd light u into something beauti-, 399
Chapter LXIV, Book VII, Omeros, from, 310
Chestnuts fell in the charred season, 540
Childhood dotted with bodies, 448
Childhood Ideogram, 423
Children under, say, ten, shouldn't know, 547
Chin, Marilyn, 534
Chord, 275
Christmas comes like this: Wise men, 380
Christmas Comes to Moccasin Flat, 380
Cisneros, Sandra, 523
City Limits, The, 237
Classic Ballroom Dances, 354
Claudette Colvin Goes to Work, 490
Clifton, Lucille, 335
Clouds at Evening, 71
Cofer, Judith Ortiz, 485
Collins, Billy, 381
Composed in the Tower before his execution, 215
Composed Near the Bay Bridge, 536
Contend in a sea which the land partly encloses, 42
Corso, Gregory, 298
Corsons Inlet, 238
Cottage Street, 1953, 208

Crane, Hart, 120
Creation, The, 7
Credo, 71
Creeley, Robert, 244
Crescent, 466
Crows in a Strong Wind, 525
Cruel time-servers, here is the crescent moon, 104
Cuba, 1962, 435
Cullen, Countee, 130
Cummings, E. E., 98

D

Dancing, The, 235
Danse Russe, 41
Dark Symphony, 106
Day Lady Died, The, 252
Daystar, 488
Dead, The, 382
Dead Color, 331
Dear John, Dear Coltrane, 348
death of fred clifton, the, 336
Death of the Ball Turret Gunner, The, 171
Death of the Hired Man, The, 12
Degrees of Gray in Philipsburg, 217
Dennis, Carl, 367
Derricotte, Toi, 383
Dickey, James, 211
Did you kill anyone over there? Angelica shifts her gaze from the Janis Joplin, 442
Different Image, A, 175
Digging, 280
Directive, 21
Disarticulated/arm torn out, 349
Disillusionment of Ten O'Clock, 33
Distances, The, 145
Dobyns, Stephen, 386
Don't play too much, don't play, 403
Don't tap your chopsticks against your bowl, 537
Doolittle, Hilda (H. D.), 65
Doty, Mark, 512

Dove, Rita, **486**
Down valley a smoke haze, 303
Dream Boogie, 128
Dream Songs, The, from, 167
    4 (Filling her compact & delicious
        body), 167
    14 (Life, friends, is boring. We must
        not say so), 167
    29 (There sat down, once, a thing on
        Henry's heart), 168
    149 (This world is gradually
        becoming a place), 168
Driving to Town Late to Mail a Letter, 243
Drunk on the Umbrian hills at dusk and
    drunk, 497
Dubie, Norman, **416**
Dugan, Alan, **213**
Dunbar, Paul Laurence, **10**
Dunbar-Nelson, Alice Moore, **28**
Duncan, Robert, **193**
Dunn, Stephen, **369**

E

Each of them must have terrified, 402
Eady, Cornelius, **525**
Eating Together, 543
Edson, Russell, **328**
Effort at Speech Between Two People, 162
Eliot, T. S., **76**
Elizabeth's War with the Christmas Bear,
    416
Ellen West, 356
Emperor of Ice-Cream, The, 36
*England Finally, Like My Mother Always
    Said We Would*, 503
Enormous cloud-mountains that form
    over Point Lobos and into the, 71
Epitaph on a Tyrant, 137
Equinox, 554
Erdrich, Louise, **528**
Errata, 483
Esta Noche, 514
Even I can't help but notice, my
    sweet, 484

Even tonight and I need to take a walk
    and clear, 337
Everyone in me is a bird, 290
Everywhere Is Out of Town, 566
Every year without knowing it I have
    passed the day, 274

F

Facing It, 441
Fairchild, B. H., **396**
Far back when I went zig-zagging,
    293
Far Cry from Africa, A, 304
Farm boys wild to couple, 211
Father and Son, 133
Ferlinghetti, Lawrence, **197**
Fiddler Jones, 2
Field Poem, 506
Filling her compact & delicious body,
    167
Final Sonnet, A, 320
Finch, Annie, **540**
Finished, 436
First Death in Nova Scotia, 150
First Fig, 97
Fish, The, 73, 147
Flounder, 559
Flower, The, 244
Flynn, Nick, **547**
For "Antrim" read "Armagh," 483
Forché, Carolyn, **467**
Forest, The, 510
For I can snore like a bullhorn, 271
Fork, 354
For My Daughter, 174
For My People, 179
For my people everywhere singing their
    slave songs repeatedly: their
    dirges, 179
For the Anniversary of My Death, 274
For the Union Dead, 190
For three years, out of key with his
    time, 54
For weeks the poem of your body, 219

4 (Filling her compact & delicious body), 167

14 (Life, friends, is boring. We must not say so), 167

Fragment, 38

Framed in her phoenix fire-screen, Edna Ward, 208

Francis, Robert, 126

Freaks at Spurgin Road Field, The, 218

Frederick Douglass, 156

Fresh Air, 225

From my mother's sleep I fell into the State, 171

From My Window, 342

From the Dark Tower, 132

Frost, Robert, 12

Fulton, Alice, 492

Funeral, The, 417

G

Gale in April, 70

Gallagher, Tess, 409

Gathering the Bones Together, 445

Geneva was the wild one, 429

Gift, The, 542

Girl Friend Poem #3, 466

Give me the summary, you said. What did, 555

Go inside a stone, 353

Goldbarth, Albert, 452

Good morning, daddy! 128

Graham, Jorie, 468

Grandfather, 351

Grandmother, 355

Grandmothers who wring the necks, 354

Grass, 29

Grimké, Angelina Weld, 38

H

Hair—braided chestnut, 102

Hall, Donald, 280

Hamby, Barbara, 494

Harjo, Joy, 472

Harlem, 129

Harlem Dancer, The, 93

Harlem Gallery, from, 110
    Psi, 110

Harper, Michael S., 348

Hass, Robert, 390

hate the people of this village, 428

Hatred, 495

Hayden, Robert, 155

Hayes, Terrance, 568

Hay for the Horses, 302

Heavy Bear Who Goes with Me, The, 165

Hecht, Anthony, 215

He climbed toward the blinding light, 369

He had driven half the night, 302

He has finished a day's work, 390

Hejinian, Lyn, 394

Helen, 65

Henry's Understanding, 169

Here, she said, *put this on your head*, 559

Here comes the man! He's talking a lot, 320

Her Kind, 287

Hermetic Definition, from, 68
    Red Rose and a Beggar, 68

Hernández Cruz, Victor, 459

He sang of life, serenely sweet, 10

He shuddered briefly and stared down the long valley, 391

He was reading late, at Richard's down in Maine, 169

He would have to put out his smoke, 465

Hill, The, 1

History of My Heart, 371

homage to my hips, 335

Home's the place we head for in our sleep, 528

Hongo, Garrett, 475

Hot Combs, 558

Howe, Marie, 470

How funny you are today New York, 250

How I Got That Name, 534

How It Is, 233

How many dawns, chill from his rippling chest, 120

How strange to be gone in a minute! A man, 320

how to do it from the beginning, 312

How to Like It, 386

Hudgins, Andrew, 477

Hughes, Langston, 127

Hugh Selwyn Mauberley, 54

Hugo, Richard, 217

Hyacinth Garden in Brooklyn, The, 204

I
_____

I, Maximus of Gloucester, to You, 141

I, Too, 127

I, too dislike it, 75

I, too, dislike it: there are things that are important beyond all this fiddle, 74

I, too, sing America, 127

I am as far as the deepest sky between clouds, 509

I am inside someone, 317

I am Marilyn Mei Ling Chin, 534

I am the woman with the black black skin, 38

I am told by many of you that I must forgive and so I shall, 557

I ask them to take a poem, 381

I bought a dollar and a half's worth of small red potatoes, 285

I cannot hold my peace, John Keats, 130

I caught a tremendous fish, 147

Idea of Ancestry, The, 314

I Do Not, 411

I do not know English, 411

I doubt not God is good, well-meaning, kind, 132

I dreamed I was digging your grave, 556

I dreamt your suicide note, 547

If the function of writing is to "express the world." My father, 433

If We Must Die, 93

If we must die, let it not be like hogs, 93

If when my wife is sleeping, 41

I had come to the house, in a cave of trees, 104

I have gone out, a possessed witch, 287

I have wanted excellence in the knife-throw, 405

I Know a Man, 244

I lay my head sideways on the desk, 423

I lie for a long time on my left side and my right side, 331

I love sweets, 356

I'm a Fool to Love You, 526

Imagining Their Own Hymns, 479

I'm half Bengali, so I went to Calcutta, 555

In 1915 my grandfather's, 351

In a Dark Time, 139

In a dark time, the eye begins to see, 139

In a dress with a black tulip's sheen, 514

In all these rotten shops, in all this broken furniture, 235

In a long text, on live TV, in an amphitheater, in the soil, 461

In a Station of the Metro, 54

In Celebration of My Uterus, 290

In Chicago, it is snowing softly, 475

Incident, 130

In cold storm light, 457

In Cold Storm Light, 457

Indian Boarding School: The Runaways, 528

In her room at the prow of the house, 209

In Just-, 98

In Just-/spring when the world is mud-, 98

In late winter, 268

In Memory of the Utah Stars, 402

In recent months I have become intent on seizing happiness: to this, 466

In Response to a Rumor That the Oldest Whorehouse in Wheeling, West Virginia, Has Been Condemned, 278

Insect, 540

Inside the veins there are navies setting forth, 243

In Singapore, in the airport, 329

Intense and terrible beauty, how has our race with the frail naked nerves, 70

In the cold, cold parlor, 150

In the final hour, our lady—Of, 544

In the Shreve High football stadium, 277

In the steamer is the trout, 543

In this blue light, 468

Into my empty head there come, 232

Introduction to Poetry, 381

I placed a jar in Tennessee, 36

I place these numbed wrists to the pane, 352

Iris, 463

I sang of quiet Achille, Afolabe's son, 310

i seemed to be drawn, 336

I Sit and Sew, 28

I sit and sew—a useless task it seems, 28

I take off my shirt, I show you, 467

It felt like the zero in brook ice, 417

I think I grow tensions, 244

It is 12:20 in New York a Friday, 252

It is a cold and snowy night. The main street is deserted, 243

It is midnight, 324

"It isn't a game for girls," 449

It may be misery not to sing at all, 10

It's wonderful how I jog, 282

It will not hurt me when I am old, 51

I've gathered the women like talismans, one, 458

I've known rivers, 127

I've never, as some children do, 477

I've stayed in the front yard all my life, 182

I wake to sleep, and take my waking slow, 138

I walk down the garden paths, 23

I went for a walk over the dunes again this morning, 238

I will grieve alone, 278

I will teach you my townspeople, 39

J

Jack Johnson Does the Eagle Rock, 525

Jarman, Mark, 497

Jarrell, Randall, 170

Jeffers, Robinson, 70

Jewel Stairs' Grievance, The, 53

Johnny the kitchen sink has been clogged for days, some utensil probably, 470

Johnson, James Weldon, 7

Jordan, June, 337

Just as my fingers on these keys, 31

Just as the earth puckered its mouth, 288

Just off the highway to Rochester, Minnesota, 277

K

Kees, Weldon, 174

Kelly, Brigit Pegeen, 479

Kid, The, 435

Kinnell, Galway, 268

Kizer, Carolyn, 222

Klink, Joanna, 562

Knight, Etheridge, 314

Koch, Kenneth, 225

Komunyakaa, Yusef, 439

Kumin, Maxine, 232

Kunitz, Stanley, 133

L

Lady Sings the Blues, 569

Lana Turner has collapsed! 251

Language, The, 245

Language Lesson 1976, 454

Language of the Brag, The, 405

Last Affair: Bessie's Blues Song, 349

Lately, I've become accustomed to the way, 316

Latin & Soul, 459

Lay down these words, 303
Legend, The, 475
Let Me Tell You, 312
Let us go then, you and I, 76
Levertov, Denise, 219
Levine, Philip, 282
Levis, Larry, 423
Life, friends, is boring. We must not say
    so, 167
Life's Tragedy, 10
Lifting, The, 406
Light of the World, The, 307
Listen: there was a goat's head hanging
    by ropes in a tree, 480
Little clown, my heart, 524
Little Clown, My Heart, 524
Li-Young Lee, 542
Locate *I/love you* some-, 245
Looking for Judas, 427
Looking into my daughter's eyes I read,
    174
Lorde, Audre, 322
Lord's lost Him His mockingbird, 155
Lost Pilot, The, 414
Louis, Adrian C., 427
Love Calls Us to the Things of This World,
    207
"Love of My Flesh, Living Death," 522
Lovers of the Poor, The, 183
Love Song: I and Thou, 213
Love Song of J. Alfred Prufrock, The, 76
Lowell, Amy, 23
Lowell, Robert, 188
Lullaby, 387
Lux, Thomas, 428
Lying in a Hammock at William Duffy's
    Farm in Pine Island, Minnesota,
    278

M

Machinist, Teaching His Daughter to Play
    the Piano, The, 396
Mackey, Nathaniel, 443
MacLeish, Archibald, 95

Madhubuti, Haki R. (Don L. Lee),
    398
Maggie's taking care of a man, 512
Marley was rocking on the transport's
    stereo, 307
Marriage, 298
Mary sat musing on the lamp-flame at
    the table, 12
Mason, David, 529
Masters, Edgar Lee, 1
Matthews, William, 402
Maximus Poems, The, from, 141
    I, Maximus of Gloucester, to You, 141
McHugh, Heather, 454
McKay, Claude, 93
Mechanic, The, 346
Medusa, 104
Meeting the British, 482
Mending Wall, 17
Menial twilight sweeps the storefronts
    along Lexington, 490
Meredith, William, 201
Merrill, James, 248
Merwin, W. S., 273
Miami Heart, 461
Mid-August at Sourdough Mountain
    Lookout, 303
Middle Passage, 157
Millay, Edna St. Vincent, 97
Miller, Jane, 461
Million Balconies, A, 555
Miniver Cheevy, 4
Miniver Cheevy, child of scorn, 4
Moonlight, 51
Moore, Marianne, 73
"More Light! More Light!, 215
Morning Swim, 232
Most men use/their eyes, 346
Mother, The, 181
Mourning Poem for the Queen of Sunday,
    155
Moving from Cheer to Joy, from Joy to
    All, 172
Mr. Flood's Party, 5
Muldoon, Paul, 482
Mullen, Harryette, 518
Musée des Beaux Arts, 136

Muse of Water, A, 222
Music divides the evening, 440
Muske-Dukes, Carol, 419
My black face fades, 441
My brother comes home from work, 284
My candle burns at both ends, 97
My daughter spreads her legs, 489
My dolls have been put away like dead, 485
My father once broke a man's hand, 424
My friend from Asia has powers and magic, he plucks a blue leaf from, 71
My friend says I was not a good son, 274
My House is the Red Earth, 474
My house is the red earth; it could be the center of the world. I've heard, 474
My Life, from, 394
    name trimmed with colored ribbons, A, 394
My mother never forgave my father, 134
My mother would be a falconress, 194
My Mother Would Be a Falconress, 194
My Papa's Waltz, 138
My sister rubs the doll's face in mud, 435
My son, my executioner, 280
My Son My Executioner, 280
My swirling wants. Your frozen lips, 296
My Wicked Wicked Ways, 523

N

Name trimmed with colored ribbons, A, 394
Nani, 502
Naturally it is night, 273
Nautilus Island's hermit, 188
Negro Speaks of Rivers, The, 127
Nelson, Marilyn, 429
Nemerov, Howard, 203
New Moon, 104

Next a Brazilian cut came, 443
Next Day, 172
"next to of course god america i, 99
next to of course god america i, 99
Night, the Porch, The, 326
Nightmare Begins Responsibility, 352
1968, 340
90 North, 170
Nocturne: Blue Waves, 504
Nothing is plumb, level, or square, 213
November Cotton Flower, 102
Now in the suburbs and the falling light, 133
Now is the time of year when bees are wild, 554
Now we must get up quickly, 447
Nude Interrogation, 442
Nye, Naomi Shihab, 498

O

Of asphodel, that greeny flower, 43
Off go the crows from the roof, 525
Off-shore, by islands hidden in the blood, 141
Of Mere Being, 36
Often I Am Permitted to Return to a Meadow, 193
O'Hara, Frank, 250
Old Eben Flood, climbing alone one night, 5
Olds, Sharon, 405
Oliver, Mary, 329
Olson, Charles, 141
Omeros, from, 310
    Book VII: Chapter LXIV, 310
Once Allen Ginsberg stopped to pee at a bookstore, 383
Once I wasn't always so plain, 522
Once on a plane, 500
Once riding in old Baltimore, 130
1 (An incident here and there), 66
One Art, 153
One Christmastime Fats Waller in a fur coat, 371

One day the Nouns were clustered in the street, 231

149 (This world is gradually becoming a place), 168

One midnight, after a day when lilies, 280

One summer afternoon when nothing much, 408

Oranges, 506

Origin of the Marble Forest, 448

Orion, 293

Orr, Gregory, 445

Our Calling, 492

Our Lady, 544

Out of burlap sacks, out of bearing butter, 283

Out of her own body she pushed, 355

Over my head, I see the bronze butterfly, 278

P
_____

Palmer, Michael, 411

Parents, 201

Parsley, 486

Patterns, 23

People of the Other Village, The, 428

Perfection, of a kind, was what he was after, 137

Perhaps he left the newspaper stand that morning, 525

Permanently, 231

Peter Quince at the Clavier, 31

Petit, the Poet, 3

Phillips, Carl, 544

Pile the bodies high at Austerlitz and Waterloo, 29

Pinsky, Robert, 371

Planetarium, 294

Plate, A, 27

Play it across the table, 29

Poem, 251

Poem About My Rights, 337

Poem as Mask, The, 163

poem at thirty, 324

Poems are bullshit unless they are, 318

Poem to Complement Other Poems, A, 399

Poem Unwritten, The, 219

Poet, The, 10

Poetry (I too, dislike it: there are things), 74

Poetry (I, too, dislike it. Reading it, however), 75

Poets, come out of your closets, 197

Populist Manifesto, 197

Pornographer, The, 390

Portrait, The, 134

Portrait in Georgia, 102

Postfeminism, 563

Pound, Ezra (Weston Loomis), 53

Power, 322

II. Powhatan's Daughter, from, 121
    The River, 121

Powwow at the End of the World, The, 557

Prediction, The, 326

Preface to a Twenty Volume Suicide Note, 316

Preludes, 80

Proem: to Brooklyn Bridge, 120

Psi, 110

Pull over. Your car with its slow, 565

Q
_____

Questions, The, 377

Quinceañera, 485

Quivira City Limits, 565

R
_____

Rain, The, 246

Randall, Dudley, 175

Reaching Yellow River, 449

Reapers, 102

Recuerdo, 97

Red Rose and a Beggar, parts 1, 2, and 5, 68–69

Red Wheelbarrow, The, 41

Return of Robinson Jeffers, The, 391

Reunion, 331

Rich, Adrienne, 293

Right now two black people sit in a jury
    room, 552

Ríos, Alberto, 502

Riprap, 303

River, The, 121

River-Merchant's Wife: A Letter, The, 53

Robinson, Edwin Arlington, 4

Roethke, Theodore, 138

Rose, harsh Rose, 65

Rowing, 291

r-p-o-p-h-e-s-s-a-g-r, 101

r-p-o-p-h-e-s-s-a-g-r, 101

Rukeyser, Muriel, 162

Ryan, Kay, 421

S
_____

Sails flashing to the wind like weapons,
    157

Saint Francis and the Sow, 271

Samurai Song, 379

Sanchez, Sonia, 324

Sandburg, Carl, 29

San Sepolcro, 468

Satin luscious, amber Beauty center-
    stage, 569

Scars, 178

Schooner Flight, The, from, 306
    II. *After the Storm, 306*

Schwartz, Delmore, 165

Science, science, science! 549

Sea Grapes, 305

Sea Rose, 65

Seeds in a dry pod, tick, tick, tick, 3

Seidel, Frederick, 340

Self-Portrait in a Convex Mirror, 254

September rain falls on the house, 149

Sestina, 149

Sex fingers toes, 348

Sexton, Anne, 287

Shall I say how is it in your clothes? 233

Shaughnessy, Brenda, 563

Sheck, Laurie, 504

Sheep Child, The, 211

She Had Some Horses, 472

She had some horses, 472

She wanted a little room for thinking,
    488

She was cleaning—there is always, 409

She was white and flown, 466

Shine, Perishing Republic, 70

Shoulder me up. Drink careless down,
    for flinching, 562

Should I get married? Should I be
    good? 298

should never be light. That kind of
    thing feels, 564

Silent Poem, 126

Silko, Leslie Marmon, 457

Silliman, Ron, 433

Simic, Charles, 353

Simple Truth, The, 285

Simpson, Louis, 221

Since you ask, most days I cannot
    remember, 288

Singapore, 329

Sitting at her table, she serves, 502

Skunk Hour, 188

Snowfall in the Afternoon, 242

Snyder, Gary, 302

Some folks will tell you the blues is a
    woman, 526

Something there is that doesn't love a
    wall, 17

Sometimes I am on a train, 178

Some Trees, 253

some waves/a wave of now, 459

*Somewhere I have never travelled,gladly
    beyond, 100*

Somewhere I have never
    travelled,gladly beyond, 100

So much depends, 41

Song, 390, 480

Song, Cathy, 538

Song in the Front Yard, A, 182

Song of the Andoumboulou: 21, 443

SOS, 318

So the distances are Galatea, 145

Soto, Gary, 506

Spare, 562

Sparrows were feeding in a freezing
    drizzle, 203

Speak to me. Take my hand. What are
    you now? 162

Spooning, 529

Spoon River Anthology, from, 1
    Fiddler Jones, 2
    Hill, The, 1
    Petit, the Poet, 3

Spring Letter, 367

Spring: the first morning when that one
    true block of sweet, laminar,
    complex, 342

Stafford, William, 176

Stallings, A. E., 561

Star-Fix, 430

Stein, Gertrude, 26

Steps, 250

Stern, Gerald, 234

Stevens, Wallace, 31

Stewart, Susan, 509

Stick your patent name on a signboard,
    121

St. John, David, 463

Stone, 353

Stone, Ruth, 178

Stone Is Nobody's, A, 328

Stopping by Woods on a Snowy Evening, 20

Strand, Mark, 326

Struck with grief you were, though only
    four, 561

Suddenly my father lifted up his nightie,
    I, 406

Summer Day, The, 330

Summer is late, my heart, 134

Sundays too my father got up early, 156

Super-cool/ultrablack, 398

Suppose Oedipus never discovers his
    ignorance, 368

Survivor, The, 537

Susie Asado, 26

Swan in Falling Snow, 220

Sweating and greasy in the dovecote
    where one of them lived, 205

Sweet sweet sweet sweet sweet tea, 26

T

Taking Off My Clothes, 467

Tantrum, The, 561

Taped to the wall of my cell are 47
    pictures: 47 black, 314

Tate, James, 414

Taylor, Henry, 408

Teasdale, Sara, 51

Tender Buttons, from, 26
    Box, A, 26
    Plate, A, 27

Thanks, 439

Thanks for the tree, 439

That hour-glass-backed, 540

That night the moon drifted over the
    pond, 326

That sail which leans on light, 305

That time my grandmother dragged me,
    384

The age/requires this task, 175

The apparition of these faces in the
    crowd, 54

The art of losing isn't hard to master,
    153

The bears are kept by hundreds within
    fences, are fed cracked, 416

The brown wrist and hand with its raw
    knuckles and blue nails, 396

The bud/stands for all things, 271

the Cambridge ladies who live in
    furnished souls, 99

The dead are always looking down on
    us, they say, 382

The deer carcass hangs from a rafter,
    445

The difference between poetry and
    rhetoric, 322

The dim boy claps because the others
    clap, 218

The earth keeps some vibration
    going, 2

The eyes open to a cry of pulleys, 207

The first time I walked, 506

The grass is half-covered with snow,
    242

The heavy bear who goes with me, 165

"The hot night makes us keep our bedroom windows open, 188

The houses are haunted, 33

The jewelled steps are already quite white with dew, 53

The man with the laughing eyes stopped smiling, 499

The medieval town, with frieze, 266

Then I Saw What the Calling Was, 163

The old dog and the old rabbit, 503

The old South Boston Aquarium stands, 189

The palm at the end of the mind, 36

The pool players, 185

The pure amnesia of her face, 419

There are times when the mind, 504

There are two kinds of people, soldiers and women, 563

There is a parrot imitating spring, 486

There is a train inside this iris, 463

There's a fresh light that follows a storm, 306

There sat down, once, a thing on Henry's heart, 168

There they are, 186

There Will Come Soft Rains, 51

There will come soft rains and the smell of the ground, 51

The rules break like a thermometer, 296

The saris go by me from the embassies, 171

These are amazing: each, 253

These are the first days of fall. The wind, 386

these hips are big hips, 335

The sky has been dark, 538

The sleep of this night deepens, 410

The whiskey on your breath, 138

The winter evening settles down, 80

They are like those crazy women, 568

They are seated in the shadows husking corn, shelling, 394

They eat beans mostly, this old yellow pair, 182

They Feed They Lion, 283

The zero of a yawn eclipses your face, 387

Thinking of Galileo, 494

XIII (The rules break like a thermometer), 296

Thirteen Ways of Looking at a Blackbird, 34

This could be a good day. It starts, 567

This is my father, 523

This is the house of Bedlam, 151

This strange thing must have crept, 354

This was gruesome—fighting over a ham sandwich, 235

This world is gradually becoming a place, 168

Those Winter Sundays, 156

Throwback, The, 484

To birth shape from the spill, 492

To John Keats, Poet, at Spring Time, 130

Tolson, Melvin B., 106

To My Brother, 521

to my last period, 336

Toomer, Jean, 102

To pull the metal splinter from my palm, 542

"To Speak of Woe That Is in Marriage," 188

To stare at nothing is to learn by heart, 326

Touch Me, 134

Tract, 39

Train Windows, 555

Traveling Onion, The, 498

Traveling through the Dark, 176

Traveling through the dark I found a deer, 176

Tree at My Window, 20

Tree at my window, window tree, 20

Trethewey, Natasha, 558

Tucson, 370

Tu Do Street, 440

Turtle, 421

29 (There sat down, once, a thing on Henry's heart), 168

Twenty-One Love Poems, from, 296

   XIII (The rules break like a thermometer), 296

Two Lines from the Brothers Grimm, 447

Two or Three Wishes, 368

U

Under Stars, 410
Unfinished, The, 505
Unholy Sonnet 13, 497
Upon the darkish, thin, half-broken ice, 220

V

Valediction Forbidding Mourning, A, 296
Vazirani, Reetika, 555
Venus Hottentot, The, 549
Victor Dog, The, 248
Visits to St. Elizabeths, 151

W

Wade / through black jade, 73
Waking, The, 138
Waking from Sleep, 243
Wakoski, Diane, 346
Walcott, Derek, 304
Walker, Margaret, 179
Walls Do Not Fall, The, from, 66
    1. An incident here and there, 66
Wanting to Die, 288
Waste Land, The, 81
Weakness, The, 384
We are not born yet, and everything's crystal under our feet, 332
Weathered gray, the wooden walls, 427
Wedding Cake, 500
Welch, James, 380
well girl, goodbye, 336
We met the British in the dead of winter, 482
We need quarters like King Tut needed a boat. A slave could row him to, 518
We Real Cool, 185
We shall not always plant while others reap, 132

We think a blink is tiny but, 452
We were characters in a story, 505
We Were Simply Talking, 477
We were simply talking, probably work, or relatives, 477
We were so poor, 521
We were supposed to do a job in Italy, 455
We were very tired, we were very merry, 97
We who must act as handmaides, 222
What about the people who came to my father's office, 377
What do we do with the body, do we, 545
Whatever it is, it must have, 221
Whatever You Want, 567
What fools they are to believe the angels, 479
What happens to a dream deferred? 129
What He Thought, 455
What Is Poetry, 266
What it must be like to be an angel, 201
What's left is the tiny gold glove, 558
What the Living Do, 470
What the Orphan Inherits, 556
When, during a weekend in Venice while standing, 494
When Americans say a man, 454
When I got there the dead opossum looked like, 234
When I had no roof I made, 379
When I see birches bend to left and right, 18
When I think how far the onion has traveled, 498
When it is finally ours, this freedom, this liberty, this beautiful, 156
When I was about eight, I once stabbed somebody, another kid, a little, 344
When I wrote of the women in their dances and wildness, it was a mask, 163
When my sister came back from Africa, 515

When the foreman whistled, 506
When the rooster jumps up on the
    windowsill, 435
When you consider the radiance, that it
    does not withhold, 237
Where are Elmer, Herman, Bert, Tom
    and Charley, 1
While Keats wrote they were
    cutting down sandalwood
    forests, 275
While my hair was still cut straight
    across my forehead, 53
While this America settles in the mould
    of its vulgarity, heavily, 70
White Elephants, from, 555
    Million Balconies, A, 555
    Train Windows, 555
Whiteman, Roberta Hill, 449
Who made the world? 330
Whose woods these are I think I
    know, 20
Who would be a turtle who could help
    it? 421
Why did you come, 68
Why Ralph Refuses to Dance, 465
Wilbur, Richard, 207
Williams, C. K., 342
Williams, Miller, 312
Williams, William Carlos, 39
Winter Stars, 424

With the warmer days the shops on
    Elmwood, 367
Woman at the Washington Zoo, The, 171
Wright, C. D., 465
Wright, Charles, 331
Wright, Franz, 519
Wright, James, 277
Writer, The, 209
Wrong Train, 320

Y

Yachts, The, 42
Yellow Stars and Ice, 509
Yesterday, 274
Yet Do I Marvel, 132
Yet/ Ere the season died a-cold, 62
You Can Have It, 284
You do look a little ill, 519
You force me to touch, 436
You might come here Sunday on a
    whim, 217
Young, Kevin, 565
Youngest Daughter, The, 538
Your face did not rot, 414
Your One Good Dress, 564
You should lie down now and
    remember the forest, 510